PENGUIN BOOKS

THE RUIN OF J. ROBERT OPPENHEIMER

Priscilla J. McMillan is an associate of the Davis Center for Russian and Eurasian Studies at Harvard University. She is the author of *Krushchev and the Arts* and the classic *Marina and Lee*. Her articles have appeared, among other places, in *The New York Times*, *The Boston Globe*, the *Los Angeles Times*, *Harper's Magazine*, *Scientific American*, and the *Bulletin of the Atomic Scientists*, where she is a member of the editorial board. She lives in Cambridge, Massachusetts.

Priscilla J. McMillan

The Ruin of
J. Robert
Oppenheimer

and the Birth
of the Modern
Arms Race

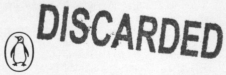

PENGUIN BOOKS

PENGUIN BOOKS
Published by the Penguin Group
Penguin Group (USA) Inc., 375 Hudson Street, New York, New York 10014, U.S.A.
Penguin Group (Canada), 90 Eglinton Avenue East, Suite 700, Toronto,
Ontario, Canada M4P 2Y3 (a division of Pearson Penguin Canada Inc.)
Penguin Books Ltd, 80 Strand, London WC2R 0RL, England
Penguin Ireland, 25 St Stephen's Green, Dublin 2, Ireland (a division of Penguin Books Ltd)
Penguin Group (Australia), 250 Camberwell Road, Camberwell,
Victoria 3124, Australia (a division of Pearson Australia Group Pty Ltd)
Penguin Books India Pvt Ltd, 11 Community Centre,
Panchsheel Park, New Delhi – 110 017, India
Penguin Group (NZ), cnr Airborne and Rosedale Roads, Albany,
Auckland 1310, New Zealand (a division of Pearson New Zealand Ltd)
Penguin Books (South Africa) (Pty) Ltd, 24 Sturdee Avenue,
Rosebank, Johannesburg 2196, South Africa

Penguin Books Ltd, Registered Offices:
80 Strand, London WC2R 0RL, England

First published in the United States of America by Viking Penguin,
a member of Penguin Group (USA) Inc. 2005
Published in Penguin Books 2006

1   3   5   7   9   10   8   6   4   2

Photograph credits appear on page 374.

THE LIBRARY OF CONGRESS HAS CATALOGED THE HARDCOVER EDITION AS FOLLOWS:
McMillan, Priscilla Johnson.
The ruin of J. Robert Oppenheimer / Priscilla J. McMillan.
p.   cm.
Includes index.
ISBN 0-670-03422-3 (hc.)
ISBN 0 14 20.0115 5 (pbk.)
1. Oppenheimer, J. Robert, 1904–1967.   2. Physicists—United States—Biography.
3. Manhattan Project (U.S.)   4. Atomic bomb—United States—History.   5. Nuclear
physics—United States—History—20th century.   6. Teller, Edward, 1908–   I. Title.
QC16.062M36 2005
530'.092—dc22   2004066103

Printed in the United States of America
Set in Adobe Garamond   Designed by Francesca Belanger

For Sam and Ethel Ballen

CONTENTS

The Ruin of
J. Robert
Oppenheimer

Introduction

ON THE MORNING of April 12, 1954, readers of the *New York Times* woke to startling news. The security clearance of the nation's best-known nuclear scientist, J. Robert Oppenheimer, had been suspended in the face of charges that he was a security risk.

The *Times*'s scoop created a sensation, for Oppenheimer was a national hero. He had been the leader of the Manhattan Project during World War II, and his name, more than that of any other American, was coupled with the building of the atomic bomb and the war's victorious end at Hiroshima and Nagasaki. After the war, as the government's number one adviser on atomic weapons, he had been privy to all its decisions about these weapons. If Oppenheimer was a security risk, did the United States have a single important secret left?

It was almost unthinkable that this man's loyalty should be in question. Except that as U.S. disagreement with the Soviet Union hardened into a state of permanent tension, the certainties that had sustained the American people during the war and the early years thereafter ebbed away, and so did some of the nation's confidence. After the defections of two people who had spied for the USSR (a Soviet code clerk in Canada named Igor Gouzenko in 1946 and a woman named Elizabeth Bentley from the U.S. Communist Party in 1948), Americans learned that key parts of the government—State, Treasury, and possibly even the White House—had been penetrated by Soviet agents. Then, in 1948, a rumpled-looking former writer for *Time* magazine named Whittaker Chambers rose in a crowded congressional committee room and, in an unforgettable televised confrontation, accused the irreproachable Alger Hiss, president of the

Carnegie Endowment for International Peace, of having handed U.S. government secrets to Russia years before, while he had been a State Department official. The confidence of Americans was shaken again in the late summer of 1949, when the Soviet Union tested its first atomic bomb, an event the CIA had not expected for at least two more years. Its atomic monopoly broken, the country learned in early 1950 that Hiss had been convicted on charges of perjury and that a serious-looking, bespectacled ex–Manhattan Project scientist named Klaus Fuchs had confessed in England to having passed atomic secrets to Russia.

After only four short years, the United States found itself shorn of its monopoly on the weapon that had given it a feeling of omnipotence, and learned that the key to its unrivaled ascendancy—the secrets of the atomic bomb—had been stolen. It was not long before ambitious politicians started to capitalize on the nation's new sense of vulnerability, and no accident that the most strident of those who tried to do so was a hard-drinking senator from the heartland of traditional isolationism. Within days of the Hiss conviction and the Fuchs confession, Joseph McCarthy stood up in Wheeling, West Virginia, and brandished a piece of paper purportedly containing the names of 205 "known" Communists who he claimed were working for the Department of State.

As McCarthy spoke, a debate that had been waged in secret about a possible next step in the arms race reached its decisive point, as President Harry Truman ordered the nation's scientists to find out whether a new weapon, the so-called hydrogen bomb, could be built in response to the Soviet success. Such a bomb would, if feasible, have a thousand times the explosive power of the atomic bomb. And, in subsequent directives, Truman made clear that the effort to build a hydrogen bomb was to be an all-out affair, and that everything about the program was to be held in utmost secrecy.

Robert Oppenheimer had been at the center of the debate over whether to try to build the hydrogen bomb. As chairman of the Atomic Energy Commission's General Advisory Committee, the group which, more than any other, made the government's decisions about atomic weapons, Oppenheimer had chaired the October 1949 meeting at which the GAC had voted 8 to 0 (a ninth GAC member was out of the country) against a crash program to develop the hydrogen bomb. Oppenheimer's committee had cited both technical and moral arguments. It had before it only one design for the weapon, and despite several years of research, it was not clear that it could ever be made to work. To launch a new stage of the arms race by committing the nation to build a weapon that had so far been proof against every effort at invention seemed to the committee members supremely irresponsible. Nor did they think it would be ethical. The new weapon, should it ever prove feasible, could be designed to carry unlimited destructive power. It would be a weapon not of warfare but, quite possibly, of genocide. As an answer to Russia's newfound possession of the atomic bomb it was, all too literally, overkill.

Oppenheimer agreed with the committee, but, contrary to accusations that were brought against him later, he had not led the GAC to its conclusions. He came to his view only in the last few days before the meeting, partly under the influence of Harvard president James B. Conant, a committee member for whom he had almost filial respect, and in the course of the meeting itself, as the consensus took shape. His feelings were less vehement than Conant's and he did not write the majority opinion, as he very often did. Nevertheless, the four-month behind-the-scenes debate over the hydrogen bomb earned him bitter foes. One was Lewis Strauss, a highly partisan Republican banker and businessman who was one of five AEC commissioners. Another was Edward Teller, the Hungarian-born scientist whom Oppenheimer had known well during the Manhattan Project years, and whom he had disappointed in 1943 by declining to make him head of Los Alamos's Theoretical Division. A brilliant administrator, Oppenheimer had kept Teller on the reservation throughout the war by allowing him to form a small group of his own. But Teller, already obsessed by the idea of the hydrogen bomb, nursed his resentments and concluded that Oppenheimer was motivated not by honest conviction but by ambition, not wanting *his* success, the atomic bomb, to be trumped by a bigger weapon.

The enmities Oppenheimer incurred during the H-bomb debate of 1949–50 became deeper afterward, for as part of his H-bomb decision, Truman also decreed that the very fact of the debate, plus everything that had been said in the course of it, was to remain supersecret. No one who had taken part was permitted even to describe the proceedings to anyone who did not have a "Q" clearance, a clearance to see top secret nuclear data. As a result Oppenheimer and the rest of the General Advisory Committee were not permitted to explain why they had reached their conclusions. Yet the GAC had urged that the American people be kept more fully informed about atomic matters, and its members were almost as disheartened by Truman's secrecy order as by the H-bomb decision itself. A few days after Truman's announcement Oppenheimer spoke on Mrs. Roosevelt's special television program against the excessive secrecy, but he was the last Q-cleared insider to do so. From then on, it was only the scientists who no longer had any official portfolio who spoke out publicly against the dangers of the thermonuclear bomb, men such as Hans Bethe of Cornell, Victor Weisskopf of MIT, retired AEC commissioner Robert Bacher, and Ralph Lapp, an expert on the effects of radiation. Oppenheimer was aware of their efforts and no doubt approved, but he had to maintain public silence. Much later, however, his early opposition to the crash program was metamorphosed into the charge that because his opposition had become known, it had discouraged other scientists and slowed down the program—all to the benefit of the Russians.

Following Truman's silencing decision, Oppenheimer took other stands that earned him enemies in high places. First, like Conant and most of the government's other scientific advisers, he opposed a pet project of the Air Force, the building of a nuclear-powered aircraft. Second, like Gordon Dean, chairman of the AEC, and nearly all his own colleagues on the General Advisory Committee, he defended the ongoing work of Los Alamos and opposed pressure from Teller and the Air Force to build a second nuclear weapons laboratory to compete with it, the laboratory that exists today in Livermore, California. After his and the GAC's defeat on this issue, Oppenheimer was forced off the GAC. Finally, he helped write the "Vista" report, a study commissioned by the Air Force in 1951, which urged that tactical nuclear weapons be made available to defend Western Europe against Soviet land armies if necessary. Instead of relying on a small number of thermonuclear bombs with which the Air Force could pulverize targets in the far-off USSR, "Vista" recommended that a large number of smaller bombs be spread among the services so that, if need be, war could be fought on the ground in Europe. The Air Force, a young and cocksure branch of the armed services, took umbrage at the notion of sharing the powerful new weapons with the other services and assumed once again that Oppenheimer was the villain.

A brilliant, charismatic man with the gift of seeing further into the future of nuclear weapons than anyone else, either then or later, Oppenheimer also had glaring vulnerabilities, chief among them the possibility that he had been a member of the Communist Party. Certainly, several of those closest to him had been: Jean Tatlock, a woman he cared about deeply, and Frank and Jackie Oppenheimer, Robert's brother and sister-in-law. Katherine Puening, whom Robert married in 1940, had belonged to the Party, as had one of her former husbands, Joe Dallet, who died a hero in the Spanish civil war. Communists and Communist sympathizers were numerous in Depression-era Berkeley, and some were physics students of Oppenheimer's who joined the Party believing him to be a member and who paid dearly for it afterward. Robert Oppenheimer himself made monthly contributions to the Party up to 1942 and, by his own admission, "belonged to nearly every fellow-traveling organization on the West Coast." But he denied that he had ever joined the Party, and the testimony of a number of close witnesses of his political activity bears him out.

Jean Tatlock was the daughter of a highly regarded professor of English literature at the University of California at Berkeley. By all accounts she was a beautiful woman, generous and warmhearted, in training to be a doctor. She and Robert Oppenheimer met in the spring of 1936 and by the fall of that year he began to court her. With the courtship, a change was observed in Oppenheimer. His lectures became simpler and more accessible. And he was happier, he said later, because he now felt more a part of his time and country. Much

of this he owed to Jean, an on-again, off-again member of the Communist Party who introduced him to her activist friends in Berkeley.

At least twice, Oppenheimer was to say, he and Jean were "close
enough to marriage to think of ourselves as engaged." He was anxious to marry her, but Jean, one friend said, "out of troubles of her
own," refused to marry him. Robert and Jean broke up in the fall of
1939, after he had met Kitty Harrison, and a year later he and Kitty
were married.[1]

In early 1943, before he left for Los Alamos, he had a telephone
call from Jean that he failed to answer. Through a mutual friend he
soon had a message that she was in distress and needed to see him. So
in June of that year he found an excuse to go to San Francisco, where
he saw Jean. The FBI followed him during every moment of the visit,
and on one of the two evenings he spent with Jean, FBI agents in a
car outside her apartment building observed that he spent the night.
The night he spent with Jean Tatlock in 1943 was brought up at his
hearing eleven years later, always as part of the charge that he was an
adulterer who disregarded demands of security by spending the night
with a known Communist. "Was that good security?" someone asked
at the hearing. "No," he admitted.

Kitty Oppenheimer knew about the meeting in advance. Knew of
it, didn't like it, and accepted it. But when Robert got into trouble over
it at the hearing, his relatives were amused. "There were dark secrets in
his life on Shasta Road," said his cousin, Hilde Stern Hein, years afterward. (Shasta Road was where he had lived as a bachelor.) "And one of
them was that Jean was lesbian." The "secret" was evidently true, but
we can only speculate about the role played by Jean's lesbianism in her
feelings toward Robert and her decision not to marry him.[2]

Whether Oppenheimer joined the Communist Party in Berkeley
during the late 1930s was a question scrutinized intently by the FBI
and Army security. The issue has been revived from time to time, most
recently when historian Gregg Herken unearthed the diary of Haakon
Chevalier's first wife. She wrote that Haakon, a lecturer in Romance
languages at the university, and Robert had belonged to a closed unit
of the Party that met every other week or so during the academic year

at the house of one or the other of them. In a letter to another historian in 1973, Chevalier, who had been a Party member and insisted that Robert had been as well, gave the names of four deceased friends who, he claimed, had belonged to their unit.[3]

Oppenheimer steadfastly denied that he had ever belonged to the Communist Party, and the U.S. government, despite its efforts, never proved that he had. But he conceded that he had been an active fellow traveler and had, through the Party, contributed to Spanish war relief and other causes favored by the Communists. At his home in Truro, Massachusetts, in 1985, Steve Nelson, head of the Party in San Francisco during the early 1940s, told the author, "Absolutely I would have known if he was in the Party, and I have no reason to deny it now that he is dead." If Oppenheimer had belonged to the Party, added the eighty-four-year-old Nelson, "I'd have been the one to collect his dues." Instead, the Party assigned Isaac "Doc" Folkoff, an older man who knew how to discuss "philosophical questions," to collect Robert's donations to the war in Spain.[4]

Nelson said that he first met Oppenheimer in 1939 at a fund-raiser in Berkeley. After they had made their speeches, Oppenheimer went up to Nelson to shake his hand. "I am going to marry a friend of yours," he said. The friend was Kitty, who had been married to Joe Dallet, a comrade of Nelson's in the Spanish war. In 1936 or so, Nelson, Dallet, and Kitty had spent a week together in Paris when the men were on their way to Spain; eight months later, it fell to Nelson to break the news to Kitty that Dallet had been killed. Later, Kitty lived briefly in New York City with Nelson and his wife, Margaret. "My association with Spain and with his wife's former husband made a bond that's a little hard to explain," Nelson said of his relationship with Oppenheimer. "I admired him. I respected him. He was an outstanding figure whom people, especially his students, looked on with awe. He was a figure with a glow. Why on earth should he have cared about the anti-Fascist cause?" Nelson thought it had something to do with Oppenheimer's exposure to anti-Semitism during his student years in Germany. But the question of asking him to join the Communist Party did not arise, Nelson claimed, in any discussion he took part in. "He's a good person, fine. He made contributions to the Party, fine. There are people who want to squeeze every drop out of a lemon. I didn't put the question to Robert. Our relationship was sensitive. I didn't want to be told no."

The Oppenheimers and Nelsons saw each other three or four times "on a personal basis," Nelson said, and other times at parties and fund-raisers. But in early 1943 Robert told Nelson he'd have to say good-bye. "I already suspected that it might be something special, maybe connected with the war effort, so I said nothing but good-bye and good luck." Robert left for Los Alamos, and they never saw each other again.[5]

Nelson's picture of Oppenheimer as close to the Party but not of it is echoed by Philip Farley, later a State Department adviser on arms control. As a graduate student in English at Berkeley, Farley saw Oppenheimer licking envelopes nights at the teachers' union, and remembered him as someone, unlike lowly graduate students such as himself, whom the Communists backed for office—Oppie was elected recording secretary—*because* he was a non-Party member who was a hero to others.[6]

Philip Morrison, a devoted student of Oppenheimer's, and David Hawkins, the Party's education director in the Bay Area, carefully distinguished their roles inside the Party from Oppenheimer's outside it. Morrison remembers lecturing on Marx, Engels, and Lenin at an old Loew's Theater in San Francisco as one of his assigned tasks, and he and Hawkins raised funds from individual donors as well. Oppenheimer donated funds but was never asked to solicit them. Years afterward, Hawkins observed that Oppenheimer was content to leave "a certain calculated ambiguity" about his relationship with the Party. Possibly it was a manifestation of his overall style of leaving things unsaid, a style which lent him an air of mystery but led others to wonder about his motives.[7]

Today, nearly seventy years later, does it matter whether Oppenheimer, along with other liberals who felt that the New Deal was not far enough left, actually belonged to the Communist Party? The Gray board, the government panel that in 1954 ruled on whether he should have a top-level security clearance, dismissed the possibility of his spying and called him "unusually discreet" with secrets of the atomic project. The question, then, is one of truthfulness. If Oppenheimer, despite his many denials, did in fact join the Party, even briefly, then he was carrying a terrible burden—both of membership and of dishonesty—during the hearings and throughout his postwar years as a government adviser.

Oppenheimer was not one to submit to the demands of Party discipline. And whether membership in what, in the parlance of the day, was called a "professional section" amounted to Party membership, as the Chevaliers claimed, may be a matter of definition. Given Oppenheimer's character and the years of scrutiny he weathered, it seems fair to assume that for a time he was, as he admitted, close to the Party, but that he did not belong to it.

Still, how could a man with so radical a record have been cleared for the Manhattan Project? The answer is that the country needed him. General Leslie R. Groves, director of the project for the Army, knew of his past connections but decided early on that Oppenheimer was the man to lead the effort and cleared him despite the objections of subordinates. Throughout the war Oppenheimer was subjected to closer surveillance than anybody else at Los Alamos: whenever he went outside the gates, he was driven in a government car by an Army security agent who listened in on his conversations. When Jean Tatlock in deep depression appealed to him and he went to her in Berkeley in 1943, FBI agents parked outside her apartment recorded the fact that he had spent the night.

After the war the surveillance continued. In the J. Edgar Hoover Building on Pennsylvania Avenue in Washington there are thousands of pages of transcripts of Oppenheimer's telephone conversations with his wife, Kitty, and others from 1946 on, all recorded by the FBI. And throughout this time he was advising the government on its policies about atomic weapons and, inevitably, its foreign policies as well. Oppenheimer knew he was being watched. Countless times, when he and Kitty were on a picnic or were stranded beside an airstrip somewhere, they and their two children would scour the ground for the four-leaf clovers they knew they would be needing someday. Although he expected lightning to strike, Oppenheimer did not trim his advice to the government. In the Acheson-Lilienthal plan, which he and his associate I. I. Rabi drafted at the end of 1945, he proposed international control of all fissionable materials although he was aware that this could—as it did—give rise to the charge that he wanted to give away the "secret" to the Russians. He opposed the H-bomb crash program although his position could—as it did—lead to the official charge that he had failed to advocate "the strongest offensive military posture for the United States." Beneath the debates, in minutes and letters that were classified for decades but are at long last available today, it is clear that he unfailingly took positions that he believed would optimize the nation's military posture.

Oppenheimer had other vulnerabilities besides his left-wing past. Ordinarily solicitous, even courtly, toward others, he also had a cruel streak. Sometimes, for no discernible reason, he would lash out at a student, a colleague, even a powerful official, with an acerbity bound to humiliate. This earned him enemies with power to retaliate and, just as much as his left-wing past or positions he had taken on major issues, paved the way to his downfall.

And there were questions about his character. While Oppenheimer did not trim his political advice in an effort to protect himself, in at least five instances he informed the government that he suspected a former student of being, or having once been, a Party member. And, spectacularly, by his own admission he had lied to Army security officials in 1943 in describing a feeler as to whether he might be willing to reveal atomic secrets to Russia—the so-called Chevalier affair.

Given these attributes, his enormous personal magnetism, his contempt for anyone he regarded as stupid or pompous or hypocritical, the fact that he was known to have lied on occasion, plus a delphic way of expressing himself that could make his pronouncements seem puzzling or double-edged, Oppenheimer was bound to become a point of anxiety to an administration which wanted to protect itself against charges that it was sheltering Communist spies. Thus, when a one-time congressional aide wrote a letter to FBI director

J. Edgar Hoover charging that Oppenheimer was "more probably than not" a spy for the Soviet Union, President Eisenhower quickly ordered that the scientist's clearances be suspended pending a hearing to determine whether he represented a danger to the nation's security.

Behind the scenes, the president was pursuing two related purposes. One was to break McCarthy's power; the other, to keep McCarthy as far as possible from the atomic energy program. As it happened, these purposes came together during the heartbreakingly beautiful Washington spring of 1954. After he had assaulted one government agency after another for alleged security lapses, McCarthy's unfriendly gaze had at last fallen upon Eisenhower's favorite institution, the U.S. Army. The commanding officer at Fort Monmouth, New Jersey, had inadvertently countenanced the promotion of a dentist named Irving Peress, who was charged by McCarthy with having been a Communist Party member. For this, McCarthy decided, the Army would have to pay. And so for the first ten days of May the secretary of the Army, Robert Stevens, occupied the witness stand in televised hearings before Congress that riveted the nation's attention. Each day after testifying, Stevens, whose career as a textile manufacturer had in no way prepared him for his ordeal, was driven back to the Pentagon to go over the testimony he had just given and be coached for his appearance the next day.

For three weeks that April and May, about the same time Stevens was suffering under the klieg lights on Capitol Hill, Oppenheimer was undergoing a comparable ordeal far out of public sight, in a dilapidated government building close by the Washington Monument. After he had testified each day and listened to the testimony of others, Oppenheimer, too, was driven across town, to the house of an attorney in Georgetown, to review the day's events and prepare for the next day's torment.

The ordeals the two men were undergoing were by no means symmetrical, for the Army secretary enjoyed the president's enthusiastic behind-the-scenes support, while the scientist endured just the opposite. The government placed obstacle after obstacle in the way of Oppenheimer's lawyers. They were denied access to documents they needed, witnesses for the defense were subjected to entrapment, and when his attorneys conferred with their client or with one another in person or by telephone, their conversations were recorded by the FBI and transmitted to the prosecution.

This wiretapping was illegal and would have caused a scandal had it been known at the time (it became public knowledge only after passage of the Freedom of Information Act more than twenty years later). In addition, nearly all the charges against Oppenheimer were wildly out of date. One accusation was that the scientist had continued to oppose the H-bomb program after it had become official policy and that his opposition had slowed down the program. Only a few days before the hearing began, however, the Atomic Energy Commission detonated a hydrogen bomb in the Pacific so powerful that it caused a diplomatic incident with Japan and gave rise to fears that thermonuclear explosions could no longer be controlled. Not only was the program successful, it was embarrassingly successful, and it had plainly outpaced that of the Russians.

Another of the accusations was that Oppenheimer had advocated the dispersal of small atomic weapons in Europe so that the West could fight a defensive war there as an alternative to mass bombing of civilians in the USSR. Testimony on this issue took up about a quarter of the transcript, yet by the time of the hearing in the spring of 1954, the measures Oppenheimer had advocated in 1951 were already the official policy of the administration that was conducting the prosecution. If Oppenheimer had committed heresy, it was the heresy of being right a year or two too soon.

During the hearing, Oppenheimer was not accused of ever having given away a government secret, nor did either of the panels that judged him find that he had done so. To the contrary, the court of first instance, the Gray board (so named after its chairman, former secretary of the Army Gordon Gray), concluded that the defendant had shown "extraordinary discretion in keeping to himself secrets," adding that had it been allowed to apply "mature common sense judgment" instead of the government's tangled security regulations, it would have cleared him. Nevertheless, citing his opposition to the

H-bomb crash program, it recommended by a vote of 2 to 1 that his clearance be withdrawn. Next, the five AEC commissioners, to whom Oppenheimer appealed the verdict, upheld the Gray board's decision by a vote of 4 to 1, this time on the entirely new ground that the scientist did not take the requirements of the security system seriously enough and that he had "defects of character" that made him a security risk.

By the conclusion of the parallel proceedings that spring, the public hearing on Capitol Hill and the secret one in the run-down building just off the Mall, Eisenhower's purposes had been achieved. In the course of the Army-McCarthy hearings the demagogic senator from Wisconsin overreached himself, and a few months later his colleagues voted to censure him, thereby ending his power. And, dominating the headlines as they did, the hearings over the Army drowned out the Oppenheimer hearing and stifled debate over the momentous questions that had led to it. As Stephen Ambrose, one of Eisenhower's biographers, pointed out, such was the furor over McCarthy that the president and Lewis Strauss got rid of Robert Oppenheimer without any public discussion of whether he had been right: whether it had been a breach of morality to build the H-bomb. The McCarthy hearings also distracted the public from fears stirred by the "Bravo" test in the Pacific that spring—the second U.S. thermonuclear test and one so enormous that it almost seemed out of control—and obscured the fact that thanks to Presidents Truman and Eisenhower, the United States was now embroiled in an all-out H-bomb race with the Russians.

But for the president, and the country, the hearing held in secret had its costs. Eisenhower respected Oppenheimer, shared his moral qualms about nuclear weapons, and knew that he was not disloyal. By allowing his officials to deceive him about Oppenheimer's alleged foot-dragging over the H-bomb and about methods used during the hearing, Eisenhower countenanced a travesty of justice that rankles in the American conscience to this day. Early in the year 2000, at a fiftieth-anniversary observance at the National Archives of McCarthy's West Virginia speech, no one—not a single member of Eisenhower's family or administration—took issue with the verdict of the historians in attendance that the Oppenheimer hearing was the single worst blot on Eisenhower's record in domestic affairs.

In writing this book, it was not my intention to write a parable for our time. But the story I tell is an old one, the story of what happens when some institution—a church, say, or a government—decides to rid itself of someone who has become anathema to it, or when it wants to change course without saying so openly.

Stories like this one do not take place in the open. Secrecy is at their heart, and so is the exclusive claim to orthodoxy. The people must be protected, whether from the taint of alien ideology or from the threat of military attack. The result is always the same. The fever passes, and most people never find out what was really at stake.

In the case of Robert Oppenheimer, the deviations from what we consider basic rules of our democracy were so egregious that even today, half a century later, the story still stirs our consciences and makes us wonder what it was all about. It was about many things. One of them was our government's decision to move to a new and deadlier level of the nuclear arms race without telling the American people. Not only was the hearing an extraordinary display of ingratitude toward a man to whom the nation owed much, but it resulted in the removal from public life of the one individual who might have helped restrain our catastrophic rush to overarmament.

This book is a look at the people and events that led to the destruction of J. Robert Oppenheimer.

There are stories like it today.

PART ONE

1945-1949

CHAPTER ONE

David Lilienthal's Vacation

FROM THE KITCHEN of his rented house on Martha's Vineyard, David Lilienthal watched on the early morning of September 19, 1949, as bluebirds flew in and out of a hole in the old knotted apple tree outside. A downy woodpecker was whacking away at the tree, along with a large flicker, a kingbird, and a pair of gray crested waxwings. The whirring sounds the birds made and the distant lapping noises of Nantucket Sound, these were nursing Helen and David Lilienthal back to life after a devastating spring and summer.

It had begun, if their current troubles could be said to have had so neat a beginning, back in May, when Republican senator Bourke Hickenlooper had demanded Lilienthal's resignation as chairman of the Atomic Energy Commission. Each day, said Hickenlooper, a member of the joint congressional committee on atomic energy, he had found new evidence of Lilienthal's "incredible mismanagement." For three months the hearings had dragged on, with Lilienthal on the witness stand day after sweltering summer day, with cameramen at his feet and glaring klieg lights in his eyes. Three months, and then Hickenlooper's Republican colleague Arthur Vandenberg had called David Lilienthal in and told him, almost casually, that the charges against him were being dropped.

Through it all, through banner newspaper headlines and nightly verbal attacks by the virulently right-wing radio commentator Fulton Lewis Jr., David and Helen Lilienthal had had over them the shadow of former secretary of defense James Forrestal, who had jumped to his death from a window of Bethesda Naval Hospital on May 22, the very day the attack on Lilienthal's "mismanagement" had begun.

Reminded in this abrupt and shocking way of what the pressures of public life could do to a man, Lilienthal felt grateful once again that he was able to count on the encouragement of his wife, Helen, and the staunch support of the president of the United States.[1]

On the Vineyard he had slept away some of his exhaustion. "I'm not a new man and never will be," Lilienthal wrote in his journal, "but I'm no longer acutely weary." It was time to think about the future. His term on the commission would be ending the following June. Nineteen years on government salaries, first as a founding director of the Tennessee Valley Authority and then as the first chairman of the AEC, had left him without much in the way of savings. He had just turned fifty, and with parents who needed help and a son and daughter who hoped to go to graduate school, he figured he had ten years left in which to put something by for his retirement. His three years at the AEC had been deeply disappointing to him in that the harnessing of atomic energy for peaceful purposes was still a long way down the road, and he knew the agency would never become what he had hoped—another TVA. On the other hand, in what the AEC had determined, to his regret, to be its main task, the commission had met its responsibility: the country had enough atomic weapons to ensure its safety for the foreseeable future.[2]

The AEC had been created in 1946, with five commissioners appointed by the president and answerable to both the White House and the Joint Committee on Atomic Energy of the House and Senate (JCAE). In addition to Lilienthal, the original commissioners were Robert Bacher, a nuclear physicist from Cornell who had worked on the Manhattan Project; Lewis Strauss and Sumner Pike, small-town boys who had been successful on Wall Street; and William Waymack, former editor of the Des Moines *Register* and *Tribune* and deputy chairman of the Federal Reserve Bank of Chicago. Because it had been created to manage atomic energy development for military as well as civilian purposes, the commission had had to take a tougher line on almost everything than Lilienthal would have liked. And of the five commissioners, the toughest had been Lewis Strauss, a strongly partisan Republican investment banker from New York. A dozen times, finding himself in a minority of one, Strauss had gone over the heads of the others to the White House, the newspapers, and even to highly placed friends such as Defense Secretary Forrestal. Strauss's habit of "shooting at one's brothers," as Lilienthal called it, had shattered the spirit of collegiality so important to Lilienthal's way of running things. He realized that he would no longer be able to lead in the way that suited him, by reconciling differences. He knew, moreover, that if he were to accept reappointment, there would probably be another ugly fight, like the one he had had with Democratic senator Kenneth McKellar of Tennessee on his confirmation in 1947 and the one he had just been through. "If we have another one," Helen told him, referring to the Hickenlooper hearings as they sat drinking coffee on the front stoop a day or two before, "*I'll* resign." Not that David Lilienthal looked with much enthusiasm on the prospect of a return to private life. For all that it cost him, the cameras and the headlines and the constant pressure to make decisions too portentous for any one man, he was in his metier as a public servant. The mere making of money held little appeal for him.

Driving home from dinner with friends in a heavy ground fog that evening of September 19, Lilienthal thought he recognized the man who, with his thumb up in a hitchhiker's gesture, was peering into the headlights. "It's Jim McCormack," he said quietly, as if he found this man every night squinting beside a goat field in dense fog. Had he parachuted in, or what?

Back at the house, the flame from the kerosene lantern made the rickety summer furniture wobble and dance as if in a Charles Addams drawing. Lilienthal gazed out the window at the Big Dipper as the visitor he called "General Jim" half apologized and half joked about being the messenger bearing bad news.

"Are you troubled?" Helen Lilienthal asked as they went to bed. "Oh, some, one of those things," her husband told her. He said he had to leave at seven the next morning, and would "probably be back by night." He did not believe it, of course, and at dawn he pumped enough water in the well to keep her supplied for two days. Before departing, he said good-bye to the birds, the slender, tufted things he had so enjoyed watching the day before. They were in a poplar tree now. Off they flew in a cloud, into the sunrise, swinging from side to side.

General Jim (Brigadier General James McCormack, director of the Division of Military Applications, AEC) filled Lilienthal in during the flight. On September 3, a weather reconnaissance plane on patrol from Japan to Alaska had picked up signs of radioactivity just east of the Kamchatka Peninsula, and more signs had been picked up during the next few days. No one in official Washington had expected the Russians to test an atomic device so soon—Secretary of State Dean Acheson had said it might occur as early as 1951 and General Leslie Groves, head of the Manhattan Project, had said it would take twenty years—and the news was bound to cause shock. William Webster, the defense secretary's deputy for atomic energy, had gone to see Lilienthal's deputy, AEC general manager Carroll Wilson, and suggested that a scientific panel be appointed to examine the evidence. Vannevar Bush, civilian director of the Manhattan Project during the war, was appointed chairman, with three Los Alamos veterans, Robert Oppenheimer, former commissioner Robert Bacher, and Admiral William S. Parsons, as members.[3]

That all of this had occurred while the chairman of the Atomic Energy Commission was allowed to rusticate in ignorance for nearly three weeks on Martha's Vineyard says worlds about the secrecy that suffused the enterprise, since no one had dared inform him by telephone or telegraph. But on Monday, September 19, at Air Force detection headquarters on G Street, the members of the Bush panel, General Hoyt Vandenberg and other high-ranking Air Force officers, a dozen scientists from various laboratories, and a small British mission gathered to question the scientists who had analyzed radioactive samples from the suspected test. Even here, however, secrecy imposed its restrictions: Oppenheimer's task of explaining what the Russians had done was the more difficult because he was not permitted to reveal how the panel had arrived at its conclusions. The assembled scientists and officers nonetheless accepted the panel's assessment that what it had seen was "consistent with the view that the origin of the fission products was the explosion of an atomic bomb" on August 29. The members of the Bush panel and the three commissioners on hand that afternoon hoped the news would be announced by the president before it leaked and before the Russians announced it. They decided to dispatch General McCormack to Martha's Vineyard to bring Lilienthal back so that he could persuade the president to announce the Soviet success without delay.[4]

When he arrived at his office on the morning of September 20, Lilienthal hoped to be told that the explosion had turned out to be something else. But Oppenheimer, looking "frantic," and a "deeply worried" Bacher assured him that the event they had feared since 1946 was upon them. Both of them urged that the news be made public right away.

Harry Truman was at his desk, reading the *Congressional Record*, when Lilienthal entered the Oval Office just before four in the afternoon. As the president joked about partisan goings-on in the Senate the day before, his mood seemed as serene as the garden outside, with the golden September sunlight streaming through it. As for this detection report—*he* raised the subject—he had known it would happen someday. Those captured German scientists had probably helped the Russians pull it off. But maybe it wasn't the real thing. Oh, yes, it was, Lilienthal assured him. The evidence had been persuasive even to the doubters. "Really?" asked the president. Still, he said, he was not going to announce it right away. The Russians had finally sent a *real* negotiator to the UN and the British were about to announce devaluation of the pound, and he wanted to let things simmer down. Another reason for silence was that announcing the test would reveal our detection capabilities to the Russians.

Lilienthal urged him to reconsider. Far from alarming the country, Truman's announcing—before it leaked—that the Russians had acquired the bomb would show that he was taking it in stride and that no one else need be upset either. And it would show that this was a president who leveled with the American people. Harry Truman heard his visitor out and accompanied him to the door, apparently still determined to take his time.

Back at commission headquarters, Lilienthal found his fellow commissioners upset by the delay. Oppenheimer was particularly unhappy, seeing it as one more case of the government's behaving as if there were some big secret when there was none, and missing the chance to bring the facts about atomic energy a little more into the open. Lilienthal agreed but, knowledgeable about the ways of government, pointed out that the decision was up to the president.

Go on back to the Vineyard, Lilienthal's secretary, Martha Jane Brown, urged him late that afternoon. Lilienthal stopped by the apartment of his friend and fellow commissioner Sumner Pike for whiskey and some talk before boarding the B-25. By 10:30 that night he was back with Helen by the fireplace on Martha's Vineyard, with the wind blowing outside, the limbs of dead apple trees dancing eerily in the firelight. The "Wuthering Heights touch again," he wrote in his journal before they went to bed.

A couple of days later Lilienthal was summoned to a neighbor's telephone on the Vineyard to take a call from acting AEC chairman Pike. The president had announced the Russian bomb that morning after all, and in the text Pike read aloud to him, Lilienthal recognized arguments he had made to President Truman three days before. The choice of words showed that the president still questioned whether the Russians really had done it—he termed it "an atomic explosion," not a full-fledged bomb test—but Lilienthal was pleased that his trip to Washington had had some effect.[5]

The General Advisory Committee of the Atomic Energy Commission happened to be meeting that day. The nine-man GAC was the tail that wagged the AEC dog, being composed of the country's wisest and most experienced nuclear scientists and engineers. Appointed by the president for fixed terms, the GAC members enjoyed an authority in nuclear affairs that no one in the Pentagon, White House, or AEC could match. The commission therefore looked to the GAC and its chairman, Robert Oppenheimer, for guidance on technical issues and much more.

Oppenheimer described the evidence that what the Russians had set off was really an atomic test. The first reaction of Glenn Seaborg, chemistry professor at the University of California and the committee's youngest member, was that the U.S. government's stringent secrecy policies had failed. Isidor Isaac Rabi, professor of physics at Columbia University, thought the Soviet bomb made war more likely. He wanted the government to take action, but he did not say what. Oppenheimer thought it too early to suggest changes in the weapons program, since it was the country's response, and not the Russian bomb, now called Joe One, that might make changes necessary. He agreed with Seaborg that if the committee were to make any response, it should be an expression of hope for a secrecy policy that made sense. When news came that the president had just announced the test—ahead of the inevitable leak or an announcement from Moscow—everyone was relieved.

Later that day Oppenheimer had a call from a former colleague, Edward Teller, in town for a meeting at the Pentagon. Teller wanted to know what *he* should do now that the Russians had tested a bomb. "Keep your shirt on," Oppenheimer told him.[6]

CHAPTER TWO

The Maneuvering Begins

No sooner had the Russian test been announced than intensive lobbying got under way, with the Joint Committee on Atomic Energy, chaired by the high-powered and ambitious senator Brien McMahon of Connecticut, taking the lead. At the end of September the JCAE's executive director, a twenty-nine-year-old veteran of World War II in Europe named William Borden, told the committee that development of a weapon a thousand times more powerful than the A-bomb, something so far unattainable called the hydrogen bomb, was the answer to the Soviet success. A few days after the president's announcement, McMahon asked General James McCormack how much the new bomb, providing it could be built at all, would "magnify the destructiveness" of the atomic bomb. McCormack replied in secret session that "if all the theory turned out," the bomb would be "infinite. You can have it any size up to the sun. . . . A million tons or more of . . . TNT."[1]

Across the ocean, a headline caught the eye of a wealthy American as he passed a newsstand in Florence, Italy. The American knew only a few words of Italian, but he grabbed the paper and puzzled out Truman's announcement. Then he sat up until three in the morning writing a letter to an old friend back in New York. The next day he carried the letter to the U.S. consul general and asked him to send it via diplomatic pouch.

The American who had spotted the president's announcement was a Wall Street investor named William Golden, and the friend to whom he sent his letter was AEC commissioner Lewis Strauss. The two men had been in the Navy together during World War II and remained friends afterward as they pursued lucrative careers in finance. After Strauss joined the commission, Golden signed on as his dollar-a-year assistant; in September 1949, he was vacationing with his wife in Europe. Years afterward Alice Strauss remembered her husband's receiving a secret message in New York that the Russians had exploded what appeared to be an atomic bomb. Dismayed and alarmed, he boarded the first flight to Washington and left her to catch up as best she could.[2]

As soon as he received Golden's letter Strauss penned a memorandum, which he read to the other commissioners on October 5. With our monopoly gone, he said, it was not enough for the United States to maintain an "arithmetical" lead in atomic weapons. Borrowing an expression from Golden, he said it was time for a "quantum jump." The only way to stay ahead was to make a commitment comparable "in talent and money . . . to that which produced the first atomic bomb." The GAC should be consulted not about whether, but about "how we can proceed with expedition."[3]

A determined man who left nothing to chance, Strauss next paid a call on Sidney Souers, another friend from naval intelligence during the war. Souers was a banker in St. Louis, Missouri, Truman's home state. Surprisingly, however, he and the president did not know each other, and it had been at Strauss's request that Souers had come to Washington to serve on an AEC security panel. Discreet and self-effacing, Souers soon won the president's trust and became executive secretary of the National Security Council (NSC). He was Strauss's man, and Strauss decided to use him as his conduit to the president. In doing so, Souers said later, Strauss had come "to the right place."[4]

Strauss asked his old acquaintance whether something called the hydrogen bomb had reached the president's attention, and if so, if Truman had made up his mind to build it.

Souers responded that as far as he knew, the president had never heard of such a bomb. "Can we build one?" he asked.

Strauss said yes.

"Then why in the world don't we build it?" Souers wanted to know.

Strauss replied that the president had not been told about the weapon because AEC chairman David Lilienthal was opposed to building it.

"See that it gets to the President," Souers said.

"I don't think I can since I'm almost alone in the Commission," said Strauss, adding that the GAC, too, was almost unanimously opposed to building the new bomb.

"That doesn't matter," said Souers. "You were appointed by the President. *You* bring it up, let your colleagues refute what you . . . recommend, and then the President can do what he thinks best."

"Check with the President, anyway," Strauss requested. "If you'll just tell me to go ahead, I'll accept that from you."

"I'll tell you right now," Souers said. "I know he would want it done."[5]

The next day Souers asked the president whether he had heard of something called the hydrogen bomb. "No," said the president, "but you tell Strauss to go to it and fast." Souers called Strauss and said nothing about talking to the president, merely that he had thought about the matter overnight, and told him to go ahead.

The memo Strauss read aloud at the commission on October 5 had its effect. Within days David Lilienthal asked Oppenheimer to call a meeting of the GAC to advise on "as broad a basis as possible" whether the atomic energy program "constitutes doing everything that it is reasonably possible for us to do for the common defense and security." Oppenheimer arranged a meeting for the final weekend of October, the earliest date at which two of his members, James Conant and Enrico Fermi, could be there.[6]

Meanwhile, a handful of scientists in Berkeley were horrified by the Soviet success. One was a tall, ruddy, intensely creative physicist named Luis Alvarez, and another was the chemist Wendell Latimer. They lost no time going to see Ernest Lawrence, director of the University of California's Radiation Laboratory, inventor of its cyclotron, and a scientist of enormous influence in political circles, who had had much to do with getting the Manhattan Project started back in 1942. Alvarez and Latimer found Lawrence worried that the Russians might already be working on the H-bomb and might succeed in building it first. The only thing to do, the three men agreed, was to get there before the Russians did. On their way to Washington for a scheduled visit, Lawrence and Alvarez decided to make a stop at Los Alamos to check with Edward Teller. On Friday, October 7, they spent a full day there talking to Teller, the Russian-born astrophysicist George Gamow, the Polish-born mathematician Stanislaw Ulam, and John Manley, the lab's associate director. Teller assured Lawrence and Alvarez, who had not done any research on the weapon, that the Super—Teller's proposed thermonuclear, or hydrogen, bomb—was feasible and, with an effort comparable to that of the Manhattan Project, could be built in about two years. Alvarez reported in his diary that the men they talked to at Los Alamos thought the Super would have a "good chance," provided there was plenty of an element called tritium—a big *if*—and provided the calculating machines at Princeton and Los Alamos could be geared up to perform the millions of mathematical calculations the project would require. Teller accompanied the visitors to their hotel in Albuquerque and stayed up half the night with them discussing how to obtain the needed supply of excess neutrons. Lawrence, in what the Hungarian took to be an exhortation to go on the stump campaigning for the H-bomb, showed Teller how to wash his shirts and hang them out to dry.[7]

At lunch three days later in Washington, Lawrence and Alvarez told Brien McMahon and California congressman Carl Hinshaw, a member of McMahon's committee, that current research on the Super was inadequate and that the "booster" test scheduled for 1951 was merely a "mincing step." According to Borden, they expressed "keen and even grave concern that Russia is giving top priority to development of the thermonuclear super-bomb. They pointed out that the Russian expert, Kapitsa, is one of the world's foremost authorities on the problems involved in light elements . . . and even went so far as to say that they fear Russia may be ahead of us. . . . They declared that for the first time in their experience they are actually fearful of America's losing a war unless immediate steps are taken on our own super-bomb project." Finally, they said that a Super could be developed in one and a half to two years if an all-out effort was mounted.[8]

Alvarez paid a visit to AEC headquarters in Washington, where he got the impression that Lilienthal felt "lukewarm" about the Super; Lilienthal wrote with disgust in his journal that Alvarez and Lawrence had come to see him, "drooling" over the H-bomb. We keep saying we have no other course, Lilienthal observed, when the real difficulty is that "we are not bright enough to see any other course."[9]

Lawrence and Alvarez were not the only ones who believed the Super was the answer. After the Soviet test, Teller went to Major General Roscoe Charles Wilson, deputy chief of the Air Force Special Weapons Group, to urge that Air Force higher-ups be briefed about the hydrogen bomb. Air Force chief of staff Hoyt Vandenberg appeared before the JCAE the day after he was briefed to plead for the weapon on the grounds that the United States had to beat Russia to the punch. General Omar N. Bradley, chairman of the Joint Chiefs of Staff, did not put it nearly so bluntly, but right after the session at which the two men testified McMahon wrote to Lilienthal that should the USSR achieve a thermonuclear bomb ahead of the United States, "the fatal consequences are obvious. . . . American efforts along this line should be as bold and urgent as our original atomic enterprise." He wanted to know whether the AEC was considering an all-out, Manhattan Project–type of effort.[10]

As busy as things were in Washington, Fuld Hall in Princeton was even busier. Fuld Hall was home of the Institute for Advanced Study, to which Robert Oppenheimer, scientific director of the atomic bomb project at Los Alamos during the war, had come as director in 1947. Of all Oppenheimer's responsibilities as adviser to the government, none meant as much to him as his chairmanship of the GAC, and during October 1949, nearly everyone in the country concerned in a high-level way with atomic energy came to Princeton to seek his counsel. The first was his close friend I. I. Rabi, and the next was another close friend, Admiral William "Deak" Parsons, the ranking military officer at Los Alamos during the war and a highly intelligent

Navy official, with whom Oppenheimer discussed everything. Then came the two top men at Los Alamos, Norris Bradbury, Oppenheimer's successor as director of the lab, and John Manley. Both men wanted a thorough review of what the laboratory was doing in light of the Russians' success. Since the Soviet test, they told Oppenheimer, scientists at the lab had been advocating everything from business as usual to an all-out program to develop the H-bomb. After the visit by the Los Alamos men, two representatives of the military side of things came, James McCormack and Robert LeBaron, of the Pentagon's Military Liaison Committee, and after them the physicists Hans Bethe and Edward Teller.

Back in 1942, Oppenheimer, aided mostly by Manley but by Teller and others as well, had scoured the country in search of talent for the Manhattan Project. The time was late, most scientists were already working on the war effort, and recruiting first-class men for a project too secret to be described had been a tough sell. But Oppenheimer had worked miracles of persuasion, and Los Alamos soon was staffed by young Americans trained during the 1930s at Berkeley, Caltech, the University of Chicago, Purdue, the University of Illinois, and East Coast universities, and by Europeans (Bethe and Teller among them) who had fled Hitler's anti-Semitism and might not have received U.S. citizenship in time to be cleared for other projects. Now Teller, perhaps in unconscious emulation of Oppenheimer's wartime effort, had embarked on a recruiting drive of his own. His first stop was Ithaca, New York, where his close friend Hans Bethe was professor of physics at Cornell.

Bethe later said that at this time he had been in "very great" internal conflict as to whether he should take part in an all-out effort to build a hydrogen bomb. He had attended the meeting at Le Conte Hall in Berkeley in the early summer of 1942, the first to consider basic thermonuclear reactions, and had taken a leading part in theoretical research during his many stints as consultant to Los Alamos since the war. Always, at the back of his mind, was the hope that he, or if not he then someone else, would succeed in proving the thermonuclear bomb impossible. Now Teller, anxious to persuade Bethe to head the theoretical effort, told him about some new ideas that might make at least one phase of the program more feasible technically than it had seemed before. Hearing about Teller's ideas in his living room, Bethe was impressed, but he still felt that building such a large bomb, and escalating the weapons race, would be a "terrible undertaking." He and his wife, Rose, discussed what he ought to do. "I was deeply troubled," he has said, and "Rose was very much against it."[11]

The two friends therefore converged on Oppenheimer's office in Fuld Hall to ask his opinion. Oppenheimer later remembered Bethe's saying, "I cannot see what we can do but build this, and I don't see that it can eventuate in anything but utter catastrophe. I cannot refuse . . . but if I go, it will be with a very heavy heart." According to Bethe, he and Teller found Oppenheimer "equally undecided and equally troubled about what should be done. I did not get from him the advice I was hoping to get" as to whether to join Teller in trying to build the bomb. When Teller presented his case, Oppenheimer did not argue for or against the bomb, but confined himself to the observation that one GAC member, James Conant, was very much against it. He pointed to a letter on his desk which he said he had just received from Conant and read part of it aloud. All Teller could remember later was that Conant had said that a crash program to develop the hydrogen bomb would be approved only "over my dead body." As for Oppenheimer, Teller remembered only his saying that if there were to be such a program, then the country should be told openly, without the hermetic secrecy that had shrouded the Manhattan Project. Bethe disagreed, and said that the fact that work was under way, and the outcome, should be kept secret. Memorably, Oppenheimer called the contest that would take place between the United States and Soviet Russia to build the bomb "a race between a piece of glass and a piece of onyx, [one] totally transparent and [the other] totally obscure."[12]

Prior to the visit, Teller had predicted that after seeing Oppenheimer, Bethe would decline to work on the bomb. But as they left Oppenheimer's office, Teller later recalled, Bethe told him, "You see, you can be quite satisfied. I am still coming."[13]

But during the weekend Bethe strolled around the Princeton campus with Victor Weisskopf, a theoretical physicist from Vienna with whom he had worked closely at Los Alamos. Weisskopf spoke in vivid terms about the costs of a thermonuclear war. He said that the world that survived would be "not worth preserving," a world in which "we would lose the things we were fighting for." Bethe later called the conversation "very long" and "very difficult . . . for both of us." Later that weekend, as Bethe, Weisskopf, and another close friend, the Czech-born physicist George Placzek, drove to La Guardia Airport, they went over it again, with both Weisskopf and Placzek urging Bethe in the strongest terms not to work on the bomb. All three speculated about the position Oppenheimer and the GAC were likely to take. After talking a full hour with Oppenheimer, Bethe said, he still did not know his opinion. So intense was the conversation that Weisskopf forgot his coat. He left it in Placzek's car and took Placzek's instead of his own, while Bethe missed his flight to Oak Ridge, Tennessee.[14]

A day or so later, Bethe called Teller to say that he had decided against working on the bomb. Then and later, Teller assumed it was Oppenheimer who had dissuaded him.

But Bethe was right—Oppenheimer had not made up his mind. Of all his colleagues on the GAC, Conant was the one Oppenheimer was closest to. Earlier that month he had stayed with the Conants during a meeting of the Harvard Board of Overseers in Cambridge. Of the visit he wrote to a colleague that he and Conant had had "a long and difficult discussion having, alas, nothing to do with Harvard." During their talk the two men apparently discussed whether the GAC should ask for a meeting with President Truman at the end of its late-October session. And on Friday, October 21, before he saw Bethe and Teller, Oppenheimer had penned his reply to Conant.[15]

"Dear Uncle Jim," he wrote, addressing Conant by his Los Alamos nickname. "We are exploring the possibilities for our talk with the President on October 30."

Oppenheimer continued:

On the technical side, . . . the super is not very different from what it was when we first spoke of it more than seven years ago—a weapon of unknown design, cost, deliverability and military value. But a very great change has taken place in the climate of opinion. On the one hand, two experienced promoters have been at work, i.e., Ernest Lawrence and Edward Teller. The project has long been dear to Teller's heart; and Ernest has convinced himself that we must learn from Operation Joe that the Russians will soon do the super, and that we had better beat them to it. . . .

What concerns me is really not the technical problem. I am not sure the miserable thing will work, nor that it can be gotten to a target except by ox cart. It seems likely to me even further to worsen the unbalance of our present war plans. What does worry me is that this thing appears to have caught the imagination, both of the congressional and of military people, as the answer to the problem posed by the Russian advance. It would be folly to oppose the exploration of this weapon. We have always known it had to be done; and it does have to be done, though it appears to be singularly proof against any form of experimental approach. But that we become committed to it as the way to save the country and the peace appears to me full of dangers.

We will be faced with all this at our meeting; and anything that we do or do not say to the President, will have to take it into consideration. I shall feel far more secure if you have had an opportunity to think about it.

I still remember my visit with gratitude and affection.

Oppenheimer had already answered Conant when Bethe and Teller visited him on October 21, but it was Conant's letter to him, and not his reply, that he chose to read aloud. Bethe speculated long afterward that Oppenheimer might already have made up his mind, but, believing that as chairman of the GAC he ought to maintain neutrality, he had let Conant's letter speak for him. But the fact is that

Oppenheimer still was uncertain. He testified at his 1954 security hearing that he had not yet made up his mind at the time he received Conant's letter, and in a 1957 interview he pointed out that the position he ultimately took was different from the one he had taken in his letter to Conant. It was Conant's arguments later, at the GAC meeting, that persuaded him.[16]

These were the discussions that were taking place as the GAC met to discuss the most important question that had ever come before it. The American people knew nothing except that Russia had tested the atomic bomb.

CHAPTER THREE

The Halloween Meeting

EACH TIME the General Advisory Committee met, the secretary, John Manley, flew to Washington a day or two early to prepare. Manley was a slight, able experimentalist who had helped Oppenheimer set up the Los Alamos laboratory early in the war and had stayed on afterward. As associate director of the laboratory and a trusted colleague of GAC chairman Oppenheimer, Manley was in a perfect position to shape the committee's agenda. This he did informally, drifting from desk to desk at AEC headquarters prior to each meeting, greeting everyone who felt like talking to him, typists to division heads, and asking what was on their minds. In this way he not only took the commission's pulse, he helped keep the advisory committee so well informed that it earned the reputation of running the commission. In late October 1949, Manley had more than the usual quantity of papers to prepare and distribute ahead of time.

He was setting out documents on the afternoon of Friday, October 28, when Robert Oppenheimer appeared in the conference room overlooking Constitution Avenue. Oppenheimer had with him someone Manley had not seen before, a slender, tall, rather dapper-looking man from the Department of State who turned out to be George Kennan, special adviser to Secretary of State Acheson. After Oppenheimer, other members of the GAC appeared: I. I. Rabi; Cyril Smith and Enrico Fermi from the University of Chicago; Oliver Buckley, head of Bell Labs in New Jersey; Hartley Rowe of the United Fruit Company; and Lee DuBridge, president of Caltech, who had been director of the radar project at MIT during the war. Two members did not appear that day: James Conant, who arrived from Boston the next morning, and Glenn Seaborg, the University of California chemist who was in Stockholm, being looked over by the Nobel Prize committee.

Kennan spoke informally to the committee that afternoon about conditions in the USSR, with a view to whether Stalin would want to embark on a new stage of the arms race so soon after the devastation of World War II. With its industry still in ruins, Kennan thought, the Soviet Union might be willing to enter an agreement to restrain nuclear weapons development, provided the United States did so as well. Kennan also believed that it would not take a huge stockpile of atomic weapons to deter the Russians from aggressive acts—a few bombs would suffice. Speaking after Kennan, Hans Bethe described the technical difficulties of igniting the Super weapon and suggested that the odds of building it were not good.[1]

On the morning of Saturday, October 29, the committee met, first with the five commissioners and other officials from the AEC, and then with Pentagon officers led by General Bradley and Air Force chief of staff General Lauris Norstad. Oppenheimer was seated at one end of the long rectangular table, with Manley behind him, taking notes. Manley was as impressed by General Bradley's homespun manner and obvious decency as he had been the previous day by Kennan's impassioned fluency and his knowledge of the Russians. But he noticed to his surprise that the generals seemed to be hearing about the hydrogen bomb for the first time. The meeting therefore devolved not into a discussion of whether the generals wanted a new, more powerful bomb, but of how, since the armies of Europe and the United States had been demobilized since the end of the war, Western Europe could be defended in the event of a Soviet attack. Manley got the impression that the two generals had not given much thought to other important questions. Would the United States, for example, respond to a Soviet attack on Europe by dropping an atomic bomb on Moscow? Norstad and Bradley did not even answer the question as to whether the armed services wanted more A-bombs. As for a hydrogen bomb, Bradley said nothing about its military usefulness, only that it might be of "psychological" value.[2]

The physicist Luis Alvarez was not a member of the GAC, but his enthusiasm for the H-bomb had prompted him to come all the way from Berkeley on his own. He stationed himself inside the entrance to the AEC to watch the generals and scientists come and go. Spotting him there at the lunch break, Oppenheimer invited Alvarez and Robert Serber, a former student now teaching at Berkeley, who had spoken before the committee on technical issues the day before, to join him at a restaurant nearby. Oppenheimer echoed Kennan's view that if the United States refrained from trying to build the Super, the Russians might do likewise. While he told his luncheon companions that negative views about the H-bomb had been expressed at the meeting on moral grounds, Oppenheimer did not say anything about the fact that in the course of discussion those views were coming to be his own. But Alvarez picked up on the tenor of Oppenheimer's remarks. Concluding, mistakenly, that he was leading the opposition and would carry the day, Alvarez gave up and flew back to California, convinced that "the program was dead."[3]

Like Oppenheimer, most GAC members had arrived with their minds not fully made up. A consensus was therefore reached only gradually, after lengthy soul-searching, in the course of which most of them changed their views. At one end of the spectrum, adamant in opposition to any effort to build an H-bomb, was James Conant who, as civilian director of the Manhattan Project in Washington during the war and Truman's original choice to be chairman of the AEC, was the senior person in the room.[4] An austere-looking New Englander whom Lilienthal described in his journal as "looking almost translucent, so grey," Conant said that mere discussion of the issue made him feel as if he were "seeing the same film, and a punk one, for the second time." Another member, Hartley Rowe, agreed—"we already built one Frankenstein." Lilienthal had the impression that Rabi was "completely on [the] other side." And Fermi gave a technical summary in which he concluded that the chances of building a deliverable thermonuclear weapon (as the H-bomb was called) were only "a little better than even."[5]

The meeting produced three documents. The main report, by

Oppenheimer and Manley, was signed by all eight members who were present. "We all hope that by one means or another the development of these weapons can be avoided. We are all reluctant to see the United States taking the initiative. . . . We are all agreed that it would be wrong at the present moment to commit ourselves to an all-out effort." Explaining that if the first problem, that of initiating an explosion, proved soluble, then deuterium, a gaseous isotope of hydrogen, could be added to the weapon to the point where "there is no limit to the explosive power of the bomb except that imposed by requirements of delivery." And if it could be delivered by ship and did not have to be dropped from the air, then, said the committee, "the weapon is from a technical point of view without limitations with regard to the damage it can inflict. . . . Its use therefore carries much further than the atomic bomb itself the policy of exterminating civilian populations." The committee recommended that, in deciding against development, the government make clear to the public the fact that the bomb would have no civilian uses and that it could be built to have unlimited destructive power.

The committee had before it only one H-bomb model, a concept invented by Edward Teller called the "Classical Super." While it had not so far proven mathematically feasible, the committee did not rule out the possibility that this or some other model might be achievable: "We believe that an imaginative and concerted attack on the problem has a better than even chance of producing the weapon within five years."

The report addressed itself also to Lilienthal's original question: was the AEC doing everything that could be done for the nation's defense? The answer, again, was no. The report urged a major effort to expand the supply of fissionable material and to adapt aircraft and weaponry to the use of smaller atomic weapons for limited, or tactical, purposes.

As against its unanimity on these issues, the committee admitted that it was divided as to the nature of its commitment not to develop the hydrogen weapon. "The majority feels that this should be an unqualified commitment. Others feel that it should be made conditional on the response of the Soviet government to a proposal to renounce such development." To the main report two appendices were added, a majority annex written by Conant and DuBridge and signed by six members, and a minority annex by Rabi and Fermi.

The majority annex read as follows:

We have been asked by the Commission whether or not they should immediately initiate an "all-out" effort to develop a weapon whose energy release is 100 to 1000 times greater and whose destructive power in terms of area of damage is 20 to 100 times greater than those of the present atomic bomb. We recommend strongly against such action.

We base our recommendation on our belief that the extreme dangers to mankind inherent in the proposal wholly outweigh any military advantage. . . . Let it be clearly realized that this is a super weapon; it is in a wholly different category from an atomic bomb. The reason for developing such super bombs would be to have the capacity to devastate a vast area with a single bomb. Its use would involve a decision to slaughter a vast number of civilians. We are alarmed as to the possible global effects of the radioactivity generated by the explosion of a few super bombs of conceivable magnitude. If super bombs will work at all, there is no inherent limit in the destructive power that may be attained with them. Therefore, a super bomb might become a weapon of genocide.

We believe a super bomb should never be produced [italics added]. Mankind would be far better off not to have a demonstration of the feasibility of such a weapon until the present climate of world opinion changes.

It is by no means certain that the weapon can be developed at all and by no means certain that the Russians will produce one within a decade. . . . Should they use the weapon against us, reprisals by our large stock of atomic bombs would be comparably effective to the use of a super.

In determining not to proceed to develop the super bomb, we see a unique opportunity of providing by example some

limitations on the totality of war and thus of limiting the fear
and arousing the hopes of mankind.

> James B. Conant
> Hartley Rowe
> Cyril Stanley Smith
> L. A. DuBridge
> Oliver E. Buckley
> J. R. Oppenheimer

The minority statement by Fermi and Rabi makes the moral case
even more strongly:

> Necessarily such a weapon goes far beyond any military ob-
> jective and enters the range of very great natural catastrophes.
> By its very nature it cannot be confined to a military objective
> but becomes a weapon which in practical effect is almost one of
> genocide.
> It is clear that the use of such a weapon cannot be justified
> on any ethical ground which gives a human being a certain indi-
> viduality and dignity even if he happens to be a resident of an
> enemy country. It is evident to us that this would be the view of
> people in other countries. Its use would put the United States in
> a bad moral position relative to the peoples of the world.
> Any postwar situation resulting from such a weapon would
> leave unresolvable enmities for generations. A desirable peace
> cannot come from such an inhuman application of force. The
> postwar problems would dwarf the problems which confront us
> at present. . . .
> The fact that no limit exists to the destructiveness of this
> weapon makes its very existence and the knowledge of its con-
> struction a danger to humanity as a whole. *It is necessarily an evil
> thing considered in any light* [italics added].
> For these reasons we believe it important for the President of
> the United States to tell the American public and the world that
> we think it wrong on fundamental ethical principles to initiate a
> program of development of such a weapon. At the same time it

would be appropriate to invite the nations of the world to join us in a solemn pledge not to proceed. . . . If such a pledge were accepted even without control machinery, it appears highly probable that an advanced stage of development leading to a test could be detected by available physical means. Furthermore we have in our possession, in our stockpile of atomic bombs, the means for adequate "military" retaliation for the production or use of a Super.[6]

Despite their strong moral language, Fermi and Rabi were proposing a practical solution. Development of the hydrogen bomb would require testing, a fact that made possible a system of control. Since any test large enough to produce debris in the atmosphere could be detected by our aircraft, American scientists would be alerted to any Soviet thermonuclear test. Having continued its research into thermonuclear processes, the United States could then go ahead with a test program of its own. Fermi and Rabi were proposing a thermonuclear test ban that was self-enforcing and would not require an intrusive system of inspection.

As they said their good-byes on Sunday, the committee members felt they had accomplished something. One of them described the spirit of the meeting as "astonishingly harmonious," and Oppenheimer called it "a meeting of sensibilities." No one had dominated; no one had even tried to win any of the others to his point of view. A consensus had evolved, and the question had become "how much we were going to say and how strongly we were going to say it."[7]

John Manley was pleased by the outcome. The GAC, he felt, had reversed the momentum created by Teller and Lawrence and pointed the way to ending the arms race. Cyril Smith, a British-born specialist in metals physics, felt the same way. On the flight back to Chicago, he and Fermi, barred from discussing sensitive matters where others could overhear them, passed the time playing mathematical games. It occurred to Smith while they were playing that the proposals they had just fashioned might be the beginning of a revolution in man's relationship to the weapons he had created. Back in Washington, however, David Lilienthal was less hopeful. He had "terrible and deeply important things" on his mind, among them the differences in kind between the ordinary atomic bomb and the Super. The Super would have no civilian by-products, and its existence was certain to increase the risk of war. It was not enough to forgo development, as the GAC had suggested: before making decisions about the future of nuclear weaponry, Americans would have to rethink where "national security" really lay. It was not something that could be left to insiders; it would have to be entrusted to citizens *outside* the government.[8]

But how to do this, given the pervasive secrecy? Not a word about the GAC meeting had appeared in the newspapers. The members had agreed not to give their views in public until the AEC gave them the go-ahead, and the go-ahead never came. Apart from a handful of officials at the very top of government, no one knew the meeting had taken place, much less its reasoning or conclusions. And the tiny group that did hear of it greeted the GAC verdict with puzzlement verging on disbelief. The Russians had broken our monopoly on the A-bomb. They had proven themselves possessors of scientific talent and industrial resources beyond anything we had supposed. The way to protect ourselves—the only way—was to build a bigger and better weapon. Against this, as this group of officials saw it, the GAC was proposing unilateral disarmament.

Unlike the scientists who had built the atomic bomb, top U.S. officials had no experience with nuclear weapons. They did not understand that the thermonuclear bomb as conceived at that time was too large to serve as a military weapon and would destroy civilian populations. And in spite of the use of the word "genocide" in both the majority and minority annexes, these officials did not understand that a weapon that could be built to carry unlimited destructive power could wipe out much of life on earth.

Nor did they comprehend that in attempting to build an H-bomb— how, in our society, could such a fact be kept secret?—we would be inviting the Russians to compete with us in building a weapon to which we were more vulnerable than they. We were surrounded by oceans, with two heavily populated coasts against which large weapons could be launched by ship—warship, barge, or submarine—whereas if we wanted to deliver a bomb on Moscow, we would have to do it from the air and would be limited to the much smaller size and weight that an airplane could carry.

Finally, there was the problem that the scientists who wrote the GAC's recommendations, and the officials who knew of them, did not speak the same language. Physicists had tried for seven years to figure out how the H-bomb could be built, and had failed. When Oppenheimer stated, as he did in the main report, that "an imaginative and concerted attack . . . has a better than even chance" of producing a weapon within five years, he was saying that the technical outlook was not promising. Senators, statesmen, and generals looked at things differently. The lesson they had drawn from recent experience with radar and the atomic bomb was that if the government threw enough money at a scientific problem, the laws of nature would succumb. They overlooked the fact that those who were warning against the Super were virtually the only influential men in the country who knew at first hand what nuclear weapons could do.

When the war ended in 1945, no one had known what to do with the laboratory that produced the atomic bomb. Los Alamos had languished, more or less, until passage of the McMahon Act in 1946 placed the atomic energy enterprise in the hands of a new civilian agency, the AEC. During that period one man held the lab together, Norris Bradbury, the lean, intense, and capable Navy commander who had succeeded Robert Oppenheimer as director. On October 8, 1945, the day he took over, Bradbury promised the scientists, in an effort to keep them at Los Alamos, that investigation of the Super's feasibility was a major reason for the lab to continue. "Another Trinity," he declared, alluding to the A-bomb test at Alamogordo in July 1945, "might even be FUN." But before the Super could be built, a smaller, more powerful A-bomb had to be designed to serve as the trigger. The emphasis had to remain on fission.

After the Halloween meeting it fell to John Manley, who helped write the GAC's conclusions and passionately agreed with them, to inform the division heads at Los Alamos that the advisory committee was unanimously opposed to an all-out program to develop the Super. Chairman Brien McMahon of the JCAE, an avid proponent of more and bigger bombs, was due for a visit November 16 to assess the lab's willingness and capability to build them. Despite the super-secrecy surrounding the Halloween meeting, it had been decided that the scientists who would be briefing McMahon on the status of H-bomb research ought to be aware of the GAC's conclusions. Carroll Wilson had therefore taken the unusual step of having the documents flown to Los Alamos by courier, and Robert Oppenheimer had given Manley permission to explain why the GAC had come to the conclusions it had.[9]

The scientists' reactions to the GAC's opinion were mixed. The first man Manley talked to, Jerry Kellogg, leader of the Experimental Division, was fearful that the decision would mean suspension of the work his division was doing. Carson Mark, head of the Theoretical Division, was "on the fence," while Darol Froman, like Manley an associate director of the lab, was all in favor of the Super. He did not think the prospective new bomb was so very different from the A-bomb, or that the public would recoil when it learned of its enormous power. Only Alvin Graves, head of the Test Division, agreed with the GAC.

Manley knew that an on-again, off-again member of the lab, Edward Teller, had been obsessed for years by the idea of a thermonuclear bomb and had been waiting for some event that would precipitate an all-out effort to build it. He was also aware that the Hungarian hoped the Soviet A-bomb would be that event. When Manley explained the GAC's thinking—that it made no sense to counter the Russians by building a new, even deadlier weapon without first trying to end the arms race—he saw that Teller was not listening. Teller did not say much, however, except to comment that if the great brains on the GAC were so sure that agreement with the Russians was possible, why hadn't they suggested some means of going about it? Manley did not know the lengths to which Teller, who was not a member of the GAC and not in possession of a "Q" clearance, had gone to learn its recommendations. When Fermi and Cyril Smith had arrived home after the Halloween meeting, Teller had met their airplane in Chicago to try to pry the news out of Fermi. When Fermi did not tell him, he had flown to Washington to see McMahon. McMahon did not tell him outright, either, but let drop that the GAC opinion made him "feel sick." Teller had the information he wanted, and Manley's briefing in Los Alamos ten days later told him nothing he did not already know.

In planning the agenda for the senator's visit, Manley had decided not to permit the visit to turn into a policy debate. He instructed the scientists to resist discussion of larger questions or even of whether the Super bomb would be militarily useful. But prior to McMahon's arrival Teller and Froman telephoned Manley repeatedly to urge that the lab formally approve the so-called crash program. Manley responded that the lab had never before taken a stand on national policy and would have no business doing so now. It was the laboratory's job to make weapons, not to decide whether they ought to be made. Teller could talk policy with McMahon outside the formal sessions if he felt like it.

But from the moment of his arrival on the morning of Tuesday, November 16, it was obvious that McMahon was thinking only about policy. The Russians, he said, had a long record as an evil people who failed to keep their promises, force was the only language they understood, and the United States must remain as strong as possible. He considered the GAC position suicidal. During lunch at Fuller Lodge, the big log building that was the lab's social center, the senator and members of his party spoke so loudly that Manley was worried about security, the lab members at tables around them not being cleared to overhear conversations of such sensitivity. McMahon compared the United States and Russia to two neighbors, of whom one possessed a machine gun and the other was building one. What sense would it make for the neighbor with the gun to throw his weapon away? Robert LeBaron, deputy to the secretary of defense for atomic energy, conceded that the armed forces had not thought much about how the Super might be used or whether it would actually be more effective than the A-bomb, but he said that "the existence of a weapon always brought forth new ideas about how it could be used." Walking back to the Tech Building after lunch, LeBaron added that the Super would be ideal for a United Nations peacekeeping force. Manley was so appalled by the idea of using a weapon a thousand times more powerful than the one that had leveled Hiroshima to carry out UN peacekeeping missions that he remembered the remark for the rest of his life.[10]

During the formal sessions, when the lab members described their thermonuclear research so far, Manley found Teller's presentation more balanced than he had expected. Teller conceded that no one knew whether a thermonuclear reaction could be made to burn and added that even if the tests scheduled for 1951 in the Pacific were successful, they would not in themselves prove that the Super bomb could be built. In private conversation with McMahon, however, outside the hearing of Manley and the other physicists, Teller painted a different picture. He told McMahon that a program to build the Super had a better than even, perhaps a much better than even, chance of success, this in spite of the fact that Teller himself had been working on it for seven years with inconclusive results.

Years afterward, it seemed to Manley that McMahon's visit marked the beginning of a change in his own feelings toward Edward Teller. He had known Teller during the mid-1940s as a colleague who refused to work on the lab's project to end the war, the atomic bomb, focusing instead on a hypothetical hydrogen bomb. Now Manley wrote in his diary that prior to the visit by McMahon, "despite many tribulations of which Teller was the cause, I had mistakenly dismissed him as forgivably eccentric, but most imaginative in compensation; almost wholly impractical but possessed of a keen mind; unaccustomed to disciplined, concentrated creativity . . . but still a valued colleague. Now I began to see a distorted human being, petty, perhaps nearly paranoid in his hatred of the Russians, and jealous in personal relations."[11]

These characteristics may have been at work in Teller's misreading of the laboratory's mood on learning that the GAC, with which it had agreed until now on nearly everything, opposed a stepped-up program to build the hydrogen bomb. He wrote to a close friend, the renowned mathematician John von Neumann, that because of the committee's opinion, "the really fine and unanimous enthusiasm which was building up at Los Alamos is now checked, at least temporarily."[12]

Von Neumann had a letter from another close friend at Los Alamos, the dashing, dark-haired Polish mathematician Stanislaw Ulam. In a letter to von Neumann at the Institute for Advanced Study in Princeton, Ulam wrote that "everybody here is against the proposals of the GAC," and predicted accurately that the GAC's verdict would "merely mean a loss of time and not any final . . . negative." Ulam, who had lost nearly all his family in the Holocaust, was in no hurry to produce a weapon a thousand times more powerful than that which had wasted Hiroshima. But he was offended by the idea of intentionally sidestepping a possible discovery. To his French-born wife, Françoise, he wondered aloud whether Newton and Archimedes would have made their great discoveries if they had had to worry constantly about the consequences.[13]

Norris Bradbury and Carson Mark, who along with Ulam were to play critical roles in bringing into being the real H-bomb—not Teller's Super, which the lab had been working on without success—felt very much as Ulam did. Protesting that "one cannot tell scientists not to think," Bradbury said, "I'll be damned if I'll let those people tell me what *not* to do." And Mark, a Canadian mathematician who had learned physics on the job, later thought it was astonishing that the GAC had taken the possibility of an H-bomb seriously enough to make a recommendation, since there was no prospect at the time of building one. Nothing had changed except the fact that the Russians had tested an A-bomb. Mark hoped to be able to prove that a thermonuclear bomb was inconsistent with the laws of nature and could not be built. But he said later that he wished the GAC had phrased its recommendations in the words Oppenheimer had used in his October letter to Conant: "It would be folly to oppose the exploration of this weapon. We have always known it had to be done. . . . But that we become committed to it as the way to save the country and the peace appears to me full of dangers."[14]

CHAPTER FOUR

The Secret Debate

SINCE ITS BEGINNING IN 1947, the Atomic Energy Commission had dealt with major questions, but never one so portentous as whether to advise that the nation embark on an all-out effort to build a thermonuclear bomb. At a meeting of the GAC in early December 1949, Robert Oppenheimer gave members a chance to reconsider their earlier recommendations. Not only did everyone stand by his original opinion, but several went further and went on record with deeply thought-out statements of their own. No one felt more strongly than Lee DuBridge, who pointed out that the Super was not suited to the annihilation of military targets and would be solely a weapon of terror. DuBridge, like Fermi, noted that with its two long coasts, the United States was more vulnerable than the USSR to attack from the sea and, like Manley, said that in embarking on a Super program, the United States would be doing Russia's research for it: the Russians inevitably would learn what we were up to. Everyone agreed that the Super was needed for neither deterrence nor retaliation, since the U.S. atomic stockpile would be sufficient to deal the Soviet Union a devastating blow even if that country had the Super and we did not.[1]

The five commissioners met several times to consider the advisory committee's recommendations, arriving at a 3–2 split; David Lilienthal, Sumner Pike, and Henry DeWolf Smyth were in agreement with the GAC and opposed to Super development "at this time," while the other two, Lewis Strauss and Gordon Dean, favored a secret effort to reach agreement with the Russians and "if this fails, then proceed with the development." All agreed that the public should be informed. Smyth later shifted to a position closer to that of Strauss and Dean.

It fell to Lilienthal to inform the president that his colleagues had failed to reach agreement. Since Lilienthal was known for the gift of bringing men of opposing views together and was anxious to present the president with an unambiguous recommendation, his friends later wondered why he had not tried harder to obtain a consensus. Did he consider building the hydrogen bomb an issue of morality too fundamental to be compromised? Or was he simply tired, worn out by years in the job and by the humiliation of the Hickenlooper hearings the summer before?

Whatever the cause of his ineffectiveness this time, Lilienthal had no second thoughts about his decision to resign and went to the president to inform him. His spirits fell as he entered the Oval Office; what would it be like never to walk through that door again? When Harry Truman glanced up from his reading, Lilienthal noted the tired look in his eyes. But the president's grin reassured the AEC chairman—maybe the conversation would not be so painful after all. "I hate like the dickens to see you go," Truman said, adding that he, too, had a tough decision to make. Lilienthal observed that McMahon and his friends in Congress seemed to think that blowing up the world was our only recourse now that the Russians had the A-bomb. He was afraid they would try to blitz the president into a quick decision. "I don't blitz easily." Truman smiled.[2]

But those who were trying to blitz him were among the heaviest hitters in Washington, ambitious, determined men who were accustomed to getting their own way. And they had access to the Oval Office: McMahon as chair of the powerful congressional committee on atomic energy and a man who aspired to the presidency, Lewis Strauss as a friend of National Security Adviser Sidney Souers, and Defense Secretary Louis Johnson as a swashbuckling donor to the Democratic Party with presidential aspirations of his own. Strauss and McMahon had joined forces early in the fall and had been bombarding the president with strongly worded letters in which they demanded an all-out effort to build the hydrogen bomb. "Brien," the

president had said to McMahon, "it's not an easy thing to order development of a weapon that will kill ten million people." But he
added that he had read McMahon's letter several times, and this persuaded the senator that Truman would side with him in the end. "He
has just got enough of Missouri common sense," McMahon told his
committee. "I can go ahead on that."[3]

When Lilienthal told the secretary of state that he had decided to
resign, Dean Acheson was sympathetic. "I don't understand how you
have stood it as long as you have, living with this grim thing all the
time." And after Lilienthal informed him that the theoretical outlook
had improved to the point where physicists considered the chances of
building the Super about even, Acheson seemed sorry to hear it. He
was "somber enough when I began," Lilienthal wrote in his journal,
"and after a few questions he was graver still. 'What a depressing
world it is,' said Dean, looking quite gray."[4]

Dean and Alice Acheson frequently spent the weekend on their
farm outside Washington. As he put his garden to bed on mellow af-
ternoons that fall, the secretary thought about the horrifying weapon
that might soon be a reality. After interminable hours testifying on
Capitol Hill, Acheson had concluded that congressional opinion was
a fairly accurate reflection of opinion in the country. Knowing that
foreign as well as domestic policy is the art of the possible, he did not
see how the president could survive a decision not to try to make the
new bomb, and he said as much to Oppenheimer. But he was appalled by the prospect of the nation's impaling itself on a deadly new
phase of the arms race, and he cast about for other options. In a
meeting with his Policy Planning Staff he floated the idea of a one-
and-a-half- to two-year moratorium on H-bomb development, accompanied by an effort to reach agreement with the Russians on a
range of issues that included arms control. Only if this effort failed
would the United States try to build the bomb. He and Lilienthal
were close for a time to recommending that H-bomb possibilities be
investigated, any decision to produce the weapon be deferred, and a
far-reaching review of foreign and domestic policies begun forthwith.

But a poorly timed leak by a member of the Joint Committee on

Atomic Energy ratcheted up pressure on the president to make a quick decision. While scolding scientists for allegedly leaking secret information, Senator Edwin Johnson of Colorado announced on television that the president was trying to decide whether to try to build a weapon a thousand times more powerful than the atomic bomb. The administration collectively held its breath, hoping no one would notice Johnson's statement. And for nearly three weeks no one did, until the *Washington Post* on November 18 reported it in a front-page story. Harry Truman hit the ceiling. He called in his attorney general and JCAE chairman McMahon and ordered them to stop the leaks. He banned government employees, even scientific advisers, from speaking about the Super except inside a tiny circle. And he named a committee comprising the state and defense secretaries and the chairman of the AEC to advise him on whether to go ahead with a crash program. Truman's order cut off discussion inside the government and meant that, with Lilienthal and Defense Secretary Johnson at odds with each other on the issue at hand and loath even to be in the same room together, Acheson's opinion would be decisive.

Although by Christmas Acheson had concluded that it would probably be necessary to launch enough of a program to determine whether the bomb could be built, he continued to seek alternatives. He consulted the head of his Policy Planning Staff, George Kennan. Kennan, known within the department—although not to the general public—for helping conceive the Truman Doctrine and the Marshall Plan and as author of the policy of "containing" Russia, pointed out that U.S. policy was based on a willingness to make "first use" of nuclear weapons. Kennan, who had discussed the matter with Oppenheimer, recommended that until the policy of first use had been reconsidered—Kennan hoped it would be abandoned—the United States should refrain from any decision about the hydrogen bomb. Acheson was put off by what an aide called Kennan's "evangelical zeal" and admonished him, "If that is your view of the matter, I suggest you put on a monk's robe, put a tin cup in your hand, and go to the street corner and announce that the end of the world is nigh." Still, he sought Conant's opinion, and had a long talk with the chairman of the Joint Chiefs of Staff, General Omar Bradley, in an effort to find out what—apart from a psychological edge over the Russians—the Pentagon wanted the H-bomb *for*.[5]

While Acheson sought answers, proponents of the Super continued to proselytize. Strauss called Sidney Souers at the White House and warned darkly that "it may be later than we think." In early January, McMahon wrote the president twice on one day alone, accusing the AEC of leaks and again demanding a quick decision. And Secretary of Defense Louis Johnson gave the president a secret Pentagon report urging that determination of the bomb's feasibility be a matter of the highest priority. These and other developments caused Truman to worry that unless he acted quickly, Congress might usurp a decision he considered part of his prerogative as president.

At a press conference on January 19, he was asked for the first time about the Super.

> *Q:* Mr. President, are you considering direct negotiations with Russia on the hydrogen bomb?
> *A:* No.

A week later, asked about the Super again, he replied that he would have nothing to say until he had made his decision. The secrecy-minded president thereby casually declassified the fact that there *was* a decision to be made and increased the pressure on himself to make it quickly. Lilienthal called the admission "a major event" and a final setback in the effort to keep the decision from being railroaded through.[6]

Acheson had had a strenuous year. Early in 1949 he had become secretary of state, succeeding the revered General George Catlett Marshall. When China fell to the armies of Mao Tse-tung and was declared a people's republic in October, Marshall, Truman's former ambassador to China, was, together with the Truman administration, accused of having "lost" China to the Communists. In addition to its defeat in Asia, the administration was plagued by espionage scandals at home. Alger Hiss, a former State Department official who was suspected of having passed secrets to the Soviet Union, went on trial for perjury for a second time in November. The case was a particular embarrassment for the secretary of state because he knew Alger Hiss and was known to be close to Hiss's brother, Donald, Acheson's former law partner and trusted assistant at the department.

Acheson had kept a comparatively open mind about the prospective new bomb longer than anyone else in the higher reaches of government. But on January 26 an event occurred that taxed even his capacity to stand above the fray. A reporter asked him to comment on the case of Alger Hiss, who had been sentenced that day to serve five to ten years in a federal penitentiary following his conviction for perjury. Conscious of "the yelping pack" at his heels and his own vulnerability to "the fall of some fool's question at a press conference," Acheson referred the questioner to a passage from Saint Matthew on the virtue of compassion, and uttered eleven words that were to haunt him for the rest of his life: "I do not intend to turn my back on Alger Hiss."[7]

He drove to the White House that afternoon and offered his resignation. Truman declined it.

Lilienthal went to see Acheson the next day, and found the secretary looking unruffled. The weather was unseasonably warm, Acheson was at work with his window open, and the two men discussed the upcoming decision about the bomb as though neither of them had another thing on his mind.

Lilienthal then changed the subject, and congratulated the secretary of state on his statement about Hiss: "I am looking at a *man*."

"After a while you get tired of the curs yiping," Acheson replied.[8]

The secretary of state sat up late on Sunday and Monday nights replying to the "flood of letters" he had received after his comment on the Hiss case. To the watchful eye of his assistant, Gordon Arneson, "the Dean" looked weary Tuesday morning as he opened the final meeting of the special committee that was to advise the president on the Super. There were eleven men in the room: Acheson, with Arneson and State Department legal counsel Adrian Fisher; Defense Secretary Johnson and three aides; Lilienthal with Commissioner Smyth; and Souers with his deputy, James Lay. Acheson led off by reading a draft recommendation that the president direct the AEC to determine whether a thermonuclear weapon was technically feasible, while deferring a decision to produce the weapon pending reconsideration by State and Defense of overall U.S. plans and objectives. Johnson objected to the proviso that a decision to produce be deferred, and even though they realized that the defense secretary was trying to accelerate building of the bomb, Lilienthal and Acheson yielded. And when Pentagon press secretary Steven Early suggested that the president not make a special announcement but merely issue a press release, Johnson weighed in again. The thing to do was "play it down, make it just one of those things."[9]

Lilienthal wanted to present his objections. The atmosphere resulting from a decision to go ahead, he said, would in all likelihood render a new approach to the atomic arms race impossible. It would confirm us on our present path and conceal from us the weakness of our position—our reliance on the atomic bomb for the defense of Europe. We were assuming that there would be no war with Russia for a few years at least. Instead of building a new bomb, why not spend a few months on "an intensive . . . re-examination of the worsening of our position as a result of our preoccupation with nuclear weapons?"[10]

Acheson agreed with most of what Lilienthal had said. But without an alternative—and in his view Lilienthal had not suggested one—the pressures for a decision had reached such a point that he did not feel he could recommend delay. To Acheson's surprise, Lilienthal agreed to join in and make their recommendation to the president unanimous, provided he be given a chance to express his objections to the president in person.

Truman was seated at his desk in the Oval Office when Johnson, Acheson, and Lilienthal appeared. Slightly surprised to see the three of them when he had expected only the secretary of defense, he greeted them with a "quick, owlish look." Acheson told him that Lilienthal had something he wanted to say. Turning to Lilienthal, Truman said he hoped we would never have to use these new weapons, but in view of the way the Russians were behaving, we had no choice but to go ahead. Lilienthal objected that he did not agree with the course the country was about to take. It would magnify our reliance on nuclear weapons and mislead the nation into thinking there was no other way. The president broke in to say that if Senator Johnson of Colorado hadn't made his televised remarks, calmer deliberation might have been possible. Now, however, so much excitement had built up that he had no alternative.[11]

At 12:45 the visitors left the Oval Office. They had been there all of seven minutes.

As his special committee had suggested, the president refrained from calling a press conference. The White House merely issued a press release: "I have directed the Atomic Energy Commission to continue its work on all forms of atomic weapons, including the so-called hydrogen or super bomb." That afternoon, acting on another Lilienthal caveat, Truman ordered State and Defense to reexamine national objectives "and the effect of these objectives on our strategic plans in light of the probable fission bomb capability and possible thermonuclear bomb capability of the Soviet Union."[12]

That afternoon David Lilienthal learned from McMahon that his committee had been on the point of demanding publicly that the president go ahead, the very act of preemption the president had anticipated.

Lilienthal later wrote that speaking up in the Oval Office had been one of the hardest acts of his life, "saying No to a steamroller." He knew that Acheson was at least as unhappy as he was about the course they were suggesting and that his own insistence on speaking out distressed the secretary, lest his doing so without putting forward an alternative merely confuse the president, who had already made up his mind. If Lilienthal had had anything but "the most unbounded admiration" for Acheson, "the deepest loyalty and fealty for the President," and compassion for the load each man had to carry, he would not have found his dissent so painful.[13]

"Now to be a good sport," he thought as he broke the news to the GAC. The mood was "like a funeral party," and became bleaker still when Lilienthal added that the president had issued a second order forbidding GAC members to speak out. Not only had the president overruled his scientific advisers; he had bound them to secrecy at a moment when they had urged that the public be more fully informed. Conant and Oppenheimer asked whether they ought to resign. Lilienthal asked them to remain.[14]

Later there was an evening gathering, the fifty-fourth birthday party Lewis Strauss gave for himself at the Wardman Park. For the GAC members it was like the second funeral they had been to that day. While Strauss celebrated, a dejected Robert Oppenheimer sat with his back to the other guests, the inevitable cigarette dangling from his fingertips. When Strauss approached to introduce his son and his son's new wife, Oppenheimer did not bother to turn around. As the Strausses remembered it, he merely extended a hand over his shoulder.[15]

Before going to bed that night, Lilienthal wrote in his journal: "This is a night of heartache. . . . We have to leave many things to God; this one He will have to get us out of."[16]

CHAPTER FIVE

Lost Opportunities

THE PRESIDENT HAD NOW committed the country to building a weapon no one knew how to make, or even whether it could be made. Against the advice of nearly all his scientific advisers, he had placed his weaponeers in a position where they *had* to produce—or make his government look catastrophically inept. And he had handed the Russians information that ought to remain secret. If they had not already embarked on a program to build the hydrogen bomb, they would do so now. And if they had begun, they would step up the pace.

We know now, as we did not know then, that the Russians were working on the H-bomb and that their physicists were just as capable as ours. After Truman's announcement of January 31, 1950, Stalin ordered them to move faster, and the Soviet scientists succeeded brilliantly. For the second time, Hiroshima having been the first, the United States had set the pace of the arms race.

Air Force officials wanted the Super because its radius of destruction—ten times that of the atomic bomb—would "compensate for bombing error." It is appalling today to read secret congressional testimony of January 1950, in which officials of the Pentagon explained that instead of ten or twelve A-bombs, a single hydrogen bomb would more efficiently do the job of wiping out a division of troops massed for a river crossing or a beachhead landing. These men understood neither the H-bomb nor the A-bomb. Air Force officials and congressional assistants such as William Borden, who drafted McMahon's emotionally charged letters to the president, had access to all the secrets. But what the H-bomb was—what it would do and what the effects would be—of this they had no understanding. The damage inflicted by the weapon could not be limited to the battlefield. A single bomb could probably "take out" any capital city in the world and, because of the pulse it emitted, wreak havoc on the communications of the country that received it. Industry, agriculture, communications, all would be so severely crippled that the conquering nation would be unable to put civilization together again. Those who understood this were the physicists, mathematicians, and engineers who had built the atomic bomb. The GAC was composed of such men, and they were horrified by the idea of a new weapon a thousand times more destructive than the one they had brought into being. But as far as the politicians were concerned, the new bomb would be bigger, therefore better, than the old, and it would be political suicide not to build it. They brushed aside any thought that it might also be a weapon of genocide.

There were other respects in which scientists and political people were at cross-purposes. The model the GAC had been looking at was the Classical Super, which Teller and others had been working on without success for more than three years. The weapon U.S. scientists ultimately developed was not the model the GAC had before it in 1949 but a new weapon, built on different principles. Thus when Oppenheimer wrote in his covering report that the GAC's recommendations "stem in large part from the technical nature of the Super," he was referring to a fact difficult for nonscientists to understand: while it had been impossible to prove the feasibility of Teller's Super, it might likewise be impossible to prove decisively that it was not feasible. The situation was an open-ended one in which the odds of the bomb's being possible did not look good enough for the nation to commit itself publicly to building it.[1]

Readers of the GAC report in Washington did not understand this. Instead, they looked at its moral language—"weapon of genocide," "necessarily an evil thing in any light"—and were put off by the fact that advisers picked for their scientific expertise had ventured into moral territory. Unaware that David Lilienthal had asked the GAC to advise on "as broad a basis as possible," the few who had seen the report believed that the GAC had bent its technical advice to fit its ethical predilections. The fact that it had dealt with the moral issue obscured its technical advice and tended to discredit its recommendations.

Why didn't the GAC press its case? Manley said later that it "leaned over backwards" not to lobby, adding that the members were not accustomed to fighting for their views, since their advice had almost always been taken. That, I. I. Rabi was to say later, left the lobbying to the other side. And lobby the other side did. While Oppenheimer, Rabi, and the rest felt inhibited from lobbying members of the legislative branch while the issue was being considered by the president, men like Strauss and Johnson were not troubled by such scruples. The same was true of the president's secrecy directives: the scientists observed the prohibition against going public, while the political men, aided by tips from a collusive FBI, felt free to leak to the press. It was not until five years later, when the transcript of the Oppenheimer hearing was published, that Americans learned that of the president's fourteen atomic energy advisers, ten had opposed an accelerated H-bomb program and one had abstained, and it had been the two nonscientists who had been most eager to go ahead.

Robert Oppenheimer had a history of thinking long thoughts about atomic weapons. In the course of six wartime visits to Los Alamos by the great Danish physicist Niels Bohr, he had become imbued with Bohr's belief in international control. Both men were convinced that once the war was over, the "secret" of atomic weapons should be shared with other nations and that the capacity to make atomic weapons should be controlled not by a single nation but by a consortium. Oppenheimer never wavered from his and Bohr's vision of international control.

As soon as the war was over, he chaired a panel to make recommendations on the future of the atomic bomb to a group consisting of Secretary of State Acheson, General Leslie R. Groves, James B. Conant, Vannevar Bush, and John J. McCloy, former assistant secretary of war. After four days' intense deliberation at the historic meeting place of Dumbarton Oaks in Washington, D.C., the group proposed that an Atomic Development Authority be created to control everything about atomic energy, from the mining of thorium and uranium to production. No nation would be allowed to make atomic bombs, and the United States would effectively give up its monopoly. The proposal, called the Acheson-Lilienthal plan, was Oppenheimer's inspiration and was drafted by him and Rabi during Christmas week, 1945, in Rabi's apartment overlooking the Hudson River. The plan, which Acheson described as "brilliant and profound," was introduced at the United Nations in amended form by the American financier Bernard Baruch, and promptly rejected by the Russians. Meanwhile Oppenheimer, as adviser to Baruch's delegation, got a chastening look at Stalin-era intransigence.

When the H-bomb issue arose in 1949, he remembered that experience. He was convinced that development of the H-bomb would make things worse, and likewise convinced that any system of inspection rigorous enough to pass the U.S. Senate would be turned down by the Russians in a way that might close the door to future negotiations. "It seems to me," Oppenheimer wrote to Kennan, "that the time for plans, proposals and systems offered unilaterally by our government is past, if it ever existed; and if we ever again come up with a set of proposals, it should be on the basis of some prior agreement."[2]

He continued to believe in international control, but he did not know how to get there. With the rest of the GAC majority, Oppenheimer considered it neither the obligation nor the prerogative of their committee to say what the president ought to do, but only to advise as to what he ought not to do. Fermi and Rabi, on the other hand, considered it incumbent on them to suggest a positive as well as a negative course of action, and proposed an attempt at a self-enforcing agreement with the Russians not to develop the bomb. Uncertainty as to which was truly the better course evidently stayed Oppenheimer's hand and kept him from fighting for the majority view. On this issue, as on a good many others, he was the possessor of a divided mind and extraordinarily divided emotions.

Why did Harry Truman come to the decision he did? The Truman of 1950 was no longer the accidental president who had, almost jauntily, it seemed, ordered the bombing of Hiroshima in the summer of 1945. Five years later, he was more confident and more humane; he understood a great deal that had been obscure to him before. In the late

1940s he told a group of military and civilian advisers, "I don't think we ought to use this thing [the atomic bomb] unless we absolutely have to. It is a terrible thing to order the use of something that is so terribly destructive. . . . You have got to understand that this isn't a military weapon."[3]

The American people, too, seem to have understood. A Gallup poll in early 1950 showed support, by 73 to 18 percent, for the president's decision, but also showed that half of those who responded wanted to try to reach agreement with the Russians before proceeding to build the hydrogen bomb. With the public, although not with the Super's more vociferous advocates in Congress and the Pentagon, the president had more leeway than he supposed.[4]

Had he been willing to brave the political fallout, Truman could have omitted any public announcement and left the scientists to continue secretly to investigate the bomb's feasibility. Meanwhile he could quietly have felt out Soviet willingness to make a deal. As long as Stalin was still alive, negotiations would not have been successful. Once Stalin was gone, however, and he died in 1953, a legacy of trying to find a solution would have been there—and might have made a difference. Khrushchev and Eisenhower might by the mid- to late 1950s have reached agreement to end the fateful competition.[5]

The outcome was a disaster for everyone. It marked a lost opportunity for the president to level with the American people on a life-or-death decision from which they would be the first to suffer and about which they showed heartening signs of common sense. And it failed to buy security for the United States. Believing that we had a greater supply of atomic weapons than we did, the Russians reversed their earlier demobilization and built their ground forces from a low of three million back up to five million men. To counter the resulting superiority of Soviet troop strength in Europe, the president ordered full steam ahead with the H-bomb. So it was to go with decision after decision for forty years, and with each upward ratchet of the arms race, each side became less secure. The decision to produce the H-bomb enshrined secrecy and made the cold war a way of life for both countries.

1950

PART TWO

1950

CHAPTER SIX

Fuchs's Betrayal

"THE ROOF FELL IN TODAY," David Lilienthal wrote in his journal on February 2. He called what had happened "a world catastrophe, and a sad day for the human race." A German-born member of the Manhattan Project had confessed in London to passing atomic secrets to the Russians. His name was Emil Julius Klaus Fuchs, and he had been a member of the British mission to Los Alamos during the war.[1]

The president was told on February 1, 1950, the day following his H-bomb announcement. To official Washington, as to the rest of the country, the news was as shattering as Joe One, the Russian atomic test, had been less than six months before. Physicists who had worked with Fuchs were appalled. Not only might his betrayal explain why the Russians had tested an atomic device sooner than expected, but it might also explain another fact—known to Oppenheimer and one or two others who had studied the debris from Joe One—that the Soviet device appeared to have similarities to the bomb we had dropped on Nagasaki. What else might Fuchs have passed on? The tiny circle of men who knew about these things quickly learned that Fuchs had attended a conference at Los Alamos on thermonuclear reactions in the spring of 1946 before going home to Britain. Had he passed H-bomb tips to Moscow? American physicists did not think so. We were on the wrong track with the H-bomb, and we had been in 1946: anything Fuchs might have transmitted could only have misled the Russians. Robert Oppenheimer expressed the belief of knowledgeable physicists when he said that if the Russians had made progress on the basis of what Fuchs could have told them, "they were marvelous indeed." Still, what Fuchs knew was important enough: that with the war barely over, the Americans already were at work on the H-bomb.[2]

One American physicist was convinced that Fuchs had given the Russians a head start with the hydrogen bomb. That physicist was Edward Teller. Teller had known Fuchs a long time, as a student in Fuchs's native Germany in 1928, and in Los Alamos during the war, when Fuchs, a bachelor, was sought after by the Tellers and other couples to babysit their children. Not only had Teller and Fuchs both been present at the 1946 Super conference, they had seen each other every year since, at the Tellers' home and elsewhere. Only a few months before, in September 1949, while Oppenheimer and Vannevar Bush in Washington were poring over fallout data from Joe One, Teller and Fuchs had made a train trip together in England. News of Fuchs's treachery must have been a fearful blow to Teller. Already he had been warning that the Russians were probably ahead with the H-bomb. Now he proclaimed it insistently.

Fuchs's betrayal had other shattering consequences, among them the growth of doubt in some quarters about Robert Oppenheimer. As early as October 1949, when the H-bomb debate was getting under way, Lewis Strauss received a tip from the FBI that Fuchs was under suspicion. Immediately, he began making inquiries of General Leslie R. Groves, director of the Manhattan Project, about Robert Oppenheimer, who was known to have had a left-wing past, and his brother Frank, a former member of the Communist Party. Strauss spent an hour with FBI director J. Edgar Hoover, apparently exchanging concerns about the Oppenheimers, and when, during the Halloween meeting in October, Robert Oppenheimer told him that he did not think the Russians would refuse to negotiate about the Super, Strauss's suspicions grew. From then on, he wondered about Oppenheimer's opposition to the H-bomb. Was Oppenheimer simply naive? Or was he, like Fuchs, trying to help the Russians? Informed that Fuchs had confessed to espionage, Strauss, in a response that spoke volumes, told Hoover that the news would strengthen the president's hand on the H-bomb decision and "make a good many men who are in the same profession as Fuchs very careful of what they say publicly."[3]

Hoover shared some of Strauss's reservations, for he informed Strauss of Fuchs's confession on the same day he told the president, thereby enabling Strauss to upstage the chairman, David Lilienthal: at the AEC's meeting on February 2, it was Strauss, not Lilienthal, who broke the news to the commissioners.

If Fuchs's espionage seemed to official Washington and much of the public to strengthen the case for secrecy, in the eyes of many Manhattan Project veterans it did the opposite. It meant, as Glenn Seaborg pointed out after learning about Joe One, that Groves's policy of compartmentalized research had failed. Most scientists believed that there were no atomic "secrets." The basic principles were widely known, and once it appeared that the bomb *could* be made, then the way was clear for others to build it. Some of the country's most distinguished physicists were convinced that had the American people been told the facts about nuclear weapons and the scientists' true opinions, they would not have supported the decision to proceed with the H-bomb. Prohibited from disclosing classified information, these physicists struggled to find a way to keep the public better informed. The way they found was to criticize the secrecy that had surrounded Truman's decision.

A day or two after the announcement of Fuchs's confession, a dozen physicists signed an appeal in the *Wall Street Journal,* describing use of the H-bomb as "a betrayal of all standards of morality and of Christian civilization itself," and calling for a pledge by the U.S. government not to be the first to use it. And a few days after that, three famed theoreticians spoke their minds on Mrs. Franklin Roosevelt's weekly television program. Characterizing the arms race as "inexorable," Albert Einstein called "each step . . . the inevitable consequence of the one before. And, at the end . . . lies general annihilation." Hans Bethe emphasized the H-bomb's genocidal nature. The only reason for developing it, he said, lay in the danger that the Russians might build it first and use it to blackmail the United States. By announcing that we would never be first to use it, we could reduce the odds that they would use it to forestall a strike by us. And Oppenheimer emphasized the "grave danger for us in that these decisions have been taken on the basis of facts held secret." The danger, he said, lay in the fact that "wisdom itself cannot flourish, nor even truth be determined, without the give and take of debate or criticism. The relevant facts could be of little help to an enemy; yet they are indispensable for an understanding of questions of policy."[4]

Oppenheimer spoke from experience: as chairman of the GAC and member of several other governmental advisory groups, he had been frustrated during the H-bomb discussions by being muzzled. Just the day before Truman's H-bomb decision, he had testified to the joint congressional committee—in tightest secrecy, of course—that it had been painful for him and others in the know to stand by "in rigid silence" while uninformed individuals had been free to say whatever they pleased, in some cases misleading the public, and in others violating security. Oppenheimer pointed to public use of the word "tritium"—a key H-bomb component—as a security violation. He added that it would be impossible to "undertake anything as interesting as this [building the bomb] and keep it quiet in this country."[5]

Oppenheimer and Bethe evidently had a conversation after their appearance on the program. Being a consultant at Los Alamos but not a government official, Bethe had greater freedom than Oppenheimer to speak out as long as he did not divulge technical secrets. Two days after their conversation Bethe wrote to his colleague Victor Weisskopf at MIT, "I had a long talk with Oppie, who agreed very much with what we had done and were doing. He emphasized the necessity of keeping the issue alive and I very much agree with him. Can you help?" Bethe's letter marked the beginning of an effort by physicists outside the official framework to keep fundamental facts about the H-bomb before the public while observing the president's security strictures.[6]

In keeping with what he and Oppenheimer had agreed, Bethe and three colleagues that spring of 1950 published a series of articles in the journal *Scientific American* and in the *Bulletin of the Atomic Scientists* in which they deplored the "authoritarian" manner in which the H-bomb decision had been made, and tried to inform the public of the principles underlying the technology. The first article, by Louis Ridenour, dean of the graduate college at the University of Illinois, called Truman's decision a "Pyrrhic reply" to the news of Joe One and noted that we were more vulnerable to the hydrogen bomb than the Russians. He praised the emphasis of Los Alamos since the war on making more efficient fission weapons instead of trying to build a hydrogen bomb, deplored the "bankruptcy" of a secrecy policy that excluded the public from life-and-death decisions, and added that the nation needed better means of delivering bombs more than it needed new, more destructive weapons.[7]

In another of the series former AEC commissioner Robert Bacher complained that the public was being given an exaggerated idea of the H-bomb's effectiveness and being denied facts that would enable it to choose between developing weapons, on one hand, and atomic power for peaceful purposes, on the other; and he warned against the belief that secrecy contributes to security: "We are dangerously close to abandoning those principles of free speech and open discussion that have made our country great," he said. And Ralph Lapp, former head of the nuclear physics branch of the Office of Naval Research, emphasized that development of the H-bomb would require a far-reaching program of civil defense and that the nation had not been informed. Since an H-bomb could level an entire metropolitan area, we would have to build a new type of city, a strip city strung along a straight line hundreds of miles long. Such a restructuring of American society could not be carried out without public assent, yet the issue had not even been raised. In the meantime Congress was making a political football of the atom.[8]

Of all the *Scientific American* articles, however, it was Hans Bethe's contribution on the moral issue that attracted the most attention. After describing the terrifying heat, blast, and radiation effects, Bethe asked, "Can we, who have always insisted on morality and human decency, introduce this weapon of total annihilation into the world?" Use of thermonuclear weapons would usher in a new dark age, with nothing left that we think of as civilization. If the Nazi experience taught anything, said Bethe, it was that physical destruction brings moral destruction, and in the struggle merely to survive, it is every man against the other. How could we, whose quarrel with the Soviet Union was largely about means, take the lead in introducing a type of warfare that was bound to bring mass slaughter? "Shall we convince the Russians of the value of the individual by killing millions of them?" Our failure to eliminate or control atomic weapons was no reason to introduce a weapon a thousand times worse.[9]

Even if the Russians were to develop the hydrogen bomb first and use it on us, Bethe said, our reserve of atomic bombs, distributed among various launching sites, would enable us to even the score. "In fact, because of the greater number available, A-bombs may well be more effective in destroying legitimate military targets. . . . H-bombs, after all, would be useful only against the largest targets, of which there are very few in the USSR." The only reason to develop the bomb would be to deter the Russians from deploying it against us, to prevent its use rather than to use it ourselves. Should we go ahead, therefore, we ought to proclaim our reason to the world and pledge that we would never be the first to use a thermonuclear weapon and would use it only if someone else had already used it in an attack on us or one of our allies.

The straightforward simplicity of Bethe's argument would have attracted attention in any event, but the circumstances in which his article appeared were sensational. On reading an advance copy, which had been delivered to the AEC, Commissioner Smyth spotted technical data which, he thought, should remain secret. The AEC immediately ordered Gerard Piel, publisher of the magazine, to stop publication and informed him that it was prepared to get a court order. Piel obeyed the AEC of his own volition and had the typeset plates, plus about three thousand copies of the magazine, destroyed. Bethe then produced a second version, which with customary prudence he had written in advance and stored in his safe, and the journal appeared, only a few days late, with this version in it. Bethe took the fuss with customary calm: the published version, he felt, was just as good for his purposes as the original. Practical as ever, he was concerned about the cost to *Scientific American*, but consoled himself by thinking that the notoriety had been "good advertising" for Mr. Piel.[10]

Bethe went further than any of the other Manhattan Project physicists to act on his disapproval of the presidential ukase. In mid-February 1950 he wrote Norris Bradbury one of the more remarkable letters in the annals of American dissent.

> You have probably heard about my feelings concerning the hydrogen bomb. . . . The announcement of the President has not changed my feelings. . . . I still believe that it is morally wrong and unwise for our national security to develop this weapon. In most respects I agree with the opinions of the General Advisory Committee although I have not seen their report itself. So much has been said about the reasons on both sides that I do not need to go into them here. The main point is that I cannot in good conscience work on this weapon.
>
> For this reason, if and when I come to Los Alamos in the future I will completely refrain from any discussions related to the super-bomb. I have not completely decided whether this should include work on the booster. This will depend essentially on the question of how many problems the super and the booster have in common. Therefore on my visits I would primarily concern myself with the problems of the implosion, with problems of neutron diffusion and of efficiency, in other words with classical Los Alamos problems. . . .
>
> Because of these very much reduced plans I think it would not be worthwhile to renegotiate my consultant's contract. . . .
>
> In case of war I would obviously reconsider my position.[11]

The letter was remarkable, among other reasons, for the willingness to sacrifice that it implied. Bethe was one of the constellation of scientific geniuses who had sought refuge from Hitler's anti-Semitism during the 1930s, and his work on the fusion of light elements in the sun was the first to point to the possibility of a weapon based on thermonuclear reactions. He was at the time a faculty member at

Cornell, which had become his home in America. Later, as director of one of the Manhattan Project's two Theoretical Divisions, he had come to think of Los Alamos, too, as home, and had returned there as a consultant every summer but one since the war. He loved gazing out at the high mesas, loved hiking in the mountains, and considered his colleagues there not only his cherished friends but his extended family. The prospect of not working with them again was painful to him.

His letter to Bradbury was unique: no one was under as much pressure as Bethe to join the program, and no one was to resist as forthrightly. Others who agreed with him that the weapon was immoral, that possessing it would not contribute to defense, or that their university research was more promising for the country than weapons work, remained silent rather than refusing outright. Bethe alone spelled out his reasons.

Meanwhile his colleague Teller had already started recruiting for the Super program. In the *Bulletin of the Atomic Scientists* that spring he wrote a summons titled "Back to the Laboratories," in which he preached that it is not the scientist's job to decide whether the hydrogen bomb *should* be built. The scientist, Teller said, is not responsible for the laws of nature: it is his job to find out how they work. The scientific community had been "out on a honeymoon with mesons. The holiday is over. Hydrogen bombs will not produce themselves. . . . If we want to live on the technological capital of the last war, we shall come out second best."[12]

Early in March 1950, Teller arranged to have dinner in Washington with Brien McMahon's assistant William Borden. He informed Borden that Oppenheimer had delayed the H-bomb program and had tried to have the Los Alamos laboratory closed after the war. "Give it back to the Indians," he quoted Oppenheimer, apparently unaware that this was the title of a popular song that Oppie must have heard somewhere. Realizing that he could not have the lab disbanded, Oppenheimer, Teller said, had tried to change it from a weapons facility into a center for basic research. While postwar director Norris Bradbury was an improvement over Oppenheimer, he added, Bradbury, too, left a lot to be desired. Under him the lab had, "miraculously," survived, but it was weak and ineffective and composed of mediocrities. It was Bradbury's fault, since he "is loyal to them and . . . refuses to supplant the mediocre with better men." Teller warned that the Fuchs case confirmed our worst fears: thanks to him, the Russians had known our most promising approach to the H-bomb since 1946 and as a result might have developed a hydrogen device concurrently with their atomic bomb. Now, with Bethe, Fermi, and Oppenheimer discouraging the younger men by refusing to join the program, our situation was "desperate." Teller hoped the president would bring his personal pressure to bear on reluctant scientists.[13]

Teller's testimony, given secretly to the congressional committee the next day, was even more alarming than what he had told Borden over dinner, but this time he did not mention Bradbury or Oppenheimer by name or suggest that the president be asked to intervene. He warned that the country was in even greater peril than during the war, since the Germans had not, after all, been working on the atomic bomb. The Russians, on the other hand, might already be ahead of us with the H-bomb. He told the committee that H-bomb work had barely progressed since the war: the best scientists had returned to basic research and many were hesitant to join because they had a bad conscience over Hiroshima. Physicists, he added, are as susceptible to the herd instinct as those of lesser intellect: they would refuse to work on the weapon if their leaders refused. Los Alamos needed to double the size of its theoretical staff and improve it by "much more than a factor of two in talent." Yet a manpower draft or other direct pressure might not be helpful, since a scientist has to put his heart in it if he is to invent something new and original. If the scientists continued to hold back, however, we might have to turn to the British and Canadians and that could be dangerous. Klaus Fuchs had, after all, been part of the British wartime mission. Was there, Teller asked, some form of suasion the committee might be willing to bring to bear? He offered a list of scientists who could be helpful.[14]

Smyth, who had come to the hearing expressly to add nuance to Teller's remarks, intervened, suggesting that an appeal by the White

House to the president of a university might be the best way to secure the services of a scientist reluctant to take time from his academic career to return to the lab. Smyth added that a scientist who did not want to work on the bomb could nevertheless contribute by training younger men to work on it, and pointed out that secrecy damaged recruitment, since it fostered the assumption that there was nothing left to do on the H-bomb but the engineering. If secrecy were eased somewhat, and scientists were told the truth, that there was still a vast amount of work to be done, it would send a signal that we had not gotten very far.[15]

In warning of a scientific boycott, Teller as usual had jumped the gun. Other shortages were more critical at that moment than highly skilled manpower; one of them was the potential shortage of tritium. No one knew how much tritium, an isotope of hydrogen, would be required for a bomb test, but it could be considerable, and the reactor facility in Hanford, Washington, the only one in the country that produced it, already was fully committed to plutonium production. In the tense atmosphere after Fuchs's confession, after an alarming Pentagon report in February that the Russians might already be working on the H-bomb, and after a formal request from the Joint Chiefs of Staff that work on the bomb receive priority status, President Truman issued the directive that put real teeth in his original order. On March 10 he secretly ordered the AEC to prepare production of the materials the weapon would require, especially tritium.[16]

Another bottleneck was the lack of computers to do the millions of computations that would be required. Just after the war a handful of scientists and their wives had performed mathematical calculations on the early IBM punch-card machines. But by 1948 it was clear that further work on either of the H-bomb designs under consideration—both Teller's Super and a simpler, layered device called the Alarm Clock, designed by Teller in 1946—would have to wait until faster machines had become available, a delay to which Teller himself agreed. Since 1948, members of the "T," or Theoretical, Division, had done hand calculations on aspects of the Super problem and had planned the calculations that needed to be done as soon as computers became available. What the lab needed most was not, as Teller thought, a famous theoretician like Oppenheimer, Fermi, Bethe, or Harvard's Julian Schwinger to replace Bradbury, but a way to cope with the staggering mathematical demands imposed by the H-bomb project.[17]

The lab eventually built a computer of its own. Even that effort, however, was slowed by something more mundane—a housing shortage that hampered the growth of personnel. Los Alamos in the spring of 1950, then, was dealing with a number of shortages, each of them related to the others and each, in time, overcome.[18]

During the period of uncertainty after the war, the man who had held the lab together was Norris Bradbury, selected by Groves and Oppenheimer to succeed Oppenheimer only a few weeks after the Japanese surrender. Bradbury was a naval commander and a specialist in ordnance; his first task had been to stanch the hemorrhaging of personnel, which had fallen from about 3,500 in the summer of 1945 to just over 1,200 six months later, and build a stockpile of fifteen or so atomic bombs that could be assembled rapidly. The lab did fission research that had been passed over during the war, especially research into design of the smaller, more efficient fission weapons that were now the country's first line of defense. Sophisticated atomic weapons were important for another reason as well: should the Super ever become a reality, the hydrogen fuel would be triggered by an atomic bomb. It was therefore of great importance to learn more about how fission worked and how fission and fusion interacted during an explosion. Bradbury was not enthusiastic about the Super, but he was convinced that "some day, someone must know the answer" to the question whether it could be built. "The use of nuclear energy," he had told the laboratory on the day he took over in 1945, "may be so catastrophic . . . that we should know every extent of its pathology. . . . One studies cancer—one does not expect or want to contract it—but the whole impact of cancer . . . is such that we must know its unhappy extent. So it is with nuclear energy . . . we must know how terrible it is."[19]

When Truman made his decision to proceed with the hydrogen

bomb, the lab under Bradbury had already held two major series of tests in the Pacific, Operation Crossroads in 1946, which studied the effects of the atomic bomb on naval vessels, and Operation Sandstone in 1948, which tested design principles for the next generation of atomic warheads. And, contrary to Teller's accusations that it was not working on the Super, the lab was preparing a series for the following year, 1951, which would include a critical test of thermonuclear principles. To prepare the series—an enormous theoretical, engineering, and logistical challenge—Bradbury in late 1949 or early 1950 set up what he called the "Family Committee" to evaluate a whole family of thermonuclear ideas—with nicknames like "Daddy," "Sonny," "Uncle," and "Little Edward"—generated by Teller, and decide which should be included in the next year's series. Teller had come up with so many ideas, some good, some not so good, that it had placed a strain on the laboratory. Aiming to harness his formidable energies without allowing them to tear the lab apart, Bradbury passed over Teller and named a tough-minded assistant, Darol Froman, who had managed the Sandstone tests, to be head of the new committee.

Bradbury's choice was preceded by some volatile history. During the war, when Bethe twice asked Teller to undertake critical assignments, Teller accepted responsibility but both times failed to follow through. After the second failure he and his group, at his request, had been relieved of work on the A-bomb, and a British team was brought in to do the work (the team that included Fuchs). It was generally felt that Teller failed to perform because he was bored by the fission bomb, a problem he considered solved, and because he was already far more interested in the H-bomb. Meanwhile the wartime director, Robert Oppenheimer, was under tremendous pressure to get the A-bomb built. To assuage Teller's resentment at not being named head of the Theoretical Division, Oppenheimer set aside an hour in his hectic schedule each week to meet with the Hungarian and listen while he poured out his suggestions. Oppenheimer also permitted Teller to form a special group of a dozen physicists and mathematicians to work on thermonuclear ideas. Years afterward members of the wartime lab still remembered with resentment Teller's having sat out what one of them called "the main event," building the atomic bomb, during the last critical year, when all hands were desperately needed. And right after the war, when Bradbury was struggling to hold the lab together, Teller had presented an ultimatum: Bradbury must promise to conduct a dozen fission tests a year, or mount a vastly stepped-up thermonuclear effort, or he would leave. The laboratory being in no condition to undertake either, Bradbury refused, and Teller returned to teaching and research at the University of Chicago.

But he did not sever his ties to Los Alamos. He had returned every summer to consult on special problems and was back at the lab on a year's leave even before the Soviet test of August 1949. With the Polish mathematician Stanislaw Ulam and the prodigious Russian astrophysicist George Gamow, he was working on the problem of ignition: how to ignite a cylinder of deuterium (an isotope of hydrogen), using a fission bomb near one end of the cylinder as the trigger. It was a daunting problem, since the deuterium would not ignite until it reached a temperature so high that the cylinder would blow apart in the fraction of a millisecond before the explosion could spread through it. With the addition of tritium, a third isotope of hydrogen, to the deuterium fuel, the temperature of ignition could be lowered sufficiently for the deuterium-tritium mixture to burn. But the amount of tritium this would require had to be established with some accuracy, since tritium, produced in the reactors at Hanford, Washington, was scarce and expensive. Producing it would mean a sacrifice of plutonium needed for the A-bomb.[20]

Teller had made several different estimates of the amount of tritium that would be required. At the time of the 1946 conference it was assumed that the Super could be ignited with fewer than four hundred grams of tritium, which was not considered prohibitive, but an estimate by Teller in September 1947 was about twice as large. In December 1949, even before Truman's H-bomb announcement, two parallel sets of calculations were begun in an attempt once again to determine the tritium requirement. One set entailed preparation of a machine calculation to go on a computer called the ENIAC, in Aberdeen, Maryland. Preparing the calculation took six months and was carried out by two husband-and-wife teams, John and Klari von Neumann in Princeton, and Foster and Cerda Evans with John Calkin in Los Alamos. The calculation went on the ENIAC in June 1950 and continued into the summer.[21]

Since the results would not be known for some time, Stanislaw Ulam and a collaborator, Cornelius Everett, undertook a second set by hand. It was expected that their work, a simplified version of the ENIAC calculation, would provide less detailed results than the ENIAC but would do so faster. The two mathematicians worked four to six hours a day, applying slide rules, pencil, and paper to a set of highly simplified calculations and filling page after page with stepwise computations. Everett, a self-effacing workaholic whom Ulam had known before the war at the University of Wisconsin, performed such a large number of calculations that his slide rule wore out, leading him to joke that the least the government could do was buy him a new one. They began their work in early winter and by the end of February 1950 concluded that it would take far more tritium to ignite the Super than any of Teller's estimates, ranging from three hundred to six hundred grams, had foreseen.[22]

Ulam and Everett then began a new calculation, one that assumed that several hundred additional grams of tritium had been added to the model. Françoise Ulam and two other wives were put to work grinding out arithmetical problems on desk calculators. But even assuming the extra tritium, this model, too, would not ignite. Thus the results of the second set of Ulam-Everett calculations, completed by early summer 1950, were even gloomier than the first, indicating that the amount of tritium required would be several times larger than previous estimates. They seemed to indicate that Teller's Super was not feasible.[23]

In April 1950, before the second set of results was known, Ulam flew east to consult the great mathematician John von Neumann, who, like Teller, hoped that the H-bomb in some form would be possible. A day or so after Ulam arrived in Princeton, Enrico Fermi, too, appeared in the busy von Neumann household, and on the afternoon and evening of April 21 the three friends spent hours discussing the implications of the first Ulam-Everett calculations. The next day they were joined by Oppenheimer, who lived near the von Neumanns in Princeton. When Ulam caught Fermi and von Neumann, the world's most accomplished mathematicians, in a minor arithmetical error, Oppenheimer winked at Ulam in amusement. Comparing Oppie's and von Neumann's attitudes toward the bomb, Ulam noticed that Oppie "liked having the difficulties confirmed, whereas von Neumann was still searching for ways to rescue the whole thing." Von Neumann "never lost heart," even after he realized that the amount of tritium required would be so great as to make the Super prohibitively expensive.[24]

Immediately after his return to Los Alamos, Ulam wrote to von Neumann that Teller had been "pale with fury" when he learned of their conclusions. Teller also wrote to von Neumann, expressing the dark thought that Ulam had biased his calculations deliberately. To this von Neumann replied that he was "sorry to see that the strain which your work puts upon you is exceedingly great." Françoise Ulam in Los Alamos was a witness to the unhappiness her husband's results caused Teller. She had enjoyed her job up to now, punching out numbers on the desk calculators. She liked working in the T Division, where her husband was, and liked joining in the midmorning coffee hour, where the lab's luminaries and its rank and file exchanged gossip and planned the next Sunday's hike in the Jemez or Sangre de Cristo Mountains. But now, down the corridor, Françoise heard Teller berating Stan and shouting that his figures were wrong. The angry scenes went on for weeks, until it seemed to Françoise that no one stood up to Teller but Stan. But what Teller denied when it came from Ulam he could accept, at least for while, from his esteemed friend von Neumann. On June 13, after more than six weeks, Ulam wrote in his diary, "Victorious end of fights with Edward."[25]

Members of the old wartime team had by now arrived for the summer. On hand to consult on fission reactions, Bethe, despite his letter to Bradbury a few months earlier renouncing work on the

Super, looked over the Ulam-Everett hand calculations and concluded that ignition would probably require a kilogram of tritium, almost twice Teller's most recent estimate. Eagle-eyed as always, Ulam noticed that Bethe began to show up more frequently, apparently in hopes of proving once and for all that the Super would not work.[26]

Another visitor was Fermi, with whom Ulam set up a calculation to explore the second, equally crucial, half of the Super problem, the problem of burning. On the dubious assumption that the deuterium could be made to ignite, would the burning "propagate" through the column of deuterium? Programmers from the lab's computing group worked with desk calculators, while Fermi used logarithms and a slide rule and his usual stunning simplifications. By late summer he and Ulam embellished this routine and made their final set of computations a race between them. Assisted by a collaborator named Miriam Plank, Fermi worked on a Marchand calculator. The many hours he spent alone with the fetching Miriam, reviewing her calculations on the Marchand and laying out new ones for her to do, caused smiles of amusement among members of the T Division.

Ulam, on his side of the competition, relied on Monte Carlo, a method of calculation that was largely his invention and that was based on random numbers. Working once again with Everett, he addressed the problem by throwing dice. The race between Fermi and Ulam ended in a draw, with the two sets of calculations producing the same answers at about the same time. Like the three sets of Ulam-Fermi calculations that had preceded them, this one also showed that the explosion would fizzle.[27]

Teller's capitulation was short-lived. Carson Mark heard him roaring in disbelief as one set of calculations came in. But Ulam and Fermi were confident of their results. Ulam's confidence went beyond the issue of accuracy. He was convinced that the work he had done with Fermi was even more important than the earlier calculations with Everett because it turned out to be basic to an understanding of thermonuclear explosions. And it was important in a way that mattered hugely for successful development of the H-bomb. For years the lab had been working on the wrong model, Teller's Super. But before a new approach could be considered seriously, the old one had to be discredited. Ulam and Everett had shown that the Super could not work, but neither of them had Fermi's prestige. His adherence to their conclusions was decisive. Los Alamos was now convinced that the Super conceived by Edward Teller would neither ignite nor burn.[28]

CHAPTER SEVEN

Fission versus Fusion

THE THEORISTS WHO gathered in Los Alamos that summer of 1950 were a stellar group. In addition to Bethe, who had come to work on fission, and Teller and Fermi, who were working on different aspects of the thermonuclear problem, another legendary physicist, John Wheeler, arrived from Paris to answer what he regarded as a patriotic summons to join the H-bomb project.

Wheeler, whose groundbreaking paper on fission with Niels Bohr before the war had identified U-235 as the isotope of uranium that could be made to fission, had been in Europe during the 1949–50 academic year for a Guggenheim-sponsored period of thinking, writing, and renewed collaboration with Bohr. With his wife and three young children, he had settled into a cozy pension on the Left Bank when, one evening in late 1949, he received a transatlantic telephone call. Wheeler took the call on the wall phone in the dining room, where a score of French guests laid down their knives and forks to listen. It was AEC commissioner Henry Smyth. Would Wheeler cut short his fellowship year and come home to work on an all-out project? The Russians, Smyth said obliquely, were almost surely working on the same thing. Wheeler had already heard from Teller and had a notion what Smyth was referring to. Other cryptic telephone calls followed from across the Atlantic.

Still hesitating two months later, Wheeler mentioned his dilemma over breakfast in Copenhagen with Niels Bohr. "Do you for a moment imagine," he heard the Danish physicist say, "that Europe would be free of Soviet control today were it not for the atomic bomb?" Wheeler, an ardent patriot, decided to go home.[1]

He brought two of his most promising Princeton graduate students, Ken Ford and John Toll, to Los Alamos, where the three of them recalculated existing bomb design ideas, altering the parameters to see if they could somehow produce a thermonuclear explosion. They thought of new designs, too, the further out the better, and ran them through the calculators. And they revived an early inspiration of Teller's, the Alarm Clock, to see how large an explosion they could get. Wheeler and his men worked in an office next to the coffee room, and members of the T Division dropped by daily to join in the brainstorming. Besides Teller and his assistant, Frederic de Hoffmann, who had come from France to help out, there were Conrad Longmire, Marshall Rosenbluth, and Emil Konopinski, all of whom were to make significant contributions. And, importantly, the patient and respected division chief, Carson Mark, would come by to ask quiet questions that had a way of ferreting out weak spots. During the morning coffee hour all of them pooled their latest ideas, especially the ones they had tried out on calculators the day before. Teller would drop in, "a dark-haired, bushy-browed prophet," as Wheeler described him, to urge that they chuck it all and try some new approach. Ulam, meanwhile, would float down the corridor from office to office and announce before leaving in midafternoon, "I don't know how you physicists do it. I can't work more than six hours a day." Then he would go home to do pure mathematics late into the night.[2]

Wheeler, too, worked evenings in the log house where he and his family were living. It was the best house on Bathtub Row, having served as the arts and crafts building for the boys' school before the war, and it had a small Indian ruin in back. The three small Wheelers loved playing with six-year-old Claire Ulam next door, and observed that, when it came to stacked-up dishes in the sink and round-the-clock hospitality, the housekeeping style of Claire's mother, Françoise, was more relaxed than that of their mother. Janette Wheeler, for her part, found Los Alamos a company town, hard to break into. When, after a year or so, the Wheelers departed for the more civilized life of Princeton, the Los Alamites detected Janette's hand. "She thought we were all savages," one of them said.[3]

While Wheeler had come to explore thermonuclear possibilities, fission exploration, too, had attracted a gifted recruit in twenty-five-year-old Theodore Taylor. A few months earlier, in the fall of 1949, Carson Mark had had a call from Robert Serber, Manhattan Project veteran and professor of physics at Berkeley. He had an outstanding graduate student who had gone to pieces during his preliminary oral exams and flunked not once, but twice. The student was exceptionally creative, and Serber could not bear to see him lost to physics. He asked Mark to try him out. Taylor, who possessed an uncanny ability to visualize the way a collection of metal and wire and high explosives would react together, used graph paper and a hand calculator to eliminate material from the designs tested at Trinity, Bikini, and Sandstone and made them lighter and more efficient. Then he rearranged what was inside the implosion systems so as to get more energy for compression of the U-235 or plutonium core. Soon it was clear that Taylor was a prodigy, capable of designing A-bombs in a whole range of sizes and yields. After his failure at Berkeley, Taylor's confidence had been at rock bottom; his freewheeling status at Los Alamos suited him perfectly. The big men were trying to figure out how to build the Super, no one cared much about fission, and he was left in peace. So little had been done to improve the early fission designs that he felt his job was like skimming cream off the top of a milk bottle. He was getting results—while everyone else at the lab was at a dead end, trying to make deuterium ignite and burn.[4]

Any number of factors, a millionth of a second in timing or the smallest deviation from perfect symmetry, could make such a difference that Taylor decided that multiple small-yield explosions, each testing a different aspect, were needed to perfect the design of his new, more efficient A-bombs. He couldn't go to the Pacific to test merely part of a bomb, and so the AEC built two sites in Nevada, the first in the continental United States, to try out Taylor's ideas. The confidence that the young theorist had lost at Berkeley rebounded. He was given increasing freedom and that precious thing, open access to the computer. Caro Taylor noticed that Hans Bethe would drop by in hiking boots to confer with her husband, that Fermi would seek him out for hikes in the mountains above Los Alamos, and that at the rare dinner party they attended, some famous physicist or mathematician would huddle with him off in a corner.

Taylor's work was partly a hedge in case the thermonuclear bomb proved impossible: indeed, two years later his design, the Super Oralloy Bomb, was tested triumphantly at the Pacific proving grounds on Eniwetok. The successful test of a fission weapon of this magnitude—at half a megaton, it produced a much bigger explosion than earlier atomic bombs and half that of the putative hydrogen bomb—was to raise the question whether the megaton weapon, the thermonuclear bomb, would be needed after all.

The constellation of geniuses at Los Alamos that summer focused on a series of tests scheduled to take place in the Pacific the following spring. The series, code-named "Greenhouse," was to test four devices, two of which would have thermonuclear components. One of these was the Booster, an atomic bomb in which a small amount of deuterium would be added to the fissionable material in order to increase the yield. At their Halloween meeting Oppenheimer and the GAC had endorsed work on this weapon because it appeared to be a promising way to use fusion to produce an enormously enhanced atomic bomb. Carson Mark and the T Division were especially committed to this test because of the information it might provide about the way the fission and fusion elements interacted.

The other test, code-named "George," was the one in which Teller was particularly interested because it was more nearly a true thermonuclear experiment than the Booster test. It was not a bomb test but an experiment to learn how a capsule of thermonuclear fuel, a mixture of deuterium and tritium (D-T), would behave if ignited by a fission explosion outside it. Instead of placing the D-T combination at the center of the explosion, as in the Booster, energy from the explosion would be channeled down a pipe, or tube, to a vial of D-T gas weighing only a fraction of an ounce. After years of trying to think of ways to ignite a D-T mixture and make it burn, Teller wanted to know what would happen once it did burn: how the temperature and density would change, all the "diagnostics" of burning.

This required that the thermonuclear mixture be at a distance from the fission trigger and studied separately. Teller hoped the test would prove that the Super on which he and the lab had lavished years of research was possible, at least in principle. But a portentous fact, to which neither he nor anyone else gave much thought at the time, was that the component of the fission explosion that would move out of the core first and down the tube toward the thermonuclear fuel would be X-radiation.

After a summer of intense theoretical exploration, the lab had continued to make headway with fission weapons. Not only was there no progress on the Super, however, but the ENIAC calculations and the hand calculations by Ulam with Everett and Fermi all had provided evidence that the Super could not be built. In August, Teller and Wheeler produced a paper in which they conceded that it was still too early to say whether a thermonuclear weapon was feasible or economically practical. Instead of blaming possible failure on statistical evidence, however, they blamed it on a shortage of the "right men," or senior theoretical physicists. The number of these, they said, was shrinking when it ought to be growing. Unwilling to give up, they expressed hope that the big new computers scheduled for completion in 1951 and 1952 might disprove the pessimistic calculations so far.

About this time Bradbury wrote a paper agreeing that the chances of success now looked poorer than before. Unlike Teller and Wheeler, however, Bradbury did not blame a shortage of talent. Thermonuclear success, he predicted, "may depend upon entirely new and as yet unforeseen approaches."[5]

At a meeting in Washington in September 1950, the GAC welcomed the laboratory's success in fission research, noting that it was now possible to make a large number of small bombs from a given amount of fissionable material and also to develop atomic weapons with ten times the destructive power of any previous design, improvements that promised effectively to double the size of the U.S. stockpile. The committee contrasted the "uncertainties" of thermonuclear development with the "great promise" of fission weapons and suggested that the laboratory concentrate on fission. The GAC made another comment that was to cause trouble later on for Chairman Oppenheimer. Taking aim at Teller's special project, the GAC expressed "misgivings as to the value and relevance" of the effort expended on the forthcoming George shot. Because of the demands preparation for the test was placing on computer time and on the T Division, the committee concluded that "there is in fact interference between the thermonuclear program and the fission weapon program."[6]

That summer an event occurred that dwarfed even the explorations at Los Alamos. On June 26, 1950, in an attack that Americans believed to have been instigated by Joseph Stalin, the troops of Communist North Korea poured over the border to the south and invaded the Republic of South Korea. With U.S. strategic interests at stake, President Truman asked the United Nations to intervene. The fighting, waged by forces of the United States and the United Nations, lasted three years and was regarded as a kind of surrogate war between the United States and the USSR.[7]

The war in Korea changed everything. With Mao Tse-tung in power in China, the outbreak of hostilities meant that the United States was engaged against Communism in Asia as well as in Europe. It led to a buildup of U.S. armed forces, a change from peace to a semiwar footing, and growing suspicion of everything remotely red at home.

Remote as they were geographically, the men on the mesa in New Mexico were very much affected. There was talk of postponing or canceling the Greenhouse tests scheduled for the spring of 1951 in the Pacific lest they interfere with Navy supply lines to Korea. Hans Bethe reconsidered his renunciation of H-bomb work and agreed to join the project. And at the higher reaches of the U.S. government, consideration was given to using the atomic bomb in Korea. This possibility enhanced the priority of fission research: Korea had no targets large enough for the hydrogen bomb, but plenty of targets for small, or "tactical," atomic weapons should Truman decide to go nuclear.

The Korean War also brought into relief a difference of emphasis in Washington between those who believed the main threat from Stalin lay in Europe and those who worried most about Asia. Those who thought the greatest danger from Communism lay in Asia wanted to give priority to better and cheaper atomic bombs, while those who worried most about Europe tended to favor the bigger bomb. The nightmare of those most concerned with Europe was that with the Americans tied down in Korea, Stalin, who had already overrun Eastern Europe, would unleash his vast land armies on Western Europe. To prevent this, they wanted priority development of a "strategic," or hydrogen, weapon with which to bomb Soviet urban areas should Stalin make a move toward the West. Brien McMahon's energetic assistant, William Borden, belonged to the Europe-first school of thought. Borden wrote a memo that summer pointing out that in addition to its larger cities, the USSR had many smaller, spread-out urban areas with factories and military bases on the outskirts. "One H-bomb would eliminate the entire complex," he wrote, while "A-bombs would be relatively ineffective." Borden also doubted the ability of U.S. bomber crews to deliver A-bombs on heavily defended pinpoint targets, especially at night or in bad weather. "Such targets," he concluded, "might succumb to the H-bomb alone." Such was the strength of Borden's feelings that he opposed use of the A-bomb in Korea not out of pacifist sentiment but because "each weapon used in Korea will leave one less to be used . . . against Russia."[8]

Ted Taylor was exposed to this attitude that fall of 1950 when he and several other New Mexico weaponeers were informed in a Pentagon briefing that Soviet land armies were capable of occupying all of Western Europe in less than six weeks. Taylor, an innocent whose experience up to then had been pretty much limited to what went on in the core of a fissioning bomb, was too startled to question whether what they were being told was true—"we were only kids from Los Alamos."

Taylor spent several weeks in the Pentagon that autumn poring over enormous photographs of Moscow, Baku, and other targets in the Soviet Union, trying to figure out whether he could design an A-bomb big enough to wipe out an entire metropolitan area. "I spent a lot of time drawing circles with ground zero on the Kremlin and the distance corresponding to various calories per square centimeter and pounds per square inch pressure." Pentagon officials were disappointed that none of his circles included the whole of Moscow. If the contents of one big bomb were divided into several smaller bombs, Taylor told them, they could destroy more of the city. "What could you do with a kiloton?" he asked rhetorically later on. "The answer was a great deal, depending on what you could package it in."[9]

Smaller bombs were a specialty of his: thanks to Taylor, a dozen small implosion designs eventually became part of the U.S. stockpile, to say nothing of the design for a tiny atomic bomb ten inches in diameter that one man could lift off the ground. But the Navy and Air Force were not interested in Taylor's boutique bombs. Frightened by the conviction that they were years behind the Russians and uncertain that the Super could be built, they wanted a one-megaton fission bomb, an atomic bomb in the hydrogen-bomb range. They hoped that the twenty-five-year-old prodigy from Los Alamos could give them the miracle they sought.

With war simmering in the Far East and Taylor at work on clever fission designs, Oppenheimer summoned the GAC to Los Alamos in late October for its twenty-third meeting. Here and there the cottonwoods were still yellow in the river valleys, but on the Hill the aspens were bare. The skepticism of the Halloween meeting just one year before had been amply borne out. Oppenheimer reminded those gathered on the mesa that the earlier meeting had been asked to judge a specific Super design and concluded that it showed too little promise to justify an all-out program. Calculations by Fermi and Ulam since then made it appear even less likely than before that the second stage of the explosion, the "propagation," would occur.[10]

The situation was equally grave, indeed it now looked nearly hopeless, with regard to the first, or "ignition," stage. Instead of the one hundred, four hundred, or six hundred grams of tritium that Teller had variously predicted, Ulam and Everett and the ENIAC calculations had shown that "a lower limit" of three to five kilograms would be required. Not only had Teller's estimates been wrong—they had been wrong by an order of magnitude.[11]

Did Teller feel chastened by his egregious miscalculations? Not in the least. He was present at the meeting, along with other members of the lab, and when Carson Mark outlined the ENIAC and Fermi-Ulam results of the summer just past, Teller charged that the assumptions on which they were based had been heavily oversimplified and that their conclusions were wrong. Fermi disagreed, suggesting that more detailed calculations would probably make the picture even bleaker. And when Chicago chemist Willard Libby, a new member of the committee, agreed with Teller that the Fermi-Ulam results had been given too much weight, Oppenheimer, Rabi, and DuBridge responded that any change would be in the direction of making success appear even more unlikely.[12]

Teller returned to the manpower issue, charging that Los Alamos did not have enough qualified personnel to do both the required theoretical work and detailed calculations—"there are just not enough of us." With more than a touch of condescension, he said the lab would be able to cope if the Super's feasibility was disproven, but should the George test the following spring show that the Super looked promising, "then for that we are not strong enough." By "we," he meant the lab and his colleagues there. Bradbury spoke up for the lab and responded that what Los Alamos needed was not larger numbers but "individuals of special abilities and judgment," especially theoreticians. He had opposed pressure to expand more rapidly, he said, lest the place become too cumbersome. Oppenheimer suggested that if the lab were to change emphasis in any way it should be in the direction of obtaining higher yields from smaller amounts of fissionable material.

With the war in Korea making the Pacific proving grounds less secure, the question arose of whether to go ahead with any of the Greenhouse tests and especially whether George, the test of ignition, or first-stage, possibilities would be useful when, in light of the work by Ulam, Everett, and Fermi, there was no apparent solution to the second, or propagation, stage.

Oppenheimer wrote a summary letter to AEC chairman Gordon Dean after the meeting, in which he conceded that the test might yield "relevant" information about burning and radiation flow. "We wish to make it clear, however, that the test, whether successful or not, is neither a proof firing of a possible thermonuclear weapon nor a test of feasibility. . . . The test is not addressed to resolving the paramount uncertainties which are decisive in evaluating the feasibility of the Super." Since George was the test to which Teller attached special importance and on which he had lavished his efforts, he and others later criticized Oppenheimer for his words and accused him of hoping for a failure. To the contrary, Oppenheimer, the GAC, and the lab thought that the test would succeed. But they considered it irrelevant to the question of whether the Super would work and believed that it "made no technical sense."[13]

Summing up the past year as the meeting ended, Bradbury concluded that the thermonuclear program had gotten nowhere. It was of utmost urgency that the lab "do first those things promising the greatest possible gain in minimum time." That meant working on atomic weapons. Bradbury had almost given up on the Super. "Practical success, if it can be attained at all without new and presently unforeseen conceptions, must be regarded as . . . distant."[14]

Teller

Soon after joining the lab, Ted Taylor found himself grounded by weather at the Phoenix airport. The only person who looked familiar to him was Edward Teller, and in the course of an eight-hour stopover, the two got to talking. Teller, who had a special liking for young people, asked Taylor what he was working on. Taylor described an idea he had for exploring reactions in the center of the current stockpile bomb by going to low-yield testing. Teller was enthusiastic.

The moment they got back to Los Alamos, Teller called a meeting and asked Taylor to lay out his idea. Carson Mark was there, and Emil Konopinski and even Enrico Fermi. Everyone said yes, that looked like a good thing to do.

That, Taylor said afterward, was Edward Teller at his best. And his best was very, very good. In originality, enthusiasm, quickness to grasp a new concept—in all of these, no one was better. Even colleagues who detested him enjoyed going to Teller's office to chew over a new idea. His math could be unreliable and he was not the person you'd ask to work a problem through patiently, with equations, but he had humor and charm and he could be immensely generous. He could also lean over backward to be fair. In 1948 he was probably the first American scientist to seek out Werner Heisenberg, Carl Friedrich von Weiszacker, and other physicists who had chosen to stay in Germany during the war. He listened to them, sought to understand the ambiguities of their position under the Nazis, and did his best to bring them back into the world scientific community. "It is wrong," he wrote to a close friend, "to act as if the only thing in the world would be politics."[1]

Teller was also astonishingly self-absorbed. Whatever his mood of the moment, that mood simply filled his universe. At such times he would extrapolate outward from his own dark mood and see the whole world in shades of black. By late fall 1950, he had sunk into one of those moods. Gone were the high hopes with which he had arrived from Chicago the year before. He blamed the lab and looked down on his colleagues there. Bradbury and the others who had stayed on after the war were what he called "the second team." His thoughts ran constantly to the first team—Fermi and Bethe and Oppenheimer—who had refused to return and work on *his* bomb as they had worked on Oppie's bomb during the war. If work on the Super was at a dead end, *they* were to blame.

Many an evening that fall and early winter, Teller trudged through the snow to the house of Kay and Carson Mark, three doors away from his own. There he sat in a big chair, chin in hand, staring at the floor, "wrapped in a black cloud you could almost touch," Kay Mark remembered. Her husband was likewise aware of that cloud of despair. Putting it in his usual mild way, Carson Mark saw that Teller was "troubled," that he was "angry and resentful." While Kay was putting the younger children to bed, Carson puffed quietly on his pipe and kept his thoughts to himself. He was reflecting that thanks largely to the man in front of him, "we had spent years working on the wrong thing. The thing Edward had peddled to Truman did not exist."[2]

There were other reasons, too, for Teller's apocalyptic frame of mind. He had received word that his father, Max Teller, had died in Budapest, leaving his mother and sister exposed to the Stalinist cruelties of Hungary's Rakosi regime. And he was tormented by indecision about his future. He had tentatively accepted a job offer from UCLA, only to learn that the regents had fired thirty-two professors who refused to take a loyalty oath. Teller's solidarity with the professors and unwillingness to take the oath himself had led to a bitter scene in Ernest Lawrence's office. Not since Nazi times, he said, had he heard a "little fascist speech" like the scolding Lawrence gave him that day. Teller actually wanted to return to the University of Chicago, but his wife, Mici, hated the place. He was toying with an offer from New York University, not because he meant to take it, but in hopes of persuading Mici that he had done his utmost to save her from the midwestern weather. All this and more Teller confided to Maria Goeppert Mayer, a brilliant former student living in Chicago, on whom he relied for counsel and support.[3]

And there was Korea. "The third world war has started," he wrote Mayer, "and I do not know whether I care to survive it." Not since Pearl Harbor had the nation faced such disaster. After a successful landing at Inchon in September 1950, General Douglas MacArthur had sent his forces up the Korean Peninsula, risking intervention by China. Sure enough, on November 25, a quarter of a million Chinese troops burst from their hiding places just south of the Yalu River and crushed the United Nations forces. President Truman created an uproar by leaving the impression at a press conference that the decision whether to use atomic weapons might be left to General MacArthur.[4]

Teller, as usual, spent much of the winter in travel mode. In December he flew in a tiny airplane from Los Alamos to Norman, Oklahoma, where he delivered a speech at the university and, even though AEC commissioner Sumner Pike was in the audience, criticized both the commission and the U.S. policy of restraint in Korea. He also traveled to Washington, where he informed Louis Ridenour, now chief scientist of the Air Force, that the AEC was dragging its feet on the H-bomb. Teller wanted to leave Los Alamos, where, he said, the research facilities were inadequate. He wanted the Air Force to set up a facility so that he could work on the problem at the University of Chicago instead. And he made a convert of Lieutenant General Elwood R. "Pete" Quesada, a renowned World War II pilot assigned to command the task force that would carry out the Greenhouse tests. Listening to Teller, Quesada realized that his service, the Air Force, stood to gain more than the other services if the H-bomb was built. It followed that he should render all the help he could. Teller warned, however, that the project had powerful opponents, the ringleader being Robert Oppenheimer. Failure of the tests would enable those opponents to argue that the effort was futile.

Teller's conviction that Oppenheimer was trying to subvert the project received reinforcement when a panel chaired by Oppenheimer made its report in December 1950. The panel, one of many on which Oppenheimer served in addition to the GAC, had been specially created by the Defense Department to advise on the long-range uses of atomic weapons. It met at a moment when hopes for the Super were at their nadir and many in Washington feared that China's intervention in Korea might be the prelude to a Soviet invasion of Europe. Since recent successes at Los Alamos had all been in fission research, the panel—like the GAC at its Halloween meeting of 1949 and its Los Alamos meeting of October 1950—agreed that priority should be given to work on the fission bomb. Only if it was understood and accepted that work on a thermonuclear bomb was long-range in nature, five years or more, could the resources of Los Alamos be freed for concentration on fission weapons. Teller disagreed, and bitterly reproached Luis Alvarez, a member of the panel, for having signed a report that, he told Alvarez, was "being used against our program. It is slowing it down and it could easily kill it."[5]

Oppenheimer had written the report, but all twelve members of the panel, which included three generals and an admiral, were in agreement. The GAC, meeting on January 6, was likewise unanimous (with Walter Whitman, director of the 1948 Lexington Study of aircraft nuclear propulsion, and Oppenheimer, who belonged to both groups, recusing themselves). But as Teller saw it, the culprit was Oppenheimer: he had a golden tongue, and the others must have succumbed to his spell. Teller did not view it as a matter of honest error or difference of opinion. Oppenheimer wanted to kill his, Teller's, program; therefore he must have a hidden motive.[6]

Teller and Bill Borden had been cultivating each other for a year. They wrote flattering letters back and forth, decried what they thought were shortcomings in the H-bomb program, and arranged to see each other over dinner when Teller was in Washington.

In March 1950, only a month after Truman's H-bomb decision, Teller had warned the committee that the country might be in even greater danger than during World War II. By the war's end we had known that the Germans did not, as we had feared, have an A-bomb program. Now, however, with the Russians, we had no such assurance: indeed, thanks to Fuchs, they might well be ahead. Between the war's end and the 1949 Russian test, Teller claimed, work on a U.S. hydrogen bomb had not gone forward "at any appreciable rate." Although he was hesitant to suggest that his colleagues actually be drafted to work on the H-bomb, the number of theoretical physicists on the project must be promptly increased by "more than a factor of two in number and much more than a factor of two in talent."[7]

Teller complained that most of the scientific community was reluctant. Many scientists, he said, were still suffering a bad conscience over the destruction wreaked by the A-bomb and questioning the morality of H-bomb work. "If some of the best among them" showed by their actions that they were doubtful about thermonuclear work, the others would also hesitate.

In his formal testimony before the committee, Teller had not named names. But at dinner with Borden the evening before, he had not hesitated to do so, blaming the scientists' reluctance on Oppenheimer and, to a lesser extent, on Bethe and Fermi also. He had charged that for two years after the war Oppenheimer had tried to have the lab disbanded—"give it back to the Indians"—or make it a center of basic research.[8]

On the strength of what Teller said that night, Borden prevailed on Senator McMahon to call the last-minute session next day in which Teller told the committee that for four years after the war no "appreciable" work had been done on the H-bomb.

Teller was well aware that the man he had chosen to confide in saw things very much as he did. Bill Borden had no training in nuclear physics, but this in no way inhibited his certainties. He shared Teller's belief that the Russians were out to do in the United States and that it was a matter of survival to stay ahead. He expected war in Europe at any moment and believed that the H-bomb could be decisive in subduing the vast territory of the USSR. The usually reticent Fermi implicitly criticized Borden's advice to the senator when he told a member of the JCAE staff that during the critical period in 1949 and 1950 when McMahon had been pushing President Truman to start a crash program, he and the JCAE had been "misinformed" about the real prospects and problems of the Super. Fermi warned that the committee ought to "think twice" before entering scientific controversies in the future, since it lacked the necessary technical competence. Coming from Fermi, who was renowned for his impartiality and cool judgment, this was devastating criticism. The conversation ended with what the staff member in his report described as "admonitory remarks about Dr. Teller. Dr. Fermi says he has the greatest respect for Dr. Teller's scientific ability and also values him as a personal friend," but that, having "very little comprehension of the scientific and engineering problems that lie between the germ of a brilliant idea and the achieving of a perfected weapon," Teller had a tendency to exaggerate the prospects for success.[9]

As for Borden, out of childish bravado and lack of genuine understanding, he made light of what the A-bomb could do. After witnessing his first atomic test, he had written a memo dismissing the impression it had made on him. He and colleagues on the committee staff who felt as he did made a point of calling atomic bombs mere "ordinaries" compared with the hydrogen bomb. He prodded Senator McMahon relentlessly to seek expansion of the program. Borden was an intelligent man who cared about duty and honor. But he was a zealot, and he had the ear of a powerful senator who wanted to be president, and as a result, he wielded an authority that far outweighed his judgment.

So zealous was Borden in pursuing his ends—larger, more powerful nuclear weapons—that he occasionally committed glaring breaches of protocol and even security. For example, after an appearance by Hans Bethe before the committee in May of 1950, Borden outlined Bethe's secret testimony in a letter to Teller that, if not technically a breach of security, was at the very least out of channels, as Borden himself acknowledged: "This information is, of course, just for your personal use. . . . I would appreciate your not circulating it."[10]

Borden's lapses of judgment were compounded by Teller's inclination to question the motives of anyone who stood in his way. Meeting with a committee staff member in Los Alamos during the spring of 1950, Teller had made what was almost—but not quite—his first suggestion to a government official that Oppenheimer might be a security risk. After entering the caveat that he "did not get along" with Oppenheimer, in part because he held him responsible for dropping the H-bomb program at the end of the war, Teller said it was "common knowledge that Oppenheimer was far to the left." Oppenheimer, he said, was "unusually close" to his brother Frank, and Frank Oppenheimer would not have joined the Communist Party if Robert had not approved. Teller believed that Robert Oppenheimer had used his influence to bring his brother to Los Alamos during the war, and he thought that this, too, was grounds for suspicion. (Frank Oppenheimer was, in fact, a first-rate experimentalist whose work checking test results at the Trinity site received high praise from everyone there.) Concluding his report, the JCAE staff member said that Teller had been "careful to explain that he himself did not have any idea that the subject was disloyal or intended to injure the best interests of the country. . . . However . . . Teller did say that were Oppenheimer found, by any chance, to be disloyal 'in the sense of transmitting information,' he could, of course, do much more damage to the program than any other single individual in the country."[11]

Borden lost no time reacting to Teller's remarks. He drafted a memo for Senator McMahon warning that the program was in the hands of highly placed individuals who had "bitterly" opposed the H-bomb decision and whose emotions might be leading them to consider the effort futile. These individuals included AEC general manager Carroll Wilson, all nine members of the GAC including Oppenheimer, and two of the commissioners, Sumner Pike and Henry D. Smyth. Borden urged that special attention be given to filling the position of general manager and vacancies on the GAC and the commission as they arose. Accordingly, when the terms of three

GAC members expired that summer, they were replaced by men who were expected to show more enthusiasm for the H-bomb project than those who were departing. By far the most notable departure was that of Fermi, quite possibly the world's greatest living physicist: his departure was pushed by a new AEC commissioner, Thomas Murray, in hopes of creating a precedent that might lead in time to the departure of Oppenheimer.[12]

The extent to which Borden shared Teller's suspicions—and, indeed, brought his own special twist to them—can be seen from a memorandum he wrote to his boss toward the end of the year:

> I spent most of last week reading several dozen personnel security files. . . .
>
> A number of the "calculated risk" clearances of distinguished scientists having irreplaceable abilities . . . left me with a feeling of apprehension. . . . Usually, too, the subject had intimate access under the Manhattan District—and if he is kept out of the program, our progress very definitely suffers.
>
> It is indeed the unhappy truth that a number of our greatest experts have long lacked—and perhaps occasionally still lack—a sense of moral outrage at the characteristics and ambitions of the Soviet government. This lack, combined with almost fantastic naivete and gullibility, has caused so many of the top scientists to join front groups, associate with Communists, etc., that any real espionage agents among them cannot be identified by reference to such activities.
>
> I conclude that we may well have another Fuchs still in the project today and that all calculations should take into account this strong possibility.[13]

CHAPTER NINE

Ulam

As HE PLAYED on the rug in his parents' house in the Polish city of Lvov, the little boy kept staring at the intricate Oriental pattern. Aware that his father was smiling at him, the boy thought, "He thinks I am childish, but these are curious patterns. I know something my father does not know."[1]

All his life, Stan Ulam was looking for patterns. All his life, too, he had the air of the detached observer. He was not yet forty-two years old when the year 1951 began, an onlooker as Edward Teller and Hans Bethe argued about thermonuclear reactions. "Amusing fights: Hans-Edward," Ulam wrote in his diary on January 18. And a few days later, "big fight fairly amusing." What the fight was about, whether and how it contributed to the pattern taking shape in Ulam's head, is not known. But on January 25 he wrote in the diary, "Discussion with Edward on two bombs."[2]

Ulam had been thinking for some time about a "bomb in a box." And in December 1950 he came upon the idea of using shock waves from an exploding fission bomb inside a "box," or container, to compress the material in a second fission device inside the same "box" to such high density that it would burn. Now it occurred to him that these ideas might be combined in such a way as to solve the problem of making a package of thermonuclear fuel burn. Ulam described the concept, that of using an exploding fission device inside a container to create so much pressure on the thermonuclear material as to maintain the burn, was called "supercompression," and it was, in fact, extreme compression compared with anything that had been contemplated before.[3]

Françoise Ulam later remembered coming home at noon on January 23, 1951, to find her husband staring out the window with a strange expression on his face. Over lunch, he told her he had had an idea that might make the Super possible. If his idea worked, he said, it would change the world. Appalled, since she had hoped the bomb would prove infeasible, Françoise asked what his next step would be. He supposed that he would have to tell Edward. Remembering Teller's fury the previous summer after he learned of Stan's results with Everett and Fermi, she asked whether he ought to try his idea on someone else first, "either Carson or Norris."[4]

Ulam appeared in Carson Mark's office that afternoon and, sketching something on the blackboard, said, "In Nevada we have to be doing something more interesting, like this. If we did it that way, it might produce such and such reactions, which would be interesting to measure." Such was Ulam's style. He seldom spelled out an idea, being so absorbed in it himself that he assumed his interlocutor was following his line of thought. Mark, frantically busy with preparations for the Greenhouse tests and for a series of smaller fission shots in Nevada, did not realize that Ulam's idea pertained to the thermonuclear problem. "It seemed like an unnecessary addition to things that were scarcely manageable as they were," he said long afterward.[5]

Ulam next showed up in Bradbury's office. This time he had no need to explain: Bradbury immediately saw what he was driving at. Both men realized that the next person Ulam had to see was Teller. Bradbury, who was given to minimizing his own role, refused to take credit in later years for so quickly grasping the relevance of Ulam's idea: he took credit only for imparting a hint or two as to how Ulam might present his idea without making Teller as angry as he had been the summer before.[6]

The next morning Teller and Ulam had their discussion "on two bombs." Teller resisted at first, but before long he, too, became enthusiastic. Later in the day he burst into the T Division office, where several of his colleagues were working. "Ulam has had an idea," he announced, "but he hasn't got it quite right." And he set the men—

Max Goldstein, Arnold Kramish, and Frederic de Hoffmann—to work on calculations to see whether the new concept might be applied to the George test in the spring. Teller went home to his piano while the others worked through the night.[7]

Ulam met with Teller several times in late January and early February 1951, half an hour or so each time. He drew a sketch, and then Teller added an idea. Ulam's idea was to compress the thermonuclear fuel by mechanical shock from an exploding fission device, while Teller's was to use radiation from the exploding device instead, in order to achieve the extreme compression required. The two men wrote a joint paper in which each described the scheme he had thought of: they had come up with parallel ways of obtaining a thermonuclear burn without using the prohibitive quantities of tritium required by all the other schemes so far. The concept was called "radiation implosion."[8]

The concept seemed simple—but only after someone had discovered it. And the title of LAMS-1225, the paper completed by the two men in late February and dated March 9, 1951—"On Heterocatalytic Detonations: I. Hydrodynamic Lenses and Radiation Mirrors—I"—hints at its extraordinary ingenuity. Hot X-rays from the exploding fission bomb would move in all directions inside the casing that contained the two bombs. The plastic material that filled the casing would then be ionized and exert a strong material pressure that would compress the secondary sufficiently to ignite the thermonuclear fuel. All of this had to occur in a millionth of a second, lest the device explode before the second bomb could ignite. In the half century since it was written, only a handful of people have read the paper, and those who have report that much of it consists of brilliant ideas of Ulam's about "staging," or arranging the components in such a way as to maximize the explosion. Although six other nations—Britain, France, China, the USSR, and probably Pakistan and India—later developed the hydrogen bomb, the Ulam-Teller paper, which lays out the key concepts of staging (Ulam's), compression (Ulam's), and radiation (Teller's), is classified to this day with no hope of declassification anytime soon, lest some would-be proliferator, whether a terrorist or a nation, learn something from it that would enable him to devise a workable bomb.[9]

Teller assigned his protégé, Frederic de Hoffmann, to do the mathematical work on a second idea he had had that was an ingenious complement to the first: the addition of a second fission element, which came to be called the "spark plug," positioned like a rod inside the thermonuclear fuel, to compress the thermonuclear component by an explosion inside as well as from the outside. The resulting paper, LA-1230, to which, knowing his mentor's emotional identification with the achievement, de Hoffmann signed only Teller's name, and not his own, is dated April 4, 1951, and likewise remains classified.[10]

Teller from the start tried to make Ulam an unperson. Not only did he assign de Hoffmann to write the April 4 paper; he refused to sign a patent application bearing Ulam's signature because it named the two of them as coinventors. Because of Teller's refusal to sign Ulam's application and failure to file an application of his own, the Teller-Ulam, or, as some might call it, the Ulam-Teller, concept, which became the basis of hydrogen bomb design, has never been patented. Teller simply took the credit.[11]

Four years later, following a conversation with Fermi on his deathbed, Teller published an article, "The Work of Many People," in which he described the contributions various scientists had made. He mentioned the calculations Ulam had done with Everett showing that the old concept would not work, but omitted Ulam's role in the breakthrough. He did it again in his book *Legacy of Hiroshima,* published in 1962, this time attributing the breakthrough to himself and de Hoffmann. Afterward, in books, articles, and interviews, he did his utmost to excise Ulam from the history books, insisting that since Ulam had not been eager for the bomb to be invented and was skeptical that it would work even after their conversations of January and February 1951, he should not receive any credit. "Ulam invented nothing!" he exclaimed on many occasions.[12]

For a time Teller's claim to sole authorship was virtually uncontested, partly because of government secrecy. Because the ideas he had contributed were considered especially sensitive, Ulam's name was for years censored out of the official literature. In the published transcript of the Oppenheimer hearing of 1954, for example, Ulam's name appears only once, with four asterisks in place of his name the other times it was mentioned in testimony; and when Bradbury, in a press conference later that year, singled out Ulam's contribution, Robert McKinney, publisher of the *Santa Fe New Mexican* and a man well versed in matters atomic, had to ask who Ulam was and how the name was spelled. Ulam declined to press his claim, considering assertiveness of that sort beneath him, and despite Bradbury's effort, the role of the Polish mathematician was for years unknown to the public, while Teller, with his reputation as "Father of the H-bomb," enjoyed tremendous standing with congressmen and Pentagon officials, who did not know the real story.[13]

This distortion of the record, for which both Teller and the system of secrecy were to blame, later became a matter of anger and embarrassment to members of the laboratory who knew how the breakthrough had occurred. Most were critical, even contemptuous, of Teller, not only for claiming credit that was not properly his, but also for the very serious action of using his public reputation to acquire his own lab at Livermore and to promote visionary schemes—the "Clean Bomb" of the 1950s, Projects "Gabriel" and "Ploughshare" in the 1960s, "Palisades of Fire" in the 1970s, and "Star Wars" in the 1980s—which they considered ill-judged and based on false scientific claims.[14] Carson Mark, in particular, felt remorse over having missed what Ulam tried to tell him that fateful afternoon of January 24, 1951. Mark believed that had he caught Ulam's drift and put the T Division to work on the new concept right away, Teller's contribution, the idea of radiation, would have occurred to the lab's theoreticians as a matter of course. In that event the T Division and Stan Ulam would have been known as mother and father, respectively, of the H-bomb. Teller would still have received credit for the single-mindedness he had brought to the quest, but he would not have had the enormous political clout that he acquired and that, in the opinion of Mark and most members of the lab, he misused.[15]

Teller's churlishness had a history, unknown until Françoise Ulam unearthed it in the lab's personnel files during the late 1980s. It was the questionnaire Teller filled out after Ulam had worked for about a year in Teller's subgroup, doing research on the Super.

War Department
Project Y

EMPLOYEE RATING OF SCIENTIFIC ACHIEVEMENT

Name of employee	Stanislaw Ulam
Success in recent work	Unsatisfactory
Theoretical ability	Outstanding
As potential member of lab research	Outstanding
Personality	Unsatisfactory

Comments: Mr. Ulam is a brilliant mathematician but does not have the proper background for the work we are doing and does not seem able to adjust himself to our work. Occasionally he has helped in our research and on the whole the group has profited by his presence.

He is an independent thinker and might conceivably turn up most important results. I think if he could work on pure research in mathematics he would be much more happily placed than in our project.

E. Teller   February 13, 1945[16]

Teller recognized Ulam's independence—and wanted no more to do with him.[17]

Something similar also happened in early 1950 when Ulam, Teller, and Gamow were looking into theoretical problems of the Super. Finding the other two uncomfortably irreverent and independent-minded, Teller seized a moment when they were both out of town to disband their three-man group.

Having shown by his calculations with Everett and Fermi during the spring and summer of 1950 that Teller's design would not work, Ulam in 1951 came up with the solution. Poker player that he was, he was pleased to have trumped Teller, to have trumped him twice, in fact, first by showing that Teller's design would not work, and then by coming up with a workable concept himself. And he had done it, as he did everything, with a beguiling air of nonchalance and not a trace of Teller's obsessiveness, which to him was unseemly and perhaps a little obscene. Ulam was annoyed by Teller's insistence on placing his stamp on the invention: as far as he was concerned, his scheme, that of achieving compression by means of mechanical shock, was enough by itself to do the job. As Ulam put it later, Teller had added a "complication." Belittling it, he said in his book that Teller "had found a parallel version, an alternative to what I had said, perhaps more convenient and generalized."[18]

But Teller's idea was crucial. Why did the idea of radiation occur first to him and not to Ulam? Carson Mark believed that Teller's concentration on George was the explanation. "Edward had just finished a year of work on the George shot," of which radiation was a feature. George was Teller's test: not only had he worked on it, he had promoted it to the point of trying to have "Item," another shot in the series, canceled. Ulam, Mark added, "did not have that immediate, close-in exposure to the radiation picture." Mark did not consider it surprising that Teller came up with the idea, since "once you try to achieve fantastic compression by means of an atomic bomb, you'd have to face the fact that radiation was there. You'd have *had* to think of it. Edward was in a better position to be aware that radiation could be decisive. He was thinking about radiation in a way that Ulam was not." Mark believed that anyone in T Division who had worked on George would have called attention, as Teller did, to radiation as a way of producing extreme compression.[19]

Another physicist, who attended the 1946 Super conference but was no longer working on weapons in 1951, agreed. "Once you think of implosion," he said, "you think of radiation. After the idea of compression occurred, a day's discussion would have produced the idea of achieving compression by means of radiation." This scientist, Philip Morrison, did not find Teller's idea surprising. Rather, what surprised him was the importance given by the new concept to "radiation mirrors."[20]

Legends surround Ulam, among them the legend that he was lazy. No one ever saw Ulam working; nor did anyone ever see him when he was not, almost visibly, engaged in thinking. Some mornings he did his thinking at home, and Bradbury would drop by at eleven or so to ask when he was coming to "work" at the two-story wooden Tech Building. There was joking at the lab that "Everett did Ulam's best work," and in later years one or two of the division chiefs were "ferociously critical" of Ulam for failing to complete his projects. But Mark, with Bradbury's support, insisted on keeping him because his presence was so stimulating to the younger scientists. Mark conceded that Ulam did not exactly "work" on things. Instead, he sowed ideas as if he were "a landed seigneur back in Poland strolling around his estates, waving a hand and ordering his minions to plant a walnut seed here, a sapling there, and leaving others to tend the young trees."[21]

Ulam was to the manor born. Stan's father, Jozef, was a lawyer; his uncle, Szymon, was a banker; and his mother, Anna Auerbach, was from a wealthy industrial family. Genius ran in the family, some of the finest buildings in Lvov being the work of an earlier Ulam, an architect. For a few years, beginning when Stanislaw was five, the family took refuge in Vienna, since Russian troops had occupied Lvov, then part of the Austro-Hungarian Empire. While still in his teens, Ulam was accepted by the coterie of mathematicians who made up the well-known Lvov school, who quickly noticed his altogether exceptional originality. Huddled in the coffeehouses and tiny inns of Lvov, these mathematicians spent hours drinking coffee and scribbling formulas on white marble tabletops. Recalling one seventeen-hour session at the Scottish Café in which the silence was broken only by occasional bouts of laughter or a pause for drinks and a bite to eat, Ulam later said that long hours of silent concentration were a requirement of creative mathematical work. But thinking very hard about the same problem for hours on end could produce severe fatigue, even breakdown. Ulam, who was as fascinated by the workings of the brain as by mathematics, wrote that he never experienced a real breakdown, but on two or three occasions he had felt "strange inside" and had to stop.

In 1932, at the age of twenty-three, he was invited to work in the Soviet Union, but because of his capitalist origins considered it the better part of wisdom to decline. Two years later, von Neumann invited him to the Institute for Advanced Study at Princeton, and in the fall of 1936 he began a three-year appointment as a junior fellow at Harvard, returning each summer to Poland. Finally, in the summer of 1939, with war impending in Europe and at his uncle's insistence, he left Poland for the United States, accompanied by his seventeen-year-old brother, Adam.

Neither Adam nor Stan ever recovered from the loss of the life they had known in Europe. Although both were to make distinguished careers in the United States (Adam as a historian), neither felt at home in what they experienced as a puritanical Anglo-Saxon culture. Nor did they know the full dimensions of their loss until after the war. Only then did they learn that the Nazis had shot their sister, Stefania, and her infant daughter; that her husband, too, had disappeared; and that the uncles and aunts who had stayed in Lvov were sent to concentration camps and died there. The Russians permitted their father, Jozef, to remain in his apartment, where he offered shelter to a seventeen-year-old student who was wanted by the authorities. During the fall and winter of 1939–1940 the two of them burned Jozef's law books for warmth and had conversations in which the older man spoke with pride about the two sons he had sent to America. Before the war ended, no one knows exactly when, Jozef died of heartbreak and ill health. The Russians, meanwhile, confiscated the family properties.[22]

Immediately after the war Stan, who was teaching at the University of Southern California, was stricken by mysterious headaches. Upon operating, the doctors found inflammation of the brain and not, as they had feared, a tumor. Their intervention relieved the intracranial pressure, and the patient recovered. But for Stan the observer of mental processes, the threat of losing his memory and capacity for logical thought had been terrifying, and he never completely recovered from the fear. After he died in 1984, his friend Gian-Carlo Rota wrote that Ulam's mental capacity had been affected by the illness, but Françoise and Adam Ulam, and two mathematicians who worked with Stan before and afterward, Mark Kac and David Hawkins, insisted that they had seen no change. When they discussed the cause of Stan's illness, colleagues speculated that he might have been trying unconsciously *not* to solve the problem of the H-bomb. But Françoise, whose mother also had died in the Holocaust, disagreed with the speculation. If Stan's illness had a psychological component, and she was by no means persuaded that it did, she thought it was caused by the realization that all of his family were gone, the old life in Europe gone forever.[23]

When Stan was invited to return to Los Alamos after his illness, he gladly accepted, and the unlikeliest part of his unlikely odyssey began. There on the dusty mesa, he managed to re-create some of the warmth and conviviality of his beloved Scottish Café: he and a colleague even opened a coffeehouse. What he missed in America was a culture in which mathematics was done orally and at leisure, in conversation upon conversation, as it had been in Warsaw and Lvov. Paradoxically, he found this culture at the lab. Being at the very frontier of science with some of the most brilliant minds in the world excited his imagination. It reminded him of Lvov. And Los Alamos, a kind of factory for most of the people who worked there, allowed him to work as he pleased.[24]

One friend said that Ulam had "not an ounce of modesty in him." Indeed, he was heard to boast, "I am the most imaginative man in the world." Aware that his greatest gift was his originality, he was at pains to conserve it. When he read a book, his eye would race down the page, plucking out the nuggets, and then he would toss the thing away, "in order not to be influenced." In conversation it was the same, with friends occasionally complaining that he gave short shrift to their ideas. When I. I. Rabi, for whom he had great respect, twice came to see him—in 1949, during the H-bomb debate, and 1954, at the time of the Oppenheimer hearings—to ask him to join the behind-the-scenes political scrimmaging, Ulam, to Rabi's annoyance, remained aloof. Similarly, although he disdained Teller's lust for the H-bomb, he refused to waste himself on anger. Indeed, some of Ulam's personal style, the air of amateurish ease, the laziness, appears to have been a cover to protect the "ability to see around corners," which, along with uncanny luck, was the Ulam signature in mathematics.[25]

Surprisingly for one so original, he required the stimulation of other minds. He was never alone if he could help it, entertained people by the hour with jokes and stories, and did nearly all his work in collaboration with others, even though, as his colleague Mark Kac put it, he was the giver 99.99 percent of the time. Ulam's work with Cornelius Everett appears to have been the exception. The two of them had written a major paper and three or four lesser ones together before they sat down to calculate tritium requirements for the Super. Everett, who combined extraordinary technical prowess with an unusual willingness to work on someone else's ideas, would listen as Ulam tossed out ideas, then check them with brilliant computations of his own. But somewhere along the way Everett, who was as reclusive and self-effacing as Ulam was outgoing, came to feel shortchanged; after his death his widow, Dolly, said that he was "disillusioned and brokenhearted" over his collaboration with Ulam. According to her and other members of her family, Everett felt that Ulam had shoved him aside and usurped the credit, as Teller was to do with Ulam.[26]

The collaboration with von Neumann was another matter. The two never wrote a paper together, yet they were so close that to understand the work of either, Françoise thought, one had to understand their relationship. The friendship went back to prewar Europe: in 1937, at Ulam's invitation, von Neumann went to Lvov, where he met Ulam's parents and visited the Scottish Café. Ulam, in turn, visited von Neumann in Budapest the following summer, met his family, and accompanied him to a mountain resort where he met two of his friend's elderly professors. And there was the matter of background. Von Neumann did not feel at ease with people whose social origins differed much from his own: he and Ulam were both well-to-do central European Jews of the third or fourth generation. Both were cultivated, with backgrounds in the Latin and Greek classics, and a wry humor was seemingly native to them both. Although something in the air stimulated them to do great work in America,

both suffered from culture shock here, and from absence of the con-
versational art. And they had a common sensibility. Although he was
six years younger and nowhere nearly as accomplished a craftsman,
Ulam sensed von Neumann's deep-seated doubt about his own ability
and knew how to tease him out of it. Especially in the early days, it
was the older man who sought out the younger one, and by some accounts Ulam was the only close friend von Neumann ever had.[27]

On the basis of Ulam's work on random processes, the two
friends, with input from Nicholas Metropolis, Stanley Frankel, Enrico
Fermi, and others, invented Monte Carlo, a method of extending the
use of computers to statistical sampling. Monte Carlo, so named because an uncle of Ulam's had borrowed money from others in the
family to fuel his frequent visits to the gaming tables, became invaluable in estimating neutron multiplication rates and predicting the explosive behavior of fission weapons. An indispensable tool in computer
science to this day, Monte Carlo exemplifies the ways in which computer development and invention of the hydrogen bomb were inextri-
cably linked.[28]

Thinking of how Ulam broke the logjam in 1951, one has to ask
whether Truman's H-bomb order made a difference. Did it speed up
the pace of Ulam's thinking? Ulam himself was dismissive. He said
that "the number of people working on something does not increase
in proportion the yield" and hinted that the visiting dignitaries and in-
flux of talent brought by Wheeler had merely been a distraction. But
Françoise Ulam at first believed that without the forcing-house atmosphere produced by the president's decision, Stan might in 1950–1951
have devoted his best thinking to some other problem. Carson Mark
had a different view, with which Françoise later came to agree. He
concluded that Ulam "resonated" neither with Truman's order nor
with Teller's enthusiasm, but with von Neumann's desire—on political as well as scientific grounds—to find a solution. Ulam did not
share von Neumann's right-wing political ideas, but he did share his
intense interest in fusion reactions. It was to von Neumann, and to the
intellectual challenge of the thermonuclear problem, that Ulam responded. Ironically, when the younger man came up with a solution,

von Neumann, the greatest mathematician of the century, felt a pang of regret that he had, once again, been trumped in originality.[29]

Ulam's enormous contribution did not at first bring him much recognition. Members of the lab were too busy with the tests of spring 1951, and then with preparing the first test of the Ulam-Teller, or Teller-Ulam, concept, to worry about questions of credit. Besides, everything Los Alamos did was a group effort: no one felt any need to sort out the question of who contributed what idea, or in what sequence, until later, when Teller's claims made it an issue. Ulam, meanwhile, disappointed by what he took to be the lab's indifference, departed for Harvard, where he spent the 1951–1952 academic year. He took no part in preparations for the "Mike" shot of autumn 1952, the first test of his ideas.

A gentle man, he was wounded more than he ever admitted by Teller's brutal rejection. While privately he despised Teller, he refrained from joining the Teller-bashing at dinner parties in Los Alamos and Santa Fe. They had needed each other once: "If either of those guys had had to work alone," Bradbury said, "each would have accomplished about one quarter of what he did." But after that brief moment in 1951 they never spoke to each other or communicated in a meaningful way again.[30]

PART THREE

1951-1952

CHAPTER TEN

Teller's Choice

LEWIS STRAUSS AND EDWARD TELLER first met in a synagogue in New York City. The year was 1948; the occasion, a speech by Teller advocating world government. After the speech an elderly woman came up to him and introduced her son. The serious-looking, bespectacled man at her elbow turned out to be AEC commissioner Lewis Lichtenstein Strauss. Despite the differences in their religious practices—Strauss, an Orthodox Jew who prayed twice a day, was distressed by the fact that Teller was nonpracticing—the two became friends, and the friendship was cemented a year later during the debate over the hydrogen bomb. From then until Strauss's death many years later, Teller and Strauss were allies who frequently acted in concert.

In February 1951, only days after Teller and Ulam had their talks in Los Alamos hammering out the concept of radiation implosion, Teller appeared on the East Coast for one of his démarches with Strauss. Strauss was no longer a commissioner, he was working in New York for the Rockefellers, and he knew nothing about the Ulam-Teller breakthrough. But he held a couple of part-time appointments that gave him leverage in Washington. As he saw it, the president had issued his order more than a year earlier and there was still no hydrogen bomb. Someone must be to blame. That someone, he decided, was Robert Oppenheimer. There were rumors that Oppenheimer had been a Communist, and two former Party members had lately surfaced and testified that they had attended a Party meeting eight years before at Oppie's house in California. Whatever his intentions, Oppenheimer was helping the Soviet Union.[1]

And so on February 9, 1951, Strauss went to see Gordon Dean, David Lilienthal's successor as chairman of the AEC. Clutching several pages of notes, he treated Dean to a scathing critique of Los Alamos: the lab was dragging its heels and Oppenheimer was "sabotaging" the project. When he described Oppenheimer as "a general who did not want to fight," Dean disagreed that the program was in the hands of people who did not believe in it. Suggesting remedies nonetheless, he noticed one in particular that Strauss did not object to—creation of an entirely new laboratory. Before the visitor left, Dean asked to keep his talking points. To his surprise, Strauss strode to the fireplace and tossed them, with a dramatic gesture, into the fire. Dean thought this a little bizarre, and was mystified further when he was told later that the notes had been intended for Truman. Dean was miffed both by Strauss's intention of going over his head to the president and by his failure to mention it. A straight shooter himself, Dean viewed it as his job to protect a president besieged by a thousand headaches. Had he read the notes, which bore the Tellerian title "The Russians May Be Ahead of Us," he would have seen what he probably suspected anyway, that Strauss's informants had been Teller and his acolyte Freddie de Hoffmann.[2]

The other member of the two-man team was also in the AEC building that day. Teller had come at Strauss's suggestion to see AEC commissioner Thomas Murray, who was also dissatisfied with thermonuclear progress. Meeting Murray for the first time, Teller attacked the panel report on long-range objectives that Strauss had criticized to Dean. Singling out the author, Oppenheimer, Teller charged that the report was "designed to discourage" enthusiasm and had effectively put the project "on ice." He added that Los Alamos had lost competent men and seemed unable to attract new ones. Time and again, Teller said, Bradbury had yanked him and others off the H-bomb project and assigned them to other work. If the program remained at Los Alamos, Bradbury should be fired and a new division created to focus on thermonuclear problems. But there was a better way: take the project away from Los Alamos and set up an entirely new laboratory.[3]

While he was in the AEC building, Teller also stopped by to see General Manager Marion Boyer and told him, too, that the program should be moved away from Los Alamos. Then he took a taxi to the Capitol, where he insinuated to William Borden that the tritium estimates by Ulam, Everett, and Fermi were wrong. He warned that the design for the upcoming George shot, the first test of thermonuclear principles, had been deliberately made highly experimental and might not succeed. Borden realized that Teller was embarrassed by his erroneous tritium estimates. Fearful that George, too, might be a failure, Teller was accusing Oppenheimer and the GAC of pushing for a premature test in hopes of a failure that would kill the whole program.[4]

Gordon Dean had been AEC chairman for about a year. At the time of his appointment, he was known in atomic energy circles mainly as Senator McMahon's onetime law partner, and his selection had been viewed as a presidential sop to the nuclear enthusiasts in Congress. Dean's appointment prompted such foreboding in Carroll Wilson, David Lilienthal's loyal deputy and the man entrusted with day-to-day management of the commission, that he had taken the unusual step of resigning publicly in protest. Wilson need not have worried, for Dean proved to be an experienced administrator and a first-rate judge of character. A Californian by birth, he had joined the Duke University law faculty at twenty-five, argued his first case before the Supreme Court at twenty-eight, served in the Justice Department's antitrust division under the legendary Thurman Arnold, and been special assistant to two of FDR's attorneys general, Homer Cummings and Robert H. Jackson. When Jackson was appointed chief U.S. prosecutor at Nuremberg, he took Dean along as an adviser.[5]

The joint descent by Teller and Strauss on the AEC, plus Teller's call on Borden and his visits to the Pentagon, planted the thought in high places that the program was lagging and a new lab might be the answer. Meanwhile, the men at Los Alamos were enjoying a breather after completing work on the Greenhouse series, and Norris Bradbury circulated a plan to reorganize the place. Bradbury was responding to a demand by Teller for a special division at Los Alamos, with himself as leader, to work solely on the thermonuclear bomb. Teller was convinced that success could come only from men who were giving it their undivided attention, a premise that made no sense to the rest of the lab. Since a small and efficient fission "primary" was the key to making the fusion "secondary" burn, and success of the weapon depended on the interaction between the two, most people were working on both.[6] Placing Teller in charge made no sense to most of them either, since Teller's idea for organizing things was to insist each day that the laboratory drop what it had been doing the day before and turn to his newest brainstorm. So while Teller—without leveling with Bradbury—was politicking in Washington for a laboratory of his own, Bradbury in Los Alamos was ceding as much as he could, short of creating a separate thermonuclear division run by Teller.[7]

In Washington again, Teller this time presented his case directly to the chairman of the AEC. It was a dark moment for Gordon Dean, who had been wrestling with a dilemma: how much of the evidence in its possession could the government use in its prosecution of Julius and Ethel Rosenberg without risking the loss of atomic secrets.[8] Dean had no sooner dealt with that issue than he learned that the Russians might be on the point of entering the war in Korea, an action that could trigger World War III. The news, a false alarm received by Pentagon Intelligence, marked the moment when the United States came closer than at any other juncture to using nuclear weapons in Korea. The Joint Chiefs asked the AEC to transfer part of its stockpile to the Air Force for possible use in the Far East, and this in turn raised the delicate issue of civilian control. And another delicate question loomed over the White House: how to handle General Douglas MacArthur, who had recently—without authorization—proposed a series of actions in the Pacific likely to expand the war. A few days after the Dean-Teller meeting, the president, at fearful political cost, fired his most famous general for insubordination.[9]

At the meeting on April 4, Teller noticed that Dean's attention seemed to wander. But the chairman's air of distraction did not restrain the scientist from giving a long and one-sided recitation on thermonuclear ideas, criticizing Bradbury's proposal for a separate thermonuclear division and discussing how and why he would hand in his resignation. Teller asked for a new laboratory devoted entirely to the thermonuclear effort and staffed by fifty senior scientists, eighty-two junior scientists, and 228 assistants. Aware of Teller's awesome political support, Dean prevailed on him to postpone any decision to quit Los Alamos.[10]

After leaving the chairman's office, Teller discovered that his zipper was broken. He thereupon attributed Dean's apparent inattention to his open fly rather than, as was in fact the case, to Dean's worry that atomic war was about to break out.[11]

Soon afterward Dean received a long memo from Teller, again asking for a new laboratory and hinting that without it he might leave the project. This was not to be the last time Teller would threaten to quit.[12]

A few weeks later Teller and Dean met again, this time on remote Eniwetok Atoll. What brought the AEC chairman all the way to the Pacific was the long-awaited George shot, on which Los Alamos had been working for two years. Detonated on May 9, local time, George produced by far the largest nuclear explosion ever: it vaporized the two-hundred-foot test tower and 283 tons of diagnostic equipment. Dean heard Teller boast that Eniwetok would not be large enough for the next test.[13]

But size was not the main thing.[14] George, in which radiation from exploding a large atomic bomb was channeled to a container of thermonuclear fuel outside it, demonstrated that with sufficient heat and pressure, tritium and deuterium could be fused.[15] The result had been expected, so beyond that was the question of the test's usefulness, since Ulam and Fermi had already shown the second part of the Super— the propagation—to be infeasible. Not only that, but during preparations for the George shot, and partly as a result of them, the Ulam-Teller idea had come along and rendered moot the problems to be addressed by the test. Theoreticians at Los Alamos were delighted all the same by the outcome, which, Carson Mark said afterward, confirmed "that the methods we were using to calculate the elements of the process were . . . accurate" and "could be relied on wherever similar processes might be involved." Mark realized that calculations for the next big test, that of the Ulam-Teller idea, would be more elaborate than any the men of the T Division had done so far. He was encouraged to know that they had been going about it the right way.[16]

Almost no one at Eniwetok had heard about the Ulam-Teller concept, but a Lawrence protégé from California named Herbert York learned of it on a warm tropical evening spent alone with Teller. The two men were in a corroded old aluminum building, and York later remembered that, using a blackboard as his prop, Teller sketched the new idea. "I instantly recognized that this was it."[17]

York was one of only a handful who had heard about the Ulam-Teller idea, and Gordon Dean decided in the spring of 1951 that it was time to inform those closest to the project of the recent developments. The new concept, known as "radiation implosion," required theoretical investigation, as did results of George and the other Greenhouse tests. In addition, Teller's 1946 Super—the concept so difficult to disprove—was still on the table. With an enormous workload ahead, Dean wanted to establish priorities. He called a meeting for mid-June at the Institute for Advanced Study, with Robert Oppenheimer as host.

All of the commissioners came, and five GAC members and, from Los Alamos, Norris Bradbury, Associate Director Darol Froman, and Carson Mark. Several consultants—Bethe, Teller, Wheeler, von Neumann, and the theoretical physicist Lothar Nordheim—were invited because of their close familiarity with the project. The gathering turned out to be the turning point in the development of the hydrogen bomb.[18]

At the meeting, which assumed the importance of the new Ulam-Teller concept, Carson Mark led off with an analysis of the Pacific test results, and Wheeler reported on ways in which findings from those tests, particularly Item and George, might be applied in a test of the radiation-implosion idea. Norris Bradbury discussed the allocation of lab time between fission and fusion; Bethe, who had been in Los Alamos checking calculations, described the new concept as hopeful; and Oppenheimer pronounced it "technically sweet." Oppenheimer's words expressed the sense of the gathering, which welcomed the breakthrough as the right course to follow.[19]

Teller apparently did not understand. Bradbury had intentionally left him and the other consultants off the Los Alamos delegation so that they could express themselves independently of the laboratory. Foreseeing trouble, Bradbury had sent a memo to Oppenheimer in which he warned that emotions were a bigger roadblock than either the physics or the engineering, and he even arranged to accompany Oppie on the train ride to Princeton to discuss how to deal with both the science and the personalities.[20]

But his omission of Teller from the lab's delegation provoked the very outburst he had been hoping to avoid: from the outset, the Hungarian treated the gathering as a "battle" for acceptance of his ideas. He listened to the speakers with growing impatience. "Finally, I could contain myself no longer. I insisted on being heard. . . . It was decided that I should be allowed to speak."[21] Outside the meeting, Bethe and Teller were overheard in some sharp exchanges, and when Gordon Dean privately asked Bethe whether there was any way to alleviate the ill feeling between Teller and the rest of the lab, Bethe sadly shook his head.[22]

During the half century since, Oppenheimer has been accused of inconsistency, at the very least, in welcoming the new ideas as "technically sweet," and many people felt that he had betrayed the principles enunciated by him and the GAC majority in 1949 when they opposed the crash program partly on moral grounds. No sooner did the bomb look feasible, critics say, than Oppenheimer tossed morality out the window. If so, Oppenheimer was not alone. Fermi was at Princeton, too, and although in 1949 he, with Rabi, had called the H-bomb "necessarily an evil thing in any light," neither Fermi nor Rabi expressed doubts now. The difference was that with the Ulam-Teller inspiration, the weapon was now within reach. In 1949, when it looked impossible, Fermi and Rabi hoped, while there was time, to agree with the Russians not to go ahead. But by 1951 it was too late. As soon as they learned of the new concept, Bethe, Fermi, and Oppenheimer, along with everyone else, realized that the bomb was possible. And if it was possible for the United States, it was possible for the Russians, too. Oppenheimer's remark announced that the landscape was irrevocably altered.

After the Princeton meeting, Bradbury asked Teller to take charge of all theoretical work on the H-bomb. Aware that many of the men he relied on would quit if he were to put Teller in overall charge, he did not offer the one thing Teller really wanted: directorship of the entire program. Bradbury did his best to "soften the blow," but each of them found the conversation so painful that neither ever again mentioned it in the other's presence. Teller for the time being stayed on, but not without a new warning to Gordon Dean, via Freddie de Hoffmann, that he might quit—and not just the lab, but the entire H-bomb program.[23]

Meanwhile the work went on, with Carson Mark and his Theoretical Division analyzing results from the Pacific tests. Twice in the summer of 1951 the unhappy Teller flew to Washington to complain to higher-ups: once over dinner with William Borden at his club, then at a meeting with Gordon Dean. Both men begged him to remain.

A few weeks later, twenty-three-year-old Richard Garwin, a protégé of Fermi's from Chicago, happened to attend a Los Alamos meeting where the schedule for Mike, the first and crucial test of the Ulam-Teller concept, was being discussed. Teller wanted the shot scheduled for July 1, 1952, while Bradbury and Marshall Holloway, leader of the Theoretical Megaton Group, said that it could not practicably be held before fall. Teller was furious. "You guys don't have your heart in it," he scolded, and he threatened to leave the lab. Garwin, who was friendly with Teller and had, at his request, done the essential early blueprint for Mike, was flabbergasted. He thought these "guys" had their hearts wholly in it, and he found their dedication impressive.[24]

About this time, late September of 1951, Bradbury made a crucial decision: he put Holloway in charge of preparations for Mike. This,

Teller's friend de Hoffmann pointed out, was "like waving a red flag before a bull." Around the lab it was said that more than anyone else, "Holloway really had Teller's number." The two men had had so many passages at arms during the preparations for the George test that Holloway, hard-shelled, even impervious, though he was, refused any longer to deal with Teller directly. Holloway would describe the calculations he needed to Carson Mark, who would go to de Hoffmann, who would then put the matter, with utmost delicacy, to Teller.[25]

Informing the AEC of his decision to elevate Holloway, Bradbury told Dean that the lab could live with Teller if he "is willing to settle down and work with the rest of us," but "after the experience of the past year I am not persuaded that this is likely." Bradbury concluded that "equally rapid and certainly more stable and unemotional progress" would be made if Teller contributed from outside, "rather than as a continually dissatisfied and rebellious member of the laboratory."[26]

For his part Teller considered Holloway cantankerous and unreasonable and altogether an insulting choice. Besides, Teller had all along wanted someone "big" to head the program— Bethe, Fermi, or Oppenheimer. Fermi and Bethe had turned it down. Now Oppenheimer, sensing that Teller was emotionally off balance, told Dean that much as he doubted he could "make the omelet rise twice," he had not closed the door on returning to Los Alamos. He telephoned Bradbury and felt him out, but sensed no eagerness on the director's part to have him back. "Oppie couldn't come here and act in a limited way," Carson Mark explained years afterward.[27]

The question of Teller's future inevitably came to a head as the AEC commissioners finally faced the decision of whether to build a second Los Alamos. Teller had been pushing this behind the scenes, telling anyone who would listen that the lab had grown stodgy, unimaginative, and unequal to the task of producing an H-bomb anytime soon. He had a supporter in former commissioner Strauss and another in Commissioner Murray. And in a speech before the U.S. Senate, Brien McMahon, chairman of the joint congressional committee, piled on the pressure by urging that all three services be equipped with nuclear weapons—"an atomic army, an atomic navy and an atomic air force."[28]

Teller's next step was to announce one more time that he was leaving Los Alamos, with the caveat that he would keep track of developments from his post at the University of Chicago and perhaps visit the lab briefly from time to time. Over lunch with Borden and another staff member from the joint committee, he made it very clear that "his primary interest . . . was the second laboratory." His departure, he pointed out, would undercut one of the chief arguments against it, since "he had already left and to that extent the new laboratory would not be cutting into the manpower" available to the old one.[29]

Gordon Dean had been staving off the pressure. First, there was the problem of personnel: a new lab would divide the small cadre of available physicists. Second was the morale factor. A new lab would constitute a staggering no-confidence vote in the men who were doing the work and showing every sign of success. Dean was impressed by Teller's cleverness and political clout, but knew that the last thing he was, was an administrator. Nor could Dean overlook the monumental self-absorption of the man who had come to him in April 1951, at a moment when Dean had thought the world was on the brink of World War III, to hand in his resignation, and had been threatening to quit ever since.

Dean and the three other commissioners who were trying to hold the line received an assist from the GAC in October when it opposed a new lab on grounds that virtually everyone qualified was at Los Alamos already, except for Teller, and that "a solution to the major thermonuclear problem" appeared likely within a year. But Oppenheimer had misgivings of his own. He considered the lab's leaders—Bradbury, Froman, Holloway, and Mark—capable but cautious and risk averse. For this or some other reason, following a visit from Teller, who again expressed doubt about the laboratory's competence, Oppenheimer invited the Hungarian to appear before the GAC. There, in December, Teller blasted the lab's senior staff for lacking imagination and failing to attract the best scientists. He did this just as the Russians announced their second and third atomic tests: these signs of progress fed anxiety in Washington that, thanks to Klaus Fuchs, they might already be ahead. Pointing to these new indicators of Soviet progress, Teller charged that even the laboratory's success at Greenhouse was proof of earlier failure to develop its potential.[30]

Despite Teller's imprecations, the GAC for the second time formally opposed a new lab, fearing it would damage Los Alamos and "create general havoc." Hoping, however, to reengage Teller and deal with its own sense that the lab had become too conservative, the committee suggested creating an advanced division to work on long-range, even far-out, ideas, with a leader who would be persona grata to both Bradbury and Teller. Bethe's name was floated, since he got along well with both men. Oppenheimer urged that the suggestion be carried out quickly, since, as he put it, "the present ambiguous situation cannot be held ambiguous very long."[31]

Bradbury was under fearful pressure. Again and again he flew east to appear before the Washington brass. Aware, as he put it, of "rather thinly veiled criticism," he nonetheless reminded skeptics that every weapon development currently under way had "arisen out of the suggestion and, in many cases, the urging, of this laboratory," and warned that siphoning off manpower and resources would only slow things down.[32]

Under tremendous pressure themselves, the lab's theoreticians, explosives experts, cryogenists, and metallurgists were working all-out to prepare two series of tests: one, a preliminary fission series in Nevada in the spring; the other, a first test of the radiation-implosion concept in the Pacific the following fall. While lab members noticed occasionally that the director was out of town, Bradbury took pains to keep them from any inkling of the ordeal he was undergoing back east. Mark, who worked with him as closely as anyone, had no idea of this pressure on Bradbury until he read a partially declassified version of Gordon Dean's diary when it was published thirty-six years later. "He never let himself sag in my presence. He kept it to himself and shielded me and the rest of us from the miserable time he was having."[33]

Why, in the midst of the enormous outlay of effort on the project, did Bradbury and the rest of the laboratory try so hard to hold on to the fractious Teller? Much of the reason lay in the man's tantalizing originality. His insight and curiosity were relentless, and he promoted his ideas with evangelical fervor. Moreover, he had been right just often enough so that each time he had an inspiration, the others strove to divine whether this might be the long-awaited stroke of genius. "It would be impossible to run a laboratory if you had no Dr. Tellers," said Max Roy, an associate director of the lab, "and equally impossible if you had all Dr. Tellers." Carson Mark put it generously: "He discussed nearly every physical detail of almost every problem. . . . He called attention to possibilities. He resolved difficulties, elucidated complicated phenomena. His speculations induced speculations in others." But Jacob Wechsler, an engineer who had to coax designs into reality, thought otherwise. "You can't take a massive program and keep changing it," he said. "Such a brilliant, destructive man! It got so that each time he came back to visit, we were terrorized. We almost hated to see him show up."[34]

No one had any idea about the true extent of Teller's disloyalty. Marshall Rosenbluth, a talented young physicist whose contributions were critical, had heard that there was tension, but commented that "it didn't make much difference" at the working level. Some lab members were amused by the Hungarian; others thought his ideas gained disproportionate attention just because he was "obnoxious." None knew how egregiously he had maligned them, and the lab, behind their backs. Teller's faith and enthusiasm were compelling—so they mostly put up with him.[35]

It was Bradbury's ironic lot, in order to save the program and build the H-bomb at the earliest possible moment, that he had to deny Edward Teller.

CHAPTER ELEVEN

The Second Lab

THOMAS MURRAY of New York was a well-known inventor and entrepreneur. A Democrat and a devout Roman Catholic layman, he had been appointed by President Truman to the Atomic Energy Commission after David Lilienthal's resignation in 1950. Murray held two hundred patents, had founded his own company, acted as receiver of the IRT subway system in New York during World War II, and had successfully arbitrated major labor disputes. But he was new to the atomic energy program.

From the moment Edward Teller appeared in his office in February 1951, Murray had been a convert to the idea of a second laboratory. Each time the matter came up at commission meetings, he had spoken strongly in favor. And each time the commissioners voted against the idea, he had written a withering dissent. Murray used Teller's criterion, the number of topflight scientists at Los Alamos engaged solely in thermonuclear work. Persuaded by Teller that a new facility was needed, Murray strove energetically to bring it about. Being a solo operator, accustomed to ignoring channels, he felt no compunction about going straight to the White House. Twice in October 1951 he expressed dissatisfaction with the thermonuclear effort directly to President Truman, then pressed the case for a new lab with Truman's national security adviser, Sidney Souers, as well.[1]

In December 1951, a few days after the GAC rejected the proposal for a new laboratory for the second time, Murray placed a call to Ernest Lawrence, Nobel laureate and inventor of the cyclotron, in Berkeley. He outlined the thermonuclear situation as he saw it and said that all of his fellow commissioners and Oppenheimer's GAC were claiming that there were too few qualified physicists to staff a second facility. Lawrence scoffed and suggested that he and Teller become the core of a new enterprise. Murray urged Lawrence to become director, saying that Lawrence's prestige would be needed if the opposition from Oppenheimer and those who thought as he did was to be overcome.[2]

At a party in Berkeley on New Year's Day, 1952, Lawrence asked a promising postdoctoral student, Herbert York, to stop by his office. York was one of a handful of men at Berkeley who had worked on the thermonuclear program, having performed diagnostic tests on the George shot the year before, and Lawrence wondered whether he had an opinion about the need for a second lab. The thirty-year-old York, whose experience until then had been mostly confined to experimental physics, told Lawrence that he had not given it much thought. And so, with the boss's blessing, he set off on a fact-finding tour. After listening to the views of Teller in Chicago, Wheeler in Princeton, and officials of the Air Force in Washington, he reported back that a new laboratory would be a good idea, the very conclusion Lawrence had hoped he would come to.

Lawrence instructed York to draw up preliminary plans. This York did, flying back and forth between Berkeley and Chicago all winter in an effort to reconcile the vastly different visions of Lawrence and Teller. Each time, he found himself editing his account so that neither man would be totally alienated by the other's concept. Teller wanted a lab focused on a single objective and staffed by world-famous scientists, like Los Alamos during the war, while Lawrence wanted something smaller, less ambitious, and in fact more open-ended. A product of the plains of South Dakota, Lawrence was the kind of leader who had little use for rank or organizational charts. He believed in selecting talented young men and giving them their head. Since York shared his predilections, the emerging plans bore the Lawrence stamp.[3]

During the winter of 1952, Teller paid a visit to Berkeley. Lawrence escorted him to the nearby townlet of Livermore amid orchards and vineyards to show him the Materials Testing Accelerator, a pet project of his. Suggesting this as a possible site for the new laboratory, Lawrence inquired whether Teller might be willing to join. Yes, Teller replied, but only if the lab worked solely on thermonuclear weapons.[4]

Back east, however, with the AEC and the GAC firm in their opposition, the drive for a new facility had stalled. In February 1952, the GAC again declared itself opposed, again praised Los Alamos, and pointed out that fission and fusion processes within the H-bomb were so closely intertwined that separation between them was impossible. The committee concluded for the third time that creating a new facility would hurt Los Alamos, while producing "no compensating advantages for many years."[5]

Over at the joint congressional committee, even Borden and committee counsel John Walker appeared resigned to the thought that it would take an impressive new advance by the Russians to rekindle enthusiasm here. One of them, however, offered a suggestion not too far removed from what eventually happened. Why shouldn't an eminent scientist, someone in private life, organize a small group of theoretical physicists to work on the H-bomb, then approach the AEC to seek funds for a new facility?

Teller, meanwhile, was his usual mercurial self. After his February visit to Lawrence he had a conversation with Murray, who advised him to lie low. Afterward Teller thanked him "for your good advice. . . . I have now a much clearer picture of the situation and consequently a much better feeling about the way I must continue to act. I shall be, as you advise me, very patient and I believe, like you do, that things will work out as we hope and as they must." Teller's optimism, as usual, was short-lived: a few days later he confided to Borden that he had given up hope.[6]

Yet events continued to unfold. In March, Murray flew to California, where he and Lawrence agreed on the need for a change of leadership. Lawrence told Teller he hoped that Oppenheimer would not be reappointed to the GAC when his term expired the next summer, that Arthur Compton of the University of Chicago would take his place as chairman, and that Luis Alvarez, leader of the Materials Testing Accelerator, would be appointed a member. Murray was a friend of fellow industrialist Henry Ford: it occurred to him and Lawrence that either the Ford Foundation or the RAND Corporation, a recently created Air Force think tank, might be persuaded to offer subsidies so that the top advisory jobs would be more appealing to those who agreed with them.[7]

Finally, to finesse a prediction attributed to Gordon Dean—that Bradbury would quit in protest if a new lab were to be set up—Murray flew home by way of New Mexico, where he was assured by Bradbury himself that he would never resign over such an issue.[8]

Meanwhile Senator McMahon, his enthusiasm for a second lab undiminished, requested a formal report from the Defense Department, an action that proved to be the turning point. Defense Secretary Robert Lovett's first response was to praise Los Alamos and declare that it would be a mistake to move the thermonuclear program. But two weeks later Lovett did an abrupt about-face, urging immediate consideration of a new laboratory and a vastly expanded thermonuclear effort.

Why did Robert Lovett, one of the most self-assured men ever to serve in Washington, suddenly have second thoughts? David Tressel Griggs, chief scientist of the Air Force, was the key. He had known Lovett very well during World War II, when Lovett was assistant secretary of war for air. Teller told a member of the joint congressional committee staff that a briefing he had given for Lovett and the three service secretaries on March 19—a briefing arranged by Griggs—had been for the express purpose of turning Lovett around, and apparently it did. Possessor of one of the early U.S. pilot's licenses, Lovett had flown countless bombing missions with the British over Germany during World War I and was a devotee of airpower and Air Force prerogatives alike. His reversal on the second laboratory came about not because of any change in his beliefs about air warfare but because of the intense campaign waged by Teller, Lawrence, and Murray to win him over. Griggs had also introduced Teller to General James H. "Jimmy" Doolittle, the Air Force hero who had led the famous incendiary raids over Tokyo during World War II. Quickly won over by Teller, Doolittle spoke to Air Force Secretary Thomas Finletter, who was hearing similar advice from his assistant, William A. M. Burden, another convert to Teller's views.[9]

Out of the blue, Teller in Chicago now received a summons from Finletter. As Teller later described it, the secretary, an austere, self-contained lawyer from New York, listened "in icy silence" as Teller described the shortcomings of Los Alamos and the likelihood that Fuchs had speeded up the Soviet program, and sketched a future with a variety of thermonuclear weapons, not just a single big bomb. A few days later, Finletter flew to Los Alamos. There he found—or thought he found—the same halfhearted attitude Teller had told him to expect. Finletter was no sooner back in Washington than Teller received another summons, this time from Lovett.[10]

As Teller waited in the outer office of the unflappable secretary of defense, his mood was shaken when Robert LeBaron, chairman of the Pentagon's Military Liaison Committee, said to him, "Edward, I've done everything I can, but it's a lost cause." In Lovett's inner sanctum, however, Teller's powers of persuasion did not fail him: "before I left the Secretary's office I knew that I had won."[11]

Finletter played the decisive role: he sanctioned the clandestine, out-of-channels meetings between David Griggs and staff members of the joint congressional committee, and he encouraged Griggs to set up half a dozen briefings by Teller and his RAND associates which added immeasurably to the pressure, especially from the Air Force. At these sessions for officials of State, Defense, and the Joint Chiefs, the RAND scientists displayed charts illustrating thermal, gamma, and shock effects from thermonuclear bombs at various megatonnages, dropped from various altitudes. Teller followed up by emphasizing the Russians' competence, the risk that Fuchs had put them ahead, and the appalling danger should the Soviet Union build the thermonuclear first. Finally, he pleaded for new talent and a new laboratory to supplement the current desultory effort. To these briefings was added the threat that if the AEC refused to establish a new laboratory, the Air Force might do so on its own.[12]

Gordon Dean was ordinarily a virtuoso at rising above pique. But he was infuriated by Teller's latest end run. Privately, he fumed that

Lovett "knows virtually nothing about the atomic program." And, in as restrained a manner as he could summon, he complained to Secretary of State Dean Acheson and to Lovett's deputy, William Foster, both colleagues on the atomic energy subcommittee of the NSC, that he had endured Teller's complaints for two years now and that "while representing the finest in scientific brains, Teller did not always have a good feel for . . . administrative headaches." To the president's incoming national security adviser, James Lay, Dean attributed Lovett's change of heart to "one man's [Teller's] kicking up a fuss with people . . . who don't know the background." It would be "the worst thing in the world . . . to disrupt the morale of the lab when they are breaking their necks" to prepare the first test of a true thermonuclear device.[13]

But Dean recognized handwriting on the wall when he saw it and reluctantly agreed to meet with Ernest Lawrence. First, however, the GAC in late April praised the existing program as "sound, constructive, and very likely indeed to lead to success," and made one last effort to deflect the pressure. Noting that scientists from Berkeley had worked on instrumentation at Greenhouse, and that York was interested in testing componentry, the committee suggested by way of compromise that the Berkeley group be invited to help with the testing program and even with broader problems—so long as it did not drain manpower from Los Alamos. Characterizing the situation as "an unhappy one in which a fairly technical decision is being forced by high-pressure methods," Oppenheimer observed that the new enterprise would "have to go fast, or it will not go at all," his way of saying that Los Alamos was on the verge of a breakthrough that would prove a new lab unnecessary.[14]

Soon afterward, the AEC echoed the GAC's praise for Los Alamos and repeated its opposition to a new laboratory. The commissioners agreed with the GAC's recommendation and invited the Berkeley scientists to join in "securing diagnostic information on the behavior of thermonuclear devices." Once established in this work, they added, the California group would be "encouraged to submit . . . proposals of areas of further thermonuclear research."[15]

Ernest Lawrence was content. Experienced entrepreneur that he was, he knew that the goals of the new operation needed no spelling out. In Washington, second lab supporters were likewise satisfied. What mattered to them was not the AEC's rhetorical opposition but the reality that it was pulling Berkeley into the program. With Lawrence in the picture, the rest would follow. But Teller disagreed, demanding a clear mandate. He distrusted the AEC and doubted that it would ever sanction a new lab devoted wholly to thermonuclear weapons, he was suspicious of Lawrence's priorities, and he considered Herbert York too inexperienced to run the place. Besides, Teller wanted to stay in Chicago, where the Air Force had, he believed, promised him a laboratory of his own. By early summer 1952, his allies—Murray, David Griggs, and Robert LeBaron of the Defense Department, and Walker and Borden of the joint congressional committee—were all trying to persuade him to go to Berkeley, while he was inclined to refuse.[16]

Teller was on hand, however, at Berkeley's Claremont Hotel in mid-July for a celebration of the new laboratory. Unexpectedly, after a considerable amount of alcohol had been imbibed by all, Teller announced that he would not be joining after all. Lawrence was unfazed, having already intimated to York that they might be better off without him. But Captain John T. Hayward of the AEC's Division of Military Applications intervened: some of those at the celebration spotted Gordon Dean racing downstairs to dictate a "warm and cordial" letter committing the AEC to the new facility's going ahead on a broad front. Teller, whose wife and children had already arrived in California, agreed to remain.[17]

The new laboratory, set in Livermore, opened officially on September 2, 1952, and was at first called Project Whitney, after the highest mountain on the West Coast. Although Lawrence continued to insist that it was not, and never would be, *the* second laboratory, within a few years it became just that, moving from diagnostics to full-scale design and development. In the beginning, Lawrence was the nominal director, with York the acting director and Teller the presiding

genius. The lab grew quickly, and it did, as proponents had prophe-
sied, draw new talent into the program. To Teller's initial chagrin,
those who came were not the world-class physicists he had dreamed
of but young, newly minted Ph.D.'s. Nearly all had been students of
Lawrence's. Charles Critchfield, a former student of Teller's, refused
to join. Like many others, he was fond of the man but did not want
to work for him—"If he's not in charge, he's not happy." Another re-
fusenik was Francis Low, a thirty-year-old postdoc at the Institute for
Advanced Study. Oppenheimer summoned Low and young Murray
Gell-Mann to his office in Princeton. He sat by without comment
while Teller made his pitch, asking the younger men to work with
him. Low drove Teller to the railway station afterward, but he did not
join the project.[18]

Besides increasing the number of physicists in the program, especially experimentalists, the new laboratory greatly expanded the number and variety of new weapons in the U.S. arsenal. That is, after
early failures—its first two tests, of uranium devices designed by
Teller, were embarrassing fizzles. But by 1956, the Livermore lab was
finally on its way. Ironically, the Air Force, which had done so much
to bring the new lab into being, continued to order its weapons from
Los Alamos, while the Army and Navy, which had not pushed for the
lab, patronized Livermore. Livermore made a specialty of building
miniaturized warheads and is perhaps best known for designing the
warhead for the Navy's Polaris missile.

The Air Force's continuing patronage of Los Alamos illustrates
what had happened. Top brass at the Air Force, including Secretary
Finletter, believed what Griggs and Teller told them, while officers at
the working level, who dealt day to day with Los Alamos, trusted
Bradbury. Bradbury did not overpromise, he did not stimulate military requirements for weapons he was not ready to produce, and he
stayed well within his cost estimates. But the higher-ups mistook his
workaday manner and his too-evident lack of enthusiasm when they
arrived on time-consuming inspection trips for absence of charisma
and lack of commitment to the program.

Herbert York in later years said that Teller's politicking failed—"It was Lawrence who rescued the enterprise." To have him, even nominally, at the helm was a gold-plated guarantee. And Lawrence wanted the lab that came into being at Livermore. The Materials Testing Accelerator, the huge device he had been building there and in which he had invested his prestige, had become an embarrassment, and he was anxious to save face. The new lab solved his problem. It likewise provided a graceful way out for the AEC, with Gordon Dean and his supporters now able to claim that it was not a new facility being created but an existing one converted to new uses.

The country now had two enormously costly laboratories competing with each other to produce ever more streamlined designs. Together, Livermore and Los Alamos created the vast arsenal of superfluous nuclear weaponry that curses us today.[19]

CHAPTER TWELVE

A New Era

THE MEN AND WOMEN of Los Alamos took creation of the new lab hard. It was an ill-deserved slap in the face, and at a moment when they were working all-out to prepare the first trial of the Ulam-Teller concept. The test, christened Mike in honor of the expected megaton yield, was scheduled to take place in the fall of 1952 on Elugelab, an island at the northern end of the Pacific atoll of Eniwetok.

The work to be done was awe-inspiring, in scale and complexity something like the logistics for one of the great Pacific landings in World War II. Sections of the test device, plus experimental and support material, were being fabricated in shops all over the United States; for reasons of secrecy, no subcontractor was told the complete story about how the parts he made were to be used. A major sea- and airborne task force would be required, with the components—hundreds of tons of them—hauled to Oakland, California, for shipment, and other parts flown directly to Eniwetok in airplanes far less capable than those used today. Making sure that the parts arrived in the right place at exactly the right moment entailed almost unimaginably close coordination.

To make the test, and analysis of the results, as simple as possible, liquid deuterium had been selected as the hydrogen fuel. This decision caused cryogenic problems never dealt with before: for these, the engineer Jacob Wechsler was in charge. Every month, sometimes more frequently, Wechsler traveled by train from New Mexico to Boulder, Colorado, where the National Bureau of Standards had built a hydrogen liquefaction plant; to Buffalo, New York, where American Car and Foundry was casting and welding the heavy steel casing and the cab under which the device would be assembled; and then to the Boston area, where the A. D. Little Cambridge Corporation was producing enormous dewars in which liquid deuterium and other liquefied gases would be stored at Eniwetok. Transporting the dewars from the East Coast to Oakland, and from there to the Pacific, was itself a vast undertaking, and one that, again, required the most precise coordination. Ultimately, to achieve, by the explosion itself, the highest temperatures ever attained on earth, the hydrogen fuel had to be cooled to minus 423 degrees Fahrenheit, one of the lowest temperatures ever generated, and maintained there in the scorching heat of the Pacific.[1]

Calculations for Mike had begun in June of 1951 and entailed millions of computations, so many that at one point, in 1952, they required the full-time use of four large calculators, the Princeton and Los Alamos MANIACs designed by John von Neumann, and two others: the UNIVAC in Philadelphia and the SEAC in Washington, D.C. The questions that were fed into these calculators originated mostly at Los Alamos, where design and engineering were directed by the Theoretical Megaton Group (also called the Panda Committee) under Carson Mark and Marshall Holloway.[2]

Years afterward, as Wechsler recalled the preparations for Mike, he gave credit first to Holloway, for managing the extraordinarily complicated logistical details, and second to Mark, for his willingness to compromise on design problems to help minimize the chances of failure. Wechsler described sitting in Mark's office trying to think of ways to channel radiation from the fission primary down the cylindrical container so that it would bombard the back of the fusion secondary. And he remembered Mark's saying, "Look, if we firm up the plan and do this, can we then hold this other thing open?" Mark considered Holloway a steady manager and someone he could rely on. For example, if the theoreticians lagged a little in delivering computations, he knew Holloway would find a margin of a week or two. "I was always sure he had a little something up his sleeve."[3]

Teller at one stage predicted that Mike would fail: because of a physical law called Taylor instability, radiation from the primary would be absorbed in the casing. But Hans Bethe, a genius at understanding the physical interaction between radiation and shell, asserted, confidently, that there would be no Taylor instability.[4]

The lab could not afford failure, or even delay. Each time a potential glitch threatened, the question was not Can the device be made perfect? but Can it be made to work at all? The result was what weaponeers call overdesign. One example was the outer casing, manufactured in Buffalo and shipped from Oakland aboard the USS *Curtiss,* disassembled, for reasons of secrecy, in heavy steel rings. To keep the device from blowing apart prematurely, the casing had welded steel walls a foot thick, which accounted for much of Mike's eighty-two-ton weight. Later, with the experience of Mike behind them, the engineers were able to design walls that were much thinner, a key to making bombs that could be carried by aircraft. But for Mike, most choices were on the conservative side. The result was a device that was not—and not meant to be—a deliverable weapon. Nicknamed "the Sausage" because of its shape, Mike has been described as "essentially a large thermos bottle," standing just over twenty feet high and not quite seven feet in diameter, with diagnostic tubes protruding at either end. Design changes were made until the moment of final assembly, with Carson Mark on hand to interpret theoretical questions into language the experimentalists could understand.[5]

Even the primary, one of the least problematic parts of the design owing to the lab's work on fission, required last-minute changes: to reduce the risk of predetonation, a new core, with altered quantities of plutonium and enriched uranium, was flown to Eniwetok and installed only a day or two before the test.[6]

While the lab was going at it full steam, four well-known scientists questioned whether the test should take place at all. In the billiard room of Washington's august Cosmos Club in the spring of 1952, Robert Oppenheimer, I. I. Rabi, and Charles Lauritsen, the president of Caltech, found themselves comparing notes about the danger that Mike would end—for all time—any hope of agreement with the Russians not to develop hydrogen weapons. Once we held a test, the USSR was sure to follow. And since any hydrogen explosion would throw up debris, secrecy was out of the question: either nation would know when the other set off a thermonuclear device. Once again, the men discussed an alternative: prepare a test, and then tell the Russians that we would not go ahead unless they did so, an idea similar to the Fermi-Rabi proposal of 1949. They telephoned their wartime colleague, Vannevar Bush, the crusty, independent-minded president of the Carnegie Institution of Washington, and asked him to join them. On Bush's arrival, they found that he was thinking along the same lines.

The Mike test was scheduled for November 1, three days before the election of a new president, and the four scientists considered it unconscionable for either candidate, Republican Dwight Eisenhower or Democrat Adlai Stevenson, to be confronted upon his election by a fait accompli of such fateful import, and with consequences for which he would be responsible. With engineers and other specialists building test components all over the country and servicemen helping in the Pacific, word could easily leak out and become an issue in the closing days of the campaign. Moreover, they were certain that a test would be invaluable to the Russians as they studied our fallout, and would help them on their way to an H-bomb of their own.[7]

Vannevar Bush, wartime director of the Office of Scientific Research and Development and a member of the Acheson-Lilienthal working group in 1945, was so concerned that Mike would end any hope of ever reaching an agreement with the Russians that after meeting with his colleagues at the Cosmos Club he immediately went to Secretary of State Acheson to urge that the test be postponed. Acheson turned a deaf ear.[8]

Hans Bethe, too, was drawn into discussions of postponement. In the early summer of 1952, he was in Los Alamos when Oppenheimer asked him to seek Bradbury's views about the consequences of a delay. Bradbury answered that a delay of ten days or so would do no harm. After that, however, bad weather might force postponement until spring. Bradbury suggested that the candidates be told of the pending test ahead of time so that the new president would be prepared for what faced him on taking office.[9]

Bethe was in a painful position. Here was someone who had, in his words, been "terribly shocked" by Truman's decision to proceed with the H-bomb, who had at first refused to work on thermonuclear weapons, who had joined the effort with great reluctance and had been cheered by every indication that the bomb might not work. Yet here he was at Los Alamos in mid-1952, doing the final calculations for Mike. About this time Gordon Dean, beset by Air Force warnings that the Russians were probably ahead, asked Bethe to compare H-bomb progress by the two countries in light of Fuchs's spying. Bethe responded in a long and thoughtful memo expressing doubt that Fuchs had been of much help to the Russians, since the ideas he was in a position to give had turned out to be invalid. He said that thermonuclear development in this country had been "about as rapid as was technically feasible" once the Ulam-Teller ideas appeared, and he pleaded for the utmost secrecy. "If we now publicly intensify our efforts, we shall force the Russians even more into developing this weapon which we have every reason to dread."[10]

Then, late that summer, Bethe wrote a second letter to Dean, pointing out that a successful test three days before the election could become a last-minute campaign issue. He urged that Mike be postponed until the day after the election or, better yet, until mid-November, when the "smoke of [campaign] battle" would have cleared. As Bradbury had done earlier, Bethe urged that Eisenhower and Stevenson be briefed. He suggested that if Dean did not wish to do the briefing, someone like Oppenheimer could do it.[11]

Oppenheimer, too, entered the discussion of test postponement once again. He had been appointed chair of a panel tasked by the secretary of state to survey relations with the Soviet Union one last time for the outgoing Truman administration and consider whether there was any way to break the impasse over arms control. The new group, called the Disarmament Panel, wanted to try for an agreement with the Russians not to engage in thermonuclear testing, and in early September, some of its members paid a call on Acheson. They, like Bethe and Bush before them, suggested that the test be postponed so that the new president would have a chance to think about thermonuclear

weapons in a much larger context, that of the U.S.-Soviet relationship overall. Once a hydrogen device had been tested, a threshold
would have been crossed, and it would be too late.[12]

Bethe, members of the Disarmament Panel, and Rabi, who had
known Eisenhower well when he was president of Columbia University, probably hoped that a postponement until mid-November
would lead to a longer delay so that the new president would have
time to test Soviet willingness to negotiate.

Displeased at seeing Oppenheimer as part of the discussion, Gordon Dean told a colleague that he was "a little concerned at Oppenheimer's recently undue interest in postponement. I can see the plays
from where I am sitting and I am not happy." Dean's position and
that of the president on the timing of the test were delicate enough
without meddling by a scientist whose left-wing past, amid the in
creasingly clamorous musings of Senator McCarthy, made him a
point of vulnerability for the atomic energy program. Truman and
Dean were Democratic loyalists who hoped for a victory by Stevenson. Years afterward, Deborah Gore Dean said that her father had
wanted the Mike test held on schedule in hopes that a successful shot
might swing the election to the Democrats, and the president probably felt the same way. In addition, he surely wanted to leave a successful test as his administration's legacy. But if he was tempted to go
ahead prior to the election on political grounds, he gave no hint, putting out word instead that he would have no objection if operational
difficulties should cause postponement. By mid-October it was clear,
however, that no such difficulties existed, and Dean instructed AEC
commissioner Eugene Zuckert, who was on his way to the Pacific, to
find out whether a brief postponement would cause problems. Zuckert's answer was yes: commanders on the ground feared a hydrogen
leak if the test was delayed.[13]

And so Mike went off as scheduled at 7:15 a.m. on November 1
(October 31 in the United States). Almost immediately an enormous
white fireball appeared in the sky like a half-risen sun, and as it rose
higher, the ocean around it turned red. Elugelab, the island on which
the shot was set off, likewise turned a brilliant red, and after burning

six hours, it disappeared. A mushroom cloud one hundred miles across rose to fill the horizon, spreading eighty million tons of radioactive earth, gases, and water into the air and atmosphere. At 10.4 megatons, it was the largest man-made explosion ever, forty-six times the size of the George shot eighteen months earlier, and a thousand times the size of the bomb that had destroyed Hiroshima. A sailor who witnessed the shot remarked: "You would swear that the whole world was on fire."[14]

With the success of Mike, the world moved into a new era just as surely as it had on that fateful day in August 1945. Proportionally, a weapon producing an explosive force of a single megaton represented as large an increase in destructive power as the atomic bomb had over a conventional high-explosive weapon. Moreover, with much of Mike's yield, more than three-quarters, coming from the layer of U-238 that surrounded the fusionable fuel, it was clear that depending on the amount of uranium used, a thermonuclear device could be built to have unlimited destructive power. As Herbert York said afterward, "fission bombs, destructive as they might be, were thought of as being limited in power. Now, it seemed, we had learned how to brush even these limits aside and to build bombs whose power was boundless."[15]

Edward Teller, who had for so long sought a weapon of unlimited destructive power, did not witness the test. Having predicted that Mike would fail, he chose to sit out the event close by a seismograph in Berkeley; when the lines on the graph registered a large explosion, he sent a triumphal telegram to Los Alamos: "It's a boy." Later he told a friend there, Fred Hoyt, that had he known Los Alamos was capable of pulling it off, he would not have insisted on a second laboratory.

Vannevar Bush viewed Mike as a lost opportunity. Gone was the possibility of an agreement with Russia never to cross that threshold. "I still think we made a grave error in conducting that test at that time and not attempting to make that simple agreement with Russia. I think history will show that was a turning point . . . that those who pushed that thing through . . . without making that attempt have a great deal to answer for."[16]

PART FOUR

1952-1954

CHAPTER THIRTEEN

Sailing Close to the Wind

THROUGHOUT THAT SUMMER and fall, the ad hoc panel appointed by Acheson and chaired by Robert Oppenheimer had been meeting to consider the largest questions of atomic policy. Besides Oppenheimer, the panel was composed of four other distinguished Americans: Vannevar Bush; John Dickey, president of Dartmouth College; Joseph Johnson, president of the Carnegie Endowment for International Peace; and Allen Dulles, deputy director of the CIA. It was a sign of the increasingly security-conscious times that the panel had to begin its work late because a question had arisen about clearing one of the distinguished members. As for Robert Oppenheimer, who had chaired innumerable government groups and was the natural leader of this one, he was sailing close to the wind—closer, perhaps, than he knew.

His enemies found an opening in the fact that his term on the GAC, along with the terms of two other members who had opposed the crash program, would expire in the summer. Commissioner Murray, an archconservative who maintained a channel of his own to J. Edgar Hoover, started the ball rolling in early 1952 by complaining to Hoover that Oppenheimer had delayed the weapons program. Soon afterward, in California, Murray discussed with Ernest Lawrence the names of possible replacements for Oppie as chairman of the GAC. Next, the California scientist Kenneth Pitzer brought matters into the open by delivering a speech in which he charged that there had been "serious and unnecessary delays" in the H-bomb program and urged that the influence of "scientific kibbitzers" be reduced. Pitzer's were not the accusations of an obscure West Coast chemistry professor: as

AEC research director, he had spent two years watching the Washington goings-on at close range. After his speech in California, when the FBI came to him, Pitzer said that in contrast to an earlier time he now had doubts, not just about Oppenheimer's judgment, but about his loyalty as well. He suggested that Teller might have something to add.[1]

Teller now made charges that carried special weight. Contacted by the FBI in New Mexico, where he was working on Mike, Teller for the nth time accused Oppenheimer of discouraging others from working on the H-bomb. Oppenheimer, he said, was motivated not by subversive tendencies but by "personal vanity": he did not want his bomb, the A-bomb, trumped by another, more powerful, weapon. According to the FBI report, Teller added that he would do "most anything to see subject separated from General Advisory Committee because of his poor advice." A couple of weeks later Teller—taking the initiative this time—sought a second FBI interview in hopes of making sure that the earlier one remained secret. To his previous comments, Teller added that as a young man, Oppenheimer had suffered "physical and mental attacks which may have permanently affected him." He warned that he "had never had the slightest reason to believe that Oppenheimer is in any way disloyal," but that he did not want it known that he had raised the loyalty question lest he be asked about Frank Oppenheimer and his Party membership. Having raised questions about both Robert Oppenheimer's loyalty and his emotional stability, Teller concluded with what was by now a trademark threat: if fellow scientists were to learn what he had said, the embarrassment would be such that he would have to "sever his connections" with the program. Keep my comments secret, he warned the FBI, or I'll quit working on the H-bomb.[2]

Teller's complaints were not new. He had made them before, to officials at various levels; but the circumstances this time were different. Senator McCarthy was now a power, and Teller was talking, not to a lowly congressional staff assistant as he had in 1950, but to agents of the FBI.[3]

Not surprisingly, with members of the scientific community being questioned by the FBI, rumors about Oppie floated to the surface that spring during the American Physical Society's annual meeting in Washington. At a Cosmos Club gathering in May 1952, James Fisk, the AEC's former director of research, picked up "almost vitriolic talk against Dr. Oppenheimer—implying that he was unpatriotic." Gordon Dean told Fisk that he, too, had "seen signs of this," and termed Pitzer's actions, in particular, "despicable."[4]

But Pitzer did not quit. He wrote a personal letter to the president asking that Oppenheimer be "eased out." (In an interview with the author years later, Pitzer denied that he had written to the president.)[5] Others, too, weighed in. Wendell Latimer, another Berkeley chemist, and Harold Urey, a nuclear chemist and Nobel Prize winner at the University of Chicago, also wrote to Truman. Berkeley physicist Luis Alvarez made a special trip east to lobby Air Force Secretary Finletter against reappointing Oppenheimer, and former commissioner Lewis Strauss, now a financial consultant in New York, raised the issue with Souers and the president in person.[6]

In addition to Strauss, Alvarez, and the chemists—none of whom had participated in the H-bomb program or knew it at first hand—others got into the act. Murray tried to enlist his fellow commissioners, and Finletter arranged to have the matter voted on by the special subcommittee of the National Security Council. Gordon Dean of this group voted to reappoint Oppenheimer, along with Conant and DuBridge, the other GAC members whose terms were expiring, while Lovett and the State Department representative who stood in for Acheson voted against.[7]

Just then, in the early summer of 1952, Gordon Dean learned something that could at any moment erupt into disaster for the atomic energy program: the Justice Department was about to indict a physicist named Joseph Weinberg for perjury. The potential for disaster lay in the fact that Weinberg, a onetime Communist Party member, had been a student and a friend of Oppenheimer's. The FBI had been tailing him for years and, in 1943, had recorded a conversation between him and the Party organizer of Alameda County, California, which seemed to implicate Weinberg in espionage. The Justice

Department now charged Weinberg with lying when he had denied to the government under oath that he had attended a Party meeting at Oppie's house in Berkeley in July 1941, at which the scientist had allegedly been present. The government had only one witness, a man named Paul Crouch, a former Communist Party organizer in California who was now a paid informer for the FBI. The charges had been simmering for a while, Oppenheimer having told a California investigating committee in 1950 that he had been in New Mexico in July of 1941 and had never attended such a meeting, much less hosted it at his house. For Gordon Dean, the disastrous potential lay in the fact that neither he nor Jay McInerny, the assistant attorney general charged with bringing the case, was convinced that Oppie had told the truth. They feared that should he be called to testify, he would lie under oath and subsequently be indicted for perjury. Dean was worried about the likelihood that such a sequence of events would make the AEC a sitting duck for McCarthy or some other red-hunting committee chairman in Congress. Dean was therefore anxious to get the count naming Oppenheimer dropped from the Weinberg indictment—and maneuver Oppie off the GAC before the press got wind of the case. Oppenheimer's attorney, Joseph Volpe, made it "crystal clear" (Volpe's words) to Oppie that Dean wanted him off the GAC. Meanwhile, ill with the brain tumor that would soon kill him, JCAE chairman Brien McMahon met with McInerny's and Oppenheimer's lawyers and brokered a deal. Oppenheimer decided not to make a fight of it, and Gordon Dean wrote him a letter of thanks—"I fully appreciate the reasons behind your unwillingness"—that hinted at the behind-the-scenes negotiations.[8]

Had Oppie chosen to fight for his place on the GAC he would not have succeeded, since National Security Adviser Sidney Souers advised the president against reappointing him. Souers said afterward that in making his decision he had discounted the "loyalty talk" against Oppenheimer but considered it time for "new blood" who "believed in the policy of the President." Despite Souers's denial, the FBI interviews with Teller, Pitzer, and Libby and the letters to the White House from Pitzer, Urey, and Latimer accomplished their goal: they persuaded Souers that Oppenheimer had been opposing the program and should be replaced.[9]

Oppenheimer enjoyed being chairman of the GAC. Volpe, Oppie's friend as well as his attorney, called him "Mr. Atom, the giant of the business. He loved being sought out for his advice and to some extent it went to his head." Now, facing the possibility that he might have to testify in a felony trial, Oppie was distressed by the likelihood that he would forfeit his enormous stature with the public, the government, and the scientific community. Kitty Oppenheimer, Volpe remembered, "took it more calmly than he did, and was extremely supportive." Gordon Dean, too, treated Oppenheimer with kid gloves. "Mr. Atom" had on occasion been a headache for Dean, personifying, as he did, traits that made the scientists difficult for a government official to deal with: they had been thrown into the public spotlight unprepared, they did not know the political game, and they enjoyed their newly acquired renown all too much. Dean felt a measure of personal attachment for Oppenheimer, however, and a respect that had risen during the second-lab affair, and did his utmost to balance fairness to the man with the best interests of the atomic energy program.[10]

The Weinberg case was like a high explosive that could blow up at any moment. Dean now made a highly unusual request: he asked the president to intervene with the Justice Department to keep Oppenheimer's name out of it. Should the prosecution call Oppie as a witness, Dean warned, "it will mean that Dr. Oppenheimer must take the stand and contradict the testimony of Crouch, the only government witness. It will be Oppenheimer's word against Crouch's. . . . Such a conflict in the atmosphere of a criminal court, involving two such colorful figures, will attract great attention. . . . Dr. Oppenheimer's good name will be greatly impaired and much of his value to the country destroyed." Such was the risk that the president overcame his reluctance to intercede and wrote to Dean, with a copy to Attorney General Tom Clark, "I am very much interested in the Weinberg-Oppenheimer connection. I feel as you do that Dr. Oppenheimer is an honest man. In this day of character assassination and unjustified smear tactics, it seems that good men are made to suffer unnecessarily." The president's words were brave, but the White House in reality was wary of embarrassment, so much so that Truman did not send his ritual letter of thanks to the outgoing members of the GAC until the eve of his departure from office.[11]

Fortunately for Dean and the AEC, the outcome was anticlimactic: the trial did not take place until March 1953, safely past the new president's inauguration; the incident involving Oppenheimer was somehow, miraculously, never mentioned; and the jury—to everyone's astonishment—found Weinberg innocent.[12]

The Weinberg affair, nonetheless, showed the difficulty of conducting rational policy with political dynamite in the air. At a meeting of the special subcommittee of the National Security Council in October, for example, Acheson suggested that the United States might use the upcoming Mike test as an opportunity to try a new arms control approach to the USSR, and Paul Nitze, chief of the State Department's Policy Planning Staff, raised the possibility of a test moratorium. At this, Secretary of Defense Robert Lovett nearly leaped out of his chair. Such ideas, he said, must be put out of mind and any documents that so much as mentioned them destroyed. The reason? Proposals such as these might be traced to "fellows like Dr. Oppenheimer, whose motivations in these matters were suspect." It turned out that Lovett had been talking with Gordon Dean about Oppenheimer and was fearful of "adverse developments," by which he meant the still ticking Weinberg case.[13]

At this very time, Oppenheimer and his colleagues on the Disarmament Panel were putting the final touches on their thoughtful and farsighted report, in which they said that nuclear weapons were not merely a military problem but were "intimately connected with the largest questions of national policy." The United States, they said, had allowed itself to become frozen in a posture of "rigidity and totality of commitment which seem to us very dangerous," and they warned of catastrophe unless our policies became more flexible. The panel singled out for special criticism the excessive secrecy whereby the public had not been told even minimal facts about the size of the nation's stockpile, about the phenomenal pace at which both sides

Robert Oppenheimer at a party in Fuller Lodge, Los Alamos, probably August 1945.

David Lilienthal a few years after his retirement as chairman of the AEC.

Lilienthal testifying at Senator Bourke Hickenlooper's "terrible mismanagement" hearings in 1949. AEC general manager Carroll Wilson sits next to Lilienthal at left, and Commissioners Gordon Dean, Henry DeWolf Smyth, and Lewis Strauss are behind him, slightly to the right.

Niels Bohr visited Los Alamos six times during the war. His views shaped
Oppenheimer's approach to postwar use of atomic knowledge.

Hans Bethe *(center)* at Wheeler Peak, a favorite hiking spot near Los Alamos.

Carson Mark *(left)* and Bethe in Ithaca, New York, during the early 1960s. They worked together on the hydrogen bomb and remained close friends and collaborators afterward.

Enrico Fermi's colleagues called him "the pope" because of his total knowledge of both theoretical and experimental physics.

Edward Teller *(left)* consulted Fermi while they were colleagues at the University of Chicago after the war. Photograph taken 1951.

John Manley *(left)* helped Oppenheimer organize the lab. He became secretary of the General Advisory Committee. Photograph probably taken August 1945.

Maria Goeppert Mayer with her teacher Edward Teller *(left);* her husband, Joseph Mayer; and James Franck, conscience of the physics community, 1930s.

Charles J. V. Murphy at Cap d'Antibes in 1949, at work on *A King's Story*, the memoir of the Duke of Windsor.

Lewis Strauss points to the area where the Bravo test took place. At this press conference, on March 30, 1954, he said that the hydrogen bomb could be made big enough to "take out" a city as big as New York.

Vannevar Bush, head of the Office of Scientific Research and Development during the war, warned the commissioners in June 1954, while they were still deliberating, that the Oppenheimer hearing might forever impair trust between scientists and the government.

A brilliant student of Oppenheimer's at Berkeley, Robert Serber *(right)* wrote what became the *Los Alamos Primer*, which was required reading for every newcomer to Los Alamos during the war. He remained close to the Oppenheimer family afterward.

Cornelius Everett at the University of Wisconsin, where he met Stanislaw Ulam in the early 1940s.

Stanislaw Ulam and
Françoise Aron, then an
exchange student at Mount
Holyoke College, during
their courtship, 1939 or
1940.

Stanislaw Ulam *(center)* with his wife, Françoise, and a Polish colleague at
the second postwar International Congress of Mathematicians in
Edinburgh, 1951.

Army general James M. Gavin, an Oppenheimer ally and a strong supporter of tactical, or "battlefield," nuclear weapons, speaks with an adversary, Edward Teller.

The AEC's director of research from 1948 to 1951, Kenneth Pitzer wrote to President Truman in 1952, opposing reappointment of Oppenheimer to the General Advisory Committee.

Henry Smyth considered his work at the International Atomic Energy Agency the most important achievement of his life, but it was his dissent in the Oppenheimer case that earned him a place in history.

I. I. Rabi *(left)* with Enrico Fermi at Westhampton Beach, New York, in 1953. Rabi was Oppenheimer's closest friend and counselor and an eloquent defender who tried to stop the hearing.

After Truman's order to develop the hydrogen bomb, Victor Weisskopf used the stature he had acquired at Los Alamos to insist that questions of weapons development be kept before the public.

OVERLEAF: After learning that he was to receive the Fermi Prize, on April 5, 1963, Oppenheimer called his friend and neighbor Ulli Steltzer and invited her to take his photograph.

were accumulating "unprecedented destructive power," or about the fact that beyond a certain number of weapons it was futile to try to meet the Soviet threat simply by "keeping ahead of the Russians." Finally, the panel urged the nation's leaders to deal more openly with the American people and reach a collective understanding with the "other major free nations" whereby the responsibility for nuclear weapons would be shared. Despite its pessimism—the panel could see no path to arms control as long as Joseph Stalin was alive—the report closed on a note of prophecy. It exhorted the U.S. government to keep channels open and listen carefully for the slightest change in attitude once the Soviet dictator passed from the scene. Two months later, the seemingly immortal Stalin lay dead.[14]

It was a measure of Robert Oppenheimer's fatalism, arrogance, and, possibly, despair that he and the panel of which he was chairman had ventured far beyond their mandate, into the deepest waters of foreign and domestic policy.

He could not have been oblivious of the storm clouds gathering in the summer of 1952. He had been maneuvered off the GAC, and the GAC itself had suffered major defeats with rejection of its H-bomb and second-lab positions. At lunch at the Cosmos Club in May 1952, he, Conant, and Lee DuBridge had discussed the "dark words" in circulation about him, as well as reports that the three of them had sabotaged the H-bomb program. He had heard about a rancorous luncheon in Georgetown that spring at which David Griggs, chief Air Force scientist, had argued about the H-bomb with two of Oppie's closest colleagues. In response to Griggs's charge that the GAC had obstructed the effort, one of them, Rabi, arranged for Griggs to meet with Oppenheimer in Princeton so that he could read minutes of the various GAC meetings at which the H-bomb project had been discussed. Griggs was disappointed, however, when Oppie showed him, not the minutes he had hoped to see, but the Halloween meeting annexes in which the GAC members spelled out their reasons for opposing a crash program. This effort at rapprochement led to disaster when Oppie's failure to make "minutes" available only deepened

Griggs's suspicions. It is not clear from existing accounts, however, which minutes Griggs had expected to see, those of the Halloween meeting—because of their sensitivity, Manley's minutes had been destroyed—or those of subsequent meetings, which, in Rabi's view, would have proven to him that the GAC had spared no effort to comply with the president's order.[15]

The meeting at Princeton veered toward acrimony, moreover, when Griggs asked whether Oppenheimer was spreading a story that Thomas Finletter had said that if only the United States had a couple of hundred hydrogen bombs, "it could rule the world." Oppenheimer bluntly replied that he believed the story and did not deny relaying it to others. Then Oppenheimer asked whether Griggs considered him pro-Soviet, or merely confused. Griggs said he wished he knew. Next, Oppenheimer asked whether Griggs had raised questions about his loyalty with Finletter and General Hoyt Vandenberg. Griggs admitted that he had. Their meeting ended with Oppenheimer's telling Griggs he was paranoid.[16]

What Oppie did not know was that a full year before, in May 1951, Finletter had canceled his Air Force clearance in the wake of a conversation with California physicist Luis Alvarez and after reading portions of Oppenheimer's FBI file. Not only were Air Force Secretary Thomas Finletter and Air Force Chief of Staff Hoyt Vandenberg convinced that Oppenheimer was a security risk, but he had infuriated the Air Force by participating in a study with Caltech scientists about ways to adapt atomic weapons to ground warfare. The study, Project Vista, had been commissioned by the Army and the Air Force as a result of their experience in Korea, where the A-bomb would have been useless against troops on the ground. The study was addressed to fears that the Russians, with their vast superiority in manpower, could roll over Western Europe and annex its industrial power. Should the Russians make such a move, the Western allies would have no way to counter them except by bombing Soviet cities and civilians. Was there a way to adapt nuclear weapons, by making them small and precisely targeted, so as to deter the Russian land armies and ward off an invasion of Western Europe?[17]

After working on the study during the spring and early summer of 1951, the chairman —Lee DuBridge—and the rest of the Vista group had invited Oppenheimer to Pasadena. With his genius at synthesizing the ideas of others, Oppenheimer redrafted the committee's work and helped write what was to become the controversial chapter 5 of the report, dealing with the question of tactical weapons. Although Oppenheimer was a latecomer to the project and his views were shared by all the other scientists who were working on it, he inevitably became the lightning rod. To the Air Force, Vista's recommendation that the Strategic Air Command relinquish its monopoly of fissionable material and share with the other services could only mean abolition of its strategic air arm. Similarly, the Air Force objected to the proposal that instead of the SAC's being assigned to carry out major bombing strikes inside the Soviet heartland, a new tactical air force be created that could drop small nuclear bombs on enemy airfields and supply lines in Europe. To the "big bomb" advocates in the Air Force, these proposals spelled heresy. And to powerful individuals already suspicious of Oppenheimer, chapter 5 of Vista smacked of treason.[18]

Oppenheimer did not help his cause when Finletter, at the suggestion of two assistants, invited him to lunch in his private dining room at the Pentagon. He arrived late, rebuffed the secretary's efforts to be gracious, and became, in the words of one of those present, "rude beyond belief." He questioned the morality of the big-bomb strategy. Finletter replied that it would be more immoral to forgo our most effective weapon before conditions were ripe for disarmament. Their meeting ended in disaster. Oppenheimer was said to have exuded contempt for everyone in the room and, the moment the meal ended, rose, turned on his heels, and walked out.[19]

The Pentagon luncheon did nothing to quell the secretary's suspicions, and, learning that a group of Vista scientists, including Oppenheimer, were on their way to Europe to present their ideas to NATO commander Dwight D. Eisenhower, Finletter tried but failed to scuttle the visit. Next, he summoned General Lauris Norstad, the ranking Air Force officer at NATO near Paris, back to Washington for a briefing. The scientists—DuBridge, Oppenheimer, Charles Lauritsen, and Walt Whitman, now chairman of the Pentagon's Research and Development Board—first called on Eisenhower, who, according to Lauritsen, was "fascinated" by the idea of using tactical airpower to defend Europe, favored publication of chapter 5, and said he wished he had written it himself. Next they met with Norstad. Fresh from his briefing at the Pentagon, Norstad at first gave an impassioned defense of the strategic concept. When the scientists saw him a second time, however, they found him calmer, and after Oppenheimer had hastily redrafted one or two provisions, Norstad pronounced himself satisfied.[20]

The Air Force in Washington was another story. Having first tried to water down the report, Finletter now moved to suppress it entirely. All copies were recalled and chapter 5 disappeared from view until its partial declassification in 1980, nearly thirty years later. Even today, it is not available in its entirety. While chapter 5 was never allowed to become part of the dialogue, the suggestions put forward there soon became policy. In early 1952, even before the complete Vista report was issued, the Joint Chiefs of Staff authorized General Eisenhower to start planning for the use of tactical nuclear weapons in Europe, and two years later NATO made a formal commitment to use them for defense. Progress in the aim and design of nuclear weapons, along with the imperatives of strategy, vindicated chapter 5 long before the Air Force could bring itself to accept it.[21]

Meanwhile, on a personal level, chapter 5 seemed once again to bear out Finletter's suspicions. If in the spring of 1951 he had judged Oppenheimer a security risk, by autumn, with the Vista affair at its height, he had concluded that the scientist might be something more sinister. One of Finletter's subordinates, Garrison Norton, came to share these suspicions, confiding to a congressional staff member that he "was awake nights worrying" about the physicist.[22]

Air Force officials were not alone. Bill Borden, executive director of the joint congressional committee and Brien McMahon's trusted right hand, had first doubted Oppenheimer's loyalty back in early 1950, following the GAC's verdict against the crash program and Fuchs's arrest for espionage. Since then Teller had fueled Borden's doubts by telling him repeatedly that the thermonuclear program was lagging, and Oppenheimer was to blame. All this time Borden had been engaged in a dialogue with himself over whether Oppenheimer took the positions he did because he was (a) an agent of the Soviet Union or (b) simply wrongheaded. In the space of just a few days in the spring of 1952 Borden took several contradictory actions. He drafted a letter for McMahon to send to the president warning that the scientist might have been in touch with the Soviet spy network even before the opening of Los Alamos, and an alternative suggesting that "sincere and patriotic" as Oppie's motives might be, his influence was nonetheless harmful. And he wrote a memo to himself summarizing the FBI's most up-to-date file. "The whole trend and connotation of this summary is to the effect that Dr. Oppenheimer is not that which might be most feared."[23]

With Borden engaged in debate with himself, he and McMahon decided to hire Frank Cotter, a former FBI agent with a year's experience at Los Alamos. On the morning Cotter reported for work in June 1952, Borden handed him the transcript of the FBI's interview with Fuchs in England, told him it hinted that there had been a second spy in the Manhattan Project, and instructed him to find out whether it was Oppenheimer.

The thirty-year-old Cotter, whose fair hair, blue eyes, and open countenance belied his extensive experience as a street agent, had grown up in the Bronx and attended New York University, where— he later pointed out—every tenth professor had been a Marxist. The idea that someone might be a real, live Communist didn't faze him. But as he read the AEC files on Oppenheimer, Cotter was appalled by the fact that Oppenheimer had kept on making monthly payments to the Party even after the Hitler-Stalin pact of 1939. Cotter knew that many Communists, especially Jewish members, had abandoned the Party after that, and he thought it remarkable that Oppenheimer should have kept up his payments. Then he noticed that nearly everyone close to the scientist—his brother, wife, sister-in-law, former students, friends—had been Party members. And he noticed that San Francisco police records of the death, thought to be suicide, of Oppie's onetime fiancée, Jean Tatlock, were missing from the file. She, too, had belonged to the Party. Was there cause for suspicion in this apparent disappearance of records?[24]

On sweltering evenings that summer of 1952, Cotter sat in the joint congressional committee offices on the Hill and talked over his findings with Bill Borden, who, to his surprise, now seemed to take Oppie's side. "No, no," Borden would say at Cotter's newest discovery. "That doesn't make him a spy." Cotter looked up an acquaintance, Maurice "Gook" Taylor, a field agent whose judgment he respected, and every week or two they met for a beer after work. Taylor, who dealt with coded messages coming in to the FBI via Soviet cable traffic, was unequivocal. There was, he said, "no way" someone as big as Oppenheimer could be engaged in espionage without its coming through the signals system. And after four months working on the case and finding nothing, Cotter was persuaded. Not only Taylor, but Don Walters and Charlie Lyons, agents whose job it was to tail Oppenheimer when he was in town, assured Cotter that the scientist was beyond suspicion.[25]

Cotter reported these assurances to Borden and other congressional staffers who had taken part in their discussions. He was therefore very much surprised in the fall of 1952, after what must have been fifty or sixty hours of conversation, to find that he and Borden had switched sides. Cotter's suspicions had been allayed. Borden's had flared up again.

Although McMahon chose not to send either of Borden's draft letters in May warning the president about Oppenheimer, he had sent Truman a third missive, also drafted by Borden and apocalyptic in tone, which demanded production of H-bombs by the hundreds, and had attached a forty-page history of the nuclear weapons program compiled by the joint committee staff. Realizing that a new administration would soon take office and that he might no longer enjoy his accustomed influence, Borden now churned out more of these papers, or "Chronologies," critical of Oppenheimer and the AEC. By the fall of 1952, John Walker, committee counsel and a Yale Law School friend of Borden's, was putting final touches on an H-bomb chronology that Borden hoped to have on the new president's desk as soon as he was inaugurated. Lewis Strauss, like Borden a fervent believer that the bomb had been dangerously delayed, contributed material from his copious files, and Teller invited committee staffers to spend two weeks with him in California so that he, too, might contribute.[26] Since the document was filled with theoretical material, Walker and Borden sought a consultant. In view of the report's criticisms of the GAC, Oppenheimer, and the AEC for allegedly obstructing the H-bomb program, they dared not turn to a scientist from Los Alamos or the AEC. Instead they chose John Wheeler, who had sided with them in the H-bomb and second-lab controversies and was currently director of a project in Princeton that was doing sensitive computations on the H-bomb. One of the world's great physicists and philosophers, Wheeler was notoriously absentminded, and somewhere on the train ride between Princeton and Washington on January 6, 1953, he managed to misplace the six highly classified pages that Borden had sent to him by registered mail. Those pages have never been recovered.

No document could have been of greater help to a would-be enemy: it revealed the basic concepts of staging, compression, and radiation implosion; the existence of the spark plug; and the length of time it had taken the United States to progress from discovery of radiation implosion to its first test of the concept. The pages also mentioned names for secret devices and codes and summarized a highly classified debate between Bethe and Teller about the American H-bomb program. A panel comprising Bethe, Bradbury, Teller, and von Neumann quickly concluded that, together with information gleaned from the Mike test of November 1, the document lost on that train ride could be the basis for a full-scale Soviet thermonuclear program.[27]

By the time news of Wheeler's gaffe had filtered through the bureaucracy, Dwight Eisenhower was in the Oval Office. Appalled by the episode, and convinced that it had been an "inside job" perpetrated by Soviet intelligence, Ike treated the five AEC commissioners to a display of temper the likes of which they had never before experienced. Painstakingly, Gordon Dean laid the facts before the president. The

AEC was in no way responsible for what had happened. It had not originated the document and had, indeed, never seen it. Wheeler, Dean explained, was far from being an agent of the worldwide Communist conspiracy. He was a distinguished theoretician and much too valuable for the program to lose.

Borden, too, was called to account, and by the committee that employed him. In breathtaking defiance of logic and common sense, he tried to place responsibility on the AEC, against whom his démarche had in fact been directed. He even blamed the commission for his and Walker's decision to send the document, classified top secret, by registered mail rather than by armed courier. Borden's presumptuousness, his conviction of his own rightness, his certainty that he was duty-bound to act as he thought best without even consulting the senators he worked for—all of these foreshadowed the still larger event in which his failed judgment was to lead not to a stand-alone breach of security, serious as it was, but to a national calamity.[28]

CHAPTER FOURTEEN

Strauss Returns

DWIGHT EISENHOWER RAN for president in 1952 to keep the Republican Party from being captured by its isolationists, led by Senator Robert A. Taft of Ohio. Eisenhower had done as much as anyone to save Europe from Hitler, he felt committed to the nations he had helped liberate, and he did not want the United States to retreat from its new responsibilities abroad. Even though he had been commander of NATO, however, he was not up-to-date on nuclear weapons. He was astonished when—nearly three weeks after the fact—Gordon Dean told him about Mike, the test in the Pacific held days before his election. Ike was subdued when he learned about Mike's enormous explosive power and the fact that the island on which it was detonated had disappeared, giving way to a vast underwater crater. Hearing about the world's first thermonuclear test, he worried that mankind would prove unequal to the challenge of managing such awesome power and would stumble into the destruction of all life on earth. And he expressed hope that news of the breakthrough could be kept secret.

Against this inclination toward secrecy, the new president had a countervailing inclination toward openness. Shortly after his inauguration in January 1953, he met with Oppenheimer and other members of the Disarmament Panel and was impressed by what they told him, and especially by their recommendation that his new government share more information with the American people about how nuclear weapons were growing exponentially in power. Indeed, he was so impressed that he devoted one of the first meetings of his National Security Council to the panel's suggestions, especially its plea for greater openness. Almost immediately thereafter, however, Ike made an appointment that was to doom the panel's proposals; he named Lewis Strauss to a new post, that of White House adviser on atomic energy. The president knew that Strauss was a successful banker and an early Taft supporter who had made amends by helping the Eisenhower campaign in New York. What he did not know was that Strauss was entering his new job with an agenda of his own.[1]

That agenda was, in part, to reduce the public stature of Robert Oppenheimer. Within days of acceding to his new office, Strauss made his first move. He had lunch with a man whose role in the events that lay ahead was to be truly extraordinary. Charles J. V. Murphy was a writer for *Fortune* and *Life* magazines and had for years been a close friend of the publisher, Henry R. Luce. But in addition to writing on defense and intelligence issues for Luce's influential publications, Murphy wore another hat, that of lieutenant colonel in the Air Force Reserve. Somehow enjoying special status, he had the run of the Pentagon and served as speechwriter and part-time adviser to outgoing secretary Finletter and his undersecretary, Roswell Gilpatric, Air Force Chief of Staff Hoyt Vandenberg, General Jimmy Doolittle, and others. Even before his luncheon with Strauss on March 12, Murphy had been thinking about a story for *Fortune* on the hydrogen bomb program, in which, he agreed with the Air Force chieftains, there had been "literally criminal negligence."[2] Pursuing his story, he had flown to Independence, Missouri, to call on the newly retired president. To Murphy's amazement, Harry Truman refused to speak to him about his decision to accelerate development of the H-bomb. Undeterred, Murphy flew on to Pasadena to interview Vista scientists Lee DuBridge, Willy Fowler, and Charles Lauritsen. Then he flew to Boston to see MIT physicist Al Hill. All the while he kept working his Air Force sources.[3]

A spellbinding Irishman from Massachusetts, Murphy had accompanied Admiral Richard E. Byrd to the Antarctic and spent two years there, and had ghostwritten Byrd's bestselling books on his Antarctic expeditions. During Murphy's years as a Luce reporter he had acquired champagne tastes—first-class restaurants, the finest private schools for his four children, and a house in Georgetown, in the nation's capital. To sustain these tastes, he juggled ghostwriting tasks along with his magazine assignments, and on a given day that spring of 1953, the afternoon might find him in New York City discussing a writing project over tea at the Waldorf with the Duke of Windsor, while in the evening he might be in Georgetown discussing air strategy with influential columnist Joseph Alsop or downing martinis with some hero of covert action at the CIA. Editors at *Time* could count on a Murphy story to be sweeping and portentous, yet the author of those stories had an odd way of taking a backseat. Though always strapped for cash, Murphy might quixotically refuse payment for a ghostwriting stint, and invariably he made the heroes of his articles larger, nobler characters than they were in real life. Such were his enthusiasms that one didn't lightly enlist him in a cause lest one find oneself mounted on a charger that might slip its harness. Only one man could keep Charlie Murphy in harness, and that was Henry R. Luce.[4] Still, Lewis Strauss tried, and his meeting with Murphy over lunch marked the confluence of two conspiracies to end Oppenheimer's influence, one masterminded by Strauss, the other by officials in the Air Force.

The highest of these officials, Thomas Finletter and Roswell Gilpatric, spent hours with Murphy that spring as they said their good-byes in Washington and moved back to their old law firms in New York. Finletter, whose conversations with Murphy covered the entire range of strategic issues confronting the Air Force, was tight-lipped and contained, not given to expressing what were said to be powerful currents of emotion underneath.[5] Thus it fell to Gilpatric, over drinks, dinners, and late-night conversations at his apartment, to provide the details. Questioned years afterward as to why he had given so much of his time to the project, Gilpatric explained that before his stint in the Air Force, as an attorney for Henry R. Luce, he had vetted Murphy's articles for *Life*, and that he had known the writer socially for years. The interviews dealt with dissension inside the Air Force over what type of aircraft should carry the H-bomb, why Finletter had supported the second lab, and Finletter's suspicion that the so-called delay in building the H-bomb was somehow tied to Oppenheimer's support of Vista. "As this conviction took hold," Gilpatric explained, the secretary "fought for giving Teller a free hand."[6]

Three years before his death in 1996, Gilpatric expanded on the personal aspect. He explained that while Finletter had relied on his assistants, William Burden and Garrison Norton, to handle the scientists, there was one scientist whom he made a point of seeing personally. That was Edward Teller. Gilpatric's office was next to the Air Force secretary's, he was aware that Teller was "in the building all the time," and he knew that Finletter frequently had Teller to lunch. Describing the secretary as "completely sold" on Teller, Gilpatric added that, "carried along by the force of his personality," Finletter had championed Teller with the other services. To Gilpatric it had seemed that his boss was "under a spell," and he did not understand how Finletter, who appeared "unemotional and moved solely by cold logic," could make an exception for this one man. He also noticed that much as Finletter resented Oppenheimer's meddling in Air Force policy, he made no objection when Teller did the same thing.[7]

This complaint, that Oppie was meddling where he did not belong, became the theme of Murphy's article, "The Hidden Struggle for the H-Bomb: The Story of Dr. Oppenheimer's Persistent Campaign to Reverse U.S. Military Strategy," which was published anonymously in the May 1953 issue of *Fortune* magazine. A hysterical, overwritten account of an alleged life-and-death struggle over Air Force policy, "it contained so many errors," one scientist said, "that it wasn't even wrong." It scolded Oppenheimer and the GAC for allegedly obstructing the H-bomb program, blocking Teller at every turn, and campaigning to give up the Air Force advantage in big bombs in favor of smaller, defensive weapons. It accused the GAC scientists of hubris in "trying to settle such grave national issues alone, inasmuch as they do not bear responsibility for the successful execution of war plans." The article's admonitory tone, and the fact that it was unsigned, lent it an ominous, somehow official, air, and made it the shot across the bow of Oppenheimer and the other "liberal" scientists that much of the scientific community had been expecting.

Teller, whom Murphy had not interviewed for the story, was one of its heroes, and another was Strauss, who can be seen from the notes of Murphy's interviews to have been the source of many of its fallacies. In explaining the GAC scientists' alleged opposition to the H-bomb, for example, Strauss told Murphy that they had mistakenly assumed that the Russians would be unable to produce an atomic bomb for decades, if ever (most scientists actually expected that it would be about five years after Hiroshima); that it was he who insisted on convening the GAC after the AEC met in the fall of 1949 (it was Lilienthal, the chairman, who convened the GAC before the AEC met); that Strauss was the only AEC commissioner who favored a crash program (Gordon Dean favored it also); and that, among GAC members, "only Fermi forthrightly supported Strauss" (Fermi, with Rabi, forthrightly dissented).[8]

These and other falsehoods added up to what Joseph Alsop, a sometime friend and sometime foe of Murphy's, called a "rich compost of hints, inaccuracies and special pleadings."[9] But even these paled before the article's most astonishing invention, a cabal called ZORC, supposedly made up of scientists who were accused of promoting a futuristic system to defend North America at the expense of the Strategic Air Command. ZORC, Murphy claimed, got its initials from its members, Jerrold Zacharias, Robert Oppenheimer, I. I. Rabi, and Charles Lauritsen, who were said to be guilty of believing that defense was more moral than offense. Outside the Air Force, where the imaginary ZORC had been the subject of rumors for some time, no one, and certainly not the scientists for whom it was supposed to be named, had ever heard of it. Murphy's source was a shadowy retired lieutenant colonel by the name of Thaddeus F. "Teddy" Walkowicz.[10]

ZORC—later to assume crucial importance in the Oppenheimer security trial—was not Walkowicz's only fabrication. He told Murphy that the Greenhouse George shot in May 1951 had been "an experiment to determine whether you could use a fusion bomb as a match to light a fission weapon," when the opposite was true.[11] Walkowicz, whose misinterpretation of secret intelligence data had led to a false alarm in 1951 that the Russians had beaten the United

States to a working thermonuclear device, was the source with whom Murphy, sometimes accompanied by Jimmy Doolittle, had met more frequently than anyone else while preparing his story.[12]

Who was this character who emerged from the Pentagon from time to time to spread dire and misleading reports? Tall, handsome, and in his forties, Walkowicz, like Murphy, was a mesmerizing story-teller whose presence could electrify a room. But he was a much darker character than Murphy, a heavy drinker and a "black Catholic" whose father had arrived in 1908 on a cattle boat from Poland. A member of the Murphy family described the friendship between the two men as "a dark chapter," while Walkowicz left so much human wreckage behind that it is difficult to find an acquaintance or family member who will speak of him at all. Brilliant in technical matters, Walkowicz had degrees in aeronautical engineering from Caltech and MIT, had been executive officer of the Scientific Advisory Board of the Air Force, and in the spring of 1953 was a financial adviser to the Rockefeller brothers. Someone who knew him well described him as "hateful," and for all his success—by the 1980s he was a board member of NASA, Eastern Airlines, and the Civil Aeronautics Board—he remained angry and sometimes violent toward those who were close to him. Rabidly anti-Communist, he was so convinced that war between the United States and the Soviet Union was about to break out that throughout his years at 30 Rockefeller Plaza, he kept a fallout detector on his desk.

After cutting his first draft from 6,600 to 3,400 words, Murphy cleared the article with Strauss, who pronounced it "accurate" as far as his role was concerned. Murphy sent the final draft to Finletter and Gilpatric, went over "last points" with Walkowicz, and twice visited Finletter at his apartment to check last-minute changes. "He had few more corrections to make and was enthusiastic," Murphy commented, adding that a final check with Gilpatric produced the same result.[13]

The article created a sensation, especially the ZORC accusation with its dark suggestion that four of the government's top advisers had formed a conspiracy to weaken the United States. And, as it happened, at the very moment of its appearance in May 1953, two longtime friends of Oppenheimer's were summoned before the Senate Internal Security Subcommittee and its chairman, Senator William Jenner of Indiana. One was Philip Morrison, professor of physics at Cornell who had been Oppenheimer's student, and the other was David Hawkins, a philosopher of science who had been Oppenheimer's administrative assistant at Los Alamos. Back in the 1930s, in Berkeley, the two men had been Communist Party activists and devoted supporters of Loyalist Spain. Appearing before a session of the Jenner committee in Boston, each took the "diminished Fifth," meaning that he agreed to answer questions about himself, but not about anyone else.[14] In closed session on the morning of May 7, Morrison was asked—and refused to answer—a series of questions about Oppenheimer. During the lunch break Morrison explained to his attorney that he was not the committee's real target. It was Oppenheimer. The attorney, Arthur Sutherland of the Harvard Law School, did not believe it. "But he's an overseer of Harvard," Sutherland objected, by which he meant that someone so respected could not possibly be under suspicion. But when, in open session that afternoon, lawyers for the committee omitted the questions about Oppie that they had asked in secret session earlier in the day, Sutherland, in Morrison's words, "nearly fainted," and accepted what Morrison, Hawkins, Rabi, and other friends of Oppenheimer's had known for years: that eminent as Oppie was, he was not too eminent to be the object of a political vendetta. Someone in Washington, however, judging the moment not yet ripe, apparently telephoned the committee's lawyers during the lunch break and ordered them to drop the questions about Oppenheimer. The famed scientist was still above public attack.[15]

And what of Oppenheimer? How did he react to the article in *Fortune* and to news that two of his old and close friends, both former members of the Communist Party, had been called before a congressional committee and asked questions designed to incriminate *him*? Oppenheimer had had plenty of warnings. He had lost his place on the GAC and, over cocktails at his house in Princeton in late 1952,

had heard from colleagues the rumors that he was about to come under attack by the Air Force.[16] Oppenheimer had long known that his
left-wing past made him vulnerable, and with Senator McCarthy as-
cendant, the danger now was even greater than before. Over the years,
Joe Volpe had seen the scientist trying to ingratiate himself with such
powerful senators as Hickenlooper and McMahon, seen him flatter
them and treat them like high priests of atomic energy, only to make
fun of them later behind their backs. "He was a genius in some respects and a child in others," Volpe commented. There were individuals, especially those he regarded as stupid, with whom Oppenheimer
could not hold himself back. With them he was capable of unleashing a fusillade of feline, almost involuntary, cruelty which witnesses
never forgot and the victims—some of them, anyway—never forgave. Volpe saw Oppie make mincemeat of Pitzer at a meeting of the
GAC, watched him ridicule Strauss at the Halloween meeting of
1949, and even saw him make withering remarks to Commissioner
Henry D. Smyth, with whom Oppenheimer was mostly in agreement
but whom he did not regard as a first-rate physicist.

     Was he aware of the effect his sharp tongue had on others? "Yes
and no," Volpe thought. "Oppie was his own worst enemy. If he did
not like someone, he was not content just to win the argument. His
propensity for destroying an adversary led to his downfall." Volpe, a
vigorous, direct, and wise counselor, called him on it repeatedly and
told him to cool it. Oppenheimer would thank him, but somehow
that didn't stop him next time.[17]

     The decisive occasion with Lewis Strauss was a congressional
committee hearing in May 1949 which had been called to discuss the
shipment of iron isotopes abroad, a step Strauss bitterly opposed because he feared that the isotopes might be put to military use. Strauss
was seated in the hearing room with his fellow AEC commissioners,
Oppenheimer with Volpe at the witness table. "No one," Oppie
started out, "can force me to say that you cannot use these isotopes
for atomic energy. You can use a shovel for atomic energy. In fact, you
do. You can use a bottle of beer for atomic energy. In fact, you
do. . . . My own rating of the importance of isotopes in this broad

sense is that they are far less important than electronic devices but far more important than, let us say, vitamins, somewhere in between." As laughter punctuated these remarks, Volpe stole a look at Strauss. His eyes had become narrow slits; the muscles in his jaws were working; his face had reddened and taken on a menacing look.

Afterward Oppenheimer turned to Volpe like a triumphant schoolboy. "Well, Joe, how did I do?"

"Too well, Robert, much too well."

"Somewhere along the way," Volpe said later, "he had learned to go for the jugular."[18]

What made this particular put-down different from the others was the fact that it happened in public. Strauss did not enjoy being mocked in closed meetings before Fermi and Rabi and Conant, of whose intellectual stature he was in awe, but he truly hated having the same thing happen within camera range, hated reading about it the next day in the *Washington Post*.[19]

The one response Oppenheimer did not evoke was indifference. According to Volpe, there were those who disliked him, those who disliked him a lot, and those who disliked him to the point of enmity. But those who liked him, loved him. Louis and Eleanor Hempelmann were among those who loved him without reservation. Dr. Hempelmann was a broad-shouldered, handsome man with deep-set eyes who had been trained in the unusual—for the times—subject of radiology at Washington University in St. Louis and the Brigham Hospital in Boston. He and Oppenheimer first met during the 1930s in Berkeley, where he was working with John Lawrence, brother of Ernest, on radiation treatment for cancer. They saw each other again in Chicago in 1942, when Oppenheimer asked Hempelmann to come to Los Alamos. The two couples became close friends, and Eleanor Hempelmann, a member of the Pulitzer family of Maine and St. Louis, became close to Kitty. The Hempelmanns were still at Los Alamos when Kitty and Robert returned to New Mexico for a visit in 1946. Dining with the Oppenheimers at the La Fonda Hotel in Santa Fe, the Hempelmanns noticed that Robert turned to the walls from time to time and made announcements for the benefit of the microphones he assumed were implanted there. Here, they reflected, was Robert Oppenheimer, hero to the entire nation, still under surveillance, as he had been throughout the war. Another time they were visiting the Oppenheimers at their ranch in the Pecos Mountains and the two couples spent hours on hands and knees, scouring the earth for four-leaf clovers. But when Louis Hempelmann came upon a rare five-leaf clover, Kitty was upset: the five-leaf clover was thought to bring bad luck, rather than the good luck she and Robert knew they would be needing.[20]

CHAPTER FIFTEEN

Two Wild Horses

THE DISARMAMENT PANEL, led by Oppenheimer, had summed up the Truman administration's accomplishments in arms control and made further suggestions for the incoming Republican administration. Paradoxically, although the panel had recommended far greater openness in nuclear matters, the report itself was held in tightest secrecy. In hopes of getting its suggestions before movers and shakers of the Eastern Establishment, Oppenheimer in February 1953 presented an unclassified version in a speech before the Council on Foreign Relations in New York. He had been encouraged by the new president's favorable response to the panel's suggestion of greater candor. In Paris a year or so before, Oppenheimer had heard Eisenhower—then NATO commander in Europe—complain about excessive secrecy. Therefore he was not surprised that of all the panel's suggestions, it was the candor proposal that the new president responded to first. If the government were to share more weapons information with the public, Oppenheimer believed, other priorities—the need for better defensive measures at home, more exchange of information with our allies, reconsideration of the mindless buildup of redundant weapons—would sooner or later fall into place. As he told an interviewer, "the only way to bring this candor into being is through the President. He is the only person who has the right to do it, the only person who has the authority to transcend the racket of noise, mostly consisting of lies, that has been built up around this subject. Only the President can make this known. All I can do is make it easier for the President to do it."[1]

On May 28, 1953, Oppenheimer visited the Oval Office and

handed the president a draft of an article he had written for *Foreign Affairs,* the influential journal of the Council on Foreign Relations, based on his speech the winter before. Eisenhower gave the article to his national security adviser, Robert Cutler, and it was published with Cutler's approval in July. Oppenheimer had written that because of secrecy, he had to tell about the arms race "without communicating anything. I must reveal its nature without revealing anything." He pointed out that merely staying ahead of the Russians did nothing for our security because "our twenty-thousandth bomb will not in any deep strategic sense offset their two thousandth." To be ready if an opportunity to negotiate with the Russians should present itself, the leaders of the two sides needed to get past the rigidity imposed by the "terrifyingly rapid accumulation of nuclear weapons." He compared the situation of Russia and the United States to that of "two scorpions in a bottle, each capable of killing the other, but only at the risk of his own life."[2]

Lewis Strauss, apostle of secrecy, did not stand idly by while Oppie was scoring points with the president. Before the scientist's visit to the Oval Office at the end of May, Strauss warned the president that he had misgivings about Oppenheimer's security record. And when the president invited Strauss to add the AEC chairmanship to his portfolio as White House adviser, Strauss is said to have told the president, before accepting, that he "could not do the job" if Oppenheimer had anything to do with the nuclear weapons program. Meanwhile, intent on keeping the threads in his own hands, Strauss helped head off a threatened investigation of Oppenheimer by Senator McCarthy, warning Senate majority leader Robert Taft that "some of the so-called evidence will not stand up. The McCarthy committee is not the place for such an investigation and the present is not the time."[3]

On June 30 Gordon Dean completed his three-year term as AEC chairman. For months after Strauss's appointment as White House atomic energy adviser, the two men had been working in tandem. Dean disliked and distrusted Strauss but had chosen to finish out his term partly because the new president asked him to, and partly

because he had been appalled by the incoming administration's ignorance about nuclear weapons. Oppenheimer, who no longer held an
advisory position and—as the unsigned *Fortune* article had made
clear—was facing brisk headwinds from the Air Force, now asked
Dean to extend his AEC consultancy. From that perch, he would still
have access to classified information and still be able to influence policy. Dean agreed. Oppenheimer's Q clearance was good for another
year, until June 30, 1954.[4]

Now that he would be wearing both hats, that of White House
atomic energy adviser and chairman of the AEC, Strauss was again in
touch with Charlie Murphy, this time about a second article for *Fortune.* The new article reported that Oppie's advocacy of greater openness had placed him "once more squarely in conflict" with Strauss, "a
man of rare sagacity, enlightenment and courage." Before the draft
went to press, however, Strauss asked Murphy to "omit the references
to me, even though they are very flattering. . . . For the next month
or two, until I am firmly in the saddle, I would like to remain very
much in the background." Accordingly, the piece appeared without
the praise of Strauss, but with a small photograph of him and a cap-
tion saying that he wanted to "keep a tight lid" on atomic secrets. The
article was mainly an attack on Oppenheimer, accusing him of a cardinal sin, that of advocating publication of—holy of holies—the
number of weapons in our atomic stockpile. It also criticized the
president—because he favored relaxation of nuclear secrecy. Murphy
met with Strauss four times while he was preparing the article, which
appeared, not anonymously like the one in May, but under Murphy's
byline, in the August issue of *Fortune.*[5]

Murphy rarely pulled his punches. If a man is a traitor, then, to
his way of thinking, get rid of him! Strauss's desire to stay in the
background disappointed Murphy, who decided that the new chairman was a trimmer. But Murphy knew only part of the story. Strauss
had another steed in his stable, and that was the obsessive Bill Borden. At the end of April 1953, badly compromised by his handling of
the Wheeler affair and a Democrat who stood to lose his job with the
new Republican Congress, Borden carried a mysterious "paper" to

Strauss and spoke with him briefly. The content of his "paper" is not known but was probably a compilation of Borden's suspicions about Oppenheimer. The May issue of *Fortune,* containing Murphy's anonymous attack on the scientist, was about to appear on the news-stands. Strauss telephoned several opponents of Oppenheimer at this time, probably to warn them that a public attack was imminent, and he may have used Borden's paper as backup.[6]

Borden spent May struggling with the question that had nagged at him for so long. He asked to see Oppenheimer's AEC security file one more time, and a day or so before he left Washington, he handed his successor at the joint committee a fifteen-page document. The document's 189 questions about Oppenheimer's record were mainly a brief against the FBI for sloppy investigatory procedures. But Borden also appended a separate, handwritten document in which he painstakingly weighed the scientist's actions: had Oppenheimer been acting "under a directive from his own conscience or a directive from the Soviet Union?" Borden considered either explanation consistent with the evidence, but concluded that "Dr. Oppenheimer's influence upon atomic policy has been more harmful to the United States than even would have been the betrayal of all the military-atomic information in his possession from 1940 to the present."[7]

Borden then repaired for the summer to his family's place in Chaumont, New York, near Lake Ontario, where he spent six weeks alone, without his wife and sons, ruminating over the unfinished business he had left behind. He spoke to Lewis Strauss by telephone during the summer, and in the fall he moved his family to Pittsburgh. But before starting on his new job, at the Westinghouse Electric Corporation, Borden felt that he would not have done his duty until he had reached a verdict on Oppenheimer. This he did, and in November he sent his verdict to the FBI.

The verdict was that "more probably than not," Oppenheimer had for years been acting as an espionage agent of the Soviet Union. Borden sent the letter to J. Edgar Hoover, rather than the head of the AEC or some other government agency, because he thought that the

FBI had grown lax and he hoped it would reopen its investigation of Oppenheimer.[8]

What sort of man was William Borden and what led him to his conclusion? Did Strauss know about his letter in advance? Had Strauss put him up to it? One August afternoon two years earlier, Borden and Strauss had had a lengthy conversation about Oppenheimer. Since then, they had remained in contact. It seems likely that during the early fall of 1951, the two men had agreed on some kind of joint action with regard to Oppenheimer, but, faced by a long absence from Washington and an apparent cooling in Strauss's regard, Borden had gone off on his own and taken a step the older man did not anticipate. But Borden's colleagues in the schoolboyish, rather Yale atmosphere at the joint congressional committee disagreed with this reading of Borden's actions. They did not think that Strauss was implicated in what Borden had done. It was not Borden's nature to conspire, they insisted, "and besides, he didn't like Strauss." He had even nicknamed Strauss "Luigi" because he considered him Machiavellian. And he still blamed Strauss for inspiring the 1949 Hickenlooper hearings, for which Borden had had to write the final, embarrassing report saying that there was nothing to the charges of "terrible mismanagement" by Lilienthal.[9]

Borden was a child of Washington. He was born there in 1920 and attended the select St. Albans School and then Yale. On his graduation in 1942 he enlisted in the Army and became a bomber pilot over Europe. One night near the end of the war, flying his B-24 home after a mission to Holland, he saw a German V-2 rocket whizzing past him on its way to London. From then on Borden was haunted by the horror that could be wrought by marrying rocket technology to that of the atomic bomb. At twenty-six, he wrote a book called *There Will Be No Time,* arguing for world federation. After graduating from Yale Law School, he was singled out by Brien McMahon, father of the Atomic Energy Act and a neighbor of his parents, to work for the JCAE.

Borden was from a protected, orderly world. The mother who left her imprint on him was known for her upright character; his father was a Washington surgeon famous for having barred from his operating room an intern who had arrived only five seconds late to assist him. There was military tradition in the family, and an uncle Liscum (Borden's middle name) who had won the Congressional Medal of Honor. Lacking much experience of everyday life, young Liscum, or "Lic," as he was known to his friends, believed things happen in a tidy, logical way. Upon becoming staff director of the joint congressional committee, he had been shaken to discover how few atomic weapons the U.S. stockpile contained—he was not told the precise numbers but was able to make a rough guess—and right away set to work to expand it. His writing had a kind of hysteria to it: he wrote lines for Senator McMahon like "total power in the hands of total evil equals total destruction" that illustrate the absolute cast of his thought. If x or y was obvious to him, he wondered, why wasn't it obvious to a genius like Oppenheimer? From there it wasn't far to the question, How can someone as clever as Robert Oppenheimer take the positions he does if he is not an agent? Extrapolating from his own character, Borden knew that *he* could not have taken those stands unless he had been an agent.[10]

Borden was a liberal Democrat. He had a strain of idealism and was an active board member of the Experiment in International Living, which sought to improve international understanding by sponsoring exchanges between European and American students. He loathed Joe McCarthy and agreed with Oppenheimer's proposal for greater candor. Far from being obsessed by security, he had been known to look the other way when something was not as it ought to have been in the dossier of a loyal congressional committee staff member. He was decent and courteous and might enjoy three or four scotches during an evening's conversation, but he would not countenance an obscenity or a dirty joke. Everyone who knew him uses the word "integrity," as in "he had more integrity than anyone I ever met." He was an exceptionally conscientious man, driven by what he saw as his duty. But he was an intense workaholic, and one colleague said, "I think that destroys judgment." Those who worked with Borden liked and respected him. Said one, "The most negative thing I thought was that he might have flown a few too many missions during the war."[11]

Why did this man who ordinarily showed little interest in people, and no interest whatever in sizing them up, focus on Oppenheimer—and reach the conclusion he did? Frank Cotter thought it was Teller, who saw Borden every time he came to Washington. They were not close personally—Borden was not close to anyone—but their views on policy were very close indeed. "An impressionable man like Bill, hearing someone of Teller's stature tell him that Oppenheimer was sabotaging the program, and always with the innuendo that he was a Communist, that would have done it."[12]

When Borden's colleagues at the joint committee read his letter to the FBI that fall, they were horrified. John Walker, J. K. "Ken" Mansfield, Frank Cotter, Corbin Allardice—none of them agreed with him about Oppenheimer. They thought his isolation that summer had contributed to his taking such a drastic step and that talking things over with them every day, as he had done at the committee, would have tempered his judgment. They noticed that he missed Senator McMahon, missed the give-and-take, missed writing over-heated letters for the boss that the boss sometimes did not send. McMahon's death in the summer of 1952, they believed, left him feeling that it was up to him to carry the burden of national security alone and removed a restraint from his actions. They thought it was tragic, that it was bound to destroy both Oppie and Borden, and that Borden would carry the weight of it with him to his grave. And they were certain that he and Strauss had not been in collusion.

But it was not so simple. Although not nearly as devious as Strauss, Borden, too, could be manipulative, his handling of the JCAE's thermonuclear history of January 1, 1953, the so-called Walker-Borden report, being a case in point. Borden had told Carl Durham, the inexperienced interim chairman of the joint congressional committee, that the report was a "compilation," not the one-sided attack on Oppenheimer and the AEC that it actually was. He had tried to withhold it from the AEC, he had delayed several hours before informing the FBI that Wheeler had lost an extract, and he had given misleading answers to members of the JCAE at their hearing on the episode. He had even used threats against Gordon Dean in an effort to force the AEC to assume responsibility. Similarly, Borden's correspondence shows him trying to manipulate Teller, and his exchanges with Strauss are so conspiratorial in tone as to suggest shared purposes that they did not care to put in writing.[13]

Borden had all along funneled information to Strauss, who in turn assumed that he could count on the younger man when the time was right. But what Strauss seems to have had in mind was some action that would tarnish Oppenheimer's public image and reduce his influence, not a dramatic move that might force the president to act.[14]

Lewis Strauss had two wild horses in his stable, and one of them threw off his harness. Only, it wasn't the spirited Charlie Murphy who got out of hand, but quiet, intense Bill Borden.

CHAPTER SIXTEEN

The Blank Wall

ON SATURDAY EVENING, November 7, 1953, Bill Borden, anxious to rid himself of the burden that was weighing on him, drove to the main post office in downtown Pittsburgh and mailed a copy of his three-and-a-half-page letter to Lou Nichols, an FBI acquaintance, to be passed along to J. Edgar Hoover. He sent the letter, which contained highly sensitive material, by ordinary mail and with a covering note in cramped handwriting, and with errors that might suggest that the author had had two or three drinks, or was under severe stress.[1]

Borden's letter stated that Oppenheimer, as member or chairman of more than thirty-five advisory groups, had shaped more government policies and been in a position to compromise more secrets than any other individual in the country. It gave twenty-one reasons why it was Borden's "exhaustively considered opinion, based on years of study, that more probably than not J. Robert Oppenheimer is an agent of the Soviet Union."

When Hoover received Borden's letter, he treated it like a grenade that might go off at any moment. He had been living with the Oppenheimer problem for years, saw nothing new in the letter, and was only too aware of Oppenheimer's formidable standing in the scientific community. Six months earlier, Hoover had headed off Joe McCarthy when the rambunctious senator—primed by Murphy's anonymous blast in *Fortune*—had come to see him about investigating Oppenheimer. Hoover also agreed with Strauss that there should be no public move against Oppie without the most careful preparation. The thing Hoover cared most about was not the arrogant physicist but protecting the FBI's sources. His FBI had kept Oppenheimer under surveillance for years. Ever since 1946 the bureau had, intermittently, opened Oppenheimer's mail, tapped his telephones, and followed his movements, and it was of utmost importance to Hoover that these methods—most of which were illegal—not be compromised. Mindful of the adage that if you strike at a king, you must kill him, he was convinced that the destruction of this particular king could not be accomplished without the use of every bit of ammunition in the FBI's arsenal. The best way to handle Borden's charges, Hoover believed, was for the Defense Department—to which, along with the White House and the Justice Department, he had sent Borden's letter—to abolish the only official board on which Oppenheimer was currently serving and thereby, in effect, cancel his clearance without the hazards of a public hearing. And there were other considerations. For one, Hoover seems to have been wary of Strauss, lest the AEC chairman in his zeal give away FBI methods, particularly its use of wiretaps. And there was the uncomfortable fact, which Hoover had until now forgotten, that back in 1947, with a single caveat, he had signed off on Oppenheimer's Q clearance.[2]

Responding to a hurry-up call from the White House on the afternoon of December 2, Lewis Strauss found the president, his adviser Robert Cutler, and one or two others in an anxious huddle in the Oval Office. Borden's bombshell had landed in a highly charged situation: Attorney General Herbert Brownell had accused former president Truman just a few weeks earlier of having knowingly protected a Communist spy in the Treasury, and McCarthy had followed up with an attack on Truman that was seen in the White House as an attack on the new president as well. Resisting the pleas of some in his entourage that he take on McCarthy openly, Eisenhower had that very morning told an aide that he would "not get in the gutter" with the Wisconsin senator. But he could not afford to open himself to the charge that he, like Truman, had knowingly protected a security risk. Strauss helped Ike reach his decision that afternoon, and the next morning Eisenhower told his national security advisers that he had decided to lower a "blank wall" between Oppenheimer and the nation's secrets. How it was to be done was left to them to decide.[3]

Robert Oppenheimer was in Europe, delivering the BBC's prestigious Reith Lectures, and was scheduled to return in mid-December. It was decided that he must be kept in the dark lest—nightmare of Hoover and Strauss—he slip off to Russia as the suspected Soviet spies Guy Burgess and Donald Maclean had done three years before. But defense installations and AEC laboratories were notified right away that Oppie's clearance had been suspended. At the Pentagon, Rear Admiral William S. "Deak" Parsons, head of ordnance at Los Alamos during the war and the closest of friends with Robert and Kitty Oppenheimer, heard about the "blank wall" order on December 4 and made up his mind to protest to the secretary of the Navy. But he was stricken with chest pains in the night and died at Bethesda Naval Hospital the next day. In the minds of Martha Parsons and their daughters there was never any doubt that Deak's heart attack had been precipitated by the news about their friend.[4]

For the next couple of weeks Hoover, Strauss, AEC general manager Ken Nichols, Commissioners Murray and Smyth, Assistant Secretary of Defense Donald Quarles, Attorney General Brownell, and National Security Adviser Robert Cutler all tried to devise a way to rescind Oppie's clearance without provoking a public outcry. Murray wanted to cancel Oppenheimer's AEC consultancy, while Smyth favored a secret hearing that he hoped would clear the scientist. Nichols wanted to hand the whole thing over to McCarthy, and Quarles was so concerned about feeling in the scientific community that he wanted to do nothing about the charges and let the government go on living with the risk. Cutler, a Harvard overseer along with Oppenheimer, preferred to inform the scientist in secret that his clearance was being revoked and ask him, for the nation's sake, not to make a fight of it. Everyone understood that if challenged in public, Oppenheimer would have to defend himself. Finally it was decided that on Oppie's return from Europe, Strauss would present him with a letter of charges and leave it to him whether to give up his clearance quietly or insist on a hearing.[5]

Lewis Strauss later falsified the events of those days in an effort to minimize his own role—and for many years he got away with it.[6] In his book *Men and Decisions,* published in 1963, Strauss claimed that the president summoned him "in the chill of late afternoon" on Thursday, December 3, to help him decide what to do. After meeting with his national security advisers, Strauss said, the president informed them that he was lowering a "blank wall" between Oppenheimer and all classified information. But from Strauss's own daybooks and from notes by his assistant Bryan LaPlante, it is clear that Strauss first saw the president "in the chill of late afternoon" on December 2, a day earlier than he wrote in his book, and for the second time at a National Security Council meeting the next morning, at the close of which Eisenhower announced his "blank wall" directive. Why, nine years after the event, did Strauss choose to make it appear that he had seen the president only once, and only after Eisenhower had already decided to lower the "blank wall"? Because it was he who suggested the "blank wall," and he did so on December 2.[7]

There is more. On December 1, Strauss spent an hour and a half with Edward Teller. Two days later, returning from his second visit to the White House, Strauss found Teller awaiting him again, this time for a luncheon appointment. Teller returned to California later in the day. That evening Strauss sent him a telegram: "Take no action on personal matter we discussed. Nichols will call you." And the next day Ken Nichols telephoned to inform Teller of changes in his "previous instructions by Mr. Strauss on Thursday, December 3, 1953." In an interview many years later, Teller could not recall what the "personal matter" was.[8]

In later years Teller described the AEC chairman as extremely upset on his return from the White House that day. "I just had a terrible piece of news," he quoted Strauss as saying. "The President insists that we open the case" of Oppenheimer's clearance. Strauss, Teller added, did not want this known, because he hoped to settle it without a public hearing. He cited Strauss's secretary, Virginia Walker, as saying that Strauss was "horrified and deeply disturbed" by the president's order. Was Strauss actually "appalled," as John MacKenzie, his personal assistant, described him, or was he secretly gratified to be going head-to-head with his nemesis at last? Someone who knew him very well, and from a position of equality, was William Golden, the self-made financier who had from time to time helped Strauss at the AEC as an unpaid, highly respected adviser. Golden thought that Strauss and Oppenheimer were in some ways alike. Each of them was courtly in manner, each had the capacity to mask his feelings, and each was, above everything, "inscrutable." Golden believed that Strauss, out of deep partisanship as a Republican and deep animosity toward Oppenheimer, had been capable of urging the "blank wall" on Eisenhower, and then coming back to his office and feigning dismay. Victor Mitchell, who worked for Strauss for three years, and his wife, Donna, who also knew the chairman well, agreed.[9]

So inscrutable was Strauss that it is still impossible to say whether he was horrified when he read Borden's letter or whether Frank Cotter was closer to the truth when he said that "Borden accidentally and without design gave Lewis Strauss the thing he wanted most in life."[10]

CHAPTER SEVENTEEN

Hoover

HAROLD GREEN, a thirty-two-year-old lawyer in the AEC's Security Division, was not surprised that someone had pulled the trigger. He had expected something like this ever since he had learned from Bryan LaPlante, one of Strauss's closest aides, that Strauss had made an unsolicited promise to Hoover that he would purge four officials at the AEC, including Oppenheimer, whom he knew to be anathema to the FBI chief. Neither Green nor others in his division considered Oppenheimer a security risk despite his appalling dossier. They simply hoped to muddle through until expiration of his clearance without another close call such as they, and Gordon Dean, had experienced with the Weinberg case.[1]

A Chicago native and graduate of the University of Chicago Law School, Green had had extensive experience evaluating security files during his three years at the AEC. He was nonetheless surprised when William Mitchell, general counsel of the AEC, called him in on the afternoon of Friday, December 11, and showed him a copy of Borden's letter. Mitchell pointed to an enormous stack of papers—the AEC's investigative files on Oppenheimer—and told Green to draft a statement of charges for the commissioners to consider on Monday morning. He instructed Green not to include Oppenheimer's opposition to the H-bomb: the commissioners did not want the scientist placed on trial for his opinions.[2]

If Green had been surprised by Mitchell's telling him to draft the charges, he was still more surprised by the behavior of Ken Nichols that weekend at AEC headquarters. Nichols, who was to be the signatory to the charges, called Green again and again that weekend and summoned him twice to his office. He told Green how difficult Oppenheimer had been to work with during the war, when he was General Groves's deputy. He described Oppenheimer's arrogance and indifference to security, and recounted the bad advice he had given the government. His attitude toward Oppie was anything but dispassionate. "Be sure you get *that* in," he would say. "I've got the son of a bitch now. I don't want him wriggling off the hook." Green thought it peculiar that a man who would probably be a judge in the case should be doing double duty behind the scenes as prosecutor.[3]

Green finished early on Sunday and decided to try his hand at adding charges about the H-bomb, doing it in such a way as to test Oppenheimer's truthfulness, rather than the validity of his advice. To the counts he had already written, Green added seven more, based on Teller's interviews with the FBI in May 1952. When Mitchell came in later on Sunday, he approved. "Let's try it on Nichols tomorrow."[4]

On Monday, Green got another surprise: a call from one of Hoover's closest assistants inviting him to call on the FBI if he needed help. Green was astonished, since in the hundreds of security cases he had handled, the FBI had until then met his requests for assistance with hostility and had helped out grudgingly if at all.[5]

Strauss, meanwhile, had outraged three of his fellow commissioners. In a hurry to accompany the president to a conference in Bermuda on December 4, he had told the two who happened to be in town about Borden's letter—but had said nothing about the president's "blank wall" directive. Nor had he told his supposedly coequal colleagues that he had for months been meeting with C. D. Jackson, the president's assistant for psychological warfare, to draw up a plan for international atomic cooperation. Under the plan, which Strauss had embraced in hopes of subverting Oppenheimer's call for candor, the United States and the USSR would contribute a pool of fissionable material to the United Nations to be devoted to peaceful purposes. The first Strauss's colleagues knew of the proposal, which had been christened "Atoms for Peace," was on December 8, when the president, on his way home from Bermuda, unveiled it at the UN General Assembly to enthusiastic applause. At dinner that night Gerard

Smith, assistant to Commissioner Murray, heard Harry Smyth describe the plan as "a thoroughly dishonest proposal" and express anxiety over the danger that it would spread nuclear know-how to
nations that did not have it. It was to avert such contingencies that
the commission had traditionally had a scientist member. While
Smyth, the current scientific member, worried that Atoms for Peace
would put tightly guarded secrets at risk, the security-obsessed
Strauss, whether ignorant of reactor physics or simply elated at having his plan adopted and Oppenheimer's proposal foiled, appeared
serenely unconcerned with the danger.[6]

Smyth and Zuckert were so unhappy with the chairman's decisions
and his abuse of commission prerogatives that by the time Strauss
called his colleagues together on December 10, they were thinking seriously about resigning. Once again Strauss failed to level with them,
neglecting to inform them that he had spoken with the president
about the Oppenheimer matter and had himself had a role in the
"blank wall" order. Now it was too late: Hoover had already sent Borden's letter and a sixty-nine-page summary of Oppenheimer's FBI file
to several government agencies, the president's "blank wall" directive
had been circulated, and the Defense Department had notified its installations at home and abroad that Oppenheimer's clearance had been
suspended. The only thing left for the commissioners to decide was
how—not whether—to implement the president's order.[7]

Commissioners Murray, Smyth, and Zuckert remained unhappy,
and with good reason. The H-bomb charges drafted by Green were
neither discussed at a meeting of the commissioners nor formally
approved by them. Twice, Harry Smyth objected to inclusion of the
H-bomb count in the letter that General Manager Nichols was to present to Oppenheimer, and he gave up only after being told—falsely—
that his colleagues were going along. Informed of AEC decisions only
after they had been taken, misinformed and even lied to, the restive
commissioners found at every step that their options—above all, the
option of keeping the matter quiet—had been foreclosed.[8]

In the middle of December the president summoned Hoover,
Brownell, Strauss, and two other high officials. They decided that

Strauss would tell Oppenheimer that his security status had been challenged and that the president had suggested that the AEC investigate the charges. The scientist would be given a choice between resigning and asking for a hearing. If he chose the latter, his case would be heard by an ad hoc AEC committee with provision for review.[9]

That meeting was a turning point for Hoover. Returning to the bureau that day, he informed his underlings that "this is a most important and urgent project" on which they were to give the AEC "the fullest cooperation," provided only that the bureau's confidential techniques—especially its bugging and wiretapping practices—be protected. For years, Hoover had been watching, gathering evidence, and waiting for his opening. Now at last he committed the FBI to an all-out effort to banish Oppenheimer from the councils of government. His decision was, in part, the culmination of a protracted courtship between him and Strauss. For years, in and out of public office, Strauss had volunteered information to the FBI; the bureau, on the other hand, had, at his request, checked the security status of faculty appointees to the Institute for Advanced Study at Princeton and the Brookings Institution in Washington, of which he was a trustee. FBI agents had greeted him at Orly Airport when he went to France and met his mother-in-law at Idlewild (now John F. Kennedy International) Airport when she returned from abroad. He had promised the FBI chief that he would get rid of Oppenheimer, and Hoover at last was persuaded that the effort was likely to succeed.[10]

Ex–FBI man Frank Cotter explained the director's change of heart. From Gook Taylor, Cotter's friend who monitored the Soviet intelligence cables, and from others, Hoover knew perfectly well that Oppenheimer was not an espionage agent. His reason for hating him could even have been mere conviction that Oppenheimer was an adulterer. But "Hoover was a master politician. Eisenhower was going a certain way, so he did, too."[11]

Kitty and Robert Oppenheimer spent their final evening in Europe with Haakon and Carol Chevalier at the Chevaliers' apartment in the Montmartre section of Paris. Haakon, a professor of Romance

languages, and Robert had been the closest of friends in Berkeley before the war, sharing a love of French poetry and French culture generally. Chevalier, a Communist Party member, and Oppenheimer,
who during the late 1930s had probably occupied a niche just outside
the Party, had also shared a great deal politically in their sympathy for
Republican Spain and for the Soviet experiment in Russia. As the evening of December 7, 1953, drew to a close, it struck Chevalier that his
old friend seemed apprehensive, as if he felt that trouble might await
him in America.[12]

A couple of weeks later, Oppenheimer was facing Lewis Strauss in
Strauss's office, the one man stocky, balding, with heavy spectacles
shielding a partially blind right eye, the other man angular, rumpled,
with large, almost transparent blue eyes. Strauss had gotten where he
was on his own, from itinerant shoe salesman in Virginia, to protégé
of Herbert Hoover in European war relief in 1919, to fabulously successful investment banker who married the boss's daughter. Strauss
was controlling and conniving: a man who would walk into a social
gathering, pick his moment, and dominate the room by telling stories. What one man had by effort, the other had by birthright, as son
of a German Jewish immigrant who had made a fortune selling suit
linings and real estate and left his sons an inheritance of Cézannes
and Van Goghs. A natural of such magnetism that he could hold a
roomful in his hand just by being there. Agnostic bohemian versus
dutiful elder of an Orthodox Jewish congregation. One might almost
have taken it for an even match.[13]

The two men sat there, and one of them told the other that he was
in trouble. A former government official had raised questions about
Oppenheimer's right to a security clearance, Strauss explained, and
the president had ordered an inquiry. Oppenheimer looked over the
letter of charges and asked whether anyone with such a record had
ever been cleared in a formal hearing. The two discussed the possibility of Oppenheimer's resigning his contract, thereby obviating the
need for a hearing. Strauss tried not to make a recommendation, but
it was clear to the other man that this was the course Strauss wanted
him to take. Oppenheimer asked for a few days to think it over:

Strauss pressed for an answer right away. He would be at home after eight that evening, and Oppenheimer could reach him there. The scientist was not even allowed to take the letter of charges with him. He could have a copy only if and when he decided to go through with a hearing.[14]

As he was leaving, Oppenheimer said that he was going to see his friend and attorney, Herbert Marks, and Strauss loaned him his official Cadillac. But the scientist changed his mind and at the last minute went instead to the office of Joe Volpe, where they were joined by Marks. Unknown to the three of them, the FBI had anticipated Oppenheimer's moves and placed a tap in the offices of both Volpe and Marks, with the result that Oppie's very first conversation with his attorneys was recorded. The three men later proceeded to Marks's house in Georgetown, where Anne Marks cooked steaks and the four of them reviewed Robert's options.[15]

The next day Oppenheimer sent Strauss his answer.

> Yesterday, when you asked to see me, you told me for the first time that my clearance by the Atomic Energy Commission was about to be suspended. You put to me as a possibly desirable alternative that I request termination of my contract as a consultant. . . . I have thought most earnestly of the alternative suggested. Under the circumstances this course of action would mean that I accept and concur in the view that I am not fit to serve this government that I have now served for some twelve years. This I cannot do. If I were thus unworthy I could hardly have served our country as I have tried, or been the Director of our Institute in Princeton, or have spoken, as on more than one occasion I have found myself speaking, in the name of our science and our country.

About this time Hoover, at Strauss's request, asked the attorney general for permission to "install a technical surveillance" on Oppenheimer's telephone at home or at "any address to which he may later move." Authorization arrived the next day. Although Attorney General

Brownell told the author many years later that he had not been "directly involved" in the Oppenheimer affair, this decision was one of many he signed off on.[16]

Oppenheimer saw Strauss a second time to accept the letter of charges. It was Strauss's impression that the scientist preferred to "terminate his contract quietly," but that his attorneys, seeing "a big fee in it for themselves," had advised otherwise. (In fact, they represented him free of charge.)[17]

Among the humiliations visited upon the Oppenheimers was a visit to their house on Christmas Eve. Their caller was Roy Snapp of the AEC, who presented them with a letter ordering Robert to hand over any official documents remaining in his possession. Oppenheimer and Snapp had had many dealings when Oppie was riding high, and the occasion can only have been excruciating for them both. Eleanor Hempelmann, on hand with her husband for the holiday, later described Oppenheimer's "consummately polite, even courtly" behavior toward the visitor. "He put on a wonderful performance."[18]

Oppenheimer suffered a disappointment after he visited the leading law firm in Washington to ask the highly regarded attorney John Lord O'Brian to represent him. O'Brian was anxious to do so but, after consulting his colleagues, felt obliged to decline. The firm's founding partner, Edward Burling, had an affectionate relationship with a younger member, Donald Hiss, who, like his brother, Alger, was the subject of espionage rumors. Because of its refusal to fire Donald Hiss, the firm had lost four or five major clients, and in the atmosphere of the day, the partners did not want O'Brian to take the case. O'Brian's stature, talent, and devotion were such that his inability to handle the case came as a severe blow to Oppenheimer.[19]

About this time FBI special agent Kenneth Commons in Newark telephoned Washington headquarters to report that the "technical surveillance" reflected the scientist's search for an attorney. Because of the danger that the wiretaps might disclose an attorney-client relationship, the agent wondered whether to continue. He was told to do so.[20]

From now on, the FBI's wiretap reports were the AEC's main source of information about Oppenheimer's search for an attorney, his attorneys' conversations with him and one another, and other defense preparations. To obscure the fact that the information had been obtained illegally, most of the reports were written in the form of letters from Hoover to Strauss that started out "according to a reliable confidential informant," code for wiretapped information. In addition to reports obtained from telephone taps, others were derived from physical surveillance. On receipt of one report, Strauss wrote to Hoover: "This is to acknowledge and thank you for your letter of February 1, 1954, concerned with the reported discussion between Dr. Oppenheimer, his counsel, and other individuals." But Strauss tired of penning acknowledgments, and a few days later wrote a letter with the notation "Strauss asked if it were necessary for him to acknowledge each letter from bureau. He was advised not necessary since letters were delivered personally to him." The person who carried the FBI reports to Strauss was Hoover's liaison to the AEC, Charles W. Bates.[21]

Hoover had chosen his go-between with care. At the age of thirty-four, Bates, a good-looking, gregarious man with slicked-back dark hair, dark skin, and, sometimes, dark glasses, had become part of Strauss's inner circle. "An able but shadowy figure," as Harold Green described him, Bates did not so much enter a room as burst in, as if he were leading an FBI raid. He spent nearly all his time at the AEC and had entrée to everyone in the building. Not only did he deliver the FBI's wiretap reports, but he carried verbal messages between Hoover and Strauss. Bates had been around politics for a long time. Raised in a tiny town in north Texas where his mother worked at the polls and his aunt was secretary to Collin County congressman Sam Rayburn, Charlie Bates and his twin brother remembered visiting Rayburn's house as children and being given lemonade and watermelon. They looked to Rayburn as a father and even carved the wooden gavel with which he called the U.S. House of Representatives to order when he was first elected Speaker in 1940.[22]

Impressed by Bates and the Rayburn connection, J. Edgar Hoover elevated the young man to the rank of supervisor when he was only twenty-seven. Bates now looked on Hoover, too, as a second father,

and came up with pretexts to drop in at his office now and then. It
got so that Hoover would address Bates by name when they saw each
other in the elevator and sound off about whatever was on his mind:
"Hoover," Bates said, "always had something he wanted to talk to
you about." Bates got along with Strauss, too, but not to the point
where he viewed him as another father. Strauss called the younger
man "Charlie," while Bates called him "Admiral" and sometimes
"Lewis." Eventually Strauss relied on Bates and sometimes turned to
him for advice. Hoover relied on Bates too—to help him gauge
Strauss's frame of mind. For, as the weeks went by, the Admiral was
less and less a cool customer who wanted to rid himself of his quarry
gracefully, more and more an implacable foe who wanted to destroy
him as ruthlessly as possible. Hoover wanted to make sure that matters did not slip out of hand.[23]

Oppenheimer spent the first three weeks of 1954 seeking an attorney.
His friend Herb Marks thought he should be represented by someone
whose stature was comparable to his own, yet it was asking a good deal
to expect a prominent attorney to accept any case, let alone this one,
on such short notice. O'Brian had advised Oppenheimer to settle for
no one but Simon Rifkind, senior partner in the New York firm of
Paul, Weiss, Rifkind, Wharton and Garrison, but for reasons of health
and at his wife's insistence, Rifkind turned him down. At that point
Rifkind's partner, Lloyd Garrison, volunteered, and Oppenheimer accepted with relief. He and Garrison were on friendly, respectful terms
already, since Garrison was a trustee of the Institute for Advanced
Study. A great-grandson of famed abolitionist William Lloyd Garrison, Lloyd K. Garrison was intensely public-spirited, a national leader
in civil rights, civil liberties, and labor arbitration. He cleared his calendar and took the case on a pro bono basis, his only payment the
firm's out-of-pocket expenses. Assisting him would be Marks; Samuel
Silverman, a litigator in Garrison's firm; and Allan Ecker, an associate
in the firm who had written a 1948 cover story on Oppenheimer for
Time. Eighty-year-old John W. Davis, Democratic candidate for president three decades earlier, was to serve as senior counselor.

The AEC, too, was seeking a lawyer. Strauss had no one in his general counsel's office whom he trusted—all of them being holdovers from Democratic days—so he asked the Justice Department to lend him an attorney. When Brownell refused, Strauss asked the FBI to suggest a former agent. Hoover likewise refused. Finally, on the recommendation of Deputy Attorney General William P. Rogers, Strauss hired Roger Robb, a Washington attorney who represented McCarthyite radio commentator Fulton Lewis Jr. and who, as a district prosecutor, had acquired a reputation as a fierce cross-examiner. Hoover approved, commenting that Robb had been "cooperative and honorable" with the bureau and agreeing to expedite his security clearance.[24]

That Strauss, certain to be a judge in the event of an appeal to the commissioners, should select the prosecuting attorney was remarkable enough. Equally remarkable, he also chose the chairman of the Personnel Security Board, in effect, foreman of the jury that would hear the case. His choice, seconded by President Eisenhower, was Gordon Gray, a Democrat, former secretary of the Army, and president of the University of North Carolina. (As it happened, Gray, Brownell, and Robb had all attended Yale Law School at the same time.) It was felt that the board should also include a captain of industry, and it fell to AEC general counsel William Mitchell to make the choice: Thomas Morgan, a North Carolina native who had risen from a hands-on job repairing gyrocompasses to the presidency of the Sperry Gyroscope Corporation.

The third member was to be a scientist. Lee Hancock, a onetime FBI man employed by the AEC, happened to be on hand when C. Arthur Rolander, an AEC employee who was assisting General Manager Nichols with the prosecution, appeared at the AEC Security Division for help in finding someone to fill the third slot. Rolander was seeking a scientist who had served on other Personnel Security Boards and had "the right attitude toward security." Members of the division checked the transcripts of board hearings all over the country, looking for individuals who had taken a tough line, and they chose a retired chemistry professor at Loyola University with a record of exceptional severity. His name was Ward Evans. Hancock considered the process a "cold, calculating exhibition of trying to stack the deck."[25]

During the weeks and months that followed, Hancock received an education in what a politically motivated prosecution could be. Carpooling from Virginia to work each day, Hancock found himself coaching the neophyte Rolander on AEC rules and procedures. During the commute, and at lunches with Strauss's assistant Bryan LaPlante, Bates, and others, Hancock became aware of the pervasive "get Oppie" atmosphere on the AEC team. He constantly heard remarks like "Strauss wants to win" and "if we deliver, our futures will be taken care of." And on days when Robb joined them for lunch, it was "the Republican Party needs this." Bates described the pressure in a report to Hoover: "Strauss felt the importance of the Oppenheimer case could not be stressed too much. He felt that if the case is lost the atomic energy program . . . will fall into the hands of left-wingers. If this occurs, it will mean another Pearl Harbor as far as atomic energy is concerned. Strauss feels that the scientists will then take over the entire program. Strauss stated that if Oppenheimer is cleared, then anyone can be cleared regardless of the information against them."[26]

The charges fell into two categories. The first twenty-three had to do with Oppenheimer's alleged Communist and left-wing associations in California between 1938 and 1946: organizations he had sponsored; publications he had subscribed to; the Communist Party memberships of his brother, wife, sister-in-law, and former fiancée; funds he had donated to the Party for Spanish war relief; fund-raisers he had attended; claims by Party organizers that he was a covert member; and, by far the most important, the Chevalier affair. In that contretemps, Oppenheimer's close friend Haakon Chevalier in late 1942 or early 1943 passed on a feeler as to whether Oppenheimer would provide information to the Russians through a Soviet consular official in San Francisco. Oppenheimer immediately refused, but he delayed several months before reporting the feeler to Army intelligence and then lied about the circumstances in the hope of protecting Chevalier. The AEC's charges also included Kitty and Robert's continuing friendship with the Chevaliers after the war, until 1947.

Appalling as these charges appeared to anyone reading them for the first time, General Leslie R. Groves and his top security man, John Lansdale, had known about nearly all of them when they cleared Oppenheimer for the Manhattan Project in 1943, and the AEC had reviewed the charges, updated to include the Chevalier affair, in 1947 and cleared Oppenheimer without a dissenting vote. Among those who had agreed to the clearance were Strauss and J. Edgar Hoover, with Hoover stipulating that he had no reservations about Oppenheimer's loyalty but only about the Chevalier matter, which he considered a matter of bad judgment, and not disloyalty.

The final charges had to do with the hydrogen bomb. Oppenheimer was accused of having altered his estimates over the years as to the bomb's feasibility, of having opposed its development for moral and political reasons, and of having continued to oppose the bomb and declining to cooperate fully even after Truman's order to go ahead. He was also accused of having tried to turn the top scientists at Los Alamos against the project by instructing John Manley to disseminate the GAC reports there in November 1949, and of having persuaded colleagues not to work on the bomb; and he was told that the opposition, "of which you are the most experienced, most powerful and most effective member, has definitely slowed down its development."[27]

Ironically, while Oppenheimer was preparing to defend himself against charges that he had delayed the hydrogen bomb, Strauss was on Bikini Atoll, witnessing the largest test the United States had ever detonated. It was called Bravo, and it exploded with a force of fifteen megatons, three times as large as expected and more than seven hundred times as powerful as the Hiroshima bomb. Bravo's size prompted rumors that it had gotten out of control, and even the president said publicly that "something must have happened that we have never experienced before." And it was not just a matter of size. Eighty-two nautical miles to the east of Bikini, twenty-three Japanese sailors on a ship called the *Lucky Dragon* sickened from fallout, and one of them died. Once again, America had inflicted nuclear damage on Japan. Seeking to distract the U.S. public from its fear of fallout,

Strauss told a press conference on his return from the Pacific that the H-bomb "can be made as large as you wish . . . large enough to take out a city." A city as big as New York? someone asked. "The metropolitan area, yes," Strauss replied, adding measurably to the panic. A photograph taken as they left the press conference showed Eisenhower scowling. "I wouldn't have answered that one that way, Lewis," the president chided. "Other than that, I thought you handled it well."[28]

Bravo was the first in a series of tests in the spring of 1954, the Castle series, that ushered in a new, more advanced phase of thermonuclear development. But U.S. officials continued to worry: six months earlier, the USSR had tested "Joe Four" (after Stalin), the first Soviet device that involved thermonuclear reactions. In Los Alamos, poring over debris that had been gathered by aircraft, Hans Bethe, Enrico Fermi, and Carson Mark concluded that while the Soviet Union was on the track, it had not yet discovered radiation implosion. Joe Four consisted of alternating layers of uranium and lithium deuteride, like our Alarm Clock. It was a single-stage and not a multistage device, like ours, and it used high explosives, not radiation, to achieve compression. Without radiation compression, the Russians would be unable to explode a megaton weapon.[29]

Ever since Joe One five years before, the United States had known that it had underestimated the talent of Soviet physicists and the capacity of the Soviet industrial machine. Americans had lost their complacency and tried incessantly to assess their lead—if indeed they still had one—over the USSR. Yet it seemed strange, at the very moment of reassurance, when the United States had just set off a device so enormous as to engender first and foremost the fear that it might get out of control, to be trying a man for having delayed development of the hydrogen bomb. The hydrogen bomb, or at least a thermonuclear device that could be weaponized with comparative ease, was already a fact. And we knew that the Russians did not yet have it.

CHAPTER EIGHTEEN

The Hearing Begins

ONE MORNING IN JANUARY, a Scottish-born reporter for a famous newspaper was looking for a seat on an airplane out of Washington. He found one next to a rumpled-looking blue-eyed man who did not seem happy to see him. Well aware of the man's identity, the reporter engaged Robert Oppenheimer in chitchat about Eisenhower's first year in office. Although he steered away from topics he thought might be troublesome, the man noticed that his companion nonetheless seemed nervous and under strain.[1]

That was all James Reston needed. On his return to the capital, he started asking around. What he found was dynamite, and before long Lloyd Garrison confirmed Reston's scoop: the government had confronted the scientist with charges, suspended his clearance, and scheduled a hearing. Garrison asked Reston, Washington bureau chief of the *New York Times,* not to publish until Oppenheimer had had time to complete his response, so that charges and rebuttal could appear simultaneously. The *Times*'s publisher, Arthur Hays Sulzberger, agreed, and for six weeks the paper held the story amid worries that Senator Joseph McCarthy or a *Times* competitor might break the news at any moment. Finally, only days before the Oppenheimer hearing was to begin, McCarthy charged on nationwide TV that Communist sympathizers in the government had caused a "deliberate eighteen-month delay" in the hydrogen bomb, a figure he had apparently lifted from Charles Murphy's anonymous article in *Fortune* the year before. Eisenhower replied that he knew of no such delay.

Anxious to trump McCarthy, Lewis Strauss and presidential press secretary James Hagerty concocted a strategy to trigger publication, and on April 13, the second day of the hearing, Reston's story appeared on page 1 of the *New York Times*. Gordon Gray, chairman of the hearing board, was outraged. Garrison had promised that he would try to restrain publication, and Gray thought Garrison had double-crossed him. Since no one at the AEC or the White House informed him that it was they who had double-crossed him, Gray scolded Garrison as the hearing opened and in the weeks that followed reprimanded him repeatedly for having—so Gray thought—broken his promise. The duplicity of this maneuver, whereby high officials of the AEC and the White House deceived their own hand-picked chairman, was typical of what was to happen in the weeks ahead.[2]

Oppenheimer's friend Joseph Volpe later said the proceeding was "like a hearing on your wife after you've been married twenty years." In his dozen years of government service Oppenheimer had been through four high-level reviews, among them the 1947 review in which Hoover and Strauss had agreed to clearance.[3] This new proceeding was unlike any of the others in that it resembled a criminal trial, with the burden of proof on one side only: the defense. It was held in a dilapidated government building with only lawyers, witnesses, and a handful of officials present. The location was not announced, reporters were not permitted—indeed, they were not formally told that it was happening—and each witness was informed as he took the stand that the proceeding was "confidential," meaning that he was not supposed to speak about it with anyone outside the hearing room and that government representatives would not do so either. On completion of the proceeding, the Gray board was to vote on whether Oppenheimer's clearance should be restored, and it was understood that, either way, the verdict would be appealed. The defense decided at the outset that, should it lose, it would not appeal within the federal court system. Instead, the five commissioners would act as the court of final appeal. In an improvised, and egregious, intermediate step, once the Gray board rendered its decision, AEC general manager Kenneth Nichols, who had signed the original letter of charges, sent the commissioners his recommendations. The government made up rules as it went along, and the defense was not consulted about what the rules should be. Lloyd Garrison objected again and again that he did not know what type of proceeding it was—was it a trial, with the normal protections of the courtroom?—but in the fear-laden climate of the day, his objections were overruled, and Chairman Gray even reprimanded him for making them.

The whole affair was after the fact: Oppenheimer's contract as an AEC consultant was to expire on June 30, and Strauss was free at any time before that to cancel the contract, which would automatically have precipitated revocation of his Q clearance. Instead, paradoxically, members of the Gray board and the AEC commissioners had to rush the writing of their opinions in order to get a verdict in before the contract was to lapse. With common sense turned on its head, it is impossible to escape the conclusion that Strauss's determination to win at any cost was colored by an implacable desire for revenge.

The week before the hearing began, Gray, Morgan, and Evans were closeted with three thousand pages of documents—Borden's letter, the denunciations by Pitzer, Teller, and Latimer, other items from Oppenheimer's FBI file—compiled by the prosecution. Roger Robb, the outside prosecutor hired for the case, and his chief assistant, C. Arthur Rolander, were on hand to interpret, and with the board members taking meals together every day, Robb very often ate with them. Not only was the defense prevented from seeing the documents the board members were reading: it was not told what the documents were or what they contained. Silverman called the board's prehearing immersion in files that the defense was not allowed to see "unheard of," while Green later said that the board members emerged "brainwashed," coming to the presentation of testimony steeped in the prosecution's case and on friendly terms with the prosecutor himself. But when Garrison asked to meet with the board, he was brusquely refused. There was no discovery process and no rules of evidence. The defense, mistakenly assuming that the proceeding might bear some resemblance to a normal trial, furnished the prosecution with the names of its witnesses ahead of time, but when Garrison asked for a list of prosecution witnesses, Robb refused and was upheld by Gordon Gray. Meanwhile, knowing in advance who the defense witnesses were to be, Robb repeatedly embarrassed them with disclosures from their FBI files.

The biggest handicap of all for the defense was its lack of security clearance. Many of the documents entered in testimony had been confiscated from Oppenheimer's files and some had even been written by Oppenheimer himself, but now they were classified and no one on the defense team was permitted to see them. Prior to the hearing, the AEC had offered to expedite a clearance for Garrison but refused to extend the offer to Silverman and Marks, and Garrison withdrew his request. (The truth, which the prosecution did not want to tell Garrison, was that they anticipated difficulty clearing Marks, a liberal who had been a close adviser to Acheson in the State Department.) As opening day approached, however, Garrison, anxious that Oppenheimer not be left unrepresented in the hearing room, renewed his request for clearance. Strauss refused outright, instructing Nichols to "make it perfectly clear to Garrison that we offered to do this last January and . . . we won't give any special consideration to this and should not give him emergency clearance." (Robb, of course, had been cleared in just a few days.) Several times Robb declassified a document on the spot, while questioning a witness, but refused to let the defense attorneys see it on grounds that they were not cleared. Barred by classification rules even from seeing Oppenheimer's FBI file, the defense lawyers were unaware both of derogatory items they should try to answer and positive items that might help their client. It was like trying to defend someone while blindfolded and with one arm tied behind one's back.[4]

Most ironic of all, the hearing was a massive breach of security. Roger Robb would ask bluntly about the core of the hydrogen device, while the witness—Oppenheimer, Bethe, or Rabi—would do his best to answer without giving anything classified away. All of the defense witnesses were more careful about secrecy than the government prosecutor, and Rabi was especially outspoken. He insisted that James Beckerley, the government's classification officer, be present at every moment while he was on the stand. He was afraid, he said, that the hearing would make it easier for the Russians to get the H-bomb by enabling them to put "bits and pieces together" and by "the attrition of the security of technical information." Beckerley remarked afterward, "If Oppenheimer or his witnesses had given anything away, they'd have been had up for it, but they knew better than the prosecution what ought not to be said." Their efforts did not wholly succeed. Scientists all over the world pored over the transcript after it was published, and the official British historian Lorna Arnold wrote that the transcript of the Oppenheimer hearing helped British weaponeers invent an H-bomb of their own.[5]

Since the defense attorneys were denied access to material they needed, Oppenheimer and Marks served instead as their historical memory, and Silverman, chief litigator for the defense, was astonished at how much they remembered. Oppenheimer also served as Silverman's tutor in physics. Silverman called these sessions "fantastic," but added that because of security Oppie censored what he told him even when a fuller explanation might have made his case more persuasive. "Oppenheimer was very careful even with us, his counsel. If a thing was classified, he didn't tell us." It was one of innumerable respects in which the government assumed Oppenheimer's loyalty and discretion even as it challenged them.[6]

A final crippling circumstance, which Garrison and Oppenheimer suspected but may have underrated, was that every detail of their strategy was known to the prosecution in advance because of the wiretapping, euphemistically called "electronic surveillance," of the Oppenheimers' conversations with their attorneys and the attorneys' conversations with one another. Robb had detailed information about Oppenheimer's state of mind, his search for an attorney, the presence of former secretary of state Acheson at dinner at the Oppenheimers' in Princeton just prior to the hearing, Kitty Oppenheimer's approach to General Groves at a New York cocktail party in an effort to find out what he was going to say on the witness stand, and Robert's conversations with potential witnesses, to say nothing of evidence the defense attorneys planned to introduce.

Charles Bates, Hoover's liaison to the AEC, carried the wiretapped reports, plus letters and memoranda from the FBI files—sometimes as much as a briefcaseful—from the FBI to Strauss, and from Strauss to Robb or his assistant Art Rolander. Bates, who strongly favored the prosecution, read all the messages stamped "via Liaison," since it was his job to advise Strauss or the FBI recipient about the matter at hand and deliver an oral reply. He would run errands and schmooze at the AEC, then return to the FBI in late afternoon. During the first six months of 1954, before, during, and after the hearing, he carried at least 273 wiretapped reports to Strauss or Robb, as well as oral messages back and forth between the two men, including Strauss's suggestions as to the questions Robb should ask witnesses.[7]

Over twenty years later, on December 1, 1976, Judge Roger Robb of the United States Court of Appeals for the District of Columbia wrote a letter to Samuel B. Ballen, a businessman in Santa Fe, New Mexico, about his role in the Oppenheimer case. "I had no knowledge of any bugging. Neither did I have any information about any conversation between Oppenheimer and his lawyer, and the suggestion that I used such information in 'strategy planning' is preposterous. I trust you will not persist in circulating false and libelous statements about my professional conduct." Robb sent a copy of his letter to Gordon Gray, and published a similar letter in *Life* magazine. As an attorney, Robb had represented clients as diverse as Earl Browder, chairman of the U.S. Communist Party, and Barry Goldwater, Republican candidate for president in 1964, and there was no way he did not know the source of the FBI documents he used in prosecuting Oppenheimer. Asked in the mid-1970s whether he would be interested in an appointment to the U.S. Supreme Court, Robb indicated that he would not, perhaps in part because he feared that his use of illegally obtained evidence in the Oppenheimer case would come to light.[8]

The hearing opened on Monday morning, April 12, in T-3, a run-down temporary building off Constitution Avenue within sight of the White House. Room 2022, where the hearing took place, was a long, rectangular office that had been converted into a makeshift courtroom. When he was not on the stand, Oppenheimer sat on an old leather couch just behind it. Roger Robb's desire to throw the defendant off balance was manifest even in the old courtroom trick of placing the couch at such an angle that Oppenheimer had to squint into the sun throughout the proceedings.[9]

Oppenheimer started off with panache. Under Lloyd Garrison's gentle probing he described his years of service to the government, beginning with Los Alamos, his efforts after the war to get an atomic energy bill passed by Congress, and his work on the Acheson-Lilienthal plan. He described the reasoning behind the GAC's advice against a crash program to build the H-bomb and denied that he had ever attempted to dissuade anyone from working on it.

But the wind went out of his sails under cross-examination when Robb grilled him about the Chevalier affair. The facts were that one evening in late 1942 or early 1943, when Oppenheimer was already involved in the secret project, his close friend Haakon Chevalier, on a visit to the Oppenheimers, passed along a feeler from George Eltenton, a Communist Party member with whom they were both acquainted. Eltenton, a British-born engineer who had lived in the USSR, had asked Chevalier to inform Oppenheimer that he knew of a way to transmit information to our then ally, the USSR, through the Soviet consulate in San Francisco. Oppenheimer, shaking a pitcher of martinis in the kitchen, immediately responded, "But that would be treason," or words very like those. The two men dropped the subject, and Oppenheimer tried to forget the conversation. Six or seven months later, on a visit to Berkeley from Los Alamos, hearing that Army security was worried about espionage at the Berkeley laboratory, he dropped by the Army security office on campus and told Lieutenant Lyall Johnson, the officer on duty, that George Eltenton, an employee of the Shell Development Company in the Bay Area, might bear watching.

Johnson's superior, Boris Pash, head of Army counterintelligence on the West Coast, was stunned. He ordered Johnson to place a wire in the office and, when Oppenheimer appeared the next day, pressed him for the name of the intermediary who had passed on Eltenton's approach. Anxious to protect Chevalier, Oppenheimer equivocated.

All he had meant to convey, he said, was that it would be a good idea to keep an eye on Eltenton.

Oppenheimer returned to New Mexico, and Army security went into overdrive. General Groves and his deputy for security, John Lansdale, tried without result to pry more out of Oppenheimer. Finally, about a year after the initial approach, Oppenheimer yielded and gave Groves the name of Haakon Chevalier.

Oppenheimer testified about these events on the third day of the hearing. Under questioning by Robb, he admitted that in Pash's office in 1943 he had, in his words, "invented a cock and bull story":

> Q: Did you tell Pash that X had approached three persons on the project?
> A: I am not clear whether I said there were 3 X's or whether X approached three people.
> Q: Didn't you say that X had approached three people?
> A: Probably.
> Q: Why did you do that, Doctor?
> A: Because I was an idiot.
> Q: Is that your only explanation, Doctor?
> A: I was reluctant to mention Chevalier.
> Q: Yes.
> A: No doubt somewhat reluctant to mention myself.[10]

Robb next read from the transcript of the 1943 interview to show that Oppenheimer had said more than he had reported in earlier testimony. Much of what he had said in 1943 had been false, and Oppenheimer, unnerved at hearing his own words read back to him, commented: "This whole thing was a pure fabrication except for the one name Eltenton."[11]

Robb concluded, "Isn't it a fair statement . . . that you told not one lie to Col. Pash, but a whole fabrication and tissue of lies?" Oppenheimer lamely answered, "Right."[12]

When he went home that night, Robb said to his wife, "I've just seen a man destroy himself."[13]

But if Oppenheimer destroyed himself, Robb had supplied the script. He had prepared with the utmost care, then handed a piece of rope to the man on the gallows.

The defense attorneys were dismayed. Robb's bullying, his innuendos, his heavy-handed insistence on yes-or-no answers, all these, along with Gray's supine failure to rein him in, soon made them realize that they were in an uphill battle. "There was a general feeling of depression," Silverman said later.[14]

On Easter Sunday, April 18, Joe Volpe was asked to the house of Randolph Paul, Garrison's law partner, in Georgetown. The Oppenheimers were staying there, and Robert, miserable over the way things were going, wanted Volpe's advice. After Garrison and Marks described what had gone on in the hearing room so far, Volpe told them that if things continued this way, they should pack their bags and walk out. Randolph Paul agreed.[15]

Volpe had been counsel to the AEC in the early days and helped draw up its security regulations. He and Herb Marks had designed the AEC security board hearings to be nonadversarial, to bring out the favorable as well as unfavorable sides of an individual's record and weigh the "whole man," in part because the AEC could not otherwise attract the highly qualified personnel it was looking for. It was clear to Volpe that the proceedings in room 2022 were a long way from long-standing AEC procedures, which were known to be the fairest and most effective in government.

Events a day or so later proved the point. On Monday the nineteenth, preparing to testify, David Lilienthal visited the AEC building to review documents about Oppenheimer's 1947 clearance and the GAC's Halloween meeting. He was assigned a desk and files that purportedly contained the documents he was seeking. Once he was on the stand, however, it became apparent that the documents he was being questioned about had been purposely lifted from the files to make it appear that he had forgotten critical facts and that his testimony should be discounted. Garrison protested that Robb's trick made "a lapse of memory seem like a deliberate falsification," adding that the hearing as a whole was more like a criminal prosecution than an inquiry to find the truth. Robb accused Garrison of challenging his professional integrity and went on questioning Lilienthal unabashed. All without a peep from Gordon Gray.

Lilienthal's entrapment was just the sort of outrage Volpe had had in mind when he had advised the defense lawyers to walk out. But Silverman explained years afterward that they had not taken the idea seriously. "In those days you didn't protest. We just accepted that this was the way things were. And who would we have appealed to?"[16]

Had he known what was happening behind the scenes, the pessimism of the forty-six-year-old Silverman might have turned to anger. The tiny basement office in building T-3 that had been assigned to the defense to work in at night was wired. Oppenheimer and Garrison correctly assumed that they could talk privately in the evenings only at the Pauls' house, but the more innocent Silverman thought they were "paranoid" and remained unaware of the tapping until passage of the Freedom of Information Act more than twenty years later gave it away.

In his testimony, Oppenheimer conceded almost every charge having to do with his life in Berkeley prior to World War II. A product of the Cambridge-Göttingen-Berkeley Ivory Tower, he had known almost nothing about events in the world outside physics, learning of the 1929 stock market crash, for example, only some time after it occurred. But after falling in love in 1936 with Jean Tatlock, a Communist Party member, he, too, became close to the Party and was eventually, in his own words, a "fellow traveler." He sympathized with the effort to create an egalitarian society in Soviet Russia, but what he cared most about was the rise of fascism in Europe and the cause of Republican Spain. Like other leftists of that era, he hoped for a defeat of fascism in Spain that would deter Hitler from unleashing war on the rest of Europe. People joked that the easiest way to find Oppenheimer was to attend a fund-raiser for victims of the Spanish civil war. What the ultrarespectable Gordon Gray and his colleagues made of Oppenheimer's life on the bohemian left in Berkeley during the 1930s has to be guessed at, since it did not remotely resemble their own experience, and like most Americans, they were not touched personally by the Spanish war. The Chevalier affair was the most damning, not because it was about espionage or treason—it was not——but because it was about lying. Oppenheimer in 1943 had lied to protect a friend. Throughout the hearing, the question that hung over room 2022 was, would he do it again? Would he put loyalty to a friend ahead of loyalty to his country? The question was the more pointed because Oppenheimer admitted that he had seen Chevalier from time to time after the war, and revealed—a startling fact that became known to the prosecution only when Oppenheimer mentioned it in his testimony—that he had seen Chevalier on two separate occasions in Paris in December 1953, only four months before the hearing.

One after the other, witnesses for the defense argued not only that Oppenheimer would place loyalty to the country above loyalty to a friend but that he had already done so. They emphasized that he, like the rest of them, had changed and grown when it came to accepting the need for security. John von Neumann, the world's greatest mathematician, who occupied the office next to Oppenheimer's in Princeton, emphasized the strange new world of espionage and counterespionage into which they had all been thrust. "We were little children," he said. "We suddenly were dealing with something with which one could blow up the world. . . . We had to make . . . our code of conduct as we went along." Even if Oppenheimer's 1943 version of the Chevalier approach had been true, von Neumann said, "it would just give me a piece of information on how long it took Dr. Oppenheimer to get adjusted to this Buck Rogers universe, but no more." Later he "learned how to handle it, and handled it very well." Robb asked a final question. "Doctor," he said to von Neumann, "you have never had any training as a psychiatrist, have you?" Von Neumann was only one of several distinguished witnesses who attested to Oppenheimer's loyalty, only to be faced by insulting innuendo.[17]

Emphasizing that events of the early 1940s, such as the Chevalier affair, had to be weighed in terms of the period in which they occurred, Gordon Dean conceded that had he first met Oppenheimer in Berkeley in 1939 or 1940, he might not have cleared him. But, "I feel quite differently having watched him closely and . . . evaluated quite carefully his service to his country." Here, said Dean, was "one of the few men who can demonstrate his loyalty to his country by his performance." Lee DuBridge, who had spent five years with Oppenheimer on the GAC, agreed: "There is no one who has exhibited his loyalty to this country more spectacularly."[18]

George Kennan, the expert on Russia whose last official post had been that of ambassador to the USSR, defended Oppenheimer against any implication that he had bent his policy advice in the Soviet Union's favor. Pointing out that the gifted individual is less likely than others to have led a wholly conventional life, Kennan said that Oppenheimer had one of the great minds of his generation. "A mind like that is not without its implications," he added. "You might just as well have asked Leonardo da Vinci to distort an anatomical drawing as . . . ask Robert Oppenheimer to speak responsibly to the sort of questions we were talking about and speak dishonestly."[19]

While all twenty-eight defense witnesses—most of them far more distinguished in American life than any prosecution witness—praised Oppenheimer's contributions, Vannevar Bush, director of the wartime Office of Scientific Research and Development and the most venerable of them all, treated the board with defiance. It ought to have rejected Nichols's letter of charges and sent it back for redrafting, he said, to eliminate any suggestion that Oppenheimer was being tried for advice he had given the government. The board's failure to do so, scolded the austere New Englander, had resulted in "a very bad mess" in the government's relations with the scientists. The National Academy of Sciences and the American Physical Society would be holding their annual meetings in Washington the following week, and he hoped "they would do nothing foolish," such as decide to boycott government programs. The scientific community was alarmed that a colleague who had "rendered great service to his country, service beyond almost any other man, is now being pilloried and put through an ordeal because he had the temerity to express his honest opinions. . . . When a man is pilloried for doing that, this country is in a severe state."[20]

But the witness who may have gone furthest of all was Rabi, a close friend of Oppenheimer's since 1929 and his successor as chairman of the GAC. Rabi conceded that Oppenheimer's failure to report the Chevalier feeler accurately "was a great mistake in judgment" but, as von Neumann had, pointed out that Oppie need not have reported it at all. "I read no sinister implication in it." Asked about his attempts to persuade Strauss to call off the hearing, Rabi replied that he had told Strauss from the outset that the suspension of Oppenheimer's clearance was "a very unfortunate thing and should not have been done. In other words, there he was; he is a consultant, and if you don't want to consult the guy, you don't consult him, period. . . . It didn't seem to me the sort of thing that called for this kind of proceeding at all against a man who had accomplished what Dr. Oppenheimer has accomplished. There is a real positive record . . . we have an A-bomb and a whole series of it, and what more do you want—mermaids? This is just a tremendous achievement. If the end of that road is this kind of hearing, which can't help but be humiliating, I thought it was a pretty bad show. I still think so."[21]

Behind the scenes, Rabi had made six attempts to have the hearing called off, only to be foiled each time by Strauss. Once, before the proceeding began, he telephoned the White House to request an appointment with the president. Spotting Strauss in the outer office, the president's secretary asked who Rabi was. Strauss intercepted the call and then obtained a commitment from the president to refer any call from Rabi—who had seen a good deal of Eisenhower during his brief time as president of Columbia University—back to Strauss. Another time, a few days after the start of the hearing, Rabi asked the AEC chairman to request a formal presidential directive to call it off. This time, worried about criticism that was beginning to appear in the press and wary of a scientific boycott, Strauss asked Robb to curtail his questioning of prosecution witnesses.[22]

Rabi let Strauss know later on that he would be appearing as a defense witness and would testify that Oppie was not a security risk. Strauss tried to warn him off and cautioned that Rabi might find himself trapped on the stand if he had not seen Oppenheimer's FBI file. Strauss got an okay from J. Edgar Hoover to let Rabi see the file, but found himself outmaneuvered when Rabi mentioned offhandedly on the witness stand that Strauss had already shown it to him. Thrown into disarray by the revelation that Strauss had shown the witness the highly classified dossier, Robb asked for an immediate recess.[23]

Finally Rabi informed Strauss that the GAC had passed a resolution declaring it the intention of all nine members to appear as witnesses for the defense, and Strauss answered that he refused to be blackmailed.[24]

Neither man wanted to alienate the other, since both were keenly interested in the Atoms for Peace conference, which was to take place in Geneva the following year. Strauss needed Rabi, a Nobel Prize winner known all over Europe, for the conference, while Rabi wanted the world to get something besides weapons out of the atom. Rabi later explained, "My way of keeping straight with Strauss was to tell him at every point what I was doing and what I thought. I never hid what I thought. Had I taken part in the defense—gone over to Oppenheimer or his damn-fool lawyers—the outcome might have been different, but I wouldn't have had my Geneva conference." Rabi was angry at Oppie and thought he had brought the whole thing on himself. Had he been part of the defense team, he said, he would have urged him to tell his accusers, " 'who the Hell are you to try *me,* who saved your country for you?' " Disgusted by Oppie's caving in under Robb's savage cross-examination, Rabi said of his friend, "He was such a great actor, so he played the role of victim. That is what they wanted of him, and he did it."[25]

Still, Rabi regretted all his life that he hadn't done more. As a member of the GAC, he held a presidential appointment and was entitled to approach the president directly, and afterward—perhaps not remembering that he had been intercepted on precisely such a mission by Strauss—he blamed himself for failing to tell Eisenhower in person that he should call the whole thing off. He did go up to the president at a White House reception one night intending to speak to him, but before he could open his mouth, Otis Chandler, publisher of the *Los Angeles Times* and backer of the Republican Party, broke in with some comment to Ike about Oppie's romance with Jean Tatlock. Rabi could not summon the heart to talk to the president that night.

It was as though Rabi, as steady as anyone could be, was standing like a rock beside Oppie and trying to impart to him the staunchness he needed. He loved Oppenheimer for the power of his mind and his superb education, so much better, he felt, than his own. He relished being with him, discussing history, philosophy, literature, and psychology with him—and knew precisely what he lacked. Oppenheimer's brain, Rabi thought, was too much for his frail body and his emotional capacity. He could be "sublime" when things were going his way, but he was not a street fighter. "Kitty was better in that way. She supplied the backbone."[26]

Groves at Los Alamos, Rabi thought, had understood what Robert lacked and supplied the "backbone" himself. And if he was too busy or was off somewhere, Groves brought in others to supply it. During the early days, in 1943, some of the Europeans thought that they were greater scientists than Oppie and that one of them should be leading the project. At moments when Oppie seemed to doubt himself, Groves would encourage Rabi or Bacher to fly in from the Radiation Lab at MIT to buck him up. Now, in the spring of 1954, Kitty Oppenheimer, herself the possessor of a keen fighting spirit, was doing her best to shore Robert up. And Rabi, as loyal in his way as Kitty was in hers, tried, quite simply, to make a gift to Robert of the staunchness, the stiffness of spine, that he himself had and that his brilliant, mysterious friend lacked.

The cost to Kitty was beyond reckoning. On weekends during the hearing, the two of them went back to Princeton. Robert caught up with institute affairs, and they spent time with their children, Toni, aged ten, and Peter, fourteen, who especially needed comforting. One spring evening Harold Cherniss, an art historian at the institute, and his wife, Ruth, a childhood schoolmate of Robert's, were with the Oppenheimers. After dinner, Robert walked them to their car. As the three of them were saying good-bye, they heard a prolonged wail coming from the house, like the baying of a wounded animal.[27]

CHAPTER NINETEEN

Smyth

THE OPPENHEIMERS would have been surprised had they known what was going on in the household of another couple—whom they knew, but were not close to—who were just as upset as they were, and on their account. AEC commissioner Henry Smyth was Oppie's senior by six years and had received his Ph.D. from Princeton in 1921, before quantum mechanics arrived in the United States. Oppenheimer respected Smyth but did not consider him a first-class physicist and had, on more than one occasion, let him know it. But Smyth, who had a lively sense of justice and an overriding desire for the well-being of the atomic energy program, was not one to hold Oppie's attitude against him. So acute was his feeling, and that of his wife, that what was happening to Oppie was unjust, outrageous, and bad for the country, that the redoubtable Mary deConingh Smyth kept a detailed record of their actions throughout this period and left it behind for history.

A little over six feet tall, with an angular face and wavy gray hair parted on one side, clad always in subdued grays and browns, Henry DeWolf Smyth was the picture of austere rectitude. A commissioner for five years, he had been disappointed when Eisenhower passed him over for AEC chairman in the spring of 1953 and selected Strauss instead. By the autumn of that year he was thinking seriously of returning to his professorship at Princeton, not because he had been passed over but because he deeply distrusted the new chairman. Once he realized that the hearing was to take place, however, he put his personal plans on hold. He knew Strauss too well not to fear a collision between scientists and the administration that could endanger the weapons program.[1]

After New Year's, 1954, he and Mary stayed up nights discussing the resignation and worrying what would happen to Oppie if no one was left at the AEC to stand up to Strauss. Mary wrote in her diary on January 11, "We decide what is right for H to do about RO." And an evening or two later, "H so tired from worry over RO. We talk late." They shared hard truths about themselves, too: walking in Rock Creek Park one Sunday, husband and wife discussed their "real incompatibility," and Mary wrote later that she was "sunk." They had their lighter moments, too. Klari and Johnny von Neumann stayed with them the week Johnny testified—he had not wanted to appear, and rumor had it that Klari threatened him with divorce if he did not testify in Oppie's favor—and another time Rabi came for dinner and stayed overnight: "Rabi here for dinner. Wonderful ping-pong."[2]

The week of April 26, the last full week of the hearing, scientists converged on Washington from all over the country for their annual meetings. Despite the warning to each witness that the hearing was to be treated as "confidential," news had spread throughout the physics community as to what kind of proceeding it was. Hans Bethe, president of the American Physical Society, invited Oppenheimer to sit on the dais during dinner at one of the big Washington hotels. When Bethe introduced the worn and tired-looking physicist he received a standing ovation.

All of the government witnesses testified that final week: the prosecution had arranged it that way so that hostile testimony would be fresh in the minds of the board members when they made their decision. During that frantic week, Strauss managed to squeeze time for four prosecution witnesses into his schedule. On Monday he saw Wendell Latimer and Kenneth Pitzer, the professors of chemistry at Berkeley who had informed against Oppie to the FBI two years earlier and were to testify against him that week. And late Tuesday he had a visit from Edward Teller, who was scheduled to testify on Wednesday.[3]

After seeing Strauss, Teller stopped by the office of Roger Robb, who had interviewed him six weeks earlier in California. On that occasion Teller had told Robb about an episode in 1942 or so when Oppenheimer had sought his advice as to whether he should accept leadership of the Manhattan Project in view of left-wing friendships he had had during the 1930s, and Teller had urged him to go ahead. Robb now told Teller that since their meeting in California, Oppenheimer had testified to an involvement with the Communist Party far more extensive than the one he had described to Teller. Robb showed Teller the passage in Oppenheimer's testimony in which the scientist admitted that he had given Pash in 1943 a false story about Chevalier, and Teller professed to be shocked. "Oppenheimer lied to me," he said, adding that his father had taught him as a boy that a half-truth was as bad as a lie.

When Teller returned to his hotel that evening, three of his oldest friends begged him not to testify for the prosecution. Thirty-two years later John Wheeler still remembered Teller's pacing back and forth in his room at the Wardman Park Hotel, worrying about the flaws in Oppie's character, while Hans and Rose Bethe also sorrowfully recalled pleading with Teller that night. Teller and Bethe had met in 1928, as students of Arnold Sommerfeld in Munich. When Bethe arrived in the United States in 1935 as a refugee from Hitler, he had gone straight to the Tellers' home in Washington, D.C., and a year or so later the Tellers had chaperoned Bethe and Rose Ewald, then in their courtship, on an automobile trip across the United States. Bethe had already implored Teller to testify *for* Oppenheimer, and Rose, too, now begged him not to turn against their old friend. This time Teller did not mention the "issue of character" of which he had spoken to Wheeler, nor did he question Oppie's loyalty. Instead he deplored his opposition to the H-bomb and complained that he had slowed down another program, the nuclear reactor effort, as well. As the old friends said good night, the Bethes knew they had failed.[4]

Teller did not mention his session with the prosecutor that day to either Wheeler or the Bethes. But in later years he insisted that his afternoon meeting with Robb—which he remembered, inaccurately, as having taken place early Wednesday morning, April 28, when he was on his way into the hearing room—changed his mind. Until that moment, he claimed, he had intended to limit his testimony to his belief that Oppie had slowed the H-bomb program and given bad advice.

But on reading Oppie's admission that he had lied, he had decided to say more.

Robb proceeded with surgical delicacy the next day. Asked whether he thought that Oppenheimer was disloyal, Teller answered that he had always considered him a loyal citizen. Describing his old colleague as "intellectually most alert" and "very complicated," Teller volunteered that "it would be presumptuous and wrong on my part if I would try in any way to analyze his motives." Robb moved in for the kill: "Do you or do you not believe that Dr. Oppenheimer is a security risk?"

"In a great number of cases," Teller answered, "I have seen Dr. Oppenheimer act in a way which for me was exceedingly hard to understand. I thoroughly disagreed with him in numerous issues and his actions frankly appeared to me confused and complicated. To this extent I feel that I would like to see the vital interests of the country in hands which I understand better and therefore trust more. In this very limited sense I would like to express a feeling that I would feel *personally more secure* if public matters would rest in other hands" (italics added).[5]

With these words, the deed was done. In California only a few days before, Teller had told an AEC official that he was sorry the case was being "brought on security grounds because such charges were not tenable." But in their session Tuesday night, Robb evidently persuaded Teller to utter the word "secure." And the moment he did so, Robb switched abruptly to a different line of questioning. He aimed at all costs to avoid giving Teller a chance to take back the words he had spoken.[6]

Teller then said under oath that Oppenheimer was "just a most wonderful and excellent director" of Los Alamos during the war. But if scientists had gone to work on the H-bomb immediately after World War II—a course he said Oppenheimer had discouraged—the United States could have had the weapon four years earlier than it had, indeed possibly as early as 1947. And he added that Oppenheimer's influence and that of the GAC had been "a brake rather than encouragement" to the thermonuclear program, "more frequently a hindrance than a help."

Toward the end of Teller's testimony Gordon Gray asked whether he thought the common security would be endangered if Oppenheimer were allowed to keep his clearance. If it was a question of intent, the answer would be no, Teller replied. Oppenheimer would not "knowingly and willingly" do anything to endanger the nation. But "if it is a question of wisdom and judgment, as demonstrated by actions since 1945, then I would say that it would be wiser not to grant clearance."[7]

As he left the stand, Teller turned to Oppenheimer, who was seated behind him on the sofa, and put out his hand. Stunned, Oppenheimer took it. "I'm sorry," Teller said. "After what you've just said, I don't know what you mean," Oppenheimer replied. Teller turned and limped from the room.[8]

Strauss and Robb were disappointed by the failure of another witness to make it to Washington that week. That witness was Ernest Lawrence, the only leader whose stature in the scientific community came close to that of Oppenheimer. A few weeks earlier, talking with Robb, Lawrence had bitterly criticized Oppenheimer: his hypnotic influence, his opposition to the H-bomb and the second lab, and his participation in Project Vista. Strauss, who for nearly twenty years had helped Lawrence acquire expensive equipment for his laboratory, had told Lawrence that it was his duty to testify, and Lawrence had reluctantly consented. Reluctantly because Lawrence and Oppenheimer went back even further than Lawrence and Strauss, and had been the closest of friends and collaborators during the 1930s. So close were they that Lawrence had named his younger son Robert after him. Lawrence, as leader, had very much at heart the "unity" part of the words "scientific community." He was a man of unusually deep loyalties, and the idea of reading Oppie out of that community pained him. But he felt betrayed. It wasn't just Oppie's left-wing opinions—Lawrence thought he had outgrown them—but the fact that prior to his recommending Oppenheimer's younger brother Frank for a teaching job at the University of Minnesota, Robert had assured him that Frank had never belonged to the Communist Party, knowing full well that he had.

Because of his bitterness, because he believed that Oppenheimer's advice had been mistaken and maybe dangerous, and also perhaps out of irritation that Oppenheimer seemed to enjoy his fame all too much, Lawrence had given Strauss his word that, on the way home from a meeting on reactors in Tennessee, he would stop in Washington to testify. Lawrence had allowed himself to be persuaded that the proceeding was Oppenheimer's fault: Strauss had given him a chance to renounce his clearance quietly; it was Oppie who had insisted on a hearing.

The woods outside Topoca Lodge in the Great Smoky Mountains were breathtakingly beautiful that last weekend of April 1954 as the country's best-known specialists on nuclear reactors met under the auspices of the AEC. They had gathered to discuss technical problems, but the immolation of Oppenheimer dominated their meeting. Lawrence was surprised by the unanimous sympathy for his old friend. When he said that Oppenheimer himself was to blame, they told him that, to the contrary, Oppie had had no choice but to ask for the hearing once he was charged as a security risk. When Lawrence argued that fame had gone to Oppie's head and he had strayed from science into moral preachment, they asked whether being a scientific adviser to the government meant that a man must renounce his beliefs. Was it his duty to approve a course of action that offended his moral code? And was it a crime to be wrong, assuming that Oppenheimer had been wrong in opposing the hydrogen bomb? Lawrence heard the words "martyrdom" and "persecution" applied to the goings-on in Washington, and approval of Oppie's stance on the H-bomb. And when one of the conferees pointed out that the hostile testimony so far had all come from Berkeley, Lawrence found himself defending his lab from the charge that it was waging a vendetta. But the arguments that weighed most with him had to do with the scientific community—the damage a split would cause, not just to science, but to the weapons program and the country.[9]

The discussions exacted a toll, and Lawrence suffered an attack of the ulcerative colitis that was eventually to kill him. Before he flew home—to California and not Washington—he summoned three other conferees to his bathroom and showed them the blood he had lost, so they would not think that he had lost his nerve.[10]

Luis Alvarez in Berkeley was surprised to receive a call from Lawrence, before he left Tennessee, telling him not to testify. Lawrence added that the four of them, Lawrence, Alvarez, Ken Pitzer, and Wendell Latimer, were viewed as a Berkeley cabal bent on destroying Oppenheimer, and that he was afraid the lab would suffer reprisals if he and Alvarez took the stand. Alvarez canceled his flight to Washington.

That evening he had another call, this one from Lewis Strauss. Maybe Lawrence had caved in because of illness, Strauss scolded, but what was Alvarez's excuse? Lawrence had ordered him not to go, Alvarez objected, and it was Lawrence he worked for. Strauss told Alvarez that it was his duty to appear; Alvarez responded that he had already done his duty to the country—during the war, at Los Alamos. Strauss became more and more exercised, and finally warned that if Alvarez failed to show up the next day, he would be unable to look at himself in the mirror for the rest of his life.

Alvarez reconsidered. He poured himself a drink and booked a seat on a midnight flight to Washington. On the drive to the airport, he reflected that it was the first time he had ever disobeyed Ernest Lawrence.[11]

CHAPTER TWENTY

Borden

ON WEDNESDAY EVENING Allan Ecker, a junior member of the defense team, was in the AEC building reading declassified transcripts of the day's testimony when he heard the crackling sounds of an ancient recording machine through the thin wall between him and the office next door. As he left the building that night, Ecker saw Roger Robb leaving with two men Ecker later recognized on the witness stand: Luis Alvarez, just in from California, and Boris Pash.[1]

When his turn came the next day Alvarez, like his Berkeley colleagues Latimer and Pitzer, testified that Oppenheimer had persuaded others, especially younger men, not to work on the H-bomb. But all three of them hedged a little. Pitzer said, "I am not myself a physicist," and Latimer, "my impressions would be based very largely on what Dr. Teller has told me." Alvarez put it this way: "This I have been told by Edward Teller. That is my only source of information on this point." Along with Teller, all of them emphasized Oppenheimer's persuasiveness—"one of the most persuasive men that has ever lived," Alvarez said—to back up the prosecution's claim that Oppenheimer had discouraged fellow scientists from working on the project. And when Robb asked whether Oppenheimer was still essential to the weapons program, Pitzer, Teller, and Latimer answered emphatically that he was not. Interestingly, Strauss had seen the three other men, and probably coached them on this very point, before they gave their testimony, but saw Alvarez, who was not asked that question, only for a brief moment Friday morning, after he had testified. Strauss apparently did not coach Alvarez but presumably thanked him for coming all the way from California: Lawrence's change of heart had, in a sense, left Teller out to dry, left him the only Berkeley physicist to take on Oppenheimer, Latimer and Pitzer being chemists. And, having seen Teller twice that week, on Tuesday, before he testified, and on Thursday, afterward, Strauss knew how shaky his star witness felt. Alvarez had no more firsthand knowledge of the thermonuclear program than Pitzer or Latimer, but at least he was a physicist and could be counted on because of his long-standing, and well-known, animosity toward Oppenheimer.[2]

Unlike the other four, a fifth prosecution witness, Major General Roscoe Charles Wilson, had no personal animus against the defendant and appeared only reluctantly, on orders of the Air Force chief of staff. Wilson had known Oppenheimer since 1944, when as Air Force liaison officer to General Groves he had helped pick Alamogordo as the site of the first atomic bomb test. He testified that despite his admiration for Oppenheimer, he had warned the director of Air Force intelligence in early 1951 about a "pattern of activity" on the scientist's part that he thought could "jeopardize the national defense." The "pattern" included Oppenheimer's advocacy of internationalizing atomic energy (the Acheson-Lilienthal plan) at a time when this country still had a monopoly, his opposition to two of three devices favored by the Air Force for detecting a possible test by the Soviet Union, and his opposition, on technical grounds, to development of a nuclear-powered airplane. In the fall of 1949, immediately after Joe One, Wilson had been briefed by Teller, who sent him to top Air Force officials to alert them to the fact that something called the hydrogen bomb might be the answer to the Soviet A-bomb. The intervention by Teller and Wilson led Air Force chief of staff Hoyt Vandenberg to testify in favor of the H-bomb in Congress, on October 14, 1949, only the day after he had learned that the bomb might someday be a possibility.[3]

Calling himself "a big bomb man," Wilson described his testimony as "one of the great sorrows of my life." Years afterward he explained that Oppenheimer had been "remarkably kind to me, and really a great mind, an incredible mind. . . . I liked Oppenheimer," he said, "we were friends. I have been to his house many times. . . . As I

sat there I could see tears running down the guy's face. . . . This really
has been on my conscience."[4] (Joe Volpe later denied that Oppenheimer wept at any time during the hearing.)

If Lawrence's defection left Teller out on a limb, Thomas Finletter's decision not to testify left the Air Force's other witness, David
Tressel Griggs, very much on the spot as well. Ivan Getting, a former
Air Force scientist and close friend of Griggs's, stopped by Griggs's
house in Los Angeles one day in 1954 and found his friend talking on
the telephone to someone back east. That someone was their old boss,
the former secretary of the Air Force, breaking the news to Griggs that
he was not going to appear. Getting noticed that Griggs looked
"ashen" and "let down."[5]

Griggs nonetheless appeared during the final week to support the
prosecution's case that Oppenheimer had engaged not in a single act
but a pattern of actions designed to weaken the Air Force and its offensive arm, the Strategic Air Command. Griggs described the 1951
Vista meetings at Caltech and a meeting outside Boston in September
1952 on air defense of the United States. During the Boston meeting,
Griggs testified, he had seen Professor Jerrold Zacharias of MIT go to
the blackboard and write the letter Z at the top, followed by the letters
O, R, and C, in capitals eighteen inches high, diagonally to the bottom of the board. The initials were those of Zacharias himself, and of
Oppenheimer, Rabi, and Charles Lauritsen, who, Griggs alleged, had
conspired to weaken SAC, if not abolish it altogether. The charge that
there was a cabal called ZORC had created a sensation when, as mentioned earlier, it appeared in Charles Murphy's *Fortune* article of May
1953, and was raised again at the hearing to suggest a conspiracy. Although Zacharias denied writing the fateful letters on the blackboard
and MIT physicist Al Hill, who was also present at the Boston meeting,
testified that the episode never took place, the ZORC story had staying
power: Ivan Getting believed it and in 1989 sent the author a letter from
a scientist who had allegedly been present, offering to swear under oath
that he had seen Zacharias write the initials on the blackboard. However, after the hearing two prominent scientists who had attended the
Boston meeting, Emmanuel Piore and Carl Overhage, told the FBI

that they had never witnessed such a scene nor heard of ZORC prior to Murphy's story in *Fortune*. Griggs himself was unsure: three weeks after testifying at the hearing he told the FBI, according to bureau records, that "doubts have arisen in his mind as to whether his recollection was true. . . . He said that he is somewhat confused concerning this matter and stated also that he has a poor memory."[6]

Guyford Stever, an aeronautics specialist who became science adviser to President Gerald Ford, in later years recalled seeing Zacharias at the blackboard, writing down names of those who had taken responsibility for drafting parts of a paper or report. "It was a simple technique, and not a consequential thing," Stever said, adding that after Zacharias had written down the four names, or initials, he exclaimed, "Look at that, ZORCH."[7]

From FBI interviews of May and June 1954, it appears that the ZORC story sprang from the brain, and almost certainly the imagination, of Air Force Colonel Teddy Walkowicz, the author of much other misinformation. This, for example, from an FBI report in June: "On June 12, Mr. Charles J. V. Murphy was interviewed. . . . He stated that he had no direct or first-hand knowledge relative to the origin of . . . the term ZORC. It is Murphy's recollection that Teddy Walcowicz [*sic*], former Air Force officer, was Murphy's main and possibly only source of information."

Griggs's story, with its accusation that Oppenheimer had been leader of a conspiracy, was unsupported by any other witness at the hearing. But it was allowed to stand. Unlike so much else that had found its way into the FBI files, Griggs's refutation in May was not leaked to the press, nor was Murphy's of June 12. The bureau had both when the commissioners sat down to consider their verdict in late June. There is no evidence that they were informed.[8]

On Friday, April 30, Boris Pash, whom Allan Ecker had seen emerging from Robb's office on Wednesday evening, testified about the meeting in Lyall Johnson's office in the summer of 1943, when Oppenheimer described the feeler from Soviet intelligence that had been relayed to him by Haakon Chevalier. The recording made by Pash, the Army's counterintelligence chief at the Presidio of San Francisco at the time, had already been played to the Gray board, and Pash now testified to his belief that Oppenheimer was a security risk, that he was merely pretending to have changed his allegiances, and that he had been in 1943 and probably remained a member of the Communist Party. (Pash was the sole prosecution witness whose testimony was not based in part on information supplied by Teller.)

Dramatic as the statements of Griggs and Pash had been, the appearance of the week's final witness was the most stunning event of all. On Friday afternoon the blond, slight, thirty-four-year-old William Borden entered the hearing room and raised his right hand while his November 7 letter to Hoover was handed to lawyers for the defense. Until this moment, they had not known about the letter. Now, seeing it for the first time, they were appalled, both because the board members had had it in front of them the entire time, and because of its conclusion: Borden's "exhaustively considered opinion . . . that more probably than not J. Robert Oppenheimer is an agent of the Soviet Union." The letter even said that Oppenheimer could have been acting on Soviet orders as far back as the time when he chose atomic weapons as his specialty in the early 1940s, and that in addition to performing espionage, he had probably also "acted under a Soviet directive in influencing United States military, atomic energy, Intelligence and diplomatic policy." Lloyd Garrison was quick to point out that in introducing accusations that were not part of the AEC's original letter of charges and that had not arisen at the hearing, "we now have a new case," and even Gray dissociated himself and his fellow board members from Borden's claim that Oppenheimer might have volunteered information to the Russians. The board had no evidence before it to show that Oppenheimer was an espionage agent, Gray said, to Borden's chagrin and the outrage of his friends, one of whom later protested that "Gray kicked Borden in the teeth."[9]

By the time Borden had read his letter aloud, it was 4:30 p.m., early enough in the afternoon for the defense to start cross-examination before adjournment for the weekend. But defense attorneys were at odds among themselves as to whether they even wanted to cross-examine, and a recess was called. Silverman did not want to give Borden a chance to make Robb's case for him or to spread innuendo on the record. Herb Marks, on the other hand, wanted to question Borden on every single assertion. By Sunday night, however, Marks had come around to Silverman's view, and the defense decided not to cross-examine. Even after Borden's surprise appearance, Silverman later admitted, it was several days before he began to suspect that this was the letter that had triggered the hearing.[10]

On Thursday, May 6, the hearing ended with a three-hour extemporaneous summation by Garrison, who stated that the hearing should not have been brought at all in view of Oppenheimer's overall record and the fact that there had been no new security information against him since his clearance in 1947. The charges, Garrison said, fell in two categories: Oppenheimer's opposition to the H-bomb, in which he had been joined by nearly all the top scientists, and the Chevalier affair. The latter, he concluded, "must be judged in perspective. It happened in a wholly different atmosphere from that of today. Russia was our so-called gallant ally. The whole atmosphere toward Russia, toward persons who were sympathetic with Russia, everything was different from what obtains today. I think you must beware of judging by today's standards things that happened in a different time and era." With that, after three and a half weeks, and nineteen days of testimony, the board adjourned. The members departed for their homes, Morgan and Gray for North Carolina, Evans for Chicago.[11]

When they reconvened on May 17, Gray and Morgan found, to their surprise, that Evans, whom they had believed to be firmly in the prosecution's camp, had changed his mind. Aware of Gray's concern that, in light of the 1947 clearance, the hearing might violate rules against double jeopardy, and that he might vote in Oppenheimer's favor, Strauss and Robb decided to act. Shortly after noon on May 20, they had Charles Bates telephone the FBI with a request that Hoover meet with the board members. They "feel that the board may be trying to find a way out to clear Oppenheimer," and wanted to "come over and talk to the director before the board does." A series of follow-up calls ensued. At 12:20 p.m., Robb called the FBI, said that it would be "a tragedy if the decision of the board goes the wrong way," and declared it "a matter of extreme urgency" that Hoover meet with the board. Ten minutes later Strauss placed a telephone call to Alan Belmont, Hoover's top counterintelligence official, and said he had just come from the White House, implying that he had spoken to the president. Things were "touch and go," Strauss said, and "a slight tip of the balance could cause the board to commit a serious error." Therefore Robb and the board members would gladly go to Hoover's out-of-town location, wherever he might be, in order to meet with him. Hoover, of course, refused. "I think it would be highly improper for me to discuss Oppenheimer case now with anyone connected with AEC or the board—JEH."[12]

Fully as remarkable as the request itself were the reactions years afterward of two participants in the approach to Hoover. In 1978, when BBC producer Peter Goodchild showed Robb, by then a federal district judge in Washington, D.C., a recently declassified FBI memo outlining the events of May 20, 1954, Robb responded, "Damned if I remember this." He subsequently dictated a statement: "I specifically and categorically deny that I ever encouraged a meeting between the board and the director for the purpose of having the director influence the board [and] have no knowledge whatsoever of any conversation between Admiral Strauss and Mr. Belmont. I never heard of any such conversation, had nothing to do with it if it occurred, and any implication to the contrary is unwarranted."[13]

Yet Robb failed to sue to prevent Goodchild's TV program from being shown in the United States. Appointed by the chief justice of the United States about this time to a panel on ethics, he subsequently named special prosecutors to investigate alleged wrongdoing by President Carter's chief of staff Hamilton Jordan, and two Reagan cabinet officers, including Attorney General Edwin Meese.

Before making his 1978 statement to Goodchild, Robb telephoned Gordon Gray; Art Rolander, his assistant at the hearing; and Charles Bates, who had carried the May 20 messages between Robb and Strauss on one hand, and high officials of the FBI on the other. Five years afterward, in an interview with the author, Bates strenuously defended Robb against any suggestion that he had wanted to influence the hearing board. "Roger is too honorable a man. It would have been suicide," he said. In an interview two weeks later, however, confronted again by Robb's statement to Goodchild and the May 20 FBI memo, Bates defended the memo's accuracy and grew angry at Robb. He had not had the memo in front of him when Robb called him in 1978, and had not known that it was declassified. "If he had shown me *that* memo, I'd have stood by it, *absolutely*" (the emphasis is Bates's). Pointing to a remark Robb had made to Goodchild, he added, "Here, he admits he took the first step. If I had him up on the witness stand, he'd be in a lot of trouble." Bates concluded by saying that he resented the Freedom of Information Act's placing him in the situation he had just been in. He had handled many high-profile cases for the FBI—Patty Hearst, the Chicago Seven, the Black Panthers— and had managed to request a transfer out of Washington just in time to avoid Watergate, but he had been sued repeatedly because of FOIA, he said, and did not like having to defend actions he had taken thirty years earlier in a different context and atmosphere.[14]

Caesar's Wife

GORDON GRAY was born at the top and had never had a failure in his life. In North Carolina as he was growing up his father was president of the R. J. Reynolds Tobacco Company. After graduating from the Yale Law School, Gray had spent two years practicing corporate law in New York City. He enlisted in the Army during World War II, rose to the rank of captain, and in 1949 was appointed secretary of the Army by President Truman. When Eisenhower asked him to serve on the board that was to hear the Oppenheimer case, he was president of the University of North Carolina and might have seen the security board as a step on the way back to public life in Washington.

Besides being virtually above criticism, Gray, a forty-four-year-old widower and father of four young boys, had a reputation for fair-mindedness. Despite this, and despite his own feeling that he had leaned over backward to protect Oppenheimer, Gray's rulings were tilted harshly against the defense, so harshly that a reader of the transcript might get the impression that he had had no training in the law and very little notion what due process was. With Oppenheimer's clearance due to expire on June 30, Gray's effort to speed up the proceeding led him at least twice to turn down requests from an exhausted Lloyd Garrison for a half hour's delay in the start of testimony the next day. But the notes he made in North Carolina during the board's ten-day recess in May show that Gray made an effort to be fair as he weighed the imperatives of security against Oppenheimer's contributions. He was impressed by the prominence of the defense witnesses and the solidarity of the scientific community in defense of Oppenheimer, and he attached special weight to the suggestion of George Kennan in his testimony that men of unusual brilliance should be held to a different standard than those of more modest capacities.[1]

On their return to Washington he and the board devoted ten days to their deliberations. Finally, by a vote of two, Gray and Morgan, against one, Evans, they decided that Oppenheimer's clearance ought not to be reinstated. The majority opinion, written by Gray and released on May 27, found nearly all of the charges having to do with the scientist's left-wing associations in Berkeley before the war to be "substantially true." Despite "poor judgment" in continuing some of those associations to the present day, however, the board found "no evidence of disloyalty. Indeed, we have before us much responsible and positive evidence of the loyalty and love of country of the individual concerned." Its decision against clearance was based on the twenty-fourth, or H-bomb, count. It found Oppenheimer inconsistent in changing his views between 1945 and 1949 as to whether the H-bomb was feasible, and inconsistent—or, worse, untruthful—in testifying that what he opposed in 1949 was only the "crash program," when he had in fact signed the GAC recommendation that the "super bomb should never be produced." While it found that Oppenheimer had done nothing actively to obstruct the H-bomb project, the board declared that his failure to make his support known among the scientists had had a negative effect on recruitment, since his "enthusiastic support" would have led others to join the program. The board believed that the opposition of many scientists, of whom Oppenheimer was the "most experienced, most powerful and most effective," had slowed development of the H-bomb. Although it considered Oppenheimer "a loyal citizen" with "a high degree of discretion reflecting an unusual ability to keep to himself vital secrets," it nonetheless ruled that clearance would not be "clearly consistent with the security interests of the United States." He was "susceptible to influence," his conduct and associations showed "serious disregard for the requirements of the security system," his conduct over the H-bomb had been "disturbing," and he had been "less than candid in several instances in his testimony."

While tortured reasoning and a tone of regret pervaded the opinion, one caveat stood out. Astonishingly, the board said that it might have reached a different conclusion had it been "allowed to exercise mature practical judgment without the rigid circumscription of regulations and criteria established for us." The regulations to which it was referring were provisions of Executive Order 10450 of the Eisenhower administration stipulating that clearance should be withheld from anyone against whom there was reliable derogatory information. This was called the "Caesar's wife" principle, it being a truism in Roman days that Caesar's wife must be above reproach. Against this was the "whole man" standard, prevalent at AEC security hearings during the Truman years, which required that favorable information should be balanced against unfavorable information.

It might have been supposed that the Eisenhower, or Caesar's wife, rule, being the more recent, should prevail, except for a June 8, 1953, ruling by the Justice Department that the AEC's existing security program exceeded requirements of the new order and that the Eisenhower rule was inapplicable. The hearing had, then, been conducted under an ad hoc combination of both regulations—with the harsher ruling prevailing in every instance. Harold Green, who had crafted the letter of charges, felt strongly at the time and afterward that among its many failings, the entire proceeding had been conducted under the wrong rules.[2]

The only member to dissent from the majority opinion was Ward Evans, the chemistry professor from Chicago who had been specially selected to be "a hanging judge." Of Oppenheimer, Evans wrote in his opinion that "to damn him now and ruin his career and his service, I cannot do it." He concluded, "I personally think that our failure to clear Dr. Oppenheimer will be a black mark on the escutcheon of our country."

And how did Gordon Gray feel about his role in a case that in his closely knit circle divided family members from one another and tempted even close friends of his to shun him? Harold Green said later that Gray never understood the nature of the proceeding he had been party to. But the columnist Roscoe Drummond wrote at the time that Gray was profoundly upset, and the widow of his closest friend, Frank Wisner, agreed, saying that she thought the case "bothered him the rest of his life." Some members of the Gray family disagree. Gray's second wife, Nancy, said Gray had "moved on" by the time she met him six months after the hearing, and his son Boyden, with whom he had many conversations over the years, said that his father told him he "never lost any sleep" over the case. But the oldest son, Gordon junior, who spent hours with his father at Walter Reed Hospital in the two weeks before he died, believed that Gray went to his grave "with very serious doubts." Again and again the father told his son how much he had admired Oppenheimer, how sorry for him he had been during the hearing, how he had worried that Oppie might break down, and how he had tried to get the hearing called off. "My father had very few failures," said the younger Gray. "He had an unblemished record, and this was the one blot on it."[3]

After publication of the opinion at the end of May, newspaper editorials in many parts of the country approved. But opinion in the *New York Times,* the *New York Herald Tribune,* and other influential dailies ran strongly against the Gray board, and Strauss quickly regretted Gray's pledge to the witnesses that their testimony would remain secret. If people could read in Oppenheimer's own words his admission that he had lied about the Chevalier affair and had spent a night in 1943 with a woman who might be a Communist Party member, Strauss thought, then opinion among the East Coast elite would turn against him.

And so it happened one evening in the first half of June that Lee Hancock of the AEC Security Division was again kept waiting while Art Rolander made a flurry of phone calls. As they drove home along the Shirley Highway, Rolander explained what had kept him. He had been telephoning the witnesses to let them know that their testimony was being released to the newspapers. Hancock was stunned. "How could you?" he asked, thinking of Gray's promise to the forty witnesses that their testimony would be treated as confidential and that the AEC would not initiate any public release. Rolander told Hancock that Robb had learned from a telephone tap that Oppie's lawyers thought his testimony showed their client in a negative light. Hancock was stunned once again. He knew, of course, that for years Oppenheimer's mail had been opened and his telephones tapped and that he was often under physical surveillance. But Hancock never got over the shock of learning that the telephones of the defense attorneys had been wiretapped throughout the hearing.[4]

As for the witnesses, some were asked for permission to have their testimony released and agreed. I. I. Rabi later said that he was not asked but was simply told that his testimony was about to appear; Norman Ramsey asked to have his remarks about the wife of a colleague excised and was embarrassed to have his request ignored and his words published as he had spoken them; those who saw George Kennan that day believe that he was not contacted, since he was giving the commencement address at his daughter's college; and Jerrold Zacharias flatly refused permission.

Strauss briefly had a pretext for releasing the testimony when Commissioner Eugene Zuckert left a notebook containing a hundred-page analysis of the evidence in a railway car near New Haven. The notebook was soon recovered, but Strauss was able to use the loss to wangle a 4–1 vote in favor of releasing the transcript, with only Harry Smyth dissenting. Gray, whose promise to the witnesses was being broken, not only went along but urged that the transcript be published. This he was persuaded to do after Strauss and Charles Murphy, another friend, warned him—untruthfully—that Lloyd Garrison was negotiating with a public relations firm in hopes of manipulating public opinion in Oppenheimer's favor. "There appears to be no respect for truth in either client or counsel," Strauss said to Gray.[5]

As relieved as they were by the Gray board's decision, Murphy and Frank Wisner, members of an influential coterie of journalists and highly placed officials who lived in Georgetown, regarded Gordon Gray's opinion as a disaster. First, it pronounced Oppenheimer "loyal" and "discreet," which they believed to be untrue. And second, by blaming him for his failure to show enthusiasm for the H-bomb, it implied that Oppie was being punished for advice he had given the government. One evening Gray's friend Wisner, head of covert action at the CIA, invited Murphy to his house after dinner to discuss the unfortunate opinion. A day or so later Murphy discussed it again with Wisner and Strauss. "The Oppenheimer ruling haunts every conversation," Murphy wrote, adding that Gray was "hurt and disturbed" by newspaper "distortion" of his opinion. But following release of the transcript in mid-June, a strategy was worked out during a dinner at the Carlton Hotel given by James Shepley of *Time* magazine, where the guests were Gray, Strauss, Murphy, Wisner, and General Wilton D. "Jerry" Persons, political adviser to the president. In accordance with the new strategy Gray flew the next day to New York, where Murphy introduced him to Henry R. Luce and Ogden Reid Jr. The *New York Herald Tribune,* the newspaper belonging to Reid's family, published the influential Walter Lippmann, whose columns were extremely critical of the way the case had been handled, and Joseph and Stewart Alsop, the most outspokenly pro-Oppenheimer and anti-Strauss reporters in the country. "The purpose of the meeting," Murphy wrote in his diary, "was to impress upon Reid that his newspaper had not reported the Oppenheimer findings objectively."[6]

With Wisner and Murphy at work on public relations, the AEC's Ken Nichols was engaged in damage control of his own. Charged with evaluating the Gray board's findings and forwarding his recommendations to the commissioners for a final decision, he faced the difficulty that six of the eight prosecution witnesses and three-quarters of the testimony had dealt with Oppenheimer's opinions on policy. With drafting help from Roger Robb, he now shifted the ground away from Oppenheimer's views and based his recommendation—that he be judged a security risk—solely on Oppenheimer's early Communist associations, his falsehoods in the Chevalier affair, and the fact that he was no longer indispensable to the atomic energy program. This shift in the prosecution's charges, together with the fact that the defense was not allowed an appeal from them, has been called the "gravest procedural defect" in the entire case.[7]

As Harry Smyth had foreseen, publication of the transcript and the Gray board's verdict did nothing to lighten the pressures under which

the commission was working. Inside the AEC, the appetite for vindi-
cation was so strong that one employee compared the atmosphere to
that of "a lynching." With the burden now on Strauss to come up
with a persuasive and, if possible, unanimous verdict by the commissioners, the chairman was gratified to receive a telephone call on June
21 from a friend in New York. The friend was William E. Robinson,
vice president of the *New York Herald Tribune*, sometime public relations man, and later president of Coca-Cola. Robinson, a "large,
beefy Irishman who was probably Eisenhower's closest friend," urged
Strauss to seek help in drafting his verdict and suggested Charles J. V.
Murphy, author of the anonymous attack on Oppenheimer in *Fortune* the year before.[8]

Two days later Murphy and Strauss dined together, and the next
day Murphy reread the Gray report with a view to correcting the impression that Oppenheimer was being punished for his opinions.
When Strauss sent a rough draft of his proposed opinion to Murphy
at the Time Inc. office on Connecticut Avenue, Murphy immediately
found it "too short and inconclusive." To avoid the Gray board's errors, he advised that the AEC opinion should steer clear of Oppenheimer's views on policy and concentrate on "his falsehoods and his
continued association with Communists," an allusion to the Oppenheimers' luncheon and dinner with Chevalier in Paris only six months
before. In the course of a two-hour drafting session at Strauss's office
on Friday, June 25, Murphy had the impression that Strauss was "wa-
vering between optimism and apprehension" over the outcome of the
vote. The two men spent all day Saturday working together, and before Strauss departed for a black-tie dinner honoring Winston
Churchill at the White House, Murphy suggested that he bring
Roger Robb along the next morning. Robb, Strauss, and Murphy
had a four-hour breakfast on Sunday in Strauss's suite at the Shoreham Hotel and thoroughly revised the draft of the day before. "It was
the first time Strauss seemed sure of his position," Murphy observed.
That night Murphy made further changes, which he showed to
Strauss over breakfast Monday morning. Strauss left for the AEC in
what Murphy judged to be "a confident frame of mind."[9]

Meanwhile, at Harry Smyth's house on Woodland Drive, on a steep hill just behind the Shoreham, work was going forward on the dissent. Smyth knew that he would be in a minority, but he hoped to be joined by Zuckert or Murray in a 3–2 vote. But when he arrived home on Tuesday evening, June 22, Mary Smyth saw that he was in low spirits. He had learned that the vote would be 4 to 1, with his the only dissent. The other commissioners had given him some notion of the arguments they would be making, however, and he decided to address those with an opinion that was "shorter, stronger, and less philosophic" than the one he had originally had in mind. For the rest of the week he and Mary, together with Philip Farley and Clark Vogel, AEC employees whose help he had requested, stayed up into the wee hours each night working on successive drafts. On Saturday, Smyth wrote what his wife called a "good, short opinion," adding at the top of her diary, "H looks close to exhaustion."[10]

The other members of the drafting team were exhausted, too, and when AEC chief counsel William Mitchell delivered a first version of the majority opinion to the house at noon on Sunday, June 27, they did not read it right away. But late that afternoon, Smyth looked at it and saw that it was not what the other commissioners had told him to expect. With Oppie's clearance due to expire on Wednesday, he did not have much time in which to produce a wholly new opinion.

The same thing was repeated on Monday, when Roy Snapp of the AEC appeared at 3000 Woodland Drive about 7:00 p.m. with the majority opinion. Having no inkling about the sessions at the Shoreham and no idea that Murphy and Robb had worked on the decision too, Smyth was greatly surprised by the final version. The wording, the emphasis, and, above all, the tone of the new opinion differed so much from the draft he had seen on Sunday night—the Strauss-Murphy version of Friday and Saturday—that he knew he would have to start all over again. As they began work that night he worried whether his loyal secretaries, Mary Sweeney and Evelyn McQuown, would lose their AEC jobs and pensions, and he was concerned about Farley, who had been matter-of-factly informed by Nichols that helping Smyth with his opinion would do his AEC career no good. And he was aware of a car parked in the cul-de-sac down the street. He assumed it was the FBI, keeping track of their comings and goings.[11]

The decision had been hammered out by the majority commissioners during an all-day session on Monday and was signed by Strauss, Commissioner Joseph Campbell, and Zuckert. Strauss had agreed to a slight weakening of the version he had approved that morning with Murphy, probably to placate Eugene Zuckert, but it was still a stunning personal attack on Oppenheimer. Specifying at the outset that Oppenheimer's position on the H-bomb had nothing to do with its decision, the board stated that Oppenheimer was no longer entitled to the government's trust because of "fundamental defects in his character." The proof was that "his associations with persons known to him to be Communists have extended far beyond the tolerable limits of prudence and self-restraint" to be expected from one holding high positions of trust. "These associations have lasted too long to be justified as merely the intermittent and accidental revival of earlier friendships." The opinion listed six associations about which he had allegedly lied, with emphasis on the Chevalier affair, concerning which he had either lied to Boris Pash in 1943 or to the Gray board in 1954. It added that the associations themselves, and not just his lying about them, were "part of the pattern of his disregard for the obligations of security."[12]

In addition to signing the majority statement, Zuckert and Campbell each wrote a separate concurring opinion that pointedly excluded Oppenheimer's advice to the government as a factor. Thomas Murray, meanwhile, also voted to revoke Oppenheimer's clearance, but such was his resentment of the way Strauss had handled the case that he refused to sign the majority statement. Instead he produced a separate decision pronouncing Oppenheimer disloyal because he lacked loyalty to the security system as such. "It will not do to plead that Dr. Oppenheimer revealed no secrets to Communists and fellow travelers," Murray said. It was the associations themselves that offended. That Oppie should have maintained them at all was an act of disloyalty. To allow him to place himself above the security regulations was "to invite the destruction of the whole security system."[13]

Strauss had violated a promise to Smyth that he would have a full twenty-four hours in which to write his dissent, and the six of them on Woodland Drive once again worked all night, revising a passage here, putting in a stronger word there, and trying to make the dissent responsive, point by point, to the majority opinion. Smyth at one point looked up and said, "You know, I'm doing all this for a fellow I've never liked very much. Of course," he added, "I'm not doing it for *him*." He and his helpers felt that what they were doing, they were doing for history, a mission larger than the cause of justice to any one individual. And they hoped their dissent might serve as a basis for re-opening the case someday.[14]

Smyth brought up the fact, about which the majority statement maintained a stunning silence, that Oppenheimer had not been charged with, or found guilty of, ever having divulged a single secret. In this, Smyth wrote, lay proof of his future trustworthiness. "The past fifteen years of his life have been investigated and reinvestigated. For much of the last eleven years he has been under actual surveillance. This professional review . . . has been supplemented by enthusiastic amateur help from powerful personal enemies. Few men could survive such a period of investigation and interrogation without having many of their actions misinterpreted." Smyth refuted the charges having to do with Oppenheimer's personal associations and called the Chevalier affair the only "inexcusable" episode in the story (a word he later wished he had weakened). He denied that Oppenheimer had impeded the H-bomb, adding, "The history of his contributions stands untarnished." Finally, he dismissed the alleged "fundamental defects in his character," describing Oppenheimer instead as "an able, imaginative human being with normal weaknesses and failings." He said that the board should have exercised "overall commonsense judgment." It was the conclusions of the majority, he said, that were "so extreme as to endanger the security system."[15]

About four o'clock in the morning Smyth took the unfinished draft to his study and worked alone. Two hours later he emerged with the final opinion. The weary secretaries typed it up, Mary Smyth made breakfast, and Farley took the dissent to the commission, where he stood watch over the mimeograph machine to be sure that no one changed it. On the following day, June 30, Mary Smyth wrote in her diary: "We buy newspapers and wonder what we have done."[16]

As for the other commissioners, Murray was a devout Roman Catholic whose faith frequently impelled him in directions where other men did not go. For years he had maintained a special channel to his fellow Catholic J. Edgar Hoover, and in accordance with what the FBI chieftain had said to him, Murray did not think Oppenheimer was a Communist. But he felt that the issue of Oppie's observance of security regulations "outweighed any question of equity to an individual." Murray's fellow commissioners viewed him as a wild card. They had no idea how he was going to vote, but since he was not much of a writer, they assumed that someone else had written his opinion for him. They thought the author was either his son, Daniel Bradley Murray, who was then in training for the priesthood, or the worldly and highly regarded Jesuit theologian John Courtney Murray, spiritual counselor not only of Tom Murray but of Clare and Henry Luce (he was known as the "Luces' Richelieu"). Queried about his father's opinion years afterward at the boys' school outside Baltimore where he was teaching, Father Daniel Bradley Murray said that he did not know how his father had voted in the Oppenheimer case but added, however, that he had consulted John Courtney Murray about "everything." His father would "put together all the problems he had at a particular time and consult him about them all at once." While a search of John Courtney Murray's papers has turned up no early drafts or other evidence that he was the true author of Thomas Murray's opinion, it remains a good guess that he was.[17]

Strauss did not leave the votes of the other two commissioners to chance. One, Joseph Campbell, was his creature. Campbell had been chief financial officer of Columbia University when, in the early 1950s, Strauss, in behalf of the Rockefeller family, negotiated a new lease of the land under Radio City with the university. Strauss, whose acquaintance with Eisenhower dated from this period, had had Campbell

appointed to the commission and, after the hearing, had him shunted
to the post of comptroller general of the United States so that he could
make a new appointment to the AEC.[18]

Eugene Zuckert's vote was a different matter. Like Gordon Gray,
Zuckert was a Democrat and a Yale Law graduate, and his friends
were mostly New Dealers. He had been assistant secretary of the Air
Force and was later to be secretary, but at this moment his term as
commissioner was expiring and he had no new job in sight. He remembered years later that in December 1953, when the case was getting under way, Strauss had sent his car for him, had him brought to
the commission, and offered him a job as head of a foundation
Strauss had created in his mother's memory. It was such a "barefaced"
attempt to bribe Zuckert into leaving that "I was completely shocked."
What governed his opinion, Zuckert said, was concern about Oppenheimer's judgment. "I've lain awake at night. This man had national
security responsibilities of the absolutely highest order. It was a question of what his judgment would be in the ultimate case and you had
no way of predicting when that case might be presented to him. I just
didn't go along with his judgment, particularly on security matters.
The scientists tend to have contempt for security anyhow. He had a
very condescending attitude toward security." Gray wondered
whether Oppie was unstable, while Zuckert wondered about his
judgment. It seemed to Zuckert afterward that, intellectually, he and
Gray were "on the same plane."[19]

But Zuckert's written opinion seems forced, as if every word had
to be wrung out of him. After the hearing, and after his departure as a
commissioner, Strauss kept him on as a consultant and did other minor favors for him but apparently did not offer Zuckert the one thing
that might have tempted him, a new term as commissioner. Harold
Green, who admired Zuckert as "a man of massive integrity," found
him, two or three days before the vote, intending to vote in Oppenheimer's favor. Something made him reconsider, presumably something more compelling than the last-minute changes in the majority
statement that he managed to obtain from Strauss. Phil Farley, an out-
standingly objective AEC employee, considered Zuckert an ambitious

man of limited ability who was worried that he did not have a job awaiting him after his term expired. "He didn't think Oppie was a security risk, he was afraid his own career would be at risk" if he voted the wrong way. Avoiding the enmity of Lewis Strauss, Farley thought, was probably sufficient.[20]

Zuckert's later years reeked of regret, and he told friends many times that it had wounded him to reach the conclusion he did. "Here was this brilliant, accomplished man. It hurt to be objective." And he would quote Supreme Court justice Abe Fortas, whom he had known since Yale Law School days. Fortas had told him that "there are times when you have to rise above principle," meaning that he should have voted to clear Oppenheimer because Oppie was exceptional. Joe Volpe, who was close to Zuckert, was convinced that he regretted his vote as long as he lived. Asked about it a decade before he died, Zuckert nodded. "It was the saddest thing I ever took part in. It cost me a lot of friendships and I had to be on the same side as people I did not respect."[21]

Do We Really Need Scientists?

ON THE AFTERNOON of June 29, the day the AEC announced the verdict in Washington, Strauss telephoned James Hagerty at the White House with news of the 4–1 vote. The president, who had just concluded a four-day visit with British prime minister Winston Churchill, called back to congratulate him on the "fine job" he had done and said he hoped Strauss's handling of the case "would be such a contrast to McCarthy's tactics that the American people would immediately see the difference."[1]

Throughout the Oppenheimer affair Strauss had consulted regularly with presidential press secretary James Hagerty, and on critical days he had met with Hagerty or the president first thing in the morning. He met at least a dozen other times with the president alone or his assistants Sherman Adams or Robert Cutler, and on some if not all of those occasions the hearing was a subject of discussion. In addition, the president's personal assistant, the normally acidulous Ann Whitman, made an exception for Strauss, whom she called "the sweetest man I ever did see," and gave him access to the Oval Office whenever he wanted a word with the president. Strauss had told Eisenhower, untruthfully, that the Oppenheimers had stayed with the Chevaliers for several days the previous winter, instead of having had two meals together, and this misinformation is said to have weighed heavily with Eisenhower. Strauss had told the president about the trouble he was having with the Democratic members of the commission, all three of whom, Murray, Zuckert, and Smyth, had, during the hearing, testified in Congress against his effort to codify his de facto role as ruler of the commission. The president was "concerned" by what Strauss told him about growing Democratic resistance to him inside the AEC and was "more determined than ever" to appoint someone who could work with Strauss when Zuckert's appointment expired at the end of June.[2]

In addition to Hagerty and the president himself, Attorney General Herbert Brownell had had a role in the case. Three years before his death he wrote the author, "I wasn't directly involved in the Oppenheimer affair, but I do recall that President Eisenhower took an active interest in the progress of the Gray board hearings and asked me to review their findings from the standpoint of procedural due process." The record shows, however, that Brownell had taken part in all the major decisions: the president consulted him before deciding to lower the "blank wall"; he gave the FBI permission to wiretap Oppenheimer's attorneys; and the day before the hearing began he spent three hours at Strauss's farm discussing, among other things, whether Oppenheimer might be subject to criminal charges.[3]

On the afternoon of June 29, when the commissioners' decision was announced, Strauss paused to honor and to thank. He called on J. Edgar Hoover at the FBI, and had dinner with the other Hoover, the former president who had made his career and on whom he still looked as a father. A day or two later he paid an afternoon visit to the president and celebrated over dinner with Charles Murphy and Frank Wisner. In many respects it was Murphy whose contribution was the most spectacular of all. Not only had he written the 1953 *Fortune* articles opening the attack on Oppenheimer, but he had been the first to realize that the Gray opinion was a disaster for the government, since it gave the impression that Oppenheimer was being punished for his opinions. He had taken charge immediately and masterminded the campaign to turn public opinion around. And he was principal author of the savage majority opinion. Which of them it was, Strauss, Robb, or Murphy, who coined the phrase "substantial defects in his character" is anybody's guess. One individual who knew Murphy well considered him the likeliest candidate, although any of the three could have done it.[4]

Recompense was in Strauss's mind, but Murphy refused payment, viewing what he had done as a public service. So Strauss did the next best thing—he shared his incomparable contacts. After the *Fortune* articles the year before he had, unsolicited, given Murphy an introduction to young King Baudouin of Belgium, who had come to his throne in difficult circumstances and was said to be looking for public relations help. Now that the Oppenheimer case was over, Strauss sent a car for Murphy in Georgetown one evening in August 1954 and had him delivered to his country home in Culpeper, Virginia. There, he told Murphy over a magnificent dinner that his friend Helen Rogers Reid was looking for someone to buy her newspaper, the *New York Herald Tribune*. Would Murphy like to be the editor?[5]

Of the two wild men Strauss had enlisted to help diminish Oppenheimer, one, Charlie Murphy, had stayed in harness and come through with flying colors. But what of the AEC chairman's other charger, Bill Borden? Borden was now working for Westinghouse in Pittsburgh, but he had not forgotten his glory days at the congressional committee. For him it was not enough that his letter to Hoover had prompted the president to take action against Oppenheimer: the scientist's destruction was merely act 1 of a two-part scenario which he and Strauss probably concocted together in the late summer or early fall of 1951. Act 2 was to make Teller the new Oppenheimer. And so in January 1954, Clay Blair, the twenty-nine-year-old Pentagon correspondent of *Time* magazine, received a letter postmarked Pittsburgh. The author of the letter congratulated Blair on his newly published book about Hyman Rickover, father of the nuclear-powered submarine. He added that the story of Edward Teller and the hydrogen bomb was equally impressive and expressed surprise that *Time* had not yet found room for Teller on its cover. The author's name was not familiar: William L. Borden.[6]

A week or so later Blair found himself in a mansion overlooking Rock Creek Park in Washington. Down from Pittsburgh for the weekend, Borden had invited Blair to his mother's house to tell him about Teller's battle to build the hydrogen bomb over the opposition of Robert Oppenheimer. And he had a story to tell! Blair's usual beat was the Navy and he did not know much about Teller and Oppenheimer, but what he was hearing reminded him of the story he had just written: Teller fought Oppie and the GAC to build the hydrogen bomb, Rickover was said to have fought the same opponents to build his nuclear sub, and Blair wondered what Oppenheimer had been up to, opposing these projects to strengthen the United States. Borden hinted at an answer: was Oppie, with his left-wing past, trying to help the Soviet Union? Borden did not mention Oppenheimer's being in trouble with the government or say anything about a prospective hearing. He struck Blair as disinterested, idealistic, anything but a huckster with something to sell.

Blair raced back to his office at *Time* on Connecticut Avenue and informed his bureau chief, James Shepley, that this guy Teller was a hell of a story. Shepley wanted to meet Borden, and Blair introduced them over lunch. He did not see Borden again.[7]

A week or two later, Shepley and Blair found themselves at the Tellers' house in California. Mici Teller cooked a "fabulous" dinner, Edward played Beethoven on the piano, and they had a "wild" evening lasting six or seven hours. Early in the evening, as Teller and Shepley discussed philosophers, Blair realized that Teller, like Rickover, had an "awesome" mind. One bibulous evening led to another as Teller dispatched them to San Diego to see Freddie de Hoffmann, Los Alamos to see Ulam, and Livermore to see Lawrence and York. Everyone they talked to seemed enthusiastic about Teller and the H-bomb.[8]

The fifteen-thousand-word "take," or raw file, that Blair wrote after his return created a sensation at *Time*. Although it was not yet in print (being raw material for the planned cover story), everyone in the New York office was reading it. Even Turner Catledge, top editor at the *New York Times,* got a glimpse of it and said that this young fellow Blair ought to get the Pulitzer. Given Blair's story and the flap it caused, it was natural for an outgoing, fabulously well connected *Fortune* writer with a desk in *Time*'s Washington bureau to take Blair under his wing. Charles J. V. Murphy was, as usual, commuting between Washington and New York, working on a dozen projects at once, but he had lost none of his enthusiasm for the Air Force. He introduced

Blair to what Blair later called the Air Force "cabal." The most flamboyant member of the cabal was Teddy Walkowicz, like Murphy a commuter to New York, where he advised Laurence Rockefeller on aviation investments. Walkowicz's franchise at the Pentagon appeared to be the care and feeding of the in-house Hungarians: Theodore von Karmann of the rocket program, Edward Teller, and Johnny von Neumann. Blair later remembered nonstop discussions of weapons systems in a tiny room in the science area of the Pentagon. At the blackboard a bald, emaciated professor would be jotting down statistics about the number of Russians who could be wiped out by a single atomic bomb, all the while sipping from a glass of milk for his ulcers. He was W. Barton Leach, wise man of the cabal and professor of property law on leave from the Harvard Law School. Another member was Colonel Bob Orr, a frequent source of Murphy's stories on science and strategy. The cabal was anti-Army, anti-Navy, anti-Russian, and out to "kill Oppenheimer" if they could. Blair later remembered the cabalists as "fanatics," very, very different from the low-key, intellectual-appearing Borden.[9]

That spring, _Time_'s Teller cover was shelved at Teller's request. He had learned that his mother and sister were alive and still in Hungary. He was worried about them, and the U.S. government was worried about him and the pressure he would be under from both the Russians and the Hungarians should their attention be drawn to his role in building the H-bomb. Blair started to interview Strauss with the idea of converting his Teller take into a book. And, always the prodigal friend, Charlie Murphy took Blair and Shepley to lunch with his book publisher, Ken Rawson (publisher also of the Duke and Duchess of Windsor) in New York, and a contract was signed for _The Hydrogen Bomb_.

By the time Blair learned about the Oppenheimer hearing, he said later, his book was three-quarters written. Fortunately his coauthor, James Shepley, a great reporter but one who lacked fluency and did little if any writing on the book, knew Gordon Gray. One day in June, Shepley called him into his office and, pointing to a stack of papers, explained that these were galleys of the Oppenheimer hearing. Blair's surprise turned to incredulity when Shepley told him that the transcript had been leaked to him by Gordon Gray.*

By now it was almost mid-June, and the book was due at the publisher's. For three or four days Shepley and Blair stayed up around the clock, feverishly extracting anecdotes from the testimony and back-feeding them into their manuscript. No sooner had they finished than Shepley had a summons from Lewis Strauss. The two reporters arrived at the AEC in early evening and, Blair recalled, found a fire going in Strauss's office. Strauss had been up all night reading their manuscript and greeted them with an astonishing offer: if they would agree to withhold publication, he would place twenty-five thousand dollars of his own funds in a safe-deposit box and it would be theirs upon his death. If the book was published now, he explained, the scientific community, which was already overwhelmingly in favor of Oppenheimer, would turn irrevocably against Teller. And that would undermine what he was trying to do: turn Teller into the new Oppenheimer.[10]

Blair and Shepley explained to Strauss that with everyone leaking to everyone else and most of the leakers convinced that Oppenheimer was a spy, there was no way to put twenty-five thousand dollars in a safe and make the story go away.

The authors met their deadline, and throughout the summer their book was at the publisher's in New York, ticking like a time bomb.

Most of the public was shocked by the verdict. As for the physicists, nearly all of whom had agreed with Oppie about the H-bomb, they began to wonder when *they* might be hauled before some tribunal and have their reputations ruined for opinions they had expressed years before, under wholly different circumstances. Vannevar Bush spoke for virtually the entire community when he wrote in the *New York Times* in June that the partnership between government and the scientists that had grown up during the war was being destroyed by a security

---

*The author doubts that Gray leaked the transcript and believes the leak was the work of one of Strauss's minions.

system gone wild. Bush pointed out that service to the government was not a privilege, as Lewis Strauss liked to say, but a duty, sometimes a disagreeable duty, which scientists would perform wholeheartedly only if they had confidence in the government. They had shown solidarity in defense of Oppenheimer because they believed he was being persecuted for expressing opinions that were not official policy of the moment. Scientists would not boycott government projects, Bush said, but they would work with a heavy heart—and at a moment when the country needed the utmost they could offer. He urged scientists to remain united and said that ordinary citizens, too, should ask whether they were being led into the "fallacies of totalitarianism."[11]

It was August before most of the scientists at the weapons labs had time to wade through the 992-page transcript. At Los Alamos, 493 scientists signed a statement of protest, and at the Argonne National Lab in Illinois, another 214. In a letter to the *Bulletin of the Atomic Scientists* Carson Mark, self-described "midwife" of the hydrogen bomb, compared the Oppenheimer hearing to the "Salem witchcraft delusion," and Vannevar Bush declared that nuclear research was nearly at a standstill because of Strauss's "gumshoeing" against the scientists. In an effort to stanch the damage, Strauss flew to Los Alamos to award the lab a presidential citation. But "Operation Butter-up," as the Los Alamites called it, fooled no one, and the scientists angrily told Strauss that the hearing had created a "very grave morale problem." To this day it is said that after Strauss snapped some photographs, Ralph Carlisle Smith, the lab's patent officer, confiscated the film on grounds that the picture taking had been a breach of security. A month or so later Harry Smyth was sent to New Mexico to pour oil on the troubled waters.[12]

Edward Teller visited Los Alamos that summer and had an experience he did not forget. After giving an interview to Robert Coughlan of *Life* magazine, Teller joined a picnic on the terrace outside Fuller Lodge. He went up to Bob Christy, an old friend who had shared his house in Chicago, and offered his hand. Christy looked at him coldly, refused his hand, and turned away. "I realized that my life as I had known it was over," Teller wrote later.[13]

Those who had been at the lab during the war could not help remembering Teller's wartime record: he had sat out "the main event," as Carson Mark called the effort to build the A-bomb, and chosen instead to work on the hypothetical hydrogen bomb just when all hands were needed to work on a bomb that would end the war. And those who had been present later, during work on the thermonuclear bomb, remembered him as a contentious colleague whose lobbying led to the establishment of a new laboratory at the very moment when Los Alamos was going all-out to test Mike. Now, as they read his testimony, they were appalled. He was Brutus. He had sunk his knife into Oppenheimer and betrayed every one of them.

Imagine their feelings when a book called *The Hydrogen Bomb: The Men, the Menace, the Mechanism* appeared that fall, accusing Oppenheimer, Bradbury, and the lab of what amounted to treason. The authors, James Shepley and Clay Blair, had written that Los Alamos during World War II had been "loaded with Communists and former Communists" hired by Oppenheimer. After Joe One, the lab, still "soft on Communism," had opposed the hydrogen bomb, and Oppenheimer's stooge, Bradbury, had dragged his feet. Even after Truman's decision, the authors claimed, Bradbury had refused to put his best men at Teller's disposal, and the lab had remained "indifferent, more often hostile," to the H-bomb. Most of the key wartime scientists had not only refused to participate in the program but had lobbied against it while, following their elders' lead, younger scientists had "stayed away in droves." Shepley and Blair charged that most of the lab members who attended the Greenhouse test in 1951 had been hoping for a failure. And they dealt with the Ulam-Teller breakthrough merely by saying that something Ulam suggested had "turned on a small light in Teller's storehouse of ideas" and that the laboratory continued to resist Teller's new approach. Oppenheimer, they said, opposed the new concept but at the June 1951 conference at Princeton had had no choice but to give in. Finally Teller realized that he was outflanked and that the nation would be in danger if he did not leave Los Alamos. Not until Livermore opened its doors was Los Alamos finally goaded into building the H-bomb.

The truth was that in 1954, when the book was written, Livermore had been in existence for two years and had so far had nothing but failures. It had held two tests, both designed by Teller, and they had been inglorious fizzles. Because of secrecy, Bradbury was not allowed to correct the record. All he could say was that Los Alamos had "developed every successful thermonuclear weapon that exists today in the free world."[14]

Gordon Dean, chairman of the AEC during the period in question, wrote that the book was "vicious" and that Shepley and Blair were like a pair of "plumbers going to work on a delicate Swiss watch." Along with everyone else in a responsible position, he worried about the harm their hatchet job might do to the weapons program. But he and Bradbury could respond only up to a point: the H-bomb, as Dean had said, was like a delicate Swiss watch whose workings could not be described because the name of each component was secret, as was the interaction between them. Only two people were in a position to discredit the Shepley-Blair book. The president wasn't going to do it because he had been deceived by Strauss and did not know the truth. And Strauss declined pleas from two of the parties who had been libeled, Bradbury and Dean, that he repudiate the volume. Likewise, he turned down an appeal from the ten Los Alamos division leaders on the specious ground that if he spoke out, it would boost sales. Strauss's refusal to repudiate the book was an act of unbelievable disloyalty, since he was head of the AEC, Los Alamos was his lab, and the scientists were his scientists. And it was painfully clear that many of the book's so-called facts could have come only from him.[15]

Bradbury was so outraged that on September 24 he gave an extraordinary press conference at Los Alamos, only the second such appearance he had ever made. Despite the stifling secrecy regulations, he managed to answer the book's most egregious calumnies. And, in his desire to set the record straight, he did something no one would be allowed to do even today: he held aloft what he called the "Ulam-Teller" paper of March 9, 1951, to let reporters know that Teller had not invented the H-bomb alone. There had been another author, and his contribution was such that perhaps the usual alphabetical order should be reversed to "Ulam-Teller." No one in the room had heard of Stanislaw Ulam, not even the best-informed among them, Robert McKinney, publisher of the *Santa Fe New Mexican,* and Bradbury had to spell out the name Ulam.

That fall Joseph and Stewart Alsop published a column asking, "Do we really need scientists, or can we just make do with Lewis Strauss?" The Alsops said that, coming on the heels of the hearing, the Shepley-Blair volume had "turned what was formerly a brush fire into a perfect conflagration of fury." That the book was the second part of a two-part plan to destroy Oppenheimer and make Teller the leader of the scientific community, and that both parts of the plan had been set in motion by William Borden, was known to no one except, perhaps, Lewis Strauss. One observer got the drift, however. Writing in the *Reporter* magazine, Elie Abel said that the book "set out to topple a particular god from his pedestal and to raise a new one in his place. The protagonists remain larger-than-life figures, casting portentous shadows on a darkened stage."[16]

Did Teller know that he was to be the beneficiary of Oppenheimer's downfall? Probably. But he would have given his testimony without that. For years he had been saying that Oppenheimer did not have good judgment. He had made secret statements against Oppie to the FBI since 1949 and to Borden and the JCAE since 1950, and had criticized him in devastating terms to the FBI on two occasions in 1952. Teller had not expected his testimony to be made public, and fear of becoming a pariah among scientists led him, within days of the commission's decision, to draft a press statement seeking to correct the impression that he might consider someone a security risk because of his opinions. He sent his proposed statement to Strauss, who in turn sent it to Roger Robb. Robb got back to Teller with an edited text but advised that silence was best. Teller followed Robb's advice and dropped the idea.[17]

Teller wrote Strauss a letter of thanks. "It is not possible for me to tell you in any short or simple way how grateful I am to you for many things you have done. The list would be too long and *the most*

important item I cannot mention" (italics added). The unmentionable
item had to do with Teller's relatives. Strauss had already spoken to
Allen Dulles, director of the Central Intelligence Agency, about getting Teller's mother, sister, and nephew out of Hungary. Now, after
receiving Teller's thanks, he sent Dulles a reminder.[18]

But Teller still wanted to retract. About the time the Shepley-Blair
volume appeared, an article lionizing him appeared in *Life* magazine
by another writer for the Luce publications, Robert Coughlan. It was
clear that Coughlan had not only drawn on Shepley and Blair's material in the *Time* files but had had help from Teller himself. All this
deepened the animosity of the other scientists and made Teller afraid
that he would be unable to set foot in Los Alamos again. He therefore
drafted an article outlining a history of the hydrogen bomb in which
he shared the credit.

Once again he consulted Strauss, who advised against publishing.
Meanwhile he had a letter from Laura Fermi telling him that her husband, Enrico, was dying of stomach cancer. Teller flew to Chicago to
see Fermi, bringing along a copy of his draft. Anxious to mend the split
among the scientists, Fermi asked to see it. He read for half an hour or
so, then looked up and inquired, "What reason would you have *not* to
publish this?" Teller explained that after all the criticism, he no longer
knew what to do. "Enrico advised me strongly and insistently to publish it."[19]

The article, "The Work of Many People," appeared in *Science*
magazine in February 1955. After recounting the early theoretical
discoveries of George Gamow, Bethe, and Fermi, Teller described
H-bomb work at Los Alamos, naming many of those who had contributed and singling out his protégé, Freddie de Hoffmann, for special praise. He credited Ulam and Everett with showing that early
calculations on the H-bomb had been in error and eliminating the
flawed model the lab had been working on, but added only that the
impasse had been broken by two hopeful indicators, "one an imaginative suggestion by Ulam, the other a fine calculation by de Hoffmann." He was modest about his own contribution, giving himself
credit mostly for his steadfast belief that the bomb could and should

be made. "I find myself in a position of being given certainly too much credit and perhaps too much blame for what has happened." He concluded that the H-bomb ought to unite, not divide, those who had contributed to it and warned, "Disunity of the scientists is one of the greatest dangers for our country."[20]

This was the most credit Teller would ever extend to Ulam. He gave many versions of the H-bomb story in the years ahead, and Ulam's role shrank with each version. One reason for this, he said, was that Ulam had not really believed the bomb would work, since he had cast doubt on it in a letter to von Neumann in 1951 ("Edward is enthusiastic, possibly a sign that it will not work"), and that if he did not believe in his own invention, then he did not deserve credit.

But Teller's outcast status bothered him and he wanted to make amends. In 1961, when he was writing a book called *The Legacy of Hiroshima*, Teller asked Lewis Strauss for advice about his chapter on the Oppenheimer case. Strauss warned that he would be seen as a "repentant witness" and advised him not to publish the chapter. Strauss also passed it along to Charles Murphy, who met with Teller three times in an effort to dissuade him and even brought Gordon Gray along. Murphy advised: "Believe me, Edward, I know how hard all this is for you. The world is also hard. It is replete with ambushes. I suggest that you walk warily and keep a sharp look in all directions."[21]

The Legacy of Hiroshima appeared the following year without a chapter on the Oppenheimer affair.

In the decade between 1944 and 1954, Teller had settled old scores. With the AEC hearing, he avenged himself on Oppenheimer for refusing to make him head of the Theoretical Physics Division of the Manhattan Project in 1944 and, very likely, for a number of perceived slights since then. With Livermore, he took revenge on Bradbury for refusing the conditions he had put on staying at Los Alamos in 1946 and refusing to place him in overall charge of the H-bomb program in 1951: if he couldn't be master of the first laboratory, he would have a laboratory of his own. The third case, that of Ulam, was the most complicated: Ulam had trumped Teller twice, once when he proved that the Super conceived by Teller was unworkable, and again when he himself conceived two of the three ideas that made the radiation-implosion bomb possible. To get even with Ulam for undermining his proudest claim, that of being father of the H-bomb, Teller avenged himself by trying to erase his rival from the history books and make him a nonperson.

Looking at all this, the Freudian observer might say that during the decade between 1944 and 1954 Teller symbolically destroyed each of the three men who had dealt him a severe narcissistic blow. The layperson might conclude, more simply, that he sought to destroy the three men who had stood in his way.

Oppenheimer

KITTY AND ROBERT returned to Princeton, where he continued to run the Institute for Advanced Study and she gardened in the greenhouse they had built at Olden Manor. Ten-year-old Toni and fourteen-year-old Peter came home from the Hempelmanns' in Rochester, New York, where they had stayed in May, and that summer the four of them went sailing off St. John's, in the Virgin Islands. Meanwhile, Lewis Strauss tried to build a majority on the institute's board of trustees for firing Robert.

Robert did not tell his closest friends in the physics community, Rabi, Bethe, Victor Weisskopf, and Abraham Pais, about this new humiliation, and when the trustees voted on October 1 to retain him, it was with McGeorge Bundy, who had helped draft the Oppenheimer panel report two years before, Mary Bundy, and newspaper columnist Joe Alsop that Kitty and Robert celebrated at the Alsops' family home in Avon, Connecticut. Physicist friends of Robert's who still had Q clearances and had stayed on as advisers to the government found themselves in an excruciating position. Virtually everything they had discussed with him during the past dozen years, all the questions about weapons policy, were off limits now. Old friends from Pasadena like Bacher and Lauritsen made a point of visiting when they were in the East, and Bethe and Weisskopf when they were anywhere near Princeton, but as Rabi's daughter Nancy Lichtenstein said later, it was as though they had been cut off in midconversation with Robert.

The autumn after the hearing Schatzi Davis, wife of lab member Bob Davis and neighbor of the Oppenheimers' at Los Alamos, went to see them and found everything changed. Instead of dust in the air and Navajo rugs on the floor and the smell of one of Kitty's pot roasts on the stove, instead of Robert's coming home from work filled with life and eager to see his family, she found the two of them spent and rather formal and sad. Even the food and the serving of it were different—a coddled egg, a butler, a canned half peach without liqueur—and, seeing how it all had changed, Schatzi could not hold back tears. Desperate to change the mood, Robert took her to inspect their new refrigerator, then went off alone to his study.

Robert was more of a presence at the institute than he had been when he was commuting to Washington, and his friends Harold Cherniss and Freeman Dyson thought he was a better director. As he had done before at Berkeley and Los Alamos, he had built the institute into one of the world's great centers of physics, and while he no longer did much original work in physics himself, he stayed abreast through institute luminaries such as T. D. Lee and Dyson and Abraham Pais, and went right on making his famously downputting remarks at seminars. At home and abroad, he lectured on larger questions of science and human values and took up with a group of cold war intellectuals clustered around the Congress for Cultural Freedom of Paris and New York, a group later found to have been secretly funded by the CIA. One of his most valued friends in the congress and at the institute was George Kennan, whose appointment as a permanent faculty member Oppenheimer secured in 1955 over the fierce opposition of the institute's fractious mathematicians.

Dyson, who frequently came upon Kitty up to the elbows in earth in her greenhouse, and Cherniss, a great listener who saw a good deal of Robert, thought the Oppenheimers recovered surprisingly well. But nearly everyone else thought they were devastated. This was especially obvious with Kitty, who had been Robert's chief support and on occasion could still put up a valiant front. But even during Los Alamos days, Kitty used to drink more than was good for her, and now her drinking grew worse. Alcohol, together with medicine she took for her pancreatitis, made her already sharp tongue even sharper. The atmosphere around her could be withering, and the children suffered. Peter, to whom by all accounts she was not a loving parent, said years later, "My father's tragedy was not that he lost his clearance, but my mother's slow descent into the hell of alcoholism." Then he added, "Cut that word 'slow.' "[1]

Early in their marriage Kitty had made Robert break with old acquaintances, and now her biases about people and her not infrequent cruelty drove even loyal friends away. If a woman who at some time or other had meant something to Robert came to see them, Kitty would withdraw to her bedroom and make her displeasure unmistakably plain. Ruth Tolman, widow of Oppie's mentor Richard Tolman, was one of these; Anne Marks, wife and then widow of Herb Marks, was another; and so was Robert's favorite cousin, Babette, who after Hiroshima had sent him a postcard of congratulations: "We always knew you'd set the world on fire."

Peter Oppenheimer, now in his sixties, says that his father coped well. But George Kennan observed that Kitty was a grave liability in Robert's relationships with others. "He was accused of being arrogant, but she made him more arrogant than he was and would egg him on to be intolerant of this or that person. If he hadn't been a pretty strong person and had a touching devotion and a willingness to put up with almost anything, he'd have been destroyed by her as the children were. I think she was a great burden to him." Even those who agreed with Kennan—and nearly everybody did—conceded that the Oppenheimers were, in the words of one witness, "welded" to each other, that they were deeply and mutually loyal, and that, along with the destructiveness, they gave each other unqualified support.[2]

Verna Hobson, Oppenheimer's secretary, a person of great distinction, saw Robert up close. She had worked for him for nearly a year when, around Christmas of 1953, she saw that he was in trouble. After she had made what she calls, without specifying, "a gesture of trust," he invited her into his office, told her about his earlier life as a fellow traveler, and asked her to be his principal secretary. When, soon afterward, seeing the toll the hearing was taking on him, she urged him to fight tooth and nail, his response made her realize that, as he saw it, the hearing was the unavoidable outcome, not of any single misstep, such as his humiliation of Strauss at the isotopes hearing, but of his entire life and the way he had lived it. It was this sense that the government had pronounced judgment on him, not for what he had done, but for what he was, that kept him from walking out as Volpe suggested. He had to fight *his* way, and Mrs. Hobson believed it was this that led him to choose the gentlemanly Lloyd Garrison as his attorney. She had no sense that he ever felt, as Kitty and many of his friends did, that Garrison failed him.[3]

But from feeling that the hearing was inevitable, how far was it to feeling that his prosecutors were right and that he was guilty of *something*, even if not of the specific offenses with which he was charged? For a man who, for all the vaunted "arrogance," had lived most of his life in a state of existential uncertainty, what was it like to be pronounced unworthy because of "substantial defects in his character"? Was it not crushing confirmation of what, beneath the mystique, he had believed all along?

Verna Hobson later said that Oppenheimer's growth during his last ten years or so was the most exciting thing she had ever witnessed. By this she meant primarily that he grew in his capacity for relationships and in his understanding of others. His time as a Harvard undergraduate had been "perfect," he told her, except that he had had no talent for friendship then. Mrs. Hobson, like Joe Volpe, pointed to something else. After the hearing, Oppenheimer never said a word in public to disparage the AEC—much though there was to disparage. Nor was he critical of the government. Once again, just as at his trial, the government counted on his loyalty even as it tried to destroy him.

In smaller ways, Oppenheimer still fell short of the perfection he required of himself. He was a "totally demanding" boss, expecting Mrs. Hobson, when she first worked for him, to take dictation in English, French, and German and in mathematical formulas. He preempted the private lives of those who worked for him. And when the White House announced in April 1963 that President Kennedy would present him with the Fermi Prize that fall, Robert "could hardly bear it" and wanted to decline. "But of course you have to accept," she told him. "I know," he said. But he hated the whole thing—because Teller had won the year before, and because the award to him was so clearly a political gesture.

When the time came, within days of the Kennedy assassination, for President Johnson to present the award in a White House ceremony, Oppenheimer performed graciously and did not blanch even when Teller maneuvered himself within camera range in order to be photographed shaking his hand. It was a "bittersweet" occasion, Anne Marks said, and Kitty Oppenheimer saluted it in her own way. She went to New York and, for ten thousand dollars, bought a mink coat, a slender, saronglike wrap in which she was resplendent. When someone asked Robert what he was going to do with the prize money, he said, "I've already spent it."[4]

We Made It—and We Gave It Away

THE BRITISH TESTED their first hydrogen weapon in 1957, and the three thermonuclear powers, the United States, Britain, and the USSR, conducted larger and larger tests in the Pacific. The public began to worry about radioactive fallout, and when the Democratic candidate, Adlai Stevenson, proposed a self-enforcing ban on large-scale nuclear tests during the presidential election campaign of that year, he did so, ironically, on the advice of Thomas Finletter and Thomas Murray, two of the most avid proponents of the H-bomb—and opponents of Robert Oppenheimer—only a short while before. In 1957 *On the Beach*, a novel about nuclear war by Australian writer Neville Shute, was an overnight bestseller, and popular response to appeals by Bertrand Russell and Prime Minister Jawaharlal Nehru of India for a test ban showed that men and women the world over were alarmed by the dangers of nuclear testing in the atmosphere. In 1958 Nikita Khrushchev, now more or less firmly in the saddle as leader of the Soviet Union, and the safely reelected Dwight Eisenhower embarked on test-ban talks in Geneva and began a test moratorium that lasted three years.

Lewis Strauss tried to apply the brakes. In 1957 he brought three test ban opponents from Livermore, Edward Teller, Ernest Lawrence, and Mark Mills, into the Oval Office, where they promised Eisenhower that a "clean," or fallout-free, bomb could be developed with a mere seven more years of atmospheric testing. Doubts next arose about whether small tests underground could be distinguished from seismic events, such as earthquakes, and these doubts—doubts about Soviet cheating—were fanned by Teller and others for decades.

When Kennedy and Khrushchev agreed in 1963, after the Cuban missile crisis, to ban nuclear testing in the atmosphere, and a limited test ban treaty was initialed in Moscow, Teller testified against it in the U.S. Senate. To him belongs a large share of responsibility for the fact that a comprehensive test ban treaty, banning tests underground as well as in the atmosphere, was never ratified. With his heavy eyebrows, his Hungarian accent, and his only partly deserved reputation as father of the H-bomb, Teller was a mesmerizing advocate of his pie-in-the-sky schemes. Just as he persuaded President Eisenhower for a brief time in 1957 that a "clean" bomb was possible, so, twenty-five years later, he persuaded President Reagan that the perfect defensive shield known casually as "Star Wars" could be achieved.

Strauss's influence persisted, too. At first he adopted Eisenhower's Atoms for Peace idea as a way to preempt Oppenheimer's Operation Candor, but he and the president sincerely hoped by way of the Geneva conferences of 1955 and 1958 to promote the use of atomic energy for peaceful purposes. What neither Strauss nor Eisenhower understood was that the facilities required to produce electricity by way of nuclear fission could also be used to make nuclear weapons. The Russians, of course, did understand, and Soviet foreign minister Vyacheslav Molotov wasted no time asking Secretary of State John Foster Dulles what on earth the Americans thought they were doing, proposing to spread weapons-grade nuclear material all over the world. It is the ironic legacy of the secrecy-obsessed Strauss that he was promoter of a program that has contributed to the spread of nuclear knowledge—and nuclear weapons—throughout the world.[1]

Percival King, an experimental physicist who specialized in reactors, observed the consequences of Strauss's ignorance at close range. Before the Geneva conference of 1958, Strauss, as AEC chairman, offered generous funding to three laboratories for peaceful fusion research. No one, not even Teller, thought that peaceful hydrogen power lay around the corner, and one of the scientists to whom funds were offered declined it for himself and his lab. But Strauss refused to be coached in physics. He counted on a breakthrough and believed that peaceful thermonuclear power would develop rapidly enough so that by 1956 or

1957 he would be the big man. King thought there was an element of competition here. Teller was father of the H-bomb; Strauss would be the father of peaceful hydrogen power. He was certain that if he threw enough money at the problem, scientists would solve it. They, on the other hand, felt that they ought to be in on decisions such as this one—political decisions—so as to help the government avoid wasting valuable resources on projects that defied the laws of nature.

The scientists came into their own again, and Strauss's influence receded, after the Russians launched *Sputnik,* the world's first artificial satellite, in October 1957. The president took it calmly, but from his intelligence he knew that the Russians had already launched an intercontinental missile—the first in the world—and that they were developing increasingly powerful thermonuclear warheads. The fact that the boosters that had lofted *Sputnik* into space would soon be able to deliver the hydrogen bomb meant that a new era was at hand—and the president knew it. Later that autumn he convened a large group of scientists. At the meeting, I. I. Rabi asked for the floor and suggested that the president bring scientists directly into the White House to advise him on the technological problems raised by the Soviet success. Rabi was known for his genius at coming up with the right solution at the right moment, and he had the backing of the scientific community. The president accepted his proposal, and an advisory panel that had previously been attached to the State Department was upgraded, brought into the White House, and christened the President's Scientific Advisory Committee (PSAC). James Killian, president of MIT, became its chairman. From then on, President Eisenhower began to get the kind of informed scientific judgment he should have been receiving all along, and would have but for his misplaced faith in Lewis Strauss. It was ironic that scientists should have regained some of their old clout under the very president who had overseen the demolition of Oppenheimer, and typical of the scientists of that era that they served him in spite of what had happened.

And there were other ironies. During the debate over whether to build the H-bomb, there had been almost no discussion of how the bomb was to be delivered. The Air Force drove the debate, and the

Strategic Air Command begged the question by demanding more and bigger airplanes for itself. The Russians were wiser. They saw that aircraft wouldn't do, and that an H-bomb without an intercontinental missile to deliver it made little sense. So they started intensive work on rocketry well ahead of the United States. In means of delivery, if not in small, sophisticated warheads, they had outstripped us. With all its lobbying for bigger bombs and bigger bombers, and its labeling as "traitors" those, like Oppenheimer, who stood in its way, the Air Force had not helped our military posture but had held us back. The generals had failed to see that the future lay not with bombers but with missiles. Scientists on the PSAC and on a pair of other high-powered committees went to work and in time made up for what one called "seven lost years" in developing long-range missiles.[2]

Strauss, who for four years had controlled the access of scientists to the president, was furious, and sabotaged the PSAC whenever he could. Killian, not one to magnify personal differences, nonetheless noticed that Strauss could be a charming host, welcoming him and Mrs. Killian to his apartment at the Shoreham and his farm in Virginia, but that at work he battled the head of the PSAC at every turn and did his utmost to block Killian's access to the president.

Eisenhower was delighted with his new scientific advisers. People in Washington, he complained, had axes to grind, but scientists were trained to be objective. He soon began to call on the PSAC for advice in matters outside science. But he never realized how badly Lewis Strauss had served him. When Strauss left the AEC in 1959, the president nominated him to be secretary of commerce, a job Strauss coveted because it had been held by his mentor, Herbert Hoover. After long and contentious hearings, however, the nomination was rejected by the Senate, only the eighth time in American history that a cabinet nominee had been turned down. One of the reasons the senators gave was "defects of character," the very words the AEC had used when it took away Oppenheimer's clearance. The president, having no understanding of the resentments stirred by the Oppenheimer case, was enraged. And in another ironic twist, Strauss, who could be so callous in inflicting harm on others, almost literally wept on the president's shoulder. In later years Lewis and Alice Strauss visited the Eisenhowers at Gettysburg, and for the rest of their lives the two men corresponded about their hobby of cattle breeding.

At least in the short run, the two sets of hearings during the spring of 1954 served the president's purposes. The Army-McCarthy hearings led to the Senate resolution in December of that year censuring the demagogue from Wisconsin and ended by breaking McCarthy's power. And, dominating the headlines as they did, they drowned out the Oppenheimer hearing and helped stifle debate over the momentous issues that had led to it. As Eisenhower's biographer Stephen Ambrose pointed out, the uproar over McCarthy enabled the president and Strauss to get rid of Oppenheimer with no public discussion of whether it had been a breach of policy or morality to build the H-bomb. Similarly, the McCarthy hearings diverted public attention from the fears aroused by the Bravo test and obscured the fact that thanks to both Truman and Eisenhower, the United States was now engaged in an all-out hydrogen bomb race with the Russians.

Mike, the November 1952 test of the Ulam-Teller principles that Bush, Bethe, and Oppenheimer had hoped at the very least to postpone, was the watershed marking the world's entry into the thermonuclear age. By the time of the next American test, Bravo in March 1954, the Russians had developed instruments that showed that the Americans had indeed made a breakthrough. Under tremendous pressure to keep up, Andrey Sakharov and Yakov Zeldovich in Moscow also made a breakthrough and, about the time of the Oppenheimer hearing, came up with their own version of the Ulam-Teller concept. A year and a half later, in Central Asia, the Russians tested their first radiation-implosion bomb.

Once again—Hiroshima in 1945 being the first time, Truman's H-bomb announcement of 1950 the second, and Mike in 1952 the third—the United States had led the way in the competition to build weapons of mass destruction.

At the end of World War II, scientists were heroes. It was scientists who had made possible an end to the fighting in time to save the hundreds of thousands of American lives that, but for the atomic bomb, would have ebbed away on the shores of Japan. It did not occur to anyone that these same scientists would now turn their talents to the political arena.

It did occur to those who had worked on the bomb, the young Los Alamos physicist Charles Critchfield for one. On August 16, 1945, days after the Japanese surrender, Critchfield wrote a memo saying that, with the coming of peace, the responsibility for the effects of science on human beings would shift from politicians to the scientists themselves. It had to happen, he said, because scientists would be the first to understand the effects of their discoveries on humanity.

Only a few weeks later physicists, chemists, and metallurgists poured out of the laboratories that had produced the bomb—Chicago's Met Lab, Oak Ridge in Tennessee, Los Alamos in New Mexico—to protest the May-Johnson bill, legislation drawn up by the War Department that would have kept atomic energy under military control. Scientific statesmen who, under pressure of war, had found a way to cooperate with the Army—Oppenheimer, Arthur Compton, James Conant, and Vannevar Bush—favored May-Johnson and believed that the military men they had dealt with, men like General George C. Marshall and former secretary of war Henry L. Stimson, could be trusted with management of the atom. But other, mostly junior, scientists who had worked on the bomb wanted no part of the military, with its secrecy and the obedience to orders from above that were stifling to the spirit of invention. On the basis of their experience with General Groves, they wanted to keep work on atomic weapons free of the Army's system of command and open to the adventurous, questioning spirit that had made their great achievement possible.

The passion with which these men pleaded their case and the awe in which atomic scientists now were held by Congress and the public proved surprisingly persuasive, and May-Johnson was quietly shelved. In its place Congress passed the McMahon Act, which physicists and mathematicians had helped to draft and which provided for civilian control. There was no reason why the scientists' cleverness should have extended to writing laws and lobbying Congress. But those who had contributed to the stunning white flash over the desert at Alamogordo in July 1945 were aware that they had handed man a strange new power, the power to alter nature, and, as Critchfield wrote, they felt that it was up to them to exercise responsibility.

They created their own organization, the Federation of Atomic Scientists (now the Federation of American Scientists), and a journal of their own, and they taught academic courses, gave public lectures, and wrote articles in the press. But the vehicle through which they exercised their responsibility most effectively during the early years after the war was the General Advisory Committee of the Atomic Energy Commission, the civilian agency created by the McMahon Act. The nine members of the GAC, as it was called, were nearly all senior scientists who had played leading roles in the Manhattan Project. They were brilliant men with no ax to grind except passion to save the world from atomic war, and, surprisingly, they were very nearly the only people in government with any real understanding of atomic weapons. Because of the members' disinterestedness and ability, the GAC from 1947 to 1952, the Oppenheimer years, acquired remarkable authority inside the government. And much of that authority it owed to Oppenheimer himself, with his mastery of atomic physics, his brilliance at synthesizing the opinions of others, and his breathtaking command of language.

The Oppenheimer GAC suffered two major defeats: President Truman's decision in 1950 to go full steam ahead with the H-bomb, and the Defense Department's decision two years later to build a second nuclear weapons laboratory. But it was the Oppenheimer hearing that put an end to the unique partnership between scientists and the government. By taking away the clearance of the man who had replaced Albert Einstein as the public face of scientific genius, the government told the scientists: We want your work, but we don't want you. We want the fruit of your research, but we have no use for the deeper wisdom you acquired as you were exploring the laws of nature. The hearing marked the end of the scientists' putting themselves and their imaginations on the line to help government with the long-range problems they had created.

Nearly three decades later, in a speech at Los Alamos in 1983, Rabi took the scientific community to task for allowing its political power to slip away. In a speech entitled "How Well We Meant," Rabi said that he and others had known when they saw the fireball at Alamogordo that they were witnessing the end of one world and the beginning of another. "We now had a power that put humanity on a new plane. And, having given this great power to our country, we were in a position to start on a new road." At first, he said, the generals seemed to agree with the scientists, but then they returned to their old ways. The men who created the bomb, on the other hand, had no way of escaping *their* responsibility. "It's gotten out of our hands and how to recover that?" Rabi asked. "We meant well and we sort of abdicated. We gave it away. We gave away the power to people who didn't understand it." In conclusion he lamented what happens when scientists "hand over the products of their knowledge to people who don't have it, to people who don't have the fundamental feeling and appreciation, who don't have a feeling for the glory of the human spirit, who don't respect science as such."

The question at issue was secrecy. Without the suffocating effects of secrecy, none of the events of the 1945–1955 decade would have happened in the way they did and some would not have happened at all. During the Manhattan Project, Oppenheimer had navigated superbly the impasse between the scientists' desire to share their research and the Army's insistence on secrecy. But after the war, because he advocated the Acheson-Lilienthal plan and opposed the H-bomb, Oppenheimer was accused by some of wanting to "give away the secret," as if there were some single, magic secret to the atomic bomb. Lewis Strauss warned before the hearing began that if the case were lost, the atomic energy program would "fall into the hands of left-wingers." The government, he added, would have "another Pearl Harbor" on its hands and scientists would take over the program. Three decades later Charles Bates, the FBI's point man during the hearing, complained to the author that "scientists observe no restrictions. They exchange information about everything. They said that any information a scientist develops, he should be free to pass on to anyone anywhere. I got so sick of hearing that, because scientists are no different from the rest of us."[3]

"That was Oppenheimer's idea," Bates added, "but it was not his government's idea, and it was the government that was paying the bills. Without the government's resources, the bomb could not have been developed. Without the government's money, labs, and support of all kinds, the scientists could not have made these discoveries, yet they had little patience for government restrictions and felt that scientific information ought to be exchanged in complete freedom." Bates overstated the views of Oppenheimer and the other scientists, and the dilemma of which he spoke is now more complex than it was in Oppenheimer's time. A scientific discovery in our time is likely to be not the work of a solitary researcher or a small team working with improvised equipment, but the product of a big team in an expensive lab operating with government funds. In such conditions the scientist is less and less likely to speak out against government policies. Today, for example, there is scarcely a physicist who thinks the Strategic Defense Initiative or its successor, National Missile Defense, can be made to work in anything like the way the Defense Department claims. Some disbelievers, however, accept government funds for the project in hopes of making an ancillary contribution to science, and cover their doubts with silence. The public has been lied to as a result, and billions of dollars have been wasted on an illusion.

The Oppenheimer hearing claims our attention not only because it was unjust but because it undermined respect for independent scientific thinking at a time when such thinking was desperately needed. Had there been no Oppenheimer affair, the government would almost surely have tried to find some other way to chasten scientists and let them know who was boss. "The more we grew," Rabi said, "the more we, the committee [the GAC], the scientists, grew in influence, the greater the worry that they were losing power." He concluded, "Science can be misused. And it's natural to misuse it, natural for politicians, people in power. It gives them a great deal of power, personal power and national power. You give politicians and people in government more power than they have the imagination and spiritual equipment to have."[4]

Among the scientists who created the bomb there were heroes, men who understood what they had done and tried desperately, each in his way, to control the outcome. Hans Bethe was one; Philip Morrison was another; Norris Bradbury, Jerrold Zacharias, Carson Mark, Victor Weisskopf, and Andrey Sakharov tried, and there were others. Of them all, Robert Oppenheimer was the American who could see the furthest, was the most articulate, had the tragic sense. If anyone could have moderated man's rush to extermination, or at least articulated the danger with such eloquence that we would all have been forced to consider, it was Robert Oppenheimer.

Postlude

WHEN I WROTE to him in the fall of 1985, Henry DeWolf Smyth did not want to see me. "Why exhume the case now?" he wrote. "It will only reopen old wounds." He was still reluctant when I arrived at the big old wooden house in Princeton. "Oppenheimer is dead," he said to me at the door. "His wife and daughter are dead. Strauss is dead. All the others are dead."[1]

But as we entered the airy paneled library, he reproached me for another reason. "Why didn't you come to me first? After all, I wrote the only dissent." Apart from his fair skin, everything about Harry Smyth was gray. His suit was dark gray, his hair was gray, the air around him seemed gray—and charged with loneliness. There were books all over the floor, so many of them that I had trouble picking my way to a chair. Dr. Smyth explained that he was giving them away in order to make room for more. This gentleman is not going to acquire more books, I said to myself. He is getting rid of them for another reason. I thought this because each time a new name entered the conversation he would ask, "Have you been to see him—or is he dead, too?"

Dr. Smyth was eighty-seven years old when I saw him in December 1985. He had been an obscure professor of physics at Princeton forty years earlier when, after the dropping of the atomic bomb, the U.S. government published *Atomic Energy for Military Purposes,* the official story of the building of the bomb. The book was christened the *Smyth Report,* and the author became famous overnight as governments and scientists the world over vied with one another to obtain copies. With the report, Smyth's notable public career began. He served for five years (1949–1954) as a member of the Atomic Energy Commission in Washington, and in 1961 President Kennedy named him U.S. ambassador to the International Atomic Energy Agency in Vienna, a job he performed with distinction for nearly a decade.

While he felt that the job in Vienna mattered more than anything else he had done, Dr. Smyth seemed aware, with some regret, that history would remember him best for his dissent in the Oppenheimer case. Talking about the case upset him, and as he was describing the tense night of June 28, 1954, when he wrote his opinion, he called in his secretary, Grace Anderson, and instructed her to take down his words. He pointed to a leather-bound copy of the hearing transcript and told me to open it to page 1063. He had marked the page with the letter I had written asking to meet with him. Near the top of the page, there was a word he wanted to change. In an early version of his opinion, he explained, he had called Oppenheimer's conduct in the Chevalier affair "unforgivable," but Lewis Strauss had remonstrated with him: "You said it was unforgivable, but then you forgave it." So in the final version, Smyth used the weaker "inexcusable." Now, three decades later, he wanted to soften his appraisal a little more. He wished the sentence to read "The Chevalier incident involved temporary concealment of an espionage attempt and admitted lying, and is *unfortunate*" (italics added).

Did you realize how strongly Strauss felt about getting rid of Oppenheimer? I asked. "Yes," Smyth replied, and then he told me an astonishing story. When he informed Strauss, the winter before the hearing, that he planned to resign in the fall, Strauss, without a moment's pause, started offering him inducements to leave right away, so that he would be unable to vote on Oppenheimer's clearance. "Twice between January and June he offered me bribes." First he offered Smyth "a fancy job somewhere" that, Smyth found out later, had not been his to offer. Then he made an offer that was almost past belief—Oppie's job. "He said he assumed that Oppenheimer would not want to continue as director of the Institute for Advanced Study after the ordeal he was going through and therefore he, as chairman of the institute's board of trustees, was searching for a new director.

He described the qualifications he was looking for, and they were nearly identical to qualities I would like to think I possessed. He didn't go quite so far as to say that he wanted someone with degrees from both Princeton and Cambridge University, but he came close. They were qualifications no one else could have possessed." Smyth, who had engaged in a running battle with Strauss over procedures in the Oppenheimer case and other crucial issues, told me how he felt in Strauss's presence. "When I went to see him in his office, I was glad to get out. I didn't want my back to him. I'd have made a perfect target."

When I asked whether Strauss had retaliated against him for his dissent, Smyth said no; he had seen no sign, for example, of Strauss's trying to have him removed from his tenured job at Princeton. "Mrs. Smyth had money," he told me, "so there was nothing he could do." But he had been in no doubt that Strauss would have taken revenge if he could have. "After the case was over, Lewis suggested that I resign, but I refused. I said it would be bad for the country and bad for the scientific community to show that the commissioners were so badly split. I told him I would resign at the end of summer, and I did."

During the hearing Smyth carried out all his day-to-day duties at the commission. He had even flown to the Pacific for the Bravo test. Throughout that time—the hearing, the Gray board's deliberations, the month of June just before the final decision—Strauss had insisted on his right, as chairman, to act as the commission's sole spokesman. He himself saw two or three newspapermen a day but treated any other commissioner who talked to the press like a pariah. Along with two other commissioners, Smyth openly disagreed with this policy. Then he and his spirited wife, Mary, devised a way of seeing to it that the chairman's was not the only view to come before the public. On Friday, May 14, 1954, Mary Smyth wrote in her diary, "JR here for talk with M," JR being James Reston of the *New York Times,* and the next day she wrote, "Al Friendly here to talk with M." Al Friendly was a reporter for the *Washington Post.* She was pleased with the result and on Sunday wrote, "Reston article just what I wanted." The next week she wrote, "M. to see Alsop suddenly," and a couple of evenings later, "Stewart Alsop asks to talk here with us two hours." In this fashion husband and wife saw to it that the public got a fuller picture than it would have otherwise.[2]

Smyth's independence and his belief, as he wrote in his opinion, that the security "system itself is nothing to worship," were exemplified by his handling of Mary's papers after she died. Mary Smyth's diary included a day-by-day account of the Oppenheimer case and Strauss's efforts to doctor the record. After she died in 1980, Harry Smyth, correct and proper though he was in every way, shipped her diary and other papers not to the AEC's successor agency, the Department of Energy, where they might be moldering to this day under a "classified" stamp, but to the American Philosophical Society in Philadelphia. There, in her bold, penciled handwriting, any visitor can read "Items of Possible Interest in Oppenheimer File," "M's Summary on Strauss Data," and dozens of other legal-sized pages documenting Strauss's deceptions from the moment he became chairman of the AEC.

Smyth told me why he had not especially warmed to Oppenheimer. "He was arrogant, and I think that is a dangerous trait when it comes to security. But what an incredible, magnificent job he did at Los Alamos! He was just about the last person I'd have picked for it." Wondering why Oppenheimer did not walk out of the hearing, as Volpe urged him to do, Smyth had concluded that Oppie was disarmed by the sheer brutality of the attack. He had expected something, but nothing this savage. Had the hearing changed him? "Oh, yes," came the reply. "It killed him."

Smyth did not remember that Oppenheimer had expressed much gratitude to him afterward. "He may have said, 'Thank you.'" But the record is a generous one on both sides. Days after the verdict, on July 5, 1954, Oppenheimer wrote:

Dear Harry:
    For the past weeks you and Mary have been in my thoughts more than anyone else; and, since the 29th, I have thought often of the skill, fortitude and high courage of your action. . . . It has needed no telling for me to know how great a toll this effort will

have taken of you. I wish for you both some quiet and some restoration, and that peace in an act of courage and honor that you have won for all of us and for all time.

    With admiration and affection,
      Robert[3]

When Oppenheimer died in February 1967, just short of his sixty-third birthday, Smyth, who had just flown across the Atlantic to bury his mother, made a second flight back from Vienna within a day or two to deliver a eulogy at Oppenheimer's memorial service in Princeton.

Kitty died of a mysterious infection in Panama in 1972 while sailing to Japan with her friend and Robert's, Bob Serber. Toni committed suicide in 1977 after the failure of her second marriage. Peter Oppenheimer lives today in a place he loves, Santa Fe, forty miles from Los Alamos, and knows everything there is to know about the Manhattan Project. Like his father and his own three children, Peter has spent much of his life worrying about the legacy of atomic weapons that Robert Oppenheimer left behind.

ACKNOWLEDGMENTS

THIS BOOK is the work of many hands and minds besides my own, first and foremost, Samuel B. Ballen and the J. Robert Oppenheimer Memorial Committee of Los Alamos and Santa Fe. Thanks to them I met, early on, pioneers of the atomic and hydrogen bomb projects whose views have informed my own: George Bell, Hans and Rose Bethe, Norris Bradbury, Charles Critchfield, Robert Raymond Davis, Percival L. D. P. King, Jim and Betty Lilienthal, M. Stanley Livingston, John and Kay Manley, Carson and Kay Mark, Louis Rosen, Max Roy, Raemer Schreiber, Richard Slansky, Robert Thorn, Robert Walker, and Jacob Wechsler.

Through them I also met Harold P. Green; Lee Hancock; Frank, Judith, and Peter Oppenheimer; Cyril and Alice Smith; Victor Weisskopf; Jane and Robert Wilson; and Jerrold Zacharias.

I owe a particular debt to an old and dear friend, Nancy Lichtenstein, to her husband, Immanuel, and to her parents, Helen and I. I. Rabi.

Others who knew the Oppenheimers well and whom I wish to thank especially include Ruth and Harold Cherniss, Priscilla Greene Duffield, "Shotsy" Durgin, Eleanor and Louis Hempelmann, George Kennan, Anne Marks, Honora Fergusson Neumann, Abraham Pais, Joseph Volpe, and Stephen White.

Sad to say, many of these individuals, some of them dear to me, are gone now, but I thank them from the bottom of my heart.

The challenge to anyone writing about the events in this book is that for decades key materials were classified, and many remain classified still. The veil lifted a little in the late 1970s, after passage of the Freedom of Information Act, when portions of Robert Oppenheimer's FBI file were released. As far as I know, the first person to use these documents in the FBI reading room was Caroline Davidson, in the course of her research for BBC producer Peter Goodchild, and I wish to thank her for sharing her notes with me after her work was done. Next to be reviewed for declassification were papers of the Joint Congressional Committee on Atomic Energy, which were bottled up entirely until 1987 and have now been released in part. Finally, beginning in 1993, Energy Secretary Hazel O'Leary took a fresh look at her department's secrecy policies, and some of the AEC's documents on the H-bomb program, the Second Lab affair, and the Oppenheimer hearing were declassified. As these materials became available, the work of historians of nuclear weapons became intensely collegial and many of us shared our discoveries with one another. I owe a particular debt to Gregg Herken for his generosity, as well as to R. Standish Norris, Richard Rhodes, and Silvan Schweber, and to the late Stanley Goldberg and Chuck Hansen. I am indebted also to Steven Aftergood, Brian Balogh, Barton Bernstein, William Burr, James David, James Hershberg, Robert Seidel, Richard Sylves, Samuel J. Walker, and Jonathan M. Weisgall. And I owe special thanks to several individuals who shared their deep knowledge of Russian and Soviet physics with me: Gennady Gorelik, Loren Graham, David Holloway, Ed Kline, and Mark Kuchment.

I gained special appreciation for the devoted work of archivists and librarians, and I wish to thank Hedy Dunn of the Los Alamos Historical Society; Marjorie Ciarlante, William Davis, and Rodney Ross of the National Archives; Arthur Freed, Roger Meade, Mollie Rodriguez, and Linda Sandoval of the Los Alamos National Laboratory; Ronald Grele and John Verso of the Columbia Oral History Research Office; Lori Hefner of the Lawrence Berkeley Laboratory; Joseph Anderson, Jean Hrichus, and Spencer Weart of the American Institute of Physics; David Haight of the Dwight D. Eisenhower Presidential Library; Dale Mayer of the Herbert Hoover Presidential Library; Dennis Bilger of the Harry S. Truman Presidential Library; Charles Greifenstein of the American Philosophical Society;

and Susan Gardos Bleich of the Davis Center Library at Harvard University.

I thank the Davis Center and, above all, Marshall Goldman for unfailing encouragement and support, and the John D. and Catherine T. MacArthur Foundation for its research and writing grant in 1988–1989. I also wish to thank Ruth Adams, Kurt Campbell, and James Cracraft.

For enhancing the audiotape of the 1982 interview of Lee Hancock at Albuquerque Airport by Jack Holl of the Department of Energy, I thank Robert Berkovitz and Haila Darcy of Bolt, Beranek, and Newman.

For advice about wiretapping law during the 1950s, I thank John Pound, Susan Rosenfeld, Herman Schwartz, and Katherine Triantafillou, and for help in interpreting key FBI documents, I thank Paul Farrell and Guy Goodwin.

For making themselves available so that I could better understand Edward Teller's contributions, I wish to thank Greg Canavan, George Chapline, and Harris Mayer, as well as Bill Beyer for arranging our meeting.

For state-of-the-art dissertations that have, alas, not been published, I thank Anne Fitzpatrick and Sybil Francis.

For making invaluable material available, I wish to thank Captain Jack Crawford and Edythe Murphy Holbrook. For additional material, I thank Theodore Conant, Dolores Everett, Ivan Getting, Gwen Groves, Elaine Kistiakowsky, J. K. Mansfield, Phillip S. Meilinger, and Ed Regis. For their understanding of key individuals, I am indebted to William Golden, Gordon Gray Jr., Joan Harrington, and Donna Mitchell.

For their comments on all or part of my manuscript, I thank Hugh De Witt, Max Holland, William Lanouette, David E. Lilienthal Jr., Cecily D. McMillan, and Herbert York. And for the title of this book, I thank Andrew Szanton.

For support and assistance of all kinds, I thank Daniel P. Asnes, Drew Colfax, Michael Day, Allan Ecker, Joseph Finder, Lester Grinspoon, Richard and Priscilla Hunt, Coit Johnson, Steve Kaiser, Roman Laba, Cecily McMillan, Thomas McMillan, Thomas Mallon, David Metcalf, Thomas Powers, Jay Topkis, Charles Weiner, and Eunice Winslow. For their talent, experience, and sheer staying power, I thank my editors, Wendy Wolf and M. S. Wyeth Jr. And for friendship and assistance beyond price, I thank the late David Hawkins, the late Carson and Kay Mark, Emily Morrison, Philip Morrison, and Françoise Ulam.

NOTES

Abbreviations

AEC—Atomic Energy Commission

AIP—American Institute of Physics

APS—American Philosophical Society

AS—Atomic Shield: A History of the United States Atomic Energy Commission, vol. 2, *1947–1952,* by Richard G. Hewlett and Francis Duncan

BAS—Bulletin of the Atomic Scientists

CIC—Coordination and Information Center, U.S. Department of Energy, Las Vegas, Nevada

CJVM—Charles J. V. Murphy papers, property of Edythe M. Holbrook

COHP—Columbia University Oral History Project

DDEPL—Dwight David Eisenhower Presidential Library

DEL —The Journals of David E. Lilienthal: The Atomic Energy Years, 1945–1950

DOE—Department of Energy, successor to the Atomic Energy Commission, College Park, Maryland

FRUS—Foreign Relations of the United States, publication of the U.S. Department of State

GAC—General Advisory Committee, Atomic Energy Commission

HHPL—Herbert Hoover Presidential Library

HSTPL—Harry S. Truman Presidential Library

IMJRO—United States Atomic Energy Commission, *In the Matter of J. Robert Oppenheimer: Transcript of Hearing Before Personnel Security Board and Texts of Principal Documents and Letters* (published by MIT Press, 1971)

JCAE—Joint Congressional Committee on Atomic Energy

JFKPL—John F. Kennedy Presidential Library

JRO—J. Robert Oppenheimer

JRO/FBI—J. Robert Oppenheimer file no. 100–17828, FBI Reading Room, Washington, DC

LANL—Los Alamos National Laboratory

LASL—Los Alamos Scientific Laboratory
LBL—Lawrence Berkeley Laboratory
LC—Library of Congress
LLS—Lewis Strauss papers, Herbert Hoover Presidential Library
NARA—National Archives and Records Administration
NYHT—New York Herald-Tribune
NYT—New York Times
OP—Oppenheimer Papers at the Library of Congress
RG 128—Record Group 128, papers of the Joint Congressional Committee on
    Atomic Energy, located at the National Archives and Records Administra-
    tion, Washington, DC
RG 326—Record Group 326, papers of the United States Atomic Energy
    Commission, located at the National Archives and Records Administra-
    tion, College Park, Maryland
TEM—Thomas E. Murray papers, in the possession of the Murray family
UC—University of California
UCSD—University of California, San Diego

Introduction

1. Emily Morrison, interviews with author, February 2 and February 15,
1985; *IMJRO,* p. 8.

2. Hilde Stern Hein, interview with author, March 7, 1987.

3. www.BrotherhoodoftheBomb.com, Web site of Gregg Herken's *Brotherhood of the Bomb:* Herken's notes of Barbara Chevalier's diary; Chevalier to
unknown researcher, April 25, 1973.

4. Steve Nelson, interview with author, August 28, 1985.

5. Steve Nelson, interview with author, August 28, 1985.

6. Philip Farley, interview with author, February 2, 1987.

7. David Hawkins, interviews with author, January 30, 1985, and January
1, 1997.

CHAPTER ONE: David Lilienthal's Vacation

1. *DEL,* pp. 566–573.

2. When Lilienthal informed Truman on April 3, 1947, that the United
States had components for only seven complete atomic bombs, the president
was visibly upset. By the end of 1949, the United States had 235 stockpiled
warheads (Natural Resources Defense Council Table of U.S. Nuclear Warheads 1945–75, www.nrdc.org/nuclear/nudb/datab9.asp). Lilienthal earned

$8,000 to $10,000 per year as director of TVA and $17,500 as chairman of the AEC.

3. A CIA memorandum of September 20, 1949, predicted, "The earliest possible date by which the USSR might be expected to produce an atomic bomb is mid-1950 and the most probable date is mid-1953." Intelligence Memorandum 225, "Estimate of Status of Atomic Warfare in the USSR" (National Intelligence estimate from CIA records, Record Group 263, NARA, College Park, MD).

4. Robert Oppenheimer, interview with Warner Schilling, 1957, OP, box 65, and *AS*, p. 366. Oppenheimer told Schilling that the British had opposed announcement of the test, while Truman felt that the U.S. public should be told.

5. For the president's announcement, see Harry Truman's *Memoirs*, vol. 2, pp. 307–308.

6. The GAC has been criticized for going beyond the offer of technical advice at its October 29–30 meeting, but in a letter of October 22, 1949, the GAC was asked a second time, this time by Acting Chairman Sumner Pike, to provide policy advice. AEC's 1954 "Thermonuclear Weapons Program Chronology," compiled at the request of H. D. Smyth in 1954 for use by the commissioners in the Oppenheimer case, and declassified in 1982, pp. 22(c) and 22(d), RG 326, NARA.

CHAPTER TWO: **The Maneuvering Begins**

1. AEC "Thermonuclear Weapons Program Chronology," p. 21, RG 326, NARA.

2. Interview with Alice Strauss, November 28, 1990.

3. AEC "Thermonuclear Weapons Program Chronology," 1954, p. 22, RG 326, NARA.

4. Strauss to Souers, May 13, 1947, and September 2, 1947; Souers to Strauss, September 25, 1947 (LLS); Souers oral history interview, December 16, 1954, part 1, HSTPL.

5. Timing of this conversation is important: if all of it took place on October 5, 1949, as the Souers oral history interview of December 16, 1954, suggests, then Strauss was misrepresenting the facts, since Lilienthal, the AEC, and the GAC had not yet taken formal positions. The dialogue recounted in the oral history could, however, be a composite of several conversations between Souers and Strauss that fall.

6. *IMJRO*, p. 714.

7. From "Take One" of an unpublished March 7, 1954, dispatch from

Clay Blair and James Shepley to Larry Laybourne of *Time* magazine for a planned cover issue on Teller, Blair Papers, Archive of Contemporary History, University of Wyoming, Laramie; Alvarez Diary, October 5–7, 1949, RG 326, NARA; *AS,* pp. 376–377.

8. The Russian physicist Pyotr Kapitsa was under house arrest from 1946 to 1954 and did not work on the hydrogen bomb. It is illustrative of the state of Western knowledge of the Soviet bomb program that during the war the United States and Britain assumed that Kapitsa was head of the project, if there was one; the actual scientific director was Igor Kurchatov; Borden memorandum to files, October 10, 1949, RG 128, doc. no. LXVI, and Walker-Borden Chronology, p. 27, RG 128, NARA. "Take Two" of the unpublished Shepley-Blair *Time* cover file of March 7, 1954, reports on the luncheon: "Slowly a fire was ignited inside McMahon. By lunch's end, he was an enthusiastic convert. . . . Lawrence went back to California to whip up enthusiasm in the university laboratories. Meantime Teller and De Hoffmann, getting word of Lawrence's partial success in Washington, began to try to whip up support at Los Alamos."

9. Alvarez Diary, p. 29, RG 326, NARA; *DEL,* p. 577.

10. According to Phillip S. Meilinger, *Hoyt S. Vandenberg: The Life of a General,* Vandenberg's testimony was occasioned by Teller's visit to Major General Roscoe Wilson. See also Walker-Borden Chronology, p. 29, RG 128, NARA.

11. *IMJRO,* p. 328; author interview with Hans and Rose Bethe, December 3, 1986.

12. Hans Bethe, interview with Charles Weiner, part 3, May 1972, p. 24, AIP.

13. *IMJRO,* p. 328.

14. Hans Bethe, interview with Charles Weiner, part 3, May 1972, p. 25, AIP; *IMJRO,* p. 329; Victor Weisskopf, interview with author, February 25, 1985.

15. According to James Hershberg in *James B. Conant: Harvard to Hiroshima and the Making of the Nuclear Age,* p. 471, Oppenheimer was in Cambridge on October 9–10. On Wednesday, October 12, he spent a full day discussing the H-bomb dilemma with his close friend I. I. Rabi (Rabi to Bacher, October 18, 1949, Rabi Papers, LC), and on Saturday, October 15, he discussed it with another close friend, Admiral William S. Parsons. From Oppenheimer appointment books for September and October 1949; Warner Schilling interview notes, p. 19, OP, box 65.

16. *IMJRO,* p. 231; Warner Schilling's notes of June 12, 1957, pp. 6–7 (OP, box 65), quote Oppenheimer as saying that he changed his mind during the GAC meeting as a "result of Conant's intervention" and that it had been a "mistake to go along." Oppenheimer added that his confidential secretary was

surprised when she saw the GAC report, and pointed out that it was not the position he had taken earlier. "She also correctly predicted that it would get me in a lot of trouble."

CHAPTER THREE: The Halloween Meeting

1. Oppenheimer interview with Warner Schilling, June 12, 1957, OP, box 65, and letter of Cyril S. Smith to Richard Hewlett, April 27, 1967. In later years Manley, Oppenheimer, and Smith said they had been strongly influenced by Kennan's remarks; Manley and Smith added that they were also impressed by Bethe's description of the technical difficulties.

2. Manley's handwritten notes on seventeenth GAC meeting, LANL; Oppenheimer interview with Schilling, p. 10; *DEL,* p. 581.

3. *IMJRO,* p. 247; Alvarez, *The Adventures of a Physicist,* p. 172.

4. According to Theodore Conant, when Truman asked his father in 1946 to become the first chairman of the AEC, Conant declined because members of the Harvard board of overseers had warned him against serving with Lewis Strauss. Strauss, they said, was deceitful and overly ambitious, and with him as a commissioner, Conant would constantly have to be watching his back. (Conversation with the author, February 6, 1994.) Since Truman had already promised McMahon that he would appoint Strauss, the offer to Conant was moot. Truman left it to the GAC to name its chairman, and according to an FBI wiretap of a conversation between Robert and Kitty Oppenheimer, Oppenheimer assumed that either he or Conant would be elected. Meanwhile I. I. Rabi wrote to Lee DuBridge that Oppenheimer ought to be chairman because he "knows the entire field" and "is not burdened with any other important outside activity and would be able to give it the care and attention which it requires. The delicate question is whether Conant wants it for himself." DuBridge obligingly wrote to Conant that if he did not want the job, then "Robert might fit the bill," and at the GAC's first meeting, on January 3, 1947, Conant nominated Oppenheimer, who was elected without dissent. (See also James Hershberg's *James B. Conant: Harvard to Hiroshima,* pp. 307–309 and 837.)

5. *DEL,* p. 581; Oppenheimer interview with Schilling; Richard T. Sylves, *The Nuclear Oracles,* pp. 145–146.

6. Oppenheimer to Lilienthal with attachments, October 30, 1949, RG 326, NARA.

7. Oppenheimer interview with Schilling.

8. *DEL,* p. 582, and AEC 222/6, minutes of 310th AEC meeting, October 5, 1949, RG 326, NARA.

9. The Gray board concluded in 1954 that Oppenheimer had slowed the H-bomb program, and cited Manley's carrying the GAC recommendations to Los Alamos in November 1949 as evidence, despite an affidavit from Manley to the board that fully explained the circumstances.

10. Manley's diary entries for October 30–November 15, 1949, LANL.

11. Unpublished MS by John Manley, shown to the author by Manley in August 1986.

12. Teller to von Neumann, November 9, 1949, NARA.

13. Ulam to von Neumann, November 15, 1949, NARA; Françoise Ulam, interview with author, November 1991.

14. Bradbury to Chet Holifield, October 15, 1969; Carson Mark, interviews with author, April 2, 1986, and October 18, 1987.

CHAPTER FOUR: **The Secret Debate**

1. Glenn Seaborg, who had missed the Halloween meeting, was present at the December meeting but chose not to take a position. Nonetheless, in his autobiography, *Adventures in the Atomic Age: From Watts to Washington* (New York: Farrar, Straus & Giroux, 2000), he blamed Oppenheimer for allegedly suppressing the letter he had written to Oppenheimer, taking an equivocal, but mildly positive, position on the H-bomb, prior to the Halloween meeting.

2. *DEL,* p. 594.

3. JCAE meeting of January 9, 1950, appendix IV, doc. no. CXXV, RG 128, NARA.

4. *DEL,* pp. 583–584.

5. Arneson, "The H-Bomb Decision."

6. *DEL,* p. 622.

7. Acheson, *Present at the Creation,* p. 360; James Chace, "Sharing the Bomb," *Foreign Affairs,* pp. 226–228.

8. *DEL,* p. 620.

9. Lilienthal's "Memo to File," January 31, 1950, in AEC's "Thermonuclear Weapons Program Chronology," p. 110, RG 326, NARA.

10. AEC's "Thermonuclear Weapons Program Chronology," pp. 111–116.

11. Arneson, "The H-Bomb Decision"; Acheson, *Present at the Creation,* pp. 348–349; *DEL,* pp. 632–633.

12. Acheson, *Present at the Creation,* p. 349. The study ordered by Truman became NSC-68.

13. *DEL,* p. 633.

14. Ibid. At his security hearing in 1954, Oppenheimer testified that Acheson sent word to him and Conant "for heck's sake not to resign or make any

public statements to upset the applecart but accept this decision . . . and not make any kind of conflict about it" (*IMJRO*, p. 86).

15. Pfau, *No Sacrifice Too Great*, p. 123.

16. *DEL*, pp. 633–634.

CHAPTER FIVE: **Lost Opportunities**

1. In his October 21, 1949, letter to Conant, Oppenheimer called Teller's Super "singularly proof against any form of experiment."

2. JRO to George Kennan, November 17, 1949, *FRUS*, 1949, vol. 1, pp. 222–223.

3. Ferrell, *Harry S. Truman: A Life*, p. 344.

4. Bernstein and Galison, "In Any Light," p. 306.

5. York, *The Advisors*, pp. 94–106.

CHAPTER SIX: **Fuchs's Betrayal**

1. *DEL*, p. 634.

2. *FRUS*, 1950, vol. 1, p. 173.

3. Hoover to Tolson, Ladd, and Nichols, February 2, 1950, JRO/FBI; Pfau, *No Sacrifice Too Great*, pp. 113–119.

4. *BAS*, March 1950, p. 75.

5. JCAE transcript, January 30, 1950, "Development of Atomic Super Weapons," app. IV, box 4, doc. no. 1447, RG 128, NARA.

6. Bethe to Weisskopf, February 14, 1950, Bethe Papers.

7. *Scientific American* 182, no. 3 (March 1950), pp. 11–15.

8. Ibid., no. 5 (May 1950), pp. 11–15.

9. Ibid., no. 4 (April 1950), pp. 18–23. Bethe's biographer, Silvan Schweber, points out that Bethe was free to publish his article only because he had allowed his Los Alamos consultancy to lapse.

10. Hans and Rose Bethe, interview with author, December 3, 1986; Bethe with Charles Weiner, session 3, May 8–9, 1972, pp. 28–29, AIP; Hansen, *Swords of Armageddon*, vol. 3, p. 113, says there were only four deletions of which one contained disinformation and the other three, information that had appeared earlier in *Scientific American*.

11. Bethe to Bradbury, February 14, 1950, RG 326, NARA.

12. *BAS*, March 1950, pp. 71–72.

13. Borden memo, "Teller Says," March 2, 1950, RG 128, NARA.

14. JCAE meeting of March 3, 1950, on "H-bomb Personnel," RG 128, NARA.

15. *AS,* p. 416.

16. Truman followed up with his June 8 approval of construction of two new heavy-water reactors at Savannah River to produce tritium, and on July 7 asked Congress for $260 million to build them. I. I. Rabi commented, "I regard Savannah River as the way he answered the Russian success." Quoted in Ulam, *Adventures of a Mathematician,* pp. 192–193, and J. Carson Mark, "A Short Account of Los Alamos Theoretical Work on Thermonuclear Weapons, 1946–1950."

17. *AS,* p. 439.

18. Anne Fitzpatrick, "Igniting the Light Elements" (unpublished doctoral dissertation), p. 132.

19. Bradbury to Coordinating Council, October 1, 1945, LANL.

20. Fitzpatrick, "Igniting the Light Elements," pp. 111–112, says that theoretical work on the Super had begun to interfere with work on the fission bomb by spring 1944 "because Teller increasingly devoted more time to this than to the implosion problems he and his group were supposed to work on. . . . Teller . . . declined to take charge of the group that would perform very detailed calculations of an implosion weapon to devote more time to the fusion weapon." In an interview with Silvan Schweber on July 21, 1990, Teller said that the strain between him and Bethe during the war arose, not from Bethe's being placed above him as Theoretical Division leader, but from "Hans' not asking, but telling, me what to do." He added that Bethe considered his reaction "a violation of discipline."

21. To produce one gram of tritium, "one would have to forgo production of 80 grams of plutonium" (Carson Mark to Garrett Birkhoff, February 13, 1990). Fermi in 1948 estimated that in terms of plutonium sacrificed, the United States could afford to produce ten grams a year. Fitzpatrick, "Igniting the Light Elements," p. 192.

22. Carson Mark to Garrett Birkhoff, February 13, 1990; Fitzpatrick, "Igniting the Light Elements," pp. 147–148. The Ulam-Everett paper, LA-1076, "Ignition of a Large Mass of Deuterium by a Burning D-T Mixture: Problem I," March 7, 1950, remains Secret-RD at LANL. Mark remembered Ulam as "smacking his lips" when he brought Mark the negative calculations. Carson Mark, interview with author, June 12, 1990.

23. Ulam, *Adventures of a Mathematician,* p. 215; Carson Mark to Garrett Birkhoff, February 13, 1990; Fitzpatrick, "Igniting the Light Elements," pp. 147–148, citing the second Ulam-Everett report, LAMS-1124, June 16, 1950, which is still secret. Testifying in a patent case years later, Ulam declined to say that the ENIAC results had been wrong. Rather, he said, his hand calcula-

tions with Everett showed the earlier calculations to have been "incomplete" (U.S. District Court of Minnesota, Fourth Division, Honeywell, Inc., v. Sperry Rand and Illinois Scientific Developments, Inc., transcript of proceedings, vol. 47, pp. 7367–7368).

24. *AS,* p. 440; Ulam, *Adventures of a Mathematician,* p. 217.

25. Ulam to von Neumann, April 27, 1950, NARA; Teller to von Neumann, May 10, 1950, NARA; von Neumann to Teller, May 18, 1950, NARA; Françoise Ulam, memorandum of September 25, 1988, "Edward and Mici," AIP; Françoise Ulam memoir, *From Paris to Santa Fe,* AIP; Peter Galison, *Image and Logic,* p. 724.

26. Ulam, *Adventures of a Mathematician,* p. 216.

27. Fitzpatrick, "Igniting the Light Elements," p. 149, citing the Fermi-Ulam paper, LA-1158, "Considerations on Thermonuclear Reactions in Cylinders," September 26, 1950, Secret-RD; Carson Mark to author, October 17, 1991; Wheeler with Ford, *Geons, Black Holes, and Quantum Foam,* p. 209.

28. Ulam, *Adventures of a Mathematician,* pp. 218–219; S. M. Ulam, "Thermonuclear Devices"; George Bell, interview with author, March 8, 2000.

CHAPTER SEVEN: **Fission versus Fusion**

1. Wheeler with Ford, *Geons, Black Holes, and Quantum Foam,* p. 189.

2. Ibid., pp. 20, 206–207.

3. Carson Mark, interview with author, October 9, 1991.

4. John McPhee, *The Curve of Binding Energy,* pp. 58–60; Wheeler with Ford, *Geons, Black Holes, and Quantum Foam,* p. 205; Nuclear History Program oral history interview with Theodore Taylor, April 12, 1989, University of Maryland.

5. Bradbury to McCormack, August 29, 1950, cited in Hansen, *Swords of Armageddon,* vol. 3, pp. 141–142.

6. Oppenheimer to Dean, September 13, 1950, AEC Secretariat Files, RG 326, NARA.

7. With the opening of archives in the former Soviet bloc, Western historians have concluded that the impetus came from North Korean dictator Kim Il Sung, who, after several attempts, persuaded a reluctant Joseph Stalin to permit the invasion.

8. Borden to Sterling Cole, July 24, 1950, app. III, box 62, doc. no. CLXXXVIII, RG 128, NARA; Borden to McMahon, November 28, 1950, app. III, box 62, doc. no. 1785, RG 128, NARA. In 1949 Borden had been denied a top secret Defense Department document because it contained stockpile data.

When he suggested that every bomb be saved for use on Russia, he may have
believed the stockpile to be smaller than it was. According to the Natural Resources Defense Council Table of U.S. Nuclear Warheads 1945–75, by late 1950
it contained 369 strategic warheads (www.nrdc.org/nuclear/nudb/datab9.asp).

9. Taylor oral history interview; Taylor, "Circles of Destruction," *BAS*
(January–February 1996).

10. Hans Bethe wrote, "The technical skepticism of the GAC . . . had
turned out to be far more justified than the GAC itself had dreamed" ("Comments on the History of the H-Bomb," written in 1954 as a reply to Shepley
and Blair and classified until its publication in *Los Alamos Science* [fall 1982]);
JRO to Dean, November 1, 1950, AEC Secretariat Files, RG 326, NARA. In
November 1950, Oppenheimer asked Ulam whether the calculations he had
done with Everett showed conclusively that the Super was impossible. In accordance with the principle of indeterminacy, Ulam replied that the calculations
were not final.

11. The Teller-Wheeler report of August 1, 1959, said the amount of uncompressed T required to ignite uncompressed D was "of the order of a kilogram or more but not of the order of tens of kilograms" (Fitzpatrick, "Igniting
the Light Elements," pp. 222–223, citing the report itself, LAMD-443, secret-
RD). The seriousness of the mistake, and of the finding that ignition would require three to five kilograms of tritium, and not a hundred or a few hundred
grams as Teller claimed, may be seen from the fact that two years later, in the
summer of 1952, the U.S. tritium supply still was measured in grams, not kilograms. On the far-off day when the nation's laboratories might be able to
produce a kilogram a year, it would take three to five years to produce enough
tritium for a single Super bomb (Hansen, *Swords of Armageddon,* vol. 3, p. 149).
As Gordon Dean told a secret session of the JCAE in November, production
of one Super would mean sacrificing enough plutonium for between 100 and
150 atomic bombs. Walker-Borden Chronology, entry for November 30, 1950,
RG 128, NARA.

12. GAC 23, October 30–November 1, 1950, AEC Secretariat Files, RG
326, NARA, p. 17.

13. Oppenheimer to Dean, November 1, 1950, AEC Secretariat Files, RG
326, NARA.

14. Fitzpatrick, "Igniting the Light Elements," p. 276, citing Draft Memorandum to the chairman of the AEC, "Notes on the AEC-MLC, LASL Conference on Tuesday, November 14, 1950," November 17, 1950 (Secret-RD);
and p. 221, citing Bradbury to Tyler, November 17, 1950, "LASL Technical
Program of Calendar Year 1951 and Fiscal Year 1952" (Secret-RD), box 4944,
Los Alamos folder 7, RG 326, NARA.

CHAPTER EIGHT: **Teller**

1. Teller to Maria Goeppert Mayer, letters of October 9 and October undated, 1948. Mandeville Department of Special Collections, UCSD.

2. Kathleen Mark, interview with author, October 4, 1999; Carson Mark, interview with author, October 18, 1987.

3. Five undated letters from Edward Teller to Maria Goeppert Mayer, August–November 1950.

4. Undated letter of Edward Teller to Maria Goeppert Mayer from Norman, Oklahoma, probably written after November 25, 1950.

5. Luis Alvarez testimony, *IMJRO,* p. 789.

6. The other members were former AEC commissioner Robert F. Bacher, Luis Alvarez, Charles C. Lauritsen, Mervin J. Kelly, Walter G. Whitman, Major General Kenneth D. Nichols, Rear Admiral William S. Parsons, Major General Roscoe C. Wilson, and Brigadier General James McCormack Jr.

7. JCAE meeting on "H-Bomb Personnel," March 3, 1950, RG 128, NARA.

8. Borden to file, March 2, 1950. "Give It Back to the Indians" was a hit song from a 1939 Rodgers and Hart musical and was still popular in 1946, when Oppenheimer allegedly made this remark. With his talent for the vernacular, Oppenheimer might well have taken the expression from the song.

9. Borden memorandum to Sterling Cole, "The Hydrogen Bomb in Relation to the Atomic Bomb," July 24, 1950, app. III, box 62, doc. no. CLXXXVIII, RG 128, NARA; "Conversation with Dr. Enrico Fermi on September 4, 1951," memo of J. K. Mansfield, October 2, 1951, RG 128, NARA.

10. Borden to Teller, May 3, 1950, RG 128, NARA.

11. The first such suggestion appears in Oppenheimer's FBI file for July 5, 1949; Bergman to Borden, May 7, 1950, app. III, box 41, doc. no. 1531, classified general subject file, RG 128, NARA.

12. Borden memo to McMahon, May 11, 1950, app. III, box 50, doc. no. 1516, RG 128, NARA; those whose terms were expiring were Fermi, Hartley Rowe, and Glenn Seaborg.

13. Borden memo to McMahon, November 24, 1950, RG 128, NARA.

CHAPTER NINE: **Ulam**

1. Ulam, *Adventures of a Mathematician,* p. 10.

2. Galison, *Image and Logic,* pp. 724–725.

3. Carson Mark to Garrett Birkhoff, February 13, 1990. George Bell, interview with author, March 8, 2000, and Bengt Carlson, interview with au-

thor, Nov. 11, 2005. George Bell noted that the "compression" being talked about here was extreme compression, much greater than that produced by ordinary high explosives.

4. Françoise Ulam, *From Paris to Santa Fe*, AIP.

5. Carson Mark, interviews with author, August 19, 1986; September 11–12 and November 3, 1989; private memo by Françoise Ulam, August 20, 1988, "How My Conversation with Carson Came About." Mark was working on the Ranger series in Nevada, as well as the Greenhouse tests. Greenhouse included two fission tests, "Dog," detonated at Eniwetok on April 8 at 82 kilotons, and "Easy," April 21 at 47 kilotons. The others were "George," May 9 at 225 kilotons, which included a new type of fission device, and "Item," June 2 at 45.5 kilotons. He later called Item, a boosted device with both fission and fusion components, "particularly dear to my heart." Teller had not been enthusiastic about Item and at one point sought to have it canceled. Today, every U.S. nuclear weapon is boosted.

6. Ulam, *Adventures of a Mathematician*, p. 220; Françoise Ulam to the author, September 18, 1989.

7. Stanislaw Ulam to Glenn Seaborg, March 16, 1962, LANL; Arnold Kramish to Samuel B. Ballen, April 4, 2000.

8. Richard Rhodes is almost certainly correct in saying in *Dark Sun*, p. 467, that Ulam's " 'following days' comprised most of a month," since the diary indicates that Ulam wrote his part of the paper in mid-February and wrote to von Neumann informing him of his new ideas only on February 23. Ulam's diary on February 15 contains this entry: "Wrote Lenses (jointly with Teller). Heterocatalytic Detonation: Radiation Lenses and Hydrogenous Lenses" (Galison, *Image and Logic*, p. 725).

9. George Bell, interview with author, March 8, 2000; Hugh DeWitt, interview with author, March 1, 1992; e-mails from Hugh DeWitt, July 28, August 8 and 21, 2000; Hugh DeWitt, telephone interview with author, August 21, 2000; Hans Bethe, who came to the lab in June 1951 to do calculations for the new scheme, relied on what he was told at that time, and did not read the Ulam-Teller paper until August 11, 1989. After reading the paper, he said that his May 28, 1952, letter to Gordon Dean had been "wrong" and that Ulam deserved more credit than he had given him in that letter and in his essay "Comments on the History of the H-Bomb," published in 1982 (Bethe to Samuel B. Ballen, September 28, 1988). Bengt Carlson, a mathematician to whom Ulam described his "two bombs in a box" idea on Dec. 23, 1950, suspects that Teller deliberately delayed publication of his March 9, 1951, paper with Ulam, with the result that Bethe was not shown it on his arrival that spring and saw only his April 4, 1951, paper with de Hoffman. Carlson believes that this omission

subsequently led to Bethe's mistakenly attributing major credit for the radiation implosion concept to Teller instead of Ulam. Bengt Carlson, interviews with author, Sept. 6, 2005, and Nov. 11, 2005.

10. Bethe, "Comments on the History of the H-Bomb," p. 48; Rhodes, *Dark Sun,* pp. 471–472.

11. Norris Bradbury, interview with Arthur Norberg, February 11, 1976. Opinions differ to this day as to whether Teller or Ulam deserves chief credit. The lab designation is "Teller-Ulam," for alphabetical reasons, but because Ulam contributed two of the three critical ideas, I have called it "Ulam-Teller," as Bradbury did at his September 24, 1954, press conference.

12. *Science,* February 25, 1955, pp. 267–275; Teller with Brown, *The Legacy of Hiroshima,* pp. 48–50; Ulam's offending remark appeared in a letter of February 23, 1951, to von Neumann, in which he said that "Edward is full of enthusiasm about these possibilities, this is perhaps an indication that they will not work." Someone has attributed to Ulam a comment after the George test of May 1951, that its "failure" showed that radiation implosion would not work. But most of Ulam's colleagues doubt that he said this, since it was known within a few days after George that the tritium-deuterium package had emitted neutrons and that the experiment had been successful. Teller told Stanley Goldberg, Gregg Herken, Richard Rhodes, and the author on June 7, 1993, that Ulam deserved no credit because of his skepticism. But Ulam's remark to Françoise over lunch in January, and his February 23 letter to von Neumann, make clear that he knew that radiation implosion would work.

13. Bradbury press conference, September 24, 1954 (LANL).

14. Carson Mark, who served on the Committee of Senior Reviewers, did not think the system was intentionally manipulated to elevate Teller's stature, and Hugh DeWitt, a onetime whistleblower at the Lawrence Livermore Laboratory, agrees. In a charitable moment, Mark suggested that Teller's followers were more responsible than Teller himself for Teller's inflated reputation, and that the sobriquet "Father of the H-bomb" was to some extent forced on him.

15. Carson Mark, interview with author, November 3, 1987; Françoise Ulam, private memorandum of August 20, 1988.

16. Françoise Ulam, *From Paris to Santa Fe,* AIP.

17. Françoise Ulam and David Hawkins, telephone interviews with author, August 19, 2000. Françoise Ulam said that her husband stood up to Teller, as younger members of their wartime TN group did not. During this period Ulam did mathematics on his own with Oppenheimer's assistant, David Hawkins, who happened to work in an adjoining office. The two of them produced a paper on branching processes.

18. U.S. District Court, District of Minnesota, Fourth Division, Honey-

well Inc. v. Sperry Rand Corp. and Illinois Scientific Developments Inc., 4-67 Civil 1138, transcript of proceedings, vol. 47, p. 7408; Stanislaw Ulam, *Adventures of a Mathematician,* p. 220.

19. Carson Mark, interview with author, September 26, 1989; Carson Mark, telephone interview with author, February 15, 1990; George Bell, in an interview with the author on March 8, 2000, agreed with Bethe that the Teller-Ulam concept was surprising, and with Mark that the T Division would have thought of radiation implosion if Teller hadn't thought of it first.

20. Philip Morrison, conversations with author, July 25, 1990, and August 18, 2000.

21. Kathleen Mark, interview with author, October 4, 1999; Leon Heller, interview with author, October 9, 1999; Carson Mark, interview with author, June 14, 1993. The mathematician Paul Stein, who also worked closely with Ulam, said, "Stan's mind was always brimming with ideas, most of them good. It was the collaborator's job to fill in the details." Quoted by Carson Mark in notes for speech given on publication of *Los Alamos Science,* no. 15, 1987.

22. Françoise Ulam, *From Paris to Santa Fe,* chapter 6, AIP; Anna Auerbach Ulam, mother of Adam and Stan, died of cancer in 1938. After the war the student, George Volsky, wrote to Adam Ulam, describing his father's fate.

23. Françoise Ulam, conversation with author, 1993.

24. Françoise Ulam, "Fragments of Taped Conversation with M. Kac and D. Mauldin," June 8, 1984, and undated biographical profile by Françoise Ulam, AIP.

25. Samuel B. Ballen, conversation with author, November 9, 1987; Françoise Ulam, conversation with author, October 7, 1987; Gian-Carlo Rota, "Wheel of Fortune," unpublished draft of March 28, 1986; comment by Seymour Papert, July 1997; Rota, "The Lost Cafe," *Contention,* 2, no. 2 (Winter 1993).

26. Françoise Ulam, "Fragments of Taped Conversation with M. Kac and D. Mauldin"; Rota, "Wheel of Fortune," March 28, 1986; Dolores Everett and Mollie Rodriguez, interviews with author, October 17 and 19, 1991; in a telephone interview on July 23, 2000, William Everett said that within the family, he heard that "Dad did all the work and Ulam got all the credit." Françoise Ulam responded that her husband did not conceal Everett's role, as Teller concealed Ulam's. To the contrary, he frequently spoke of Everett's contribution and lamented not having more opportunities to talk with him. Still another collaborator of Ulam's confirmed the fact of Everett's bitterness and said that he, too, felt used by Ulam. "Ulam had great ideas, and expected his underlings to work them out" (William Beyer, conversation with author, February 14, 2001).

27. Françoise Ulam, interview with author, April 6, 1986; Stanislaw Ulam, *Adventures of a Mathematician,* pp. 76, 79–80, 107–111; Rota, "The Lost Cafe," pp. 48–49.

28. According to David Hawkins, Ulam during the war was able to solve linear equations much faster than other scientists because he was already, in his head, doing statistical sampling. In 1947, playing solitaire with his head still bandaged from his encephalitis operation, he thought of the Monte Carlo method and the uses to which it might be put. On his return to Los Alamos he firmed it up in his mind in letters to von Neumann and Robert Richtmyer, then head of the T Division.

29. Transcript of H-bomb symposium sponsored by Sloan Foundation at Princeton, NJ, 1982, part 1, p. 13, and part 2, p. 14; Françoise Ulam, interview with author, November 22, 1987; Carson Mark, interview with author, September 12, 1989; Stanislaw Ulam, *Adventures of a Mathematician,* p. 80, refers to Kurt Godel's discovery of undecidability; Heims, *John von Neumann and Norbert Weiner,* pp. 143–144.

30. Françoise Ulam, interview with author, November 22, 1987; Françoise Ulam memoranda February 1, 1987, and December 8, 1988, AIP.

CHAPTER TEN: **Teller's Choice**

1. Pfau, *No Sacrifice Too Great,* pp. 131–132.

2. Dean, "Memorandum of Conversation with Lewis Strauss," note of February 12, 1951, in Anders, ed., *Forging the Atomic Shield,* pp. 117–118; Pfau, *No Sacrifice Too Great,* pp. 132–133; Herken, *Brotherhood of the Bomb,* p. 241.

3. Diary of Thomas E. Murray, vol. 2, part 2, pp. 8–9, TEM. The quotations are Murray's.

4. Anders, ed., *Forging the Atomic Shield,* p. 117; Borden to file, "Conversation with Dr. Edward Teller," February 9, 1951, JCAE doc. no. CCLXXXIII, RG 128, NARA.

5. "The Reminiscences of Gordon Dean," COHP, 1959.

6. Carson Mark later explained: "There was one outfit that handled calculations. Was it to work only on the thermonuclear? The same thing was true of the chemists. And they were working well as it was. . . . In addition to the computing, there was the Experimental Physics Division. It had machines, a Cockroft-Walton, a Van de Graaff, and so on. The work of the machines could be directed toward either fission or fusion. There was no sense saying that a given machine will work only on one and not the other." Carson Mark, interview with author, October 18, 1991. Darol Froman made another objection: "What do we do with people who insist on having ideas . . . in both

fields, e.g., Ulam?" He termed the duplication of effort involved in creation of a separate division "time-consuming, wasteful, costly, geographically inappropriate . . . absurd" and added, "I believe we have, entering this reorganizational picture from both sides, a lack of faith either in the motivation of others or in their ability to carry out their parts"; Froman, memos of March 20 and March 22, 1951, LANL. In a memo of March 28, Froman offered to mediate between Teller and the rest of the lab, adding that in case of a standoff, Bradbury would make the decision. Teller would not accept Bradbury's having the final say. Bradbury's March 6 proposal was ultimately sidetracked, in Carson Mark's words, "because there was no way you could have a sensible way of working and please Teller." Carson Mark, interview with author, October 18, 1991.

7. A month after his February 9 visit to AEC general manager Marion Boyer, Teller told Bradbury: "You know that I am not pressing at present for any reorganization or change because that might disturb the harmony of the laboratory at a time when united effort is badly needed." Teller to Bradbury, March 7, 1951, LANL.

8. Anders, ed., *Forging the Atomic Shield,* pp. 106–107, 120–126. Dean was unaware that the government's case against the Rosenbergs was mostly based on the decrypted Soviet wartime cable traffic known as "Venona." The secret that the United States had decoded a portion of the Soviet intelligence cables was so tightly held that it has been claimed, probably erroneously, that even President Truman did not know of it. Existence of the decryptions was acknowledged by the U.S. government, and texts were published, only in 1995 and 1996.

9. Dean met with Truman on April 6, 1951, to discuss the JCS request, and the transfer was authorized, a decision that marked the end of exclusive civilian control over the atomic stockpile as mandated by the Atomic Energy Act. Anders, "The Atomic Bomb and the Korean War: Gordon Dean and the Issue of Civilian Control," *Military Affairs,* January 1988; Hamby, *Man of the People,* pp. 555–556.

10. *AS,* p. 541.

11. Anders, ed., *Forging the Atomic Shield,* pp. 106–107, 131–134; Teller with Brown, *The Legacy of Hiroshima,* p. 51.

12. Teller to Dean, April 20, 1951, from "ET" Files, LANL; Anders, ed., *Forging the Atomic Shield,* p. 108.

13. Hansen, *Swords of Armageddon,* vol. 3, p. 251; Anders, ed., *Forging the Atomic Shield,* pp. 143–145.

14. Actually, the hydrogen fuel did not account for much of George's power, nor had it been expected to: of the total yield of 225 kilotons, an estimated 160 to 200 were produced by the fission trigger and the rest by the fu-

sion component, prompting a young theoretician who worked on it, Robert Jastrow, to compare the test with "using a blast furnace to light a match." Jastrow, "Why Strategic Superiority Matters," *Commentary,* March 1983, p. 27.

15. Less than an ounce in weight, the tritium-deuterium mixture accounted for an estimated yield of 25 kilotons. *Race for the Superbomb,* shown on the PBS television series *The American Experience,* January 1999.

16. Carson Mark, interviews with author, September 26, 1989, and October 17, 1991; Mark to Hansen, September 18, 1989; *IMJRO,* p. 952; *AS,* p. 541.

17. York, *Making Weapons, Talking Peace,* pp. 57–58.

18. Total cost of the conference, said to have been the turning point in the H-bomb program, was $166.07 (including lunch for twenty-five on June 16 at $56, for twenty-seven on June 17 at $68, beer at $11.19, plus labor and equipment). The expense was borne by the Institute for Advanced Study after the AEC refused to pay (Smyth Professional Correspondence Series One, box 5, see Katherine Russell to Evelyn McQuown in "Boyer 1950–1953" file).

19. *AS,* pp. 542–545; Bradbury to Froman and Mark, June 6, 1951, LANL; Bradbury to Oppenheimer, June 1, 1951, LANL; Bradbury to Froman and Mark, June 6, 1951, LANL; Bethe, "Comments on the History of the H-Bomb," p. 48; "Partial Statement Made by Hans Bethe at Princeton Meeting," June 16–17, 1951, LANL; Bradbury to Tyler, July 13, 1951, LANL; Bethe to Joseph and Stewart Alsop, October 1, 1954, Joseph Alsop Papers, LC.

20. Bradbury to Oppenheimer, June 1, 1951, LANL. Oppenheimer later ascribed differences that emerged at the conference to the fact that the leading personalities represented "polar psychological types." Mansfield to file, October 3, 1951, doc. no. C 7404, RG 128, NARA.

21. Teller with Brown, *The Legacy of Hiroshima,* pp. 52–53. In his memo to Froman and Mark of June 6, Bradbury explained that their role as consultants to GAC would enable Teller, Wheeler, and Lothar Nordheim "to speak as freely as they wish . . . without any laboratory strings or restraints attached." The memo had been sent to Teller beforehand.

22. Nicholas Metropolis, interview with Silvan Schweber, August 20, 1990; *AS,* p. 545. Wheeler and Bethe both knew in advance that the Ulam-Teller ideas were to be discussed; both postponed visits to Europe in order to be present.

23. Norris Bradbury, interview with author, August 27, 1986; Anders, ed., *Forging the Atomic Shield,* p. 156.

24. Richard Garwin, interview with author, February 9, 2000.

25. Anders, ed., *Forging the Atomic Shield,* p. 164; Carson Mark, interviews with author, September 26, 1989, and June 12, 1990.

26. Bradbury to Dean teletype, September 26, 1951, LANL. Robert Serber

and one or two others later speculated that Bradbury provoked Teller into leaving because he suspected that Teller had deliberately falsified his tritium estimates for the Super.

27. Anders, ed., *Forging the Atomic Shield,* p. 164; Carson Mark, interview with author, June 12, 1990.

28. JCAE, Walker-Borden Chronology, entry for September 18, 1951, RG 128, NARA. Pressure for a major expansion was heightened by the announcement during the autumn of 1951 of the Soviet Union's second and third atomic tests.

29. John S. Walker memo, "Lunch Meeting with Dr. Teller," October 3, 1951, RG 128, NARA.

30. Mansfield to file, "Conversation with Dr. Oppenheimer," October 3, 1951, RG 128, NARA; Teller to GAC, December 13, 1951, AEC Secretariat Files, RG 326, NARA.

31. Kenneth Pitzer was also mentioned for the job, and Bradbury was said, additionally, to have considered Fred Seitz.

32. Bradbury to Fields, October 11, 1951, LANL Folder 635, "Laboratory Program 1951–1957."

33. Carson Mark, interview with Silvan Schweber, July 19, 1990. Mark added that if Bradbury "let down his hair" with anyone, it would have been with his associate director, Darol Froman.

34. Raemer Schreiber, interview with author, November 19, 1987; J. K. Mansfield memo for record, August 29, 1951, RG 128, NARA; J. Carson Mark, "A Short Account of Los Alamos Theoretical Work," LASL, 1974; Jacob Wechsler, interview with author, July 25, 2001.

35. Silvan Schweber with Marshall Rosenbluth, July 18, 1990; Max Roy, interview with author, October 11, 1991.

CHAPTER ELEVEN: **The Second Lab**

1. Murray, Thermonuclear Chronology, vol. 2, part 1, p. 10; part 2, pp. 27, 31–32, TEM.

2. Murray, Thermonuclear Chronology, vol. 2, part 2, pp. 44–45, TEM.

3. York, *Making Weapons, Talking Peace,* pp. 62–67.

4. Ibid.; Teller and Brown, *The Legacy of Hiroshima,* p. 60.

5. Oppenheimer to Dean, February 17, 1952, AEC Secretariat Files, box 1275, RG 326, NARA.

6. Teller to Murray, February 7, 1952, enclosed in Murray Diary, vol. 2, part 2, TEM; Teller to Borden, February 18, 1952, TN box 59, doc. 2646, RG 128, NARA.

7. A key here was Rowan Gaither, president of RAND and assistant to Paul Hoffman, president of the Ford Foundation (Murray Diary, vol. 2, part 2, p. 59, TEM). In a letter to Murray on March 17, Lawrence said he had mentioned Murray's idea to Gaither, and perhaps RAND could "accomplish the desired objectives."

8. Murray Diary, vol. 2, part 1, p. 15, and part 2, pp. 57–58, TEM. Bradbury added that nothing would provoke him into a protest resignation except Pentagon takeover of key civilian jobs in atomic energy, and even that might not be sufficient.

9. Ivan Getting, interview with author, October 6, 1989; Walker to Borden, April 3, 1952, RG 128, NARA; *AS*, p. 583; in a draft memo of March 15, 1952, Griggs warned Finletter that the Russians might already possess the radiation-implosion idea thanks to Fuchs. Finletter's assistant, William A. M. Burden, a New York investment banker, later said he had "recommended to Finletter, on Teller's advice, that we set up a separate laboratory . . . to work solely on the hydrogen bomb" (COHP interview with William A. M. Burden, p. 72). About the second-lab proposal and details of the thermonuclear work, two congressional aides said of the Air Force at this time: "They have bought Teller hook, line and sinker" (Walker and Borden to McMahon, April 4, 1952, CD XCIX, RG 128, NARA; Dwayne A. Day, *Lightning Rod* [my thanks to Stan Norris for this document]).

10. At Los Alamos, Bradbury refused to allow one of Finletter's party, Sidney Plesset, to attend the briefing, and the briefer, Carson Mark, no doubt disgusted by still another inspection visit by Washington bigwigs, gave an exceptionally lackluster performance.

11. Blumberg and Owens, *Energy and Conflict*, p. 289; Teller with Shoolery, *Memoirs*, pp. 336–338.

12. The briefings took place between March 6 and April 15, 1952, Walker-Borden Chronology, January 1, 1953, p. 76, RG 128, NARA; Walker to file, "Thermonuclear Background Information—Air Force," December 1952, CD DLXXXVII, TN box 59, app. 3, RG 128, NARA; Anders, ed., *Forging the Atomic Shield*, pp. 206–207; Gordon Dean memorandum, April 1, 1952, AEC Secretariat Files, box 4930, RG 326, NARA; Murray Diary, vol. 2, part 2, p. 68. The Air Force threat was effective despite the fact that its establishment of a nuclear weapons laboratory would have been a violation of the Atomic Energy Act.

13. Borden and Walker memorandum to McMahon, May 7, 1952, p. 6, doc. DXXIX, RG 128, NARA; Anders, ed., *Forging the Atomic Shield*, pp. 209–212.

14. Minutes of thirtieth GAC meeting, AEC Secretariat Files, box 1272, RG 326, NARA; Oppenheimer to Dean, April 30, 1952, AEC Secretariat Files, box 1275, RG 326, NARA; Norris Bradbury, interview with author, August 27, 1986.

15. Walker-Borden Chronology, entry for June 10, 1952, June 16, 1952, draft, doc. 3257, RG 128, NARA.

16. Murray Diary, vol. 2, part 1, pp. 18–19, and vol. 2, part 2, pp. 73–74, plus attachment to p. 74, TEM; Walker to file, "Thermonuclear Program," June 19, 1952, doc. no. 2890, RG 128, NARA; Borden and Walker to file, "Second Laboratory—Dr. Teller," June 19, 1952, doc. no. 2899, RG 128, NARA; Teller to Murray, June 20, 1952; Dean to Bethe, June 23, 1952, RG 326, NARA; LeBaron to Borden, June 30, 1952, doc. no. DXXXVII, RG 128, NARA; Walker and Hamilton, "Denver Meeting," July 1, 1952, RG 128, NARA.

17. York, *Making Weapons, Talking Peace,* pp. 67–68; Blumberg and Owens, *Energy and Conflict,* p. 291; Childs, *An American Genius,* pp. 444–445; Walker to file, "Project Whitney," November 10, 1952, TN box 60, doc. no. DCVII, RG 128, NARA.

18. Edward L. Heller to file, "Project Whitney," October 7, 1952, doc. no. 8055, RG 128, NARA; Charles Critchfield, interview with author, October 28, 1987; Francis Low, interview with author, March 4, 1999. Gell-Mann was already committed to going to Chicago. By September 1952, Lawrence had recruited 123 scientists and technicians. The Materials Testing Accelerator was originally set up to produce uranium-235, but plentiful sources had subsequently been discovered in Colorado and elsewhere in the United States.

19. This chapter also owes much to Sybil Francis, "Warhead Politics"; and Sybil Francis, "Between Science and Politics"; and Sybil Francis, Lecture at the Air and Space Museum, Smithsonian Institution, Washington, DC, February 18, 1999; Barton Bernstein, "The Struggle for the Second Laboratory"; Herbert York, interview with Chuck Hansen, September 29, 1993; Robert Seidel, "Ernest Lawrence"; and Robert Seidel, interviews with author, June 8, 1993, and May 11 and May 30, 2001.

CHAPTER TWELVE: **A New Era**

1. Hansen, *Swords of Armageddon,* vol. 4, pp. 40–59; Jacob Wechsler, interviews with author, July 25 and October 10, 2001; Rhodes, *Dark Sun,* pp. 482–512.

2. Hansen, *Swords of Armageddon,* vol. 3, p. 280.

3. Jacob Wechsler, interview with author, October 10, 2001; Carson Mark, interview with author, September 26, 1989.

4. Rhodes, *Dark Sun,* p. 487; George Bell, interview with author, March 8, 2000.

5. George Bell, interview with author, October 7, 1999; Jacob Wechsler, interviews with author, July 25 and October 10, 2001.

6. Hansen, *Swords of Armageddon,* vol. 4, p. 67; Rhodes, *Dark Sun,* p. 503.

7. Bernstein, "Crossing the Rubicon"; Stern with Green, *Oppenheimer Case,* pp. 194–195; *IMJRO,* p. 248.

8. According to a memo of John Ferguson, deputy director of the Policy Planning Staff, dated September 2, 1952, Bush gave Acheson a paper, but the text has not been found, *FRUS,* 1952–1954, vol. 2, part 2, pp. 992–993; Zachary, *Endless Frontier,* p. 363.

9. Bradbury to Oppenheimer, June 11, 1952.

10. Bethe oral history interview with Charles Weiner, session 3, May 1972, p. 27, AIP; Bethe to Dean, May 23, 1952, CD 471.6, RG 330, NARA; Dean in his reply agreed about the danger of intensifying the effort "in public." Dean to Bethe, June 23, 1952, Dean's unclassified reader file, RG 326, NARA. At this point, Bethe himself fell victim to secrecy: on August 14, 1952, Teller wrote a reply to Bethe's memorandum for Air Force Secretary Finletter and enclosed carbon copies for Bethe and Dean. In response to a July 25, 1990, query from the author as to whether he had written a classified response, Bethe wrote, "I did not know about Teller's memorandum until today, so I did not write a rejoinder."

11. Bethe to Dean, September 9, 1952, RG 326, NARA.

12. "Timing of the Thermonuclear Test," *FRUS,* 1952–1954, vol. 2, part 2, pp. 994–1008; an unsigned memorandum with the penciled notation "9/5/52" is apparently the substance of the panel's remarks to Acheson. At his security hearing, Oppenheimer testified that the panel had made its points orally, not in a written memorandum. The panel's proposal rested on an argument that a test by either side could not escape detection by the other, a premise that was undercut by Luis Alvarez's incorrectly informing Finletter that the hydrogen bomb could be developed without testing.

13. *AS,* pp. 591–592; Anders, ed., *Forging the Atomic Shield,* pp. 218–230; Deborah Gore Dean, interview with author, June 11, 2001; Eugene Zuckert, interview with author, November 28, 1990. Deborah Dean must have been reporting what her mother told her, since she was not yet born in 1952.

14. Hansen, *Swords of Armageddon,* vol. 4, pp. 70–77; Rhodes, *Dark Sun,* p. 509.

15. York, *Making Weapons, Talking Peace,* p. 69.

16. *IMJRO,* p. 562.

CHAPTER THIRTEEN: **Sailing Close to the Wind**

1. Ladd to Hoover, January 23, 1952, JRO/FBI; Hoover to Souers, March 26, 1952, JRO/FBI; Hoover to Souers, April 16, 1952, JRO/FBI. Pitzer asked to have his identity kept secret, and the FBI complied.

2. Washington Field Office 100-12253, enclosing FBI summaries of May 14 and May 27, 1952, and letter of Teller to Department of Justice, June 19, 1977.

3. FBI, Summary of May 1, 1954, "to Director FBI re JRO." The document quotes Teller as telling a JCAE staff member in 1950 that Robert Oppenheimer was "far to the left," that Frank would not have joined the Party without his brother's approval, and that if Robert were found to have given information to the Russians, "he could, of course, do more damage than any other single individual." Teller had also answered FBI questions about Oppenheimer, Robert Serber, and Philip Morrison on July 5, 1949. NLH, 90-4/32:14, FBI, April 18, 1952.

4. Gordon Dean memorandum, May 19, 1952, RG 326, NARA.

5. Kenneth Pitzer, interview with author, March 2, 1992. Pitzer's animosity apparently had an additional source: Joseph Volpe was present at a GAC meeting at which Oppenheimer subjected Pitzer, the AEC's director of research, to withering treatment. Volpe to author, December 4, 2000.

6. Pitzer to Truman, April 4, 1952; Latimer to Truman, May 29, 1952; and Urey to Truman, June 2, 1952, all at HSTPL; Kenneth Pitzer, interview with author, March 2, 1992; Walker to file, October 3, 1952, TN box 41, doc. no. 3049, RG 128; Borden to McMahon, May 28, 1952, TN box 41, doc. no. 3831, RG 128; Walker to file, May 28, 1952, TN box 41, doc. no. DXIII, RG 128, all at NARA.

7. Keay to Belmont, April 28, 1952, JRO/FBI; Borden to McMahon, May 28, 1952, TN box 41, doc. no. 3831, RG 128, NARA; Walker to file, May 28, 1952, doc. no. DXIII, RG 128, NARA.

8. Nichols to Tolson, May 29, 1952, JRO/FBI; Dean diary entries for May 16, 17, 19–23, and June 5, 11–13, 27, 1952; Dean to file, May 19, 1952; Dean to Oppenheimer, June 14, 1952, all in Dean papers, RG 326, NARA. Dean and McInerny had collaborated in framing the charges against Julius and Ethel Rosenberg in 1951 and evidently trusted each other. McMahon's staff had been relaying Griggs's reports that the Air Force believed there had been "literally criminal negligence" in the H-bomb program (Walker and Borden to McMahon, April 4, 1952, JCAE doc. no. CDXCIX, RG 128, NARA). Griggs's queries as to what they were "doing to get Oppenheimer off the GAC" (Walker to Borden, "Thermonuclear Program," April 7, 1952, JCAE doc. no. CDXCIV, RG 128, NARA) and Teller's comment, " 'Three men, one soul.' He felt very strongly that it

would be an extreme mistake to reappoint Dr. Oppenheimer" (John S. Walker, memo to file, "Conversation with Dr. Edward Teller," April 17, 1952, RG 128, NARA). Dean to Oppenheimer, June 14, 1952. In an interview on February 21, 1984, Harold Green told the author that the Justice Department had informed the AEC that it was prepared to indict Oppenheimer and bring him to trial.

9. William Hillman and David M. Noyes oral history with Sidney W. Souers, December 16, 1954, HSTPL.

10. Joseph Volpe, interviews with author, November 19 and 21, 1985; Deborah Gore Dean, interview with author, June 11, 2001; and Roger Anders, interview with author, July 19, 1989; Dean diary entries for May 16 and June 5, 1952, Dean papers, RG 326, NARA; Joseph Volpe to author, December 4, 2000.

11. Dean to Truman, August 25, 1952, and Truman to Dean, August 26, 1952, doc. no. 7693, President's Secretary's Files, HSTPL. The charge mentioning Oppenheimer was temporarily dropped at Dean's request in May 1952. The Justice Department had other reasons for its reluctance to put Oppenheimer on the stand: it would have had to reveal that it was using a paid FBI informer and possibly also that its best evidence against Weinberg was based on wiretaps.

12. McCarthy got wind of what had happened and held an executive session on September 15, 1953, at which Crouch described Truman's intervention in the Weinberg case. The transcript was released on May 5, 2003, by the Senate Permanent Subcommittee on Investigations.

13. Lovett had other informants besides Dean. According to Philip Stern, Lovett told his assistant, James Perkins, that Oppenheimer's security file was "a nightmare" and that "the quicker we get Oppenheimer out of the country, the better off we'll be." Perkins added that Lovett had mentioned the names of people who had expressed doubt to him about Oppenheimer: one of them was Lewis Strauss. Stern with Green, *Oppenheimer Case*, pp. 195–196.

14. Acheson had asked McGeorge Bundy, then dean of Harvard, to act as recording secretary, and the report was written by Bundy with Oppenheimer's participation. A slightly edited version appears as "Early Thoughts on Controlling the Nuclear Arms Race" (ed. McGeorge Bundy), *International Security* 7, no. 2 (Fall 1982).

15. *IMJRO*, pp. 751–752; Walker to file, October 3, 1952, p. 3, CD 3049, TN box 59, app. 3, RG 128, NARA; Walker to file, December 1952, "Thermonuclear Background Information—Air Force," TN box 59, app. 3, CD DLXXXVII, pp. 4–5, RG 128, NARA; Stern with Green, *Oppenheimer Case*, pp. 187–188.

16. Stern with Green, *Oppenheimer Case*, pp. 188–189. The accusation was that Oppenheimer had implied that the leaders of the Pentagon were madmen.

17. Borden to file, November 16, 1951, RG 128, NARA; Elliot, "Project Vista," pp. 163–183; Stern with Green, *Oppenheimer Case,* pp. 180–181.

18. Walker to file, "Thermonuclear Program," May 28, 1952, doc. no. DXIII, RG 128, NARA.

19. Stern with Green, *Oppenheimer Case,* pp. 189–190. Finletter's assistants, William A. M. Burden and Garrison Norton, attended the lunch, while the exchange between Finletter and Oppenheimer was described to Charles J. V. Murphy in interviews with Gilpatric and Finletter on April 1 and April 11, 1953, respectively. CJVM.

20. Charles J. V. Murphy interviews with Charles Lauritsen and Lee DuBridge, March 18, 1953. CJVM.

21. A fairly complete account by Hanson W. Baldwin did appear in the *New York Times* on June 5, 1952: "Experts Urge Tactical Air Might; Score Stress on Big Atomic Bomber"; Elliot, "Project Vista."

22. In a memo, "Project Vista," November 15, 1951, addressed to William A. M. Burden, Garrison Norton said Finletter's word was "subversive." RG 340 (records of the Office of the Secretary of the Air Force), NARA, College Park, MD. My thanks to Gregg Herken for this document. Walker to file, July 2, 1952, doc. no. 2925, RG 128, NARA. According to his Columbia oral history, Burden did not share Finletter's suspicions. Norton confined himself in a 1990 interview with the author to extolling Oppenheimer's intellect.

23. McMahon did not send either draft and told Borden that he preferred to take the matter up with the president in person, TN box 41, app. 3, doc. no. DCXXXVII, RG 128, NARA. He failed to do so, however, and because of illness or for some other reason canceled a long-standing appointment with the president. Herken, *Brotherhood of the Bomb,* p. 250, and Borden to file, May 30, 1952, RG 128, NARA.

24. Francis P. Cotter, interviews with author, November 21, 1989, and May 2, 1990.

25. The coded messages Taylor dealt with were almost certainly the "Venona" cables, existence of which was a tightly held U.S. government secret until the mid-1990s. Walters and Lyons were instructed to conduct physical surveillance of Oppenheimer from the moment his train arrived in Union Station from Princeton. In later years, Walters assured Joseph Volpe that Oppenheimer was not merely discreet but "very, very discreet." Taylor, whom Volpe saw also in later years, at their golf club, said that "no matter what you think of Oppenheimer, he wasn't a spy." Joseph Volpe, interview with author, November 21, 1985.

26. Walker and Mansfield to file, August 25, 1952, RG 128, NARA; Walker memo for file, January 13, 1953, doc. no. 3344, RG 128, NARA. The latter document contains part of what Teller told committee staffers.

27. Memo of March 2, 1953, for the commissioners from Bethe, Bradbury, Teller, and von Neumann, doc. no. DCXV, RG 326, NARA. Hansen, *Swords of Armageddon,* vol. 4, pp. 99–102.

28. Transcript of JCAE executive session, February 18, 1953, doc. no. 3281, RG 128, NARA. My thanks to Gregg Herken for this document.

CHAPTER FOURTEEN: **Strauss Returns**

1. Strauss to Hickenlooper, September 19, 1952; Hickenlooper to Eisenhower, September 26, 1952; Ralph Cake to Hickenlooper, October 10, 1952. Hickenlooper papers, HHPL. Strauss's sponsor was Herbert Hoover.

2. Walker and Borden to McMahon, April 4, 1952, doc. no. CDXCIX, RG 128, NARA. The memo continues, "It seems further that the Air Force feels that the removal of Dr. Oppenheimer [from the GAC] is an urgent and immediate necessity."

3. Murphy's work diaries for February 12, March 18, and April 8, 1953, and his interviews with Charles Lauritsen and Lee DuBridge, March 18, 1953. CJVM.

4. John Holbrook, interview with author, November 8, 1993.

5. Notes of Murphy's interview with Finletter, April 11, 1953; Murphy's work diaries for December 15, 1952, and January 15 and 23, February 6, and April 9, 14, and 16, 1953, reflect meetings with Finletter. CJVM.

6. Notes of Murphy's interview with Gilpatric, April 1, 1953; other dates when Murphy discussed the story with Gilpatric include January 23, March 31, April 14 and 16, 1953. CJVM.

7. Roswell Gilpatric, interview with author, November 30, 1993; notes of Murphy interview with Gilpatric, April 1, 1953; other dates when Murphy discussed story with Gilpatric include January 23, March 31, April 14 and 16, 1953. CJVM.

8. Murphy's interview with Lewis L. Strauss, March 12, 1953. CJVM.

9. Joseph Alsop to Murphy, October 18, 1954. Joseph Alsop Papers, LC.

10. Undated notes of Murphy's interviews with Walkowicz and Doolittle, Murphy Papers. "It is Murphy's recollection that Teddy Walkowicz . . . was Murphy's main and perhaps only source of information relative to ZORC." Hoover to Waters, June 18, 1954, FBI report 100-17828-1760, FBI/JRO. See also Hoover to Waters, June 3, 1954, FBI report 100-17828-1739, FBI/JRO; and FBI field report of June 21, 1954, by SA Joe R. Craig, FBI/JRO.

11. Notes of Murphy interview with Walkowicz, undated, CJVM. A correct way of putting it would be to say that it was an experiment to determine

whether you can use a fission bomb as a match to light a small amount of thermonuclear material.

12. Blumberg and Owens, *Energy and Conflict*, pp. 265–267; work diaries for March 24 and 31, 1953. CJVM.

13. Work diaries for April 14 and 16, 1953. CJVM.

14. On December 20, 1950, Hawkins, appearing before HUAC, took the "diminished Fifth." Schrecker, *No Ivory Tower*, p. 249. Hawkins's lawyer, Joseph Fanelli, was recommended to him by Oppenheimer.

15. Schrecker, *No Ivory Tower*, p. 157; Philip Morrison, interview with author, March 4, 2003. Morrison's interpretation was that because of Oppenheimer's stature, if he were to be attacked, it would have had to be done by the committee that was most in the public eye, the McCarthy committee, rather than the Jenner committee.

16. Killian, *Sputnik, Scientists, and Eisenhower*, p. 67. Killian says that he, Rabi, and others discussed reports that the Air Force was about to remove Oppenheimer's access to classified material, a step it had already taken in May 1951. Gregg Herken has written that it was Oppenheimer's Q clearance, for access to classified nuclear data, and not his Air Force clearance, that was in question. Herken, *Brotherhood of the Bomb*, p. 257.

17. Joseph Volpe, interviews with author, November 19 and 21, 1985; July 7 and 8, 1989; May 12, 1994.

18. Joseph Volpe, interviews with author, November 19 and 21, 1985; July 7 and 8, 1989; May 12, 1994; Stern and Green, *Oppenheimer Case*, pp. 129–130.

19. Joseph Volpe, interviews with author, November 19 and 21, 1985; July 7 and 8, 1989; May 12, 1994; Volpe to author, June 28, 2001. Contents of the "Isotopes" folder in Strauss's papers in the Hoover presidential library in West Branch, Iowa, bear out the importance of this episode to Strauss.

20. Louis and Eleanor Hempelmann, interviews with author, December 7 and 10, 1987.

CHAPTER FIFTEEN: **Two Wild Horses**

1. Gertrude Samuels, "A Plea for 'Candor' About the Atom."

2. Robert Oppenheimer, "Atomic Weapons and American Policy."

3. Belmont to Ladd, June 5, 1953, sec. 14, JRO/FBI; Bernstein, "The Oppenheimer Loyalty-Security Case Reconsidered," p. 1433.

4. Hewlett and Holl, *Atoms for Peace and War*, pp. 52–55; Deborah Gore Dean, interview with author, June 11, 2001.

5. Strauss appointment diary, 1953/1: June 1, 23, and July 10, 23, LLS;

Joanne Callahan to Strauss, July 16, Strauss memo to John Mackenzie, July 15, July 13 draft article, Murphy to Strauss, July 21, with final proof, all 1953, Murphy folder, LLS. The editor of the *Bulletin of the Atomic Scientists,* Eugene Rabinowich, later criticized a series of articles by Murphy, starting with the anonymous piece of May 1953, for violating security: Rabinowich, "Fortune's Own Operation Candor," BAS, December 1953.

6. John Holbrook, interview with author, November 8, 1993; Hewlett and Holl, *Atoms for Peace and War,* p. 47. Strauss saw Captain Hyman Rickover, Trevor Gardner of the Air Force, Willard Libby of the GAC, Kenneth Pitzer, and Luis Alvarez. Strauss tried to reach Ernest Lawrence and Leslie R. Groves, and was called by Robert Bacher and Kenneth D. Nichols. Some of them were in Washington for a meeting of the National Academy of Sciences, and their conversations with Strauss may have had nothing to do with the impending attack on Oppenheimer.

7. "Questions Raised in My Mind by JRO file—WLB," May 29, 1953, TN box 41, doc. no. DCXXXVIII, RG 128, NARA; "Comment and Recommendations," June 1, 1953, TN box 41, doc. no. DCXXXIX, RG 128, NARA.

8. William L. Borden, interview with Jack M. Holl, February 11, 1975.

9. Borden to file, August 13, 1951, app. III, JCAE doc. no. 3464, RG 128, NARA. I have dated the possible Strauss-Borden conspiracy to the late summer or early fall of 1951, when Borden drafted a letter for McMahon to Walter Bedell Smith of the State Department, inquiring about Teller's relatives. McMahon to Smith, September 28, 1951, RG 128, NARA. As for Strauss's possibly "cooling" toward Borden, Borden had asked Strauss for a job in the AEC before leaving the congressional committee. Strauss did not oblige: instead it was Hyman Rickover and Representative Chet Holifield of California who found him his job at Westinghouse. Strauss's failure to find room for Borden at the AEC may have had to do with the pending Oppenheimer affair but could also have been related to Democratic-Republican differences over the issue of public versus private power.

10. J. Kenneth Mansfield, interviews with author, May 29, May 31, and June 1, 1986; according to the *BAS,* November–December 2002, p. 103, the number of warheads, not assembled weapons, was 32 in 1947, 110 in 1948, and 236 in 1949.

11. Karl Haar, interview with author, July 11, 1990; J. K. Mansfield, interview with author, May 31, 1986; Courts Oulahan, interview with author, July 13, 1990; Frank Cotter, interviews with author, November 21, 1989, and May 2, 1990.

12. Frank Cotter, interview with author, November 21, 1989.

13. JCAE executive transcript, February 18, 1953, CD 3281, RG 128, NARA, courtesy of Gregg Herken; Harold Green, interview with author,

February 21, 1984. The author was told on excellent authority that a folder of correspondence between Borden and Strauss had been removed from Strauss's papers. This source believed that the two men worked together up to a point, but that Strauss did not have advance knowledge of Borden's letter.

14. Frank Cotter, interview with author, May 2, 1990.

CHAPTER SIXTEEN: **The Blank Wall**

1. Although most historians have said that the letter was sent by registered mail, the FBI ascertained that it came by regular mail. Nichols to Tolson, January 12, 1954, JRO/FBI; Hoover to Brownell, January 19, 1954, JRO/FBI.

2. Hoover to Tolson and Ladd, November 25, 1953, JRO/FBI; Hoover to Tolson, Ladd, and Nichols, December 3, 1953, FBI doc. no. 17828-418. Although Hoover had discouraged McCarthy from holding hearings on Oppenheimer earlier in 1953, McCarthy did hold an executive session on September 15 at which Paul Crouch described Truman's role in squelching the Weinberg prosecution.

3. Dwight D. Eisenhower, "Note for Diary," December 2, 1953, typed by Ann Whitman, Gordon Gray Papers, DDEPL.

4. Martha Burroughs's telephone conversations with author in 1985; Clarissa Parsons Fuller, interview with author, September 17, 1986; Peggy Parsons Bowditch, interview with author, July 22, 1992; Stern with Green, *Oppenheimer Case,* p. 222.

5. Bernstein, "The Oppenheimer Loyalty-Security Case Reconsidered," pp. 1383–1447.

6. Strauss got away with his deception until publication in 1989 of *Atoms for Peace and War,* the AEC's official history, by Hewlett and Holl.

7. Lewis H. Strauss, interview with author, July 6, 1989. Among those who believe that it was Strauss who urged Eisenhower to lower a "blank wall" is Strauss's son, Lewis H. Strauss, who points out that "blank wall" is the sort of expression his father would have coined. Further evidence exists in handwritten notes exchanged between Strauss and C. D. Jackson at an NSC meeting of December 18, 1953, in which Strauss wrote that "the P. himself had been consulted and had (ordered) or (concurred)." LLS, C. D. Jackson folder, HHPL. A memo by AEC security officer Bryan LaPlante, titled "J. R. Oppenheimer" and dated December 3, 1953, describes a meeting with Strauss, Nichols, and AEC general counsel William Mitchell at 3:30 p.m. that day, at which Strauss displayed a copy of the presidential order, Secretariat Files, RG 326, NARA. Thus it is clear that the president did not first consider his decision "in the chill of late afternoon" on that day, as Strauss later wrote. By 1963, when Strauss published his book, the term "blank wall" had acquired the ring

of opprobrium, as typifying the folly of the proceeding. He would logically have wanted to dissociate himself from it and deny his own role.

8. Strauss to Teller, December 3, 1953, LLS, "J. Robert Oppenheimer" folder, HHPL; Bryan LaPlante diary memo, December 3, 1953, Secretariat Files, RG 326, NARA; Teller interview of June 4, 1993, with Stanley Goldberg, Gregg Herken, Priscilla McMillan, and Richard Rhodes. During the same interview, Teller said that he had discussed the Oppenheimer situation with JCAE chairman Sterling Cole on December 2. In fact, according to Cole's 1978 oral history interview at Cornell, they discussed Atoms for Peace. This means that Strauss discussed the Atoms for Peace proposal with Teller before he told his fellow commissioners about it.

9. Blumberg and Owens, *Energy and Conflict*, p. 332; Teller interview of June 4, 1993, with Goldberg, Herken, McMillan, and Rhodes; William S. Golden, interview with author, January 3, 1990; Victor and Donna Mitchell, interview with author, November 13, 1990.

10. John MacKenzie, interview with author, February 13, 1985; Frank Cotter, interview with author, November 21, 1988.

CHAPTER SEVENTEEN: **Hoover**

1. Ladd to Hoover, March 27, 1953, sec. 14, JRO/FBI; Belmont to Ladd, April 13, 1953, sec. 14, JRO/FBI; Hoover to Tolson and Ladd, June 24, 1953, sec. 14, JRO/FBI; Belmont to Ladd, December 2, 1953, sec. 14, JRO/FBI; Green, "The Oppenheimer Case"; Lee Hancock, interviews with author, August 22, September 22, and December 13, 1983, and January 16, 1985; Hancock to Harold Green, January 22, 1966, in author's possession. The individuals Strauss had offered to purge were Carroll Wilson, former general manager of the AEC; Carroll Tyler, the AEC's former director of Santa Fe operations; Oppenheimer; and Francis Hammack of the AEC's Security Division. Strauss made the promise in March 1953, after he was appointed special White House adviser; Hoover's memo of June 24, 1953, can be read as signifying that Strauss knew the purge of Hammack was a precondition of Hoover's help in getting rid of Oppenheimer. In an interview on March 7, 1984, Harold Green told the author that he had learned of Strauss's promise to Hoover directly from AEC security officer Bryan LaPlante and indirectly, via Lee Hancock, from Francis Hammack, Charles Bates, and C. A. Rolander.

2. Mitchell did not tell Green that he had given up an attempt to do the job himself after two commissioners criticized his inclusion of charges about the H-bomb. Hewlett and Holl, *Atoms for Peace and War*, pp. 75–76; Stern with Green, *Oppenheimer Case*, pp. 223–225.

3. Harold Green, interview with author, May 14, 1984; Stern with Green, *Oppenheimer Case,* pp. 225–226; Hewlett and Holl, *Atoms for Peace and War,* p. 76.

4. Harold Green to John Manley, January 24, 1984, Manley Papers, LANL.

5. Green, "The Oppenheimer Case"; Harold Green, interview with author, May 14, 1984. Green believed that the FBI official who called him was William C. Sullivan, later head of domestic counterintelligence in the FBI.

6. Gerard Smith writes that Smyth "had a clearer idea of the dangers of the plan and its implications for nuclear proliferation than the rest of us" (Gerard Smith, *Disarming Diplomat,* p. 29). See also Mary Smyth diary entry for December 8, 1953, Smyth Papers, APS.

7. Mary Smyth's "Summary on Strauss Data," p. 2; Henry D. Smyth to Strauss, "Dr. X. Case," February 23, 1954; Henry D. Smyth to the Chairman and Commissioners, May 20, 1954; Henry D. Smyth to Cole, May 20 and June 22, 1954; Henry D. Smyth to [A. L.] Christman, August 15, 1967, all in Smyth Papers, APS; Strauss to file, December 10, 1953; Strauss memo for Smyth, December 17, 1953; Strauss memo for Snapp, December 22, 1953; Strauss memo, undated, all LLS; Hewlett and Holl, *Atoms for Peace and War,* pp. 71–72. Smyth did not learn until April 1954 that Strauss had met with the president on December 3, 1953, or that he had ordered the AEC general manager in July 1953 to discourage consultation with Oppenheimer.

8. Minutes of 957th AEC meeting (NARA), courtesy of Gregg Herken; Bernstein, "The Oppenheimer Loyalty-Security Case Reconsidered"; Mary Smyth diary entries for December 20–26, 1953, and February 3, 1954, Smyth Papers, APS. Smyth made his objections on December 18 and December 21, and was told by AEC general counsel William Mitchell that his colleagues had agreed to inclusion of the H-bomb count. He later realized that this was not the case: Zuckert had not agreed to it and there was a question as to whether Murray had agreed. Smyth, draft memo to Strauss, "Dr. X. Case," February 2, 1954; Smyth to Strauss, "Dr. X Case," April 5, 1954; Smyth to Chairman and Commissioners, May 20, 1954, Smyth Papers, APS.

9. Hoover to Tolson, Ladd, Belmont, Clavin, and Nichols, December 15, 1953, JRO/FBI. The other officials in attendance were Arthur Flemming, head of the Office of Defense Mobilization, and Robert Cutler, national security adviser to the president.

10. Hoover to Tolson, Ladd, Belmont, Clavin, and Nichols, December 15, 1953, JRO/FBI; File number 77-47503-2, Lewis L. Strauss, FBI.

11. Frank Cotter, interview with author, May 2, 1990.

12. Stern with Green, *Oppenheimer Case,* pp. 211–213 and 229–232.

13. Anne W. Marks, interview with author, August 2, 1986; Alice H. Strauss, interview with author, November 28, 1990.

14. Stern with Green, *Oppenheimer Case,* pp. 229–231; Hewlett and Holl, *Atoms for Peace and War,* pp. 78–80; Belmont to Ladd, December 21, 1953, JRO/FBI; Strauss to file, April 15, 1954, LLS.

15. Hewlett and Holl, *Atoms for Peace and War,* pp. 79–80; Stern with Green, *Oppenheimer Case,* pp. 231–232. Herbert Marks's widow, Anne, remembers the day differently: she recalls picking up Oppenheimer by car at the AEC building, his coming out white as a sheet and telling her what had happened, and her driving him home to the Markses' house, where they were joined by Volpe and Marks (Anne Wilson Marks, interview with author, August 2, 1986). But the recorded conversation in Volpe's office appears to confirm the version given here. Volpe and his partner discovered that their offices were tapped when something came up the next day in the Dixon-Yates matter that showed advance knowledge by the AEC. Harold Green reports having seen wiretapped reports for that day from Marks's and Volpe's offices (author interview of May 14, 1984). Knowing that Oppenheimer would go to either Marks or Volpe, the FBI had placed wiretaps in both offices.

16. Hoover to Brownell, December 21, 1953, JRO/FBI; Hoover to SAC Newark, December 28, 1953, JRO/FBI; Brownell to the author, September 9, 1993.

17. Belmont to Ladd, December 23, 1953, JRO/FBI. Oppenheimer's attorneys represented him free of charge throughout the hearings, and he had to pay only their out-of-pocket expenses, which, in the case of Garrison's firm, amounted to about twenty-five thousand dollars.

18. Stern with Green, *Oppenheimer Case,* pp. 235–236; Louis and Eleanor Hempelmann, interview with author, December 7, 1987. Mrs. Hempelmann's observation could have occurred either on Snapp's first visit, on Christmas Eve, or on his second visit, on New Year's Eve, when he actually retrieved the documents.

19. Stern with Green, *Oppenheimer Case,* pp. 240–241; Anne Wilson Marks, interview with author, August 2, 1986; Charles Horsky, interview with author, December 19, 1986; "Re: Dr. J. Robert Oppenheimer," January 14, 1954, an FBI field office report, quotes a "reliable confidential informant" to the effect that O'Brian told Herbert Marks that he wanted to take the case but could not do so "because of the disapproval of his partners." Covington and Burling was Acheson's law firm as well.

20. Belmont to Ladd, January 5, 1954, JRO/FBI.

21. Strauss to Hoover, February 1, 1954, LLS; Strauss to Bates, February 8, 1954, JRO/FBI. Of the 110 reports on Oppenheimer sent by the FBI be-

tween December 22 and April 12, more than 50 were disguised as personal letters from Hoover to Strauss. Hewlett and Holl, *Atoms for Peace and War,* p. 85.

22. Charles W. Bates, interview with author, October 12, 1983; Joan Harrington, interview with author, November 26, 1990.

23. Charles W. Bates, interview with author, October 12, 1983; Harold Green, interview with author, May 14, 1984; Green, "The Oppenheimer Case"; Belmont to Ladd, February 2, 1954, p. 2, JRO/FBI.

24. Hoover to Tolson, Ladd, and Nichols, February 1, 1954, JRO/FBI.

25. Lee Hancock, interview with author, August 22, 1983; Lee Hancock to Harold Green, January 22, 1966 (courtesy of Lee Hancock).

26. Hancock to Green, January 22, 1966; Belmont to Ladd, January 26, 1954, JRO/FBI.

27. *IMJRO,* pp. 3–7; Joseph Volpe, interview with author, November 19, 1985.

28. Pfau, *No Sacrifice Too Great,* pp. 163–167; Rhodes, *Dark Sun,* pp. 541–543.

29. Rhodes, *Dark Sun,* pp. 524–526. Joe Four's yield was four hundred kilotons.

CHAPTER EIGHTEEN: **The Hearing Begins**

1. Reston, *Deadline,* p. 221.

2. Hewlett and Holl, *Atoms for Peace and War,* pp. 89–91; a story by Joseph and Stewart Alsop, also sympathetic to Oppenheimer, appeared the same day on page one of the *Times*'s competitor, the *New York Herald-Tribune;* notes of James C. Hagerty, April 8–11, 1954, Hagerty Papers, DDEPL. The strategy was developed at meetings attended by Sherman Adams, Hagerty, Murray Snyder, and Wilton Persons for the White House, and Commissioners Strauss and Campbell of the AEC.

3. Oppenheimer had been cleared informally by Gordon Dean in 1950, and by Walter Whitman, chairman of the Research and Development Board of DoD, in July 1953, under the Eisenhower executive order.

4. Samuel J. Silverman, interview with author, October 5, 1989.

5. James G. Beckerley, interview with author, June 6, 1987; Arnold with Pyne, *Britain and the H-Bomb,* p. 92. At a meeting of commissioners the following summer, Smyth put his finger on the problem when he said he had been worried about "rate and scale and direction of thinking information, and specifically . . . the question of the change in the thermonuclear program and the time it occurred." Minutes of 1,017th AEC meeting, July 23, 1954, NARA. My thanks to Gregg Herken for this document.

6. Samuel J. Silverman, interview with author, October 5, 1989.

7. Charles W. Bates, interviews with author, October 5, 12, and 17, 1983; FBI file dated December 14, 1959, titled "J. Robert Oppenheimer." This file lists 428 documents, mostly wiretapped conversations, transmitted by the FBI to the Atomic Energy Commission between 1947 and 1958. General Correspondence series, JRO file/RG 128, NARA. My thanks to Gregg Herken for this document. Strauss memo to Robb, February 23, 1954, suggesting questions for Bradbury, Rabi, and Groves, LLS AEC, JRO file.

8. Roger Robb to Samuel B. Ballen, December 1, 1976; Irene Rice Robb, interview with author, November 11, 1988; Harold Tyler, interview with author, October 24, 1989; Patrick Raher, interview with author, November 11, 1991; Judge Oliver Gasch, interview with author, November 13, 1991; Mrs. Ruth Luff, interview with author, January 4, 1992; Judge Paul Friedman, interview with author, May 31, 1986.

9. Manchester, *The Glory and the Dream,* pp. 697–698.

10. *IMJRO,* p. 137.

11. *IMJRO,* p. 146. What neither Oppenheimer, Chevalier, nor Army security seems to have known then or later was that Eltenton was a physicist, not an engineer, and that he worked from 1934 to 1937 in Leningrad under Yuli Khariton, an important figure in Soviet nuclear research and later director of the Soviet H-bomb program. He was also close to Shalnikov, another prominent Soviet nuclear physicist.

12. *IMJRO,* p. 149.

13. Stern with Green, *Oppenheimer Case,* p. 280.

14. Samuel J. Silverman, interview with author, October 5, 1989.

15. Joseph Volpe, interviews with author, November 19, 1985, and July 7, 1989; Stern with Green, *Oppenheimer Case,* pp. 305–309; Goodchild, *J. Robert Oppenheimer: Shatterer of Worlds,* p. 244.

16. Samuel J. Silverman, interviews with author, October 5, 1989, and July 2, 1998.

17. *IMJRO,* pp. 649–650, 656.

18. *IMJRO,* pp. 306, 322, and 517.

19. *IMJRO,* pp. 356–357, 365.

20. *IMJRO,* pp. 566–567.

21. *IMJRO,* p. 468.

22. "Dates and times of appointments Dr. Rabi had with Mr. Strauss at AEC building during month of April, 1954," and Strauss to "Joe" [Campbell], undated, but probably April 16, 1954, in Rabi folder, LLS. Belmont to Boardman, April 17, 1954, JRO/FBI; Strauss to Robb, April 16, 1954, in Oppenheimer folder, LLS. See also James Reston, "Oppenheimer Case Stirs Re-

sentment Among Scientists," *New York Times,* April 15, 1954; Walter Lippmann, "The Oppenheimer Case," *New York Herald-Tribune,* April 15, 1954; and Drew Pearson, "Admiral Strauss Sorry He Started Fuss, Oppenheimer Made Him Look Foolish," *New Mexican,* April 20, 1954.

23. Belmont to Ladd, January 7 and 15, 1954, JRO/FBI.

24. Strauss to file, January 22, 1954, LLS; Belmont to Ladd, January 26, 1954, JRO/FBI.

25. I. I. Rabi, interviews with author, July 22, 1985, and January 31, 1986.

26. In an interview of December 11, 1985, George Kennan used almost the same words: "Oppenheimer had a brain that was outsize and too much for his physical and emotional frame."

27. Ruth and Harold Cherniss, interviews with author, December 13, 1985.

CHAPTER NINETEEN: **Smyth**

1. "M's Summary on Strauss Data," from Mary Smyth's diary, Smyth Papers, APS. Smyth learned on May 8, 1953, that he would not be appointed chairman, and on May 9 he heard, via radio, of the *Fortune* attack on Oppenheimer.

2. Mary Smyth diary entry of May 25, 1954, Smyth Papers, APS.

3. Times of visits and calls are from Strauss's appointment calendar and telephone log, April 26–30, 1954, LLS.

4. Roger Robb, memo for file, July 24, 1967, LLS; John Wheeler, interview with author, November 14, 1985; Hans and Rose Bethe, interview with author, December 3, 1986; Hans Bethe, interview with Charles Weiner, part 3, April 1972, AIP.

5. Teller's testimony appears on pp. 709–727 of *IMJRO,* this remark on p. 710.

6. Memo of Charter Heslep to Lewis L. Strauss, May 3, 1954. Years afterward, defense attorney Silverman said he had no doubt that Teller's testimony had been the result of a deal, with Robb asking, "Will you say that?" and Teller saying, "so far and no farther," and Robb knowing exactly how far Teller was willing to go. Samuel Silverman, interview with author, October 5, 1989.

7. *IMJRO,* p. 726.

8. Stern with Green, *Oppenheimer Case,* p. 340.

9. Herbert Childs, *An American Genius,* pp. 466–473; Molly B. Lawrence, interview with author, February 24, 1992. Mrs. Lawrence said that her husband was "horribly torn," did not know what he was going to say, and felt relief when he did not have to testify. She attributed his feeling of betrayal to an

incident over Frank, to passages in Oppenheimer's testimony in which he admitted lying about the Chevalier episode, and to having heard from a neighbor at Balboa Island that Oppenheimer had allegedly had a long love affair with Ruth Tolman, wife of his colleague Richard Tolman.

10. Childs, *An American Genius,* p. 473. The men he summoned to his room were Leland J. Haworth, Thomas H. Johnson, and Clarence E. Larson. Mrs. Lawrence vouched for Childs's accuracy and added that her husband was not pretending to be sicker than he was.

11. Alvarez, *The Adventures of a Physicist,* p. 180. Lawrence's defection deprived the Berkeley contingent of its heaviest heavyweight: Oppenheimer's old, old friend and one with whom he had worked closely in the 1930s.

CHAPTER TWENTY: Borden

1. Allan B. Ecker, interview with author, June 18, 1989. Ecker concluded that Robb had been playing a recording of the August 26, 1943, conversation between Oppenheimer, Pash, and Lyall Johnson. In his questioning of Pash on April 30, Robb asked: "Have you recently refreshed your recollection about this interview by looking over a copy of that transcript?" Pash said: "I have." *IMJRO,* p. 814.

2. Alvarez, *IMJRO,* pp. 770–805; Latimer, *IMJRO,* pp. 656–667; Pitzer, *IMJRO,* pp. 697–709.

3. For Wilson's testimony, see *IMJRO,* pp. 679–697; for the information about Vandenberg, see Meilinger, *Hoyt S. Vandenberg,* p. 155.

4. Interview of Lieutenant General Roscoe C. Wilson by Lieutenant Colonel Dennis A. Smith, December 1–2, 1983, Air Force Oral History Program.

5. Getting to author, March 2, 1990.

6. "To Whom It May Concern" letter of Dr. Allen F. Donovan, dated November 19, 1989, and sent to the author by Ivan Getting; FBI Report 100-17828-1739, "Hoover to Waters via Liaison," June 3, 1954, reports the denials by Piore and Overhage, as well as the remarks by Griggs cited here.

7. Guyford Stever, telephone interview with author, April 27, 1990.

8. FBI Report 100-17828-1760, "Hoover to Waters via Liaison," and marked "attention Rolander," reads in part: "On June 12, Mr. Charles J. V. Murphy was interviewed. . . . [H]e stated that he had no direct or firsthand knowledge relative to the origin of the term ZORC. It is Murphy's recollection that Teddy Walcowicz [*sic*], former Air Force officer, was Murphy's main and possibly only source of information relative to ZORC."

9. *IMJRO,* pp. 834 and 839; Courts Oulahan, interview with author, July 13, 1990.

10. Samuel J. Silverman, interviews with author, October 5, 1989, and July 2, 1998.

11. *IMJRO*, pp. 971–990; Stern with Green, *Oppenheimer Case*, p. 367.

12. Hennrich to Belmont, May 20, 1954, JRO/FBI.

13. Goodchild, *J. Robert Oppenheimer*, pp. 260–261.

14. Charles W. Bates, interviews with author, October 5 and 17, 1983.

CHAPTER TWENTY-ONE: **Caesar's Wife**

1. President Eisenhower told Philip Stern on July 19, 1967, that he "believes he talked with Mr. Gray, and asked him to serve in that capacity" (Stern to Schulz, July 21, 1967, Stern Papers, JFKPL.

2. Green, "The Oppenheimer Case."

3. Harold P. Green, interview with author, May 14, 1984; Polly Wisner Fritchey, interview with author, June 16, 1989; Mrs. Gordon Gray, interview with author, June 14, 1989; Boyden Gray, interview with author, May 3, 1991; Gordon Gray Jr., interview with author, April 4, 1989; and Joan Harrington, interview with author, November 26, 1990. Gray did try to end the hearing, but the person to whom he appealed was not, as he later told Boyden, Lloyd Garrison, but Roger Robb. Gray also gave his family the impression that he and Morgan had gone into the case expecting to clear Oppenheimer, but his notes at the time indicate that he, Morgan, and Evans all were inclined against clearance from the start and that the inclination grew stronger during their immersion in the prosecution's documents before the hearing. Notes dictated by Gray to Ardith Johnson, May 7–14, Gray Papers, DDEPL.

4. Lee Hancock, interview with author, September 22, 1983; Lee Hancock to Harold Green, January 22, 1966, author's files. Some witnesses were told that their testimony was being released and others were asked for permission. One, Jerrold Zacharias, told the author that he refused permission. His testimony was published nevertheless.

5. James Hagerty diary entry for June 15, 1954, Hagerty Papers, DDEPL; Strauss to Gray, June 11, 1954, Gray Papers, DDEPL. According to a memo by Strauss, Garrison may have talked to a public relations adviser about representing the defense in March, but there is no evidence that he did so later. Strauss to file, May 18, 1954, LLS.

6. Murphy's work diaries, June 8, 10, 14, 17, 18, 19, 1954, CJVM. Reid immediately called a high-ranking FBI official, Louis B. Nichols, for advice on how to handle Gray. Nichols to Tolson, June 18, 1954, FBI.

7. Kalven, "The Case of J. Robert Oppenheimer Before the Atomic Energy Commission."

8. Ambrose, *Eisenhower, the President,* pp. 476–477.

9. Murphy's work diaries, CJVM.

10. Mary Smyth diary, June 20–July 10, 1954; "From M's Diary: M's Summary on Strauss Data 1954"; and "Answers to Questions from Philip Stern," August 7, 1967. All in Smyth Papers, APS.

11. H. D. Smyth, interview with author, December 10, 1985; "Answers to Questions from Philip Stern," August 7, 1967, Smyth Papers, APS. Farley did not consider Nichols's warning a threat. Moreover, he was planning to leave the AEC to become assistant to Gerard Smith, chief atomic energy adviser to the Department of State. Philip Farley, telephone interview with author, February 2, 1987.

12. *IMJRO,* pp. 1049–1052.

13. *IMJRO,* pp. 1058–1061.

14. Henry DeWolf Smyth, interview with author, December 10, 1985; Philip Farley, telephone interview with author, February 2, 1987.

15. *IMJRO,* pp. 1061–1065.

16. Mary Smyth diary entry for June 30, 1954, Smyth Papers, APS; "Answers to Questions from Philip Stern," August 7, 1967, Smyth Papers, APS; H. D. Smyth, interview with author, December 10, 1985.

17. Father Daniel Bradley Murray, interview with author, November 12, 1990. John Courtney Murray's papers at the Georgetown University library document his close friendships with Thomas Murray, Henry R. Luce, and Clare Boothe Luce, whom he catechized upon her conversion to Catholicism.

18. Lewis H. Strauss, interview with author, July 6, 1989.

19. Eugene Zuckert, interview with author, November 28, 1990.

20. Harold Green, interview with author, November 13, 1991; Philip Farley, telephone interview with author, October 20, 1983.

21. Eugene Zuckert, interview with author, November 28, 1990.

CHAPTER TWENTY-TWO: **Do We Really Need Scientists?**

1. Hagerty diary entry, June 29, 1954, DDEPL.

2. Hagerty diary entry, May 29, 1954 (Strauss was considering Kenneth Pitzer as Zuckert's replacement). Between April 9 and June 30, Hagerty's diary records contacts with Strauss in person or by telephone on at least fifteen days, including one day when they spoke about the Oppenheimer case four or five times; Strauss's diary records at least four solo visits with the president and numerous other occasions when the two men saw each other in the presence of others.

3. Brownell to author, September 9, 1993.

4. Jerry Hannifin, telephone conversation with author, July 19, 2003. The author's guess is Robb.

5. Murphy work diaries, October 5, 1953, and August 18, 1954, CJVM.

6. Clay Blair, interview with author, February 22, 1993; Borden to Allardice, March 22, 1954, NND 902010, TN box 58, RG 128, NARA. Before leaving the JCAE on June 1, Borden, who wished to remain in Washington, asked Strauss whether he had a place for him at the AEC. But Strauss apparently did not want Borden in Washington, and it was Rickover and Representative Chet Holifield of California who found him his job at Westinghouse.

7. Clay Blair, interviews with author, February 22, 1993, and March 20, 1994. The author's conjecture that Borden and Strauss made such a plan in the autumn of 1951 is based on the August 13, 1951, conversation between the two men and on Borden's letter in late September 1951, to Walter Bedell Smith of the State Department, seeking help in getting Teller's relatives out of Hungary.

8. Clay Blair, interview with author, February 22, 1993.

9. Clay Blair, interviews with author, February 22, 1993, and March 20, 1994. Leach was also consulted about air strategy in Europe by James B. Conant while he was president of Harvard.

10. In an interview with the author on February 22, 1993, Blair described accompanying Shepley to Strauss's office, while Shepley, on the NBC television program *Comment*, on September 26, 1954, said Strauss had summoned him but made no mention of Blair's presence (from an unpublished article on the Shepley-Blair book by Chuck Hansen). Blair told the author that there had been a fire burning in Strauss's office at the time of his visit with Shepley. Since the meeting took place in mid-June, one wonders whether Blair's memory may have slipped and whether the fire might have been lit earlier, during one of his interviews with Strauss for the book.

11. Vannevar Bush, "If We Alienate Our Scientists."

12. Carson Mark letter of June 29, 1954, *BAS*, September 1954; excerpt from Drew Pearson broadcast, October 23, 1954, Teeple folder, LLS; minutes of forty-first GAC meeting, p. 54, box 4932, RG 326, NARA. Three members of Strauss's staff at the AEC were thought to be "gumshoeing": two of them, McKay Donkin and Bryan LaPlante, together with Strauss's secretary, Virginia Walker, reported on Smyth's activities throughout the summer of 1954.

13. Teller with Shoolery, *Memoirs*, p. 401.

14. Bradbury actually answered the charges from the condensed version in *U.S. News & World Report*, September 21, 1954, prior to the book's publication on September 28. Livermore's first successful large-scale fusion test took place only in 1956, and its first design, the W-27, did not go into production until 1958, six years after the lab was founded.

15. Gordon Dean press release of September 28, 1954, with review at-

tached, from David Lilienthal Papers, Princeton University Library; Dean to Strauss, September 10, 1954, LLS; Froman et al. to Strauss, September 28, 1954, RG 326, LANL; Strauss to Froman, October 12, 1954, RG 326, LANL. Strauss reviewed at least two drafts of the Shepley-Blair book: first in early June, prior to his attempt to purchase the manuscript, and second in early July. Chuck Hansen's unpublished article on the book cites a letter from Strauss to Pearl Carroll of Time Inc., dated July 10, 1954, with questions and suggested changes, in Strauss's handwriting. Strauss saw Shepley at least six times during May and June of 1954, most of these meetings lasting more than an hour and at least three of them with no one else present. During those visits Strauss may also have helped with *Time*'s June 14, 1954, cover story on Oppenheimer. In addition to Blair's several hours with Borden in January 1954, Shepley and Blair had been coached by Murphy, had had personal access to his sources, and had read the notes for his stories in *Fortune*.

16. Joseph and Stewart Alsop, "Do We Need Scientists?" *New York Herald-Tribune*, October 1, 1954; Elie Abel, "The Attack on Oppenheimer Continues," *Reporter*, October 21, 1954.

17. All in LLS, Teller folder, HHPL: Teller to Strauss, July 2, 1954; Strauss to Teller, July 6, 1954; Robb to Teller, July 8, 1954, with enclosure; Teller to Robb, July 30, 1954.

18. Teller to Strauss, July 2, 1954; Strauss to Dulles, July 27, 1954. In LLS, Teller folder, HHPL. After his meeting with Blair in February, Borden wrote to his successor at the JCAE and asked him to follow up a 1951 inquiry he himself had made about the relatives. Borden to Allardice, March 22, 1954, NND902010, RG 128, NARA; McMahon to [W. Bedell] Smith, September 28, 1951, doc. no. CDVII, RG 128, NARA.

19. Teller with Shoolery, *Memoirs*, p. 405. In his autobiography, the Italian-born physicist Emilio Segrè wrote that Fermi considered Teller's testimony at the Oppenheimer hearing "unethical." Segrè, *A Mind Always in Motion*.

20. Teller, "The Work of Many People," *Science*, February 25, 1955.

21. Murphy to Teller, May 17, 1961, LLS, Murphy folder, HHPL.

CHAPTER TWENTY-THREE: **Oppenheimer**

1. Peter Oppenheimer, interview with author, November 16, 1987.

2. George Kennan, interview with author, December 11, 1985.

3. Verna Hobson, interview with author, September 20, 1986.

4. Anne Marks, interview with author, November 11, 1986. (The prize money was fifty thousand dollars.)

CHAPTER TWENTY-FOUR: **We Made It—and We Gave It Away**

1. Gerard Smith, *Disarming Diplomat,* p. 37; Leonard Weiss, "Atoms for Peace," *BAS,* November–December 2003.

2. James Killian, interview with Stephen White, 1969, pp. 225–228, COHP. The author is indebted to David Holloway for the insight that the Air Force held us back.

3. Charles Bates, interview with author, October 12, 1983.

4. I. I. Rabi, interview with Chauncey Olinger, 1983, box 3, pp. 759–760 and 827–828, COHP.

Postlude

1. H. D. Smyth, interview with author, December 10, 1985.

2. Mary Smyth Papers, APS.

3. JRO to Smyth, July 5, 1954, Smyth folder, JRO Papers, LC.

SELECTED BIBLIOGRAPHY

Books

Acheson, Dean. *Morning and Noon*. Boston: Houghton Mifflin, 1965.

———. *Present at the Creation: My Years in the State Department*. New York: Norton, 1969.

———. *Sketches From Life*. New York: Harper & Bros., 1959.

Albright, Joseph, and Marcia Kunstel. *Bombshell: The Secret Story of America's Unknown Atomic Spy Conspiracy*. New York: Times Books, 1997.

Alperovitz, Gar. *The Decision to Use the Atomic Bomb and the Architecture of an American Myth*. New York: Knopf, 1995.

Alsop, Joseph W., with Adam Platt. *I've Seen the Best of It*. New York: Norton, 1992.

Altshuler, B. L., B. M. Bolotovsky, I. M. Dremin, V. Y. Fainberg, and L. V. Keldysh, eds. *Andrei Sakharov. Facets of a Life*. Gif-sur-Yvette, France: Editions Frontières, 1991.

Alvarez, Luis W. *The Adventures of a Physicist*. New York: Basic Books, 1987.

Ambrose, Stephen E. *Eisenhower, the President*. New York: Simon & Schuster, 1984.

Anders, Roger M., ed. *Forging the Atomic Shield: Excerpts from the Office Diary of Gordon E. Dean*. Chapel Hill: University of North Carolina Press, 1987.

Andrew, Christopher, and Vasili Mitrokhin. *The Sword and the Shield: The Mitrokhin Archive and the Secret History of the KGB*. New York: Basic Books, 1999.

Arnold, Lorna, with Katherine Pyne. *Britain and the H-Bomb*. Houndmills, UK: Palgrave, 2001.

Badash, Lawrence. *Scientists and the Development of Nuclear Weapons: From Fission to the Limited Test Ban Treaty, 1939–1963*. Atlantic Highlands, NJ: Humanities Press International, 1995.

Badash, Lawrence, Joseph O. Hirschfelder, and Herbert P. Broida, eds. *Reminiscences of Los Alamos, 1943–1945*. Dordrecht, the Netherlands: Reidel, 1980.

Benson, Robert Louis, and Michael Warner, eds. *VENONA: Soviet Espionage and the American Response, 1939–1957*. Washington, DC: Central Intelligence Agency, 1996.

Bernstein, Jeremy. *Hans Bethe: Prophet of Energy*. New York: Dutton, 1981.

———. *The Life It Brings: One Physicist's Beginnings*. New York: Ticknor and Fields, 1987.

———. *Oppenheimer: Portrait of an Enigma*. Chicago: Ivan Dee, 2004.

Bix, Herbert P. *Hirohito and the Making of Modern Japan*. New York: HarperCollins, 2000.

Blackett, P. M. S. *Fear, War, and the Bomb*. New York: McGraw-Hill, 1948.

Blumberg, Stanley, and Gwinn Owens. *Energy and Conflict: The Life and Times of Edward Teller*. New York: Putnam, 1976.

Blumberg, Stanley, and Louis Panos. *Edward Teller: Giant of the Golden Age of Physics*. New York: Scribner's, 1990.

Borden, William L. *There Will Be No Time: The Revolution in Strategy*. New York: Macmillan, 1946.

Bowen, Lee, and Robert D. Little. *A History of the Air Force Atomic Energy Program, 1943–1953*. 5 vols. Washington, DC: Air University Historical Liaison Office, Bolling Air Force Base.

Bowie, Robert R., and Richard H. Immerman. *Waging Peace*. New York: Oxford University Press, 1998.

Boyer, Paul. *By the Bomb's Early Light*. Chapel Hill: University of North Carolina Press, 1994.

Bradley, Omar N., and Clay Blair Jr. *A General's Life*. New York: Simon & Schuster, 1983.

Broad, William. *Star Warriors*. New York: Simon & Schuster, 1985.

———. *Teller's War: The Top Secret Story Behind the Star Wars Deception*. New York: Simon & Schuster, 1992.

Brower, Kenneth. *The Starship and the Canoe*. New York: Harper & Row, 1983.

Brown, Andrew. *The Neutron and the Bomb: A Biography of Sir James Chadwick*. Oxford: Oxford University Press, 1997.

Brown, John Mason. *Through These Men*. New York: Harper, 1956.

Brownell, Herbert, with John P. Burke. *Advising Ike*. Lawrence: University Press of Kansas, 1993.

Bundy, McGeorge. *Danger and Survival: Choices About the Bomb in the First Fifty Years*. New York: Random House, 1988.

Bush, Vannevar. *Modern Arms and Free Men*. New York: Simon & Schuster, 1949.

———. *Pieces of the Action*. New York: Morrow, 1970.

Butow, Robert J. C. *Japan's Decision to Surrender*. Stanford, CA: Stanford University Press, 1954.

Byrnes, James F. *All in One Lifetime.* New York: Harper & Row, 1958.

———. *Speaking Frankly.* New York: Harper & Bros., 1947.

Cassidy, David C. *Uncertainty: The Life and Science of Werner Heisenberg.* New York: Freeman, 1991.

Chevalier, Haakon. *The Man Who Would Be God.* New York: Putnam, 1959.

———. *Oppenheimer: The Story of a Friendship.* New York: Braziller, 1965.

Childs, Herbert. *An American Genius: The Life of Ernest Orlando Lawrence, Father of the Cyclotron.* New York: Dutton, 1968.

Christman, Al. *Target Hiroshima: Deak Parsons and the Creation of the Atomic Bomb.* Annapolis, MD: Naval Institute Press, 1998.

Cohen, Sam. *Shame: Confessions of the Father of the Neutron Bomb.* Xlibris, 2000.

Compton, Arthur. *Atomic Quest.* New York: Oxford University Press, 1956.

Conant, Jennet. *Tuxedo Park.* New York: Simon & Schuster, 2002.

Craig, William. *The Fall of Japan.* New York: Dial, 1967.

Curtis, Charles P., Jr. *The Oppenheimer Case: The Trial of a Security System.* New York: Simon & Schuster, 1955.

Davis, Hope Hale. *Great Day Coming.* South Royalton, VT: Steerforth, 1994.

Davis, Nuell Pharr. *Lawrence and Oppenheimer.* New York: Simon & Schuster, 1968.

Day, Dwayne A. *Lightning Rod: A History of the Air Force Chief Scientist's Office.* Washington, DC: Chief Scientist's Office, U.S. Air Force, 2000.

Divine, Robert. *Blowing on the Wind: The Nuclear Test Ban Debate, 1954–1960.* New York: Oxford University Press, 1978.

Donovan, Robert J. *The Presidency of Harry S. Truman, 1945–1948: Conflict and Crisis.* New York: Norton, 1977.

———. *The Presidency of Harry S. Truman, 1949–1953: The Tumultuous Years.* New York: Norton, 1982.

Dorwart, Jeffery M. *Eberstadt and Forrestal.* College Station: Texas A & M Press, 1991.

Drell, Sidney D., and Sergei P. Kapitsa. *Sakharov Remembered.* Woodbury, NY: American Institute of Physics, 1991.

Dyson, Freeman. *Disturbing the Universe.* New York: Harper & Row, 1979.

———. *Weapons and Hope.* New York: Harper & Row, 1984.

Eltenton, Dorothea. *Laughter in Leningrad: An English Family in Russia, 1933–1938.* Privately published, 1998.

Evangelista, Matthew. *Innovation and the Arms Race.* Ithaca, NY: Cornell University Press, 1988.

———. *Unarmed Forces.* Ithaca, NY: Cornell University Press, 1999.

Feis, Herbert. *Between War and Peace.* Princeton, NJ: Princeton University Press, 1960.

————. *Japan Subdued: The Atomic Bomb and the End of the War in the Pacific.* Princeton, NJ: Princeton University Press, 1961.

Fermi, Laura. *Atoms in the Family.* Chicago: University of Chicago Press, 1954.

————. *Illustrious Immigrants.* Chicago: University of Chicago Press, 1968.

Ferrell, Robert H. *The Diary of James C. Hagerty: Eisenhower in Mid-Course, 1954–1955.* Bloomington: Indiana University Press, 1983.

————, ed. *Harry S. Truman: A Life.* Columbia, MO: University of Missouri Press, 1994.

Fitzgerald, Frances. *Way Out There in the Blue.* New York: Simon & Schuster, 2000.

Ford, Daniel. *The Cult of the Atom.* New York: Simon & Schuster, 1982.

Frayn, Michael. *Copenhagen.* New York: Random House, 1998.

Furman, Necah Stewart. *Sandia National Laboratories: The Postwar Decade.* Albuquerque: University of New Mexico Press, 1989.

Gaddis, John Lewis. *The Long Peace.* Oxford: Oxford University Press, 1987.

————. *Strategies of Containment.* Oxford: Oxford University Press, 1982.

————. *The United States and the End of the Cold War.* New York: Oxford University Press, 1992.

————. *We Now Know: Rethinking Cold War History.* Oxford: Oxford University Press, 1997.

Gaddis, John Lewis, Philip Gordon, Ernest R. May, and Jonathan Rosenberg, eds. *Cold War Statesmen Confront the Bomb: Nuclear Diplomacy Since 1945.* Oxford: Oxford University Press, 1999.

Galison, Peter. *Image and Logic: A Material Culture of Microphysics.* Chicago: University of Chicago Press, 1997.

Galison, Peter, and David J. Stump, eds. *The Disunity of Science: Boundaries, Contexts, and Power.* Stanford, CA: Stanford University Press, 1996.

Gamow, George. *My World Line.* New York: Viking, 1970.

————. *Thirty Years That Shook Physics.* New York: Dover Publications, 1996.

Garthoff, Raymond L. *Détente and Confrontation.* Washington, DC: Brookings, 1985.

————. *The Great Transition.* Washington, DC: Brookings, 1994.

————. *A Journey Through the Cold War.* Washington, DC: Brookings, 2001.

Gerhart, Eugene C. *America's Advocate: Robert H. Jackson.* Indianapolis, IN: Bobbs-Merrill, 1958.

Getting, Ivan. *All in a Lifetime: Science in the Defense of Democracy.* New York: Vantage Press, 1989.

Gilpin, Robert. *American Scientists and Nuclear Weapons Policy.* Princeton, NJ: Princeton University Press, 1962.

Ginsberg, Vitaly. *On Physics and Astrophysics.* Moscow: Bureau Quantum, 1995.

Golden, William T., ed. *Science and Technology Advice to the President, Congress, and Judiciary.* New York: Pergamon Books, 1988.

Goldfischer, David. *The Best Defense.* Ithaca, NY: Cornell University Press, 1993.

Goldstein, Jack S. *A Different Sort of Time: The Life of Jerrold R. Zacharias.* Cambridge, MA: MIT Press, 1992.

Goodchild, Peter. *Edward Teller: The Real Dr. Strangelove.* London: Weidenfeld & Nicolson, 2004.

————. *J. Robert Oppenheimer: Shatterer of Worlds.* Boston: Houghton Mifflin, 1981.

Gorelik, Gennady. *Andrei Sakharov: Science and Freedom.* Moscow: RkhD, 2000.

Goudsmit, Samuel A. *Alsos.* New York: Henry Schuman, 1947.

Gowing, Margaret. *Britain and Atomic Energy, 1939–1945.* Vol. 1. London: Macmillan, 1964.

————. *Britain and Atomic Energy, 1945–1952.* Vol. 2. London: Macmillan, 1974.

Greenstein, Fred I. *The Hidden-Hand Presidency.* New York: Basic Books, 1982.

Groves, Leslie R. *Now It Can Be Told.* New York: Harper & Row, 1962.

Gusterson, Hugh. *Nuclear Rites.* Berkeley: University of California Press, 1996.

Hamby, Alonzo L. *Man of the People: A Life of Harry S. Truman.* New York: Oxford University Press, 1995.

Hansen, Chuck. *The Swords of Armageddon: U.S. Nuclear Weapons Development Since 1945.* CD-ROM. 8 vols. Chukelea Publications, 1995.

————. *U.S. Nuclear Weapons: The Secret History.* New York: Orion Books, 1988.

Hawkins, David. *Project Y: The Los Alamos Story.* Part 1, *Toward Trinity.* Woodbury, NY: American Institute of Physics, Tomash, 1983.

Haynes, John Earl, and Harvey Klehr. *Venona: Decoding Soviet Espionage in America.* New Haven, CT: Yale University Press, 1999.

Heilbron, J. L., and Robert Seidel. *Lawrence and His Laboratory: A History of the Lawrence Berkeley Laboratory.* Berkeley: University of California Press, 1989.

Heims, Steve J. *John von Neumann and Norbert Wiener.* Cambridge, MA: MIT Press, 1980.

Heisenberg, Elisabeth. *Inner Exile: Recollection of a Life with Werner Heisenberg.* Boston: Birkhauser, 1984.

Heisenberg, Werner. *Physics and Beyond.* New York: Harper & Row, 1972.

Herken, Gregg. *Brotherhood of the Bomb.* New York: Holt, 2002.

————. *Cardinal Choices: Presidential Science Advising from the Atomic Bomb to SDI.* New York: Oxford University Press, 1992.

————. *Counsels of War.* New York: Knopf, 1985.

————. *The Winning Weapon: The Atomic Bomb in the Cold War.* New York: Knopf, 1980.

Hershberg, James. *James B. Conant: Harvard to Hiroshima and the Making of the Nuclear Age.* New York: Knopf, 1993.

Hewlett, Richard G., and Oscar E. Anderson Jr. *The New World: A History of the United States Atomic Energy Commission.* Vol. 1, *1939–1946.* Washington, DC: U.S. Atomic Energy Commission, 1972.

Hewlett, Richard G., and Francis Duncan. *Atomic Shield: A History of the United States Atomic Energy Commission.* Vol. 2, *1947–1952.* Washington, DC: U.S. Atomic Energy Commission, 1972.

Hewlett, Richard G., and Jack M. Holl. *Atoms for Peace and War: Eisenhower and the Atomic Energy Commission, 1953–1961.* Vol. 3. Berkeley: University of California Press, 1989.

Hoddeson, Lillian, Paul W. Henriksen, Roger A. Meade, and Catherine Westfall. *Critical Assembly.* Cambridge: Cambridge University Press, 1993.

Holloway, David. *The Soviet Union and the Arms Race.* New Haven, CT: Yale University Press, 1983.

———. *Stalin and the Bomb: The Soviet Union and Atomic Energy, 1939–1956.* New Haven, CT: Yale University Press, 1994.

Holton, Gerald. *The Advancement of Science, and Its Burdens.* Cambridge: Cambridge University Press, 1986.

Holton, Gerald, and Robert S. Morison, eds. *Limits of Scientific Inquiry.* New York: Norton, 1978.

Hoopes, Townsend, and Douglas Brinkley. *Driven Patriot: The Life and Times of James Forrestal.* New York: Knopf, 1992.

Hughes, Emmet John. *The Ordeal of Power.* New York: Atheneum, 1963.

Immerman, Richard H. *John Foster Dulles: Piety, Pragmatism and Power in U.S. Foreign Policy.* Wilmington, DE: Scholarly Resources, 1999.

Iriye, Akira. *Power and Culture: The Japanese-American War, 1941–1945.* Cambridge, MA: Harvard University Press, 1981.

Irving, David. *The German Atomic Bomb.* New York: Simon & Schuster, 1967.

Jackson, Robert H. *That Man: An Insider's Portrait of Franklin D. Roosevelt.* Edited by John Q. Barrett. Oxford: Oxford University Press, 2003.

Jenkins, Edith. *Against a Field Sinister: Memoirs and Stories.* San Francisco: City Lights Books, 1991.

Jones, Vincent C. *U.S. Army in World War II, Special Studies, Manhattan: The Army and the Atomic Bomb.* Washington, DC: U.S. Government Printing Office, 1985.

Jungk, Robert. *Brighter Than a Thousand Suns.* New York: Harcourt Brace, 1958.

Kac, Mark. *Enigmas of Chance.* New York: Harper & Row, 1985.

Kamen, Martin. *Radiant Science, Dark Politics: A Memoir of the Nuclear Age.* Berkeley: University of California Press, 1986.

Kaplan, Fred. *The Wizards of Armageddon.* New York: Simon & Schuster, 1983.

Kennan, George F. *The Cloud of Danger.* Boston: Little, Brown, 1977.

——. *Memoirs.* Vol. 1, *1925–1950.* Boston: Little, Brown, 1967.

——. *Memoirs.* Vol. 2, *1950–1963.* Boston: Little, Brown, 1972.

——. *The Nuclear Delusion.* New York: Pantheon, 1976.

——. *Russia and the West Under Lenin and Stalin.* Boston: Little, Brown, 1960.

Kevles, Daniel. *The Physicists: The History of a Scientific Community in Modern America.* New York: Vintage, 1979.

Khariton, Yuli B., and Yury N. Smirnov. *Myths and Reality of the Soviet Atomic Project.* Arzamas 16: Russian Federal Nuclear Center, 1994.

Killian, James R. *The Education of a College President.* Cambridge, MA: MIT Press, 1985.

——. *Sputnik, Scientists, and Eisenhower.* Cambridge, MA: MIT Press, 1977.

Kipphardt, Heinar. *In the Matter of J. Robert Oppenheimer.* Trans. by Ruth Speirs. New York: Hill and Wang, 1985.

Kistiakowsky, George. *A Scientist at the White House.* Cambridge, MA: Harvard University Press, 1976.

Klehr, Harvey, John Earl Haynes, and Fridrikh I. Firsow. *The Secret World of American Communism.* New Haven, CT: Yale University Press, 1995.

Krock, Arthur. *Memoirs.* New York: Funk & Wagnalls, 1968.

Kuhns, Woodrow J., ed. *Assessing the Soviet Threat: The Early Cold War Years.* Washington, DC: Center for the Study of Intelligence, CIA, 1997.

Kunetka, James. *City of Fire.* Albuquerque: University of New Mexico Press, 1979.

——. *Oppenheimer: The Years of Risk.* Englewood, NJ: Prentice-Hall, 1969.

Lamont, Lansing. *Day of Trinity.* New York: Atheneum, 1965.

Lamphere, Robert, and Tom Shachtman. *The FBI-KGB War: A Special Agent's Story.* New York: Random House, 1986.

Lanouette, William, with Bela Szilard. *Genius in the Shadows: A Biography of Leo Szilard, the Man Behind the Bomb.* New York: Scribner's, 1992.

Lansdale, John, Jr. *John Lansdale, Jr., Military Service Record.* Privately printed, 1987.

Lapp, Ralph E. *My Life with Radiation: The Truth About Hiroshima.* Madison, WI: Cogito Books, 1985.

——. *The Weapons Culture.* New York: Norton, 1968.

Leffler, Melvyn P. *A Preponderance of Power.* Stanford, CA: Stanford University Press, 1992.

Libby, Leona M. *The Uranium People.* New York: Scribner's, 1979.

Lichtenstein, Alice. *The Genius of the World.* Cambridge, MA: Zoland Books, 2000.

Lilienthal, David E. *The Journals of David E. Lilienthal.* Vol. 2, *The Atomic Energy Years, 1945–1950.* New York: Harper & Row, 1964.

———. *The Journals of David E. Lilienthal.* Vol. 4, *The Road to Change, 1955–1959.* New York: Harper & Row, 1969.

———. *The Journals of David E. Lilienthal.* Vol. 5, *The Harvest Years, 1959–1963.* New York: Harper & Row, 1971.

MacEachin, Douglas J. *The Final Months of the War with Japan.* Washington, DC: Central Intelligence Agency, Center for the Study of Intelligence, 1998.

Macrae, Norman. *John von Neumann: The Scientific Genius Who Pioneered the Modern Computer, Game Theory, Nuclear Deterrence, and Much More.* New York: Pantheon, 1992.

Major, John. *The Oppenheimer Hearing.* New York: Stein and Day, 1971.

Malkov, Viktor. *The Manhattan Project: Intelligence and Diplomacy.* Moscow: Nauka Publishing House, 1995.

Manchester, William. *The Glory and the Dream: A Narrative History of America, 1932–1972.* New York: Bantam, 1984.

Mark, Hans, and Lowell Wood. *Energy in Physics, War and Peace: A Festschrift Celebrating Edward Teller's 80th Birthday.* Dordrecht, the Netherlands: Kluwer Academic Publishers, 1988.

McMahon, Thomas. *Principles of American Nuclear Chemistry.* Boston: Little, Brown, 1970.

McPhee, John. *The Curve of Binding Energy: A Journey into the Awesome and Alarming World of Theodore B. Taylor.* New York: Farrar, Straus & Giroux, 1973.

Meilinger, Phillip S. *Hoyt S. Vandenberg: The Life of a General.* Bloomington: Indiana University Press, 1989.

Merry, Robert W. *Taking on the World.* New York: Viking, 1996.

Michelmore, Peter. *The Swift Years: The Robert Oppenheimer Story.* New York: Dodd, Mead, 1969.

Millis, Walter, ed. *The Forrestal Diaries.* New York: Putnam, 1952.

Morland, Howard. *The Secret That Exploded.* New York: Random House, 1979.

Morrison, Philip. *Nothing Is Too Wonderful to Be True.* Woodbury, NY: American Institute of Physics, 1995.

Morse, Philip. *In at the Beginnings.* Cambridge, MA: MIT Press, 1977.

Moss, Norman. *Klaus Fuchs.* New York: St. Martin's, 1987.

———. *Men Who Play God.* New York: Harper & Row, 1968.

Moynihan, Daniel Patrick. *Secrecy.* New Haven, CT: Yale University Press, 1998.

Murray, Thomas E. *Nuclear Policy for War and Peace.* Cleveland: World Publishing, 1960.

————. *The Predicament of Our Age.* New York: Privately printed, 1955.

Nelson, Steve, James R. Barrett, and Rob Ruck. *Steve Nelson, American Radical.* Pittsburgh: University of Pittsburgh Press, 1981.

Newhouse, John. *War and Peace in the Nuclear Age.* New York: Knopf, 1989.

Nichols, K. D. *The Road to Trinity: A Personal Account of How America's Nuclear Policies Were Made.* New York: Morrow, 1987.

Nolan, Janne E. *Guardians of the Arsenal.* New York: Basic Books, 1989.

Norris, R. Standish. *Racing for the Bomb.* South Royalton, VT: Steerforth, 2002.

Nuclear Weapons Databook. Vol. 1, *U.S. Nuclear Forces and Capabilities.* Thomas B. Cochran, William B. Arkin, and Milton M. Hoenig. Cambridge, MA: Ballinger, 1984.

Nuclear Weapons Databook. Vol. 2, *U.S. Nuclear Warhead Production.* Thomas B. Cochran, William B. Arkin, Robert S. Norris, and Milton M. Hoenig. Cambridge, MA: Ballinger, 1987.

Nuclear Weapons Databook. Vol. 3, *U.S. Nuclear Warhead Facility Profiles.* Thomas B. Cochran, William B. Arkin, Robert S. Norris, and Milton M. Hoenig. Cambridge, MA: Ballinger, 1987.

Nuclear Weapons Databook. Vol. 4, *Soviet Nuclear Weapons.* Thomas B. Cochran, William B. Arkin, Robert S. Norris, and Jeffrey I. Sands. New York: Harper & Row, 1989.

Nuclear Weapons Databook. Vol. 5, *British, French, and Chinese Nuclear Weapons.* Robert S. Norris, Andrew S. Burrows, and Richard W. Fieldhouse. Boulder, CO: Westview Press, 1994.

Nuclear Weapons Databook, Working Paper. U.S.–USSR/Russian Strategic Offensive Nuclear Forces, 1945–1996. Robert S. Norris and Thomas B. Cochran. Washington, DC: Natural Resources Defense Council, 1997.

Oppenheimer, J. Robert. *Atom and Void: Essays on Science and Community.* Princeton, NJ: Princeton University Press, 1989.

————. *The Flying Trapeze: Three Crises for Physicists.* London: Oxford University Press, 1964.

————. *The Open Mind.* New York: Simon & Schuster, 1955.

————. *Science and the Common Understanding.* New York: Simon & Schuster, 1953.

————. *Uncommon Sense.* Boston: Birkhauser, 1984.

Oshinsky, David M. *A Conspiracy So Immense.* New York: Free Press, 1983.

Pais, Abraham. *Einstein Lived Here.* New York: Oxford University Press, 1994.

————. *Niels Bohr's Times.* New York: Oxford University Press, 1991.

————. *"Subtle Is the Lord."* New York: Oxford University Press, 1982.

————. *A Tale of Two Continents: A Physicist's Life in a Turbulent World.* Princeton, NJ: Princeton University Press, 1997.

Palevsky, Mary. *Atomic Fragments*. Berkeley: University of California Press, 2000.

Pape, Robert A. *Bombing to Win*. Ithaca, NY: Cornell University Press, 1996.

Peat, F. David. *Infinite Potential: The Life and Times of David Bohm*. Reading, MA: Addison-Wesley, 1997.

Peierls, Rudolph. *Bird of Passage*. Princeton, NJ: Princeton University Press, 1985.

Pfau, Richard. *No Sacrifice Too Great: The Life of Lewis L. Strauss*. Charlottesville: University Press of Virginia, 1984.

Polenberg, Richard, ed. *In the Matter of Robert J. Oppenheimer: The Security Clearance Hearing*. Ithaca, NY: Cornell University Press, 2002.

Powers, Thomas. *Heisenberg's War: The Secret History of the German Bomb*. New York: Knopf, 1993.

Rabi, I. I., Robert Serber, Victor F. Weisskopf, Abraham Pais, and Glenn T. Seaborg. *Oppenheimer*. New York: Scribner's, 1969.

Regis, Ed. *Who Got Einstein's Office?* Reading, MA: Addison-Wesley, 1987.

Reston, James. *Deadline*. New York: Random House, 1991.

Rhodes, Richard. *Dark Sun: The Making of the Hydrogen Bomb*. New York: Simon & Schuster, 1995.

———. *The Making of the Atomic Bomb*. New York: Simon & Schuster, 1986.

Rigden, John S. *Rabi*. New York: Basic Books, 1987.

Rogow, Arnold A. *James Forrestal*. New York: Macmillan, 1963.

Romerstein, Herbert, and Eric Breindel. *The Venona Secrets: Exposing Soviet Espionage and America's Traitors*. Washington, DC: Regnery, 2000.

Rosenthal, Debra. *At the Heart of the Bomb*. Reading, MA: Addison-Wesley, 1990.

Rossi, Bruno. *Moments in the Life of a Scientist*. Cambridge: Cambridge University Press, 1990.

Rota, Gian-Carlo. *Indiscrete Thoughts*. Boston: Birkhauser, 1997.

Rouze, Michel. *Robert Oppenheimer: The Man and His Theories*. Greenwich, CT: Fawcett, 1965.

Rovere, Richard H. *Senator Joe McCarthy*. New York: Harcourt Brace, 1959.

Rowny, Edward L. *It Takes One to Tango*. Washington, DC: Brassey's, 1992.

Royal, Denise. *The Story of J. Robert Oppenheimer*. New York: St. Martin's, 1969.

Sakharov, Andrei. *Memoirs*. New York: Knopf, 1990.

Schecter, Jerrold L., and Leona P. Schecter. *Sacred Secrets: How Soviet Intelligence Operations Changed American History*. Washington, DC: Brassey's, 2002.

Schrecker, Ellen W. *No Ivory Tower: McCarthyism and the Universities*. New York: Oxford University Press, 1986.

Schwartz, Stephen I. *Atomic Audit*. Washington, DC: Brookings, 1998.

Schweber, Silvan. *In the Shadow of the Bomb: Bethe, Oppenheimer, and the Moral Responsibility of the Scientist*. Princeton, NJ: Princeton University Press, 2000.

———. *QED and the Men Who Made It.* Princeton, NJ: Princeton University Press, 1994.

Seaborg, Glenn. *Kennedy, Khrushchev, and the Test Ban.* Berkeley: University of California Press, 1981.

Seaborg, Glenn T., with Eric Seaborg. *Adventures in the Atomic Age: From Watts to Washington.* New York: Farrar, Straus & Giroux, 2001.

Segrè, Emilio. *Enrico Fermi: Physicist.* Chicago: University of Chicago Press, 1970.

———. *A Mind Always in Motion.* Berkeley: University of California Press, 1993.

Seidel, Robert W. *Los Alamos and the Development of the Atomic Bomb.* Los Alamos, NM: Otowi Crossing Press, 1995.

Serber, Robert. *The Los Alamos Primer: The First Lectures on How to Build an Atomic Bomb.* Berkeley: University of California Press, 1992.

Serber, Robert, with Robert P. Crease. *Peace and War.* New York: Columbia University Press, 1998.

Shepley, James, and Clay Blair Jr. *The Hydrogen Bomb: The Men, the Menace, the Mechanism.* New York: David McKay, 1954.

Sherwin, Martin. *A World Destroyed: The Atomic Bomb and the Grand Alliance.* New York: Knopf, 1975.

Smith, Alice Kimball. *A Peril and a Hope: The Scientists' Movement in America, 1945–47.* Cambridge, MA: MIT Press, 1971.

Smith, Alice Kimball, and Charles Weiner, eds. *Robert Oppenheimer, Letters and Recollections.* Cambridge, MA: Harvard University Press, 1980.

Smith, Gerard C. *Disarming Diplomat.* Lanham, MD: Madison Books, 1996.

Smyth, Henry DeWolf. *Atomic Energy for Military Purposes: The Official Report on the Development of the Atomic Bomb Under the Auspices of the United States Government, 1940–1945.* Princeton, NJ: Princeton University Press, 1989.

Stein, Jonathan B. *From H-Bomb to Star Wars.* Lexington, MA: D.C. Heath, 1984.

Stern, Philip M., with Harold P. Green. *The Oppenheimer Case: Security on Trial.* New York: Harper & Row, 1969.

Straight, Michael. *After Long Silence.* New York: Norton, 1983.

Strauss, Lewis L. *Men and Decisions.* New York: Macmillan, 1962.

Swanberg, W. A. *Luce and His Empire.* New York: Scribner's, 1972.

Sudoplatov, Pavel, and Anatoli Sudoplatov, with Jerrold L. Schecter and Leona P. Schecter. *Special Tasks: The Memoirs of an Unwanted Witness—A Soviet Spymaster.* Boston: Little, Brown, 1994.

Sylves, Richard T. *The Nuclear Oracles: A Political History of the General Advisory Committee of the Atomic Energy Commission, 1947–1977.* Ames: Iowa State University Press, 1987.

Szasz, Ferenc Morton. *The Day the Sun Rose Twice*. Albuquerque: University of New Mexico Press, 1984.

Talbott, Strobe. *The Master of the Game: Paul Nitze and the Nuclear Peace*. New York: Knopf, 1988.

Teller, Edward. *Better a Shield Than a Sword: Perspectives on Defense and Technology*. New York: Free Press, 1987.

————. *Energy from Heaven and Earth*. San Francisco: Freeman, 1979.

————. *The Pursuit of Simplicity*. Malibu, CA: Pepperdine University Press, 1981.

Teller, Edward, and Albert Latter. *Our Nuclear Future: Facts, Dangers, and Opportunities*. New York: Criterion Books, 1958.

Teller, Edward, with Allen Brown. *The Legacy of Hiroshima*. New York: Doubleday, 1962.

Teller, Edward, with Judith Shoolery. *Memoirs: A Twentieth-Century Journey in Science and Politics*. New York: Perseus Press, 2001.

Thackara, James. *America's Children*. Woodstock, NY: Overlook Press, 2001.

Thorne, Kip S. *Black Holes and Time Warps*. New York: Norton, 1994.

Toulmin, Stephen. *Foresight and Understanding*. New York: Harper & Row, 1961.

Trachtenberg, Marc. *A Constructed Peace*. Princeton, NJ: Princeton University Press, 1999.

————. *History and Strategy*. Princeton, NJ: Princeton University Press, 1991.

Truman, Harry S. *Memoirs*. Vol. 1, *Year of Decisions*. Garden City, NY: Doubleday, 1955.

————. *Memoirs*. Vol. 2, *Years of Trial and Hope*. Garden City, NY: Doubleday, 1956.

Udall, Stewart. *The Myths of August*. New York: Pantheon, 1994.

Ulam, S. M. *Adventures of a Mathematician*. Berkeley: University of California Press, 1991.

United States Atomic Energy Commission. *In the Matter of J. Robert Oppenheimer: Transcript of Hearing Before Personnel Security Board and Texts of Principal Documents and Letters*. Cambridge, MA: MIT Press, 1971.

Van DeMark, Brian. *Pandora's Keepers*. Boston: Little, Brown, 2003.

Van der Post, Laurens. *The Night of the New Moon*. London: Hogarth Press, 1970.

von Hippel, Frank. *Citizen Scientist*. New York: Simon & Schuster, 1991.

Walker, Samuel J. *Prompt and Utter Destruction*. Chapel Hill: University of North Carolina Press, 1997.

Weart, Spencer, and Gertrude W. Szilard, eds. *Leo Szilard: His Version of the Facts*. Vol. 2. Cambridge, MA: MIT Press, 1978.

Weinstein, Allen. *Perjury: The Hiss-Chambers Case*. New York: Random House, 1997.

Weinstein, Allen, and Alexander Vassiliev. *The Haunted Wood: Soviet Espionage in America—The Stalin Era*. New York: Random House, 1999.

Weisgall, Jonathan M. *Operation Crossroads: The Atomic Tests at Bikini Atoll*. Annapolis, MD: Naval Institute Press, 1994.

Wheeler, John Archibald, with Kenneth Ford. *Geons, Black Holes, and Quantum Foam: A Life in Physics*. New York: Norton, 1998.

Wicker, Tom. *Dwight D. Eisenhower*. New York: Times Books, 2002.

Wiesner, Jerome B. *Where Science and Politics Meet*. New York: McGraw-Hill, 1961.

Wigner, Eugene. *The Recollections of Eugene Wigner*. As told to Andrew Szanton. New York: Plenum Press, 1992.

Williams, Robert C. *Klaus Fuchs, Atom Spy*. Cambridge, MA: Harvard University Press, 1987.

Williams, Robert C., and Philip L. Cantelon, eds. *The American Atom: A Documentary History of Nuclear Policies from the Discovery of Fission to the Present, 1939–1984*. Philadelphia: University of Pennsylvania Press, 1984.

Wittner, Lawrence S. *One World or None*. Stanford, CA: Stanford University Press, 1993.

Wyden, Peter. *Day One: Before Hiroshima and After*. New York: Simon & Schuster, 1984.

York, Herbert F. *The Advisors: Oppenheimer, Teller, and the Superbomb*. San Francisco: Freeman, 1976.

———. *Arms and the Physicist*. Woodbury, NY: American Institute of Physics, 1995.

———. *Making Weapons, Talking Peace: A Physicist's Odyssey from Hiroshima to Geneva*. New York: Basic Books, 1987.

———. *Race to Oblivion: A Participant's View of the Arms Race*. New York: Simon & Schuster, 1970.

Zachary, G. Pascal. *Endless Frontier: Vannevar Bush, Engineer of the American Century*. New York: Free Press, 1997.

Ziegler, Charles A., and David Jacobson. *Spying Without Spies: Origins of America's Secret Nuclear Surveillance System*. Westport, CT: Praeger, 1995.

Articles

Alsop, Joseph, and Stewart Alsop. "We Accuse!" *Harper's*, October 1954, 24–25.

Arneson, R. Gordon. "The H-Bomb Decision." *Foreign Service Journal* 46 (May 1969): 27–29; (June 1969): 24.

Baker, Richard Allen. "A Slap at the 'Hidden-Hand Presidency': The Senate and the Lewis Strauss Affair." *Congress and the Presidency* 14, no. 1 (Spring 1987): 1–16.

Bernstein, Barton J. "The Atomic Bombings Reconsidered." *Foreign Affairs,* January–February 1995, 137–152.

———. "Crossing the Rubicon." *International Security* 14, no. 2 (Fall 1989): 132–160.

———. "Eclipsed by Hiroshima and Nagasaki: Early Thinking About Tactical Nuclear Weapons." *International Security,* Spring 1991, 149–173.

———. "Four Physicists and the Bomb." *Historical Studies in the Physical and Biological Sciences* 18, part two (1988): 231–261.

———. "The H-Bomb Decisions: Were They Inevitable?" In *National Security and International Stability,* ed. B. Brodie, M. D. Intriligator, and R. Kolkowicz. Boston: Oelgeschlager, Gunn, 1983, 327–356.

———. "Oppenheimer and the Radioactive Poison Plan." *Technology Review,* May/June 1985, 14–17.

———. "The Oppenheimer Conspiracy." *Discover,* March 1985, 22–32.

———. "The Oppenheimer Loyalty-Security Case Reconsidered." *Stanford Law Review* 42 (July 1990): 1383–1484.

———. "Truman and the H-Bomb." *Bulletin of the Atomic Scientists,* March 1984, 12–18.

Bernstein, Barton J., and Peter Galison. "In Any Light: Scientists and the Decision to Build the Superbomb, 1952–1954." *Historical Studies in the Physical and Biological Sciences* 19, part 2 (1989): 328.

Bethe, Hans A. "Biographical Memoirs of the Fellows of the Royal Society" 14 (1968): 391–416.

———. "Comments on the History of the H-Bomb," *Los Alamos Science,* Fall 1982, 43–53.

———. "Rewriting the History of the H-Bomb." *Science,* November 19, 1982, 769–772.

Bix, Herbert P. "Japan's Delayed Surrender: A Reinterpretation." *Diplomatic History* 19, no. 2 (Spring 1995): 197–225.

Bliven, Naomi. "Ike." *New Yorker,* July 1, 1985, 95–97.

Brands, H. W. "The Age of Vulnerability: Eisenhower and the National Insecurity State." *American Historical Review,* Fall 1989, 963–989.

Broad, William J. "Soviets Shown to Have Lagged on H-Bomb in 50's." *New York Times,* October 7, 1990.

Bundy, McGeorge. "The Missed Chance to Stop the H-Bomb." *New York Review of Books* 29, no. 8 (May 13, 1982): 19.

Burr, William, and Hector L. Montford. "The Making of the Limited Test

Ban Treaty, 1958–1963." www2.gwu.edu/~nsarchiv/nsa/NC/nuchis/html. Posting for August 8, 2003.

Bush, Vannevar. "If We Alienate Our Scientists." *New York Times Magazine,* June 13, 1954, 9.

Chace, James. "Sharing the Atom Bomb." *Foreign Affairs,* January–February 1996.

Coughlin, Robert. "Dr. Edward Teller's Magnificent Obsession." *Life,* September 1954, 60.

———. "The Tangled Drama and Private Hells of Two Famous Scientists." *Life,* December 13, 1963, 87.

Day, Michael A. "Oppenheimer on the Nature of Science." *Centaurus* 43 (2001): 73–112.

"The Decade of Innovation: Los Alamos, Livermore, and National Security Decision-Making in the 1950s." Workshop at Pleasanton, California, February 19–21, 1992, published by the Center for Security and Technology Studies.

De Santillana, Georgio. "Galileo and J. Robert Oppenheimer." *Reporter,* December 26, 1957, 10–18.

DeWitt, Hugh E. "Labs Drive the Arms Race." *Bulletin of the Atomic Scientists,* November 1984.

DeWitt, Hugh E., and Gerald E. Marsh. "Stockpile Reliability and Nuclear Testing." *Bulletin of the Atomic Scientists,* April 1984.

Dingman, Roger. "Atomic Diplomacy During the Korean War." *International Security* 13, no. 3 (Winter 1988/1989): 50–91.

Elliot, David C. "Project Vista and Nuclear Weapons in Europe." *International Security* 2, no. 1 (Summer 1986): 163–183.

Feld, Bernard. "The Oppenheimer Case." *American Scientist,* July 1970.

Gaddis, John Lewis. "The Tragedy of Cold War History." *Foreign Affairs,* January–February 1994, 142–154.

Garthoff, Raymond L. "Assessing the Adversary: Estimates by the Eisenhower Administration of Soviet Intentions and Capabilities." Washington, DC: Brookings Institution Press, 1991.

Goncharov, German A. "Thermonuclear Milestones." *Physics Today,* November 1996, 44–61.

Goodman, Michael S. "The Grandfather of the Atomic Bomb? Anglo-American Intelligence and Klaus Fuchs." *Historical Studies in the Physical Sciences* 32, part 1: 1–22.

Gorelik, Gennady. "The Metamorphosis of Andrei Sakharov." *Scientific American,* March 1999.

Green, Harold P. "The Oppenheimer Case: A Study in the Abuse of Law." *Bulletin of the Atomic Scientists,* September 1977: 12.

———. "Q-Clearance: The Development of a Personnel Security Program." *Bulletin of the Atomic Scientists,* May 1964.

Hammond, Thomas T. "Did the United States Use Atomic Diplomacy Against Russia in 1945?" In *From the Cold War to Détente,* ed. Peter J. Potichnyi and Jane P. Shapiro. Boulder, CO: Praeger, 1976.

Hersey, John. "Hiroshima." *New Yorker,* August 31, 1946.

Hershberg, James G. "Where the Buck Stopped: Harry Truman and the Cold War." *Diplomatic History* 27, no. 5 (November 2003): 735–739.

Hoddeson, Lillian, Adrienne Kolb, and Roger Meade. "Extending the Master's Vision: Bradbury at Los Alamos and Lederman at Fermilab." Los Alamos Technical Release, Los Alamos National Laboratory, 1999.

Holloway, David. "New Light on Early Soviet Bomb Secrets." *Physics Today,* November 1996, 26–27.

———. "Soviet Scientists Speak Out." *Bulletin of the Atomic Scientists,* May 1996, 18–19.

Holton, Gerald. "The Migration of Physicists to the United States." *Bulletin of the Atomic Scientists,* April 1984, 18–24.

———. "Success Sanctifies the Means: Heisenberg, Oppenheimer, and the Transition to Modern Physics." *Transformation and Tradition in the Sciences,* 1984, 155–173.

———. "Young Man Oppenheimer." *Partisan Review,* July 1981, 380–388.

Holtzman, Franklyn D. "Politics and Guesswork: CIA and DIA Estimates of Soviet Military Spending." *International Security* 14, no. 2 (Fall 1989): 101–113.

Jastrow, Robert. "Why Strategic Superiority Matters." *Commentary,* March 1983.

Joravsky, David. "Sin and the Scientist." *New York Review of Books,* July 17, 1980, 7–10.

Kalven, Harry, Jr. "The Case of J. Robert Oppenheimer Before the Atomic Energy Commission." *Bulletin of the Atomic Scientists,* September 1954, 259–269.

Kempton, Murray. "The Ambivalence of J. Robert Oppenheimer." *Esquire,* December 1983, 236–248.

Khariton, Yuli. "USSR Nuclear Weapons: Did They Come from America or Were They Built Independently?" *Izvestia,* December 8, 1992.

Khariton, Yuli, and Yuri Smirnov. "The Khariton Version." *Bulletin of the Atomic Scientists,* May 1993, 20–31.

Lapp, Ralph E. "Atomic Candor." *Bulletin of the Atomic Scientists,* October 1954.

Leffler, Melvyn P. "The American Conception of National Security and the Beginnings of the Cold War, 1945–48." *American Historical Review* 89, no. 2 (April 1984): 346–400.

Leskov, Sergei. "Dividing the Glory of the Fathers." *Bulletin of the Atomic Scientists,* May 1993, 37–39.

Mayers, David. "Containment and the Primacy of Diplomacy: George Kennan's Views, 1947–1948." *International Security* 11, no. 1 (Summer 1986): 124–162.

Miles, Rufus E., Jr. "Hiroshima: The Strange Myth of Half a Million American Lives Saved." *International Security* 10, no. 2 (Fall 1985): 121–140.

Morland, Howard. "Errata." *Progressive,* December 1979.

Murray, Thomas E. "Morality and the H-Bomb." *National Catholic Weekly Review,* December 1, 1956.

Norris, Robert S., and William M. Arkin. "Russian/Soviet Weapons Secrets Revealed." *Bulletin of the Atomic Scientists,* April 1993, 48.

Norton-Taylor, Duncan. "The Controversial Mr. Strauss." *Fortune,* January 1955.

Oppenheimer, J. Robert. "The Atomic Bomb as a Great Force for Peace." *New York Times Magazine,* June 9, 1946.

———. "Atomic Weapons and American Policy." *Foreign Affairs* 31:4, July 1953, 526–535.

———. "International Control of Atomic Energy." *Foreign Affairs,* January 1948.

Pape, Robert A. "Why Japan Surrendered." *International Security* 18:2 (Fall 1993): 154–201.

Rabinowich, Eugene. "Fortune's Own Operation Candor." *Bulletin of the Atomic Scientists,* December 1953.

Rhodes, Richard. "I Am Become Death: The Agony of J. Robert Oppenheimer." *American Heritage,* October 1977, 72.

Rigden, John S. "J. Robert Oppenheimer Before the War." *Scientific American,* July 1995, 76–81.

Ritus, V. I. "If Not Me, Then Who?" *Priroda,* August 1990.

Rosenberg, David Alan. "American Atomic Strategy and the Hydrogen Bomb Decision." *Journal of American History* 66 (June 1979): 62–87.

———. "The Origins of Overkill: Nuclear Weapons and American Strategy, 1945–1960." *International Security* 7, no. 4 (Spring 1983): 3–71.

———. "A Smoking Radiating Ruin at the End of Two Hours: Documents on American Plans for Nuclear War with the Soviet Union, 1954–1955." *International Security* 6, no. 3 (Winter 1981–82): 3–38.

———. "U.S. Nuclear Stockpile, 1945 to 1950." *Bulletin of the Atomic Scientists,* May 1982, 25–30.

———. "U.S. Nuclear Strategy: Theory vs. Practice." *Bulletin of the Atomic Scientists,* March 1987, 20–26.

Rota, Gian-Carlo. "The Lost Cafe." *Contention* 2, no. 2 (Winter 1993): 41–61.

Sagdeev, Roald. "Russian Scientists Save American Secrets." *Bulletin of the Atomic Scientists,* May 1993, 32–36.

Samuels, Gertrude. "A Plea for 'Candor' About the Atom." *New York Times Magazine,* June 21, 1953.

Schilling, Warner. "The H-Bomb Decision: How to Decide Without Actually Choosing." *Political Science Quarterly,* March 1961, 24–46.

Schlesinger, Arthur M., Jr. "The Oppenheimer Case." *Atlantic Monthly,* October 1954.

Seidel, Robert W. "A Home for Big Science: AEC's Lab System." *Historical Studies in the Physical and Biological Sciences* 16, part 1 (1986): 135–175.

———. "The DOE Weapons Laboratories." *Los Alamos National Laboratory,* July 26, 1992.

Smith, Alice Kimball. "Scientists and Public Issues." *Bulletin of the Atomic Scientists,* December 1982, 38–45.

Smith-Norris, Martha. "The Eisenhower Administration and the Nuclear Test Ban Talks, 1958–1960." *Diplomatic History* 27, no. 4 (September 2003): 503–541.

Stimson, Henry L. "The Decision to Use the Bomb." *Harper's,* February 1947.

Suri, Jeremy. "The Surprise Attack Conference of 1958." *Diplomatic History* 21, no. 3 (Summer 1997): 417–451.

Teller, Edward. "The Work of Many People." *Science,* February 25, 1955.

Trachtenberg, Marc. "Truman, Eisenhower, and the Uses of Atomic Superiority." *International Security* 13, no. 3 (Winter 1988–89): 4–49.

Trilling, Diana. "The Oppenheimer Case: A Reading of the Testimony." *Partisan Review,* November–December 1954, 105–142.

Ulam, S. M. "Thermonuclear Devices." In *Perspectives in Modern Physics: Essays in Honor of Hans A. Bethe,* ed. R. E. Marshak. New York: John Wiley and Sons, 1966.

Ulam, S., H. W. Kuhn, and Claude E. Shannon. "John von Neumann, 1903–1957." *Perspectives in American History* no. 2 (1968): 235–269.

Unna, Warren. "Dissension in the AEC." *Atlantic Monthly,* May 1957.

Wampler, Robert A. "NATO Strategic Planning and Nuclear Weapons, 1950–1957." Occasional Paper no. 6, Nuclear History Program, University of Maryland.

Weiss, Leonard. "Atoms for Peace." *Bulletin of the Atomic Scientists,* November–December 2003, 34–44.

Ziegler, Charles, and David Jacobson. "Intelligence Assessments of Soviet Atomic Capability, 1945–1949: Myths, Monopolies, and Maskirovka." *Intelligence and National Security* 12, no. 4 (1997).

Unpublished Materials

———. "The Struggle for the Second Laboratory, 1951–54." Paper prepared for American Historical Association, 1999.

Bethe, Hans A. Letter to Messrs. Joseph and Stewart Alsop, October 1, 1954, Joseph Alsop Papers, LC.

———. "Memorandum on the History of Thermonuclear Program." May 28, 1952. Assembled by Chuck Hansen transcription of May 12, 1990.

Borden, William Liscum. "Springtime of the Nuclear Debate." Copy of manuscript, given to author by J. K. Mansfield.

Fitzpatrick, Anne. "Igniting the Light Elements: The Los Alamos Thermonuclear Weapons Project, 1942–1952." Ph.D. diss., Virginia Polytechnic Institute, 1998.

Francis, Sybil. "Between Science and Politics: Edward Teller and the Lawrence Livermore National Laboratory." Paper prepared for "The Martians: Hungarian Emigré Scientists," a workshop held at Eotvos University, Budapest, 1997.

———. "Race Horses vs. Work Horses: Competition Between the Nuclear Weapons Labs in the 1950's." Paper prepared for workshop on the weapons laboratories at Pleasanton, CA, February 19–21, 1992.

———. "Warhead Politics: Livermore and the Competitive System of Nuclear Weapon Design." Ph.D. diss., MIT, 1995.

Getting, Ivan A., and John M. Christie. "David Tressel Griggs." Paper given to author by Ivan Getting.

Holloway, David. "The Hydrogen Bomb." From a manuscript dated April 2002.

Hughes, Emmet J. Memorial speech for John Courtney Murray, January 16, 1969, Georgetown University Special Collections.

"In Memoriam: A Celebration of Thanksgiving for the Life of I. I. Rabi." Privately published.

Kuchment, Mark. "The Rosenberg Case and the Sarant-Barr Story." Paper.

Mark, Carson. "A Short Account of Los Alamos Theoretical Work on Thermonuclear Weapons, 1946–1950." Los Alamos Scientific Laboratory, 1974. LA-5647-MS, Los Alamos National Laboratory.

Messer, Robert L. "America's 'Sacred Trust': Truman and the Bomb, 1945–1949." Paper prepared for American Historical Association meeting, December 30, 1987.

Murphy, Charles J. V. Correspondence and papers, property of Edythe M. Holbrook.

Murray, Thomas E. Diary and notes, in the possession of the Murray family.

Operation Epsilon: The Farm Hall Transcripts, August 8–22, 1945. RG 77, NARA.

Oppenheimer, J. Robert. "Atomic Weapons and American Policy." Speech and discussion at Council on Foreign Relations, New York City, February 17, 1953.

———. Speech at meeting of the Association of Los Alamos Scientists, November 2, 1945, LANL.

———. Speech at Seven Springs Farm, NY, June 1963, JRO, LC.

———. Speech on Niels Bohr at Los Alamos, 1967, LANL.

Schilling, Warner. "Interview with Robert Oppenheimer." June 12, 1957. J. Robert Oppenheimer Papers, Library of Congress.

Seidel, Robert W. "Ernest Lawrence and the Founding of a Second Nuclear Weapons Laboratory at Livermore," paper presented at the Institute on Global Conflict and Cooperation Colloquium, University of California at Irvine, May 17, 1984.

Sherwin, Martin. "Policing Science in Cold War America: The U.S. Government and the Conspiracy to Destroy J. Robert Oppenheimer." Speech at Symposium on Science and Technology with a Human Face, MIT, 1992.

Smith, Cyril. Letters to Ralph Lapp, June 23, 1965; Margaret Gowing, July 16, 1965; Richard G. Hewlett, April 27, 1967. Gift of the author.

———. "Los Alamos Reminiscences." August 17, 1964. Gift of the author.

Stern, Beatrice M. "A History of the Institute for Advanced Study, 1930–1950." 2 vols. 1964, Institute for Advanced Study. Gift of Ed Regis.

Ulam, Françoise. "Stanislaw Ulam, 1909–1984: A Biographical Profile." American Institute of Physics.

Walker, John S., and William L. Borden. "Policy and Progress in the H-Bomb Program: A Chronology of Leading Events." Called the Walker-Borden Chronology in the notes. RG 128, NARA.

Weisskopf, Victor F. "Banquet Speech at the Fortieth Anniversary Conference of the Los Alamos National Laboratory," April 15, 1983, Los Alamos National Laboratory.

Author's Correspondence

Samuel B. Ballen
Hans A. Bethe
Herbert Brownell
Charles Critchfield
Lloyd K. Garrison
Ivan Getting

Barry Goldwater
Harold P. Green
Lee Hancock
John H. Manley
J. Carson Mark
Kathleen Mark
John Nuckolls
Abraham Pais
Joseph Volpe

Libraries and Oral History Collections

American Philosophical Society Library: Edward U. Condon Papers, H. D. Smyth Papers, Stanislaw Ulam Papers

Columbia University Oral History Collection: Kenneth Bainbridge, Edward L. Beach, Herbert Brownell, William A. M. Burden, Charles Coryell, Gordon Dean, Dwight D. Eisenhower, Lloyd K. Garrison, Gordon Gray, Edward S. Greenbaum, James Killian, Kenneth D. Nichols, Isidor Isaac Rabi, Norman Ramsey

Cornell University Library: Hans Bethe Papers, Sterling Cole Papers

Dwight D. Eisenhower Presidential Library: Dwight D. Eisenhower Papers, Gordon Gray Papers, James Hagerty Papers

Georgetown University Library, Special Collections: John Courtney Murray Papers

Harvard University Libraries:
> Houghton Library: Time Inc. files
> Langdell Law Library: Lloyd Garrison Papers, Walter Barton Leach Papers
> Pusey Library: James B. Conant Papers

Herbert Hoover Presidential Library: Bourke B. Hickenlooper Papers, Lewis L. Strauss Papers

John F. Kennedy Presidential Library: McGeorge Bundy Papers, Glenn Seaborg Papers, Philip M. Stern Papers

Lawrence Berkeley Laboratory Archives: Edwin McMillan Papers

Library of Congress: Joseph Alsop Papers, Vannevar Bush Papers, J. Robert Oppenheimer Papers, William S. Parsons Papers, Isidor Isaac Rabi Papers, Hoyt S. Vandenberg Papers

Los Alamos National Laboratory: Norris Bradbury Papers, John Manley Papers, Carson Mark Papers

Massachusetts Institute of Technology, Special Collections: J. Robert

Oppenheimer Oral History Collection, Philip Morrison Papers, Cyril Smith Papers, Victor Weisskopf Papers, Carroll Wilson Papers

Seeley Mudd Manuscript Library, Princeton University: Emmet Hughes Papers, David E. Lilienthal Papers, George F. Kennan Papers

National Archive and Records Administration: Joint Congressional Committee on Atomic Energy Files, RG 128, in Washington, DC; Records of the U.S. Atomic Energy Commission, RG 326, at College Park, Maryland: AEC Secretariat Files; Gordon Dean Files; J. Robert Oppenheimer Personnel Security Board Files; Henry D. Smyth Files; Lewis L. Strauss Files; Records of the U.S. Atomic Energy Commission, RG 326, at Coordination and Information Center (CIC), Las Vegas, Nevada

Harry S. Truman Presidential Library: Dean Acheson Papers, Gordon Arneson Papers, Gordon Dean Papers, Sidney Souers Papers, Harry S. Truman Papers, Eugene Zuckert Oral History

University of California, Berkeley, Bancroft Library: Herbert Childs Papers, Ernest O. Lawrence Papers

University of California, San Diego, Mandeville Special Collections: Maria Goeppert Mayer Papers

University of Illinois: Louis Ridenour Papers

University of Maryland, Center for International Security Studies, Nuclear History Program: Oral History with Theodore Taylor

University of Wyoming: Clay Blair Papers

U.S. Air Force Oral History Program: Interview of Lieutenant General Roscoe C. Wilson

U.S. Federal Bureau of Investigation Files: William Liscum Borden no. 77-37709; Lewis L. Strauss no. 77-47503-2; J. Robert Oppenheimer no. 100-17828, at FBI Reading Room, Washington, DC

Interviews

The author is indebted to these individuals, each of whom she interviewed or talked with at least six times: Gennady Gorelik, Kay and John Manley, Carson and Kay Mark, David and Frances Hawkins, Emily Morrison, Philip Morrison, and Françoise Ulam.

Adams, Ruth. April 29, 1985

Alsop, Joseph. May 28, 1986

Anderson, Grace. June 9, 1987

Appel, Leonard. Nov. 14, 1985

Arneson, Gordon. Nov. 23, 1985

Bacher, Robert F. Feb. 3 and 4, 1987

Bainbridge, Kenneth. Oct. 29, 1986

Barnett, Henry and Shirley. Feb. 19, 1985

Bates, Charles W. Oct. 5, 1983; Oct. 12, 1983; Oct. 17, 1983

Beach, Commander Edward L. Nov. 1986

Beckerley, James. June 6, 1987

Bell, Daniel. Jan. 13, 1986

Bell, George. Oct. 7, 1999; March 8, 2000

Bethe, Hans. Dec. 3, 1986; Feb. 2, 1987; Aug. 11, 1997

Beyer, William. April 28, 2001; Oct. 20, 2001

Blair, Clay, Jr. Feb. 22, 1993; March 3, 1993; March 20, 1994 (telephone)

Bowditch, Margaret Parsons. July 22, 1992

Bradbury, Norris. Jan. 8, 1985; Aug. 27, 1986

Brooks, Harvey. May 22, 1986

Bundy, McGeorge. April 22, 1986

Bunkin, Irving. Dec. 4, 1987

Burroughs, Martha Parsons. March 12, 1985; April 8, 1985; May 24, 1985; May
    27, 1985; June 10, 1985 (all by telephone)

Carlson, Bengt. Oct. 8, 2001; Sept. 3, 2005; Sept. 6, 2005; Nov. 11, 2005; Nov.
    12, 2005; Nov. 14, 2005.

Carothers, James. Feb. 26, 1992 (telephone)

Carter, Ashton. June 4, 1985

Chalk, Rosemary. May 13, 1987

Cherniss, Harold. Dec. 13, 1985

Cherniss, Ruth Meyer. Dec. 13, 1985; Feb. 10, 1986

Conant, Theodore. Nov. 1993

Cooper, Necia. Aug. 27, 1986

Corbett, Peggy Felt. Nov. 6, 1987

Cotter, Francis P. Nov. 21, 1985; May 2, 1990

Cowan, George. Sept. 28, 1997

Crawford, Jack. Nov. 28 and 30, 1990

Critchfield, Charles. Sept. 22, 1983; Oct. 28, 1987; Nov. 5, 1987

Davis, Robert Raymond. Jan. 10, 1985

Day, Michael. Feb. 26, 2000

Dean, Deborah Gore. June 11, 2001

Deutsch, Martin and Suzanne. Oct. 14, 1998

DeWitt, Hugh. March 1, 1992

Diamond, Luna. May 1, 1991

Dow, Sterling. Feb. 15, 1985

Drell, Sidney. Jan. 30, 1987

Duffield, Priscilla Greene. Jan. 16, 1985; Nov. 13, 1987

Durgin, Charlotte Warner Davis. Nov. 5, 1985; Jan. 14, 1986

Dyson, Freeman. Dec. 13, 1985

Ecker, Allan B. June 15 and 18, 1989

Edsall, John. July 3, 1988

Elliot, David C. Feb. 4, 1987

Erdmann, Andrew. April 29, 1999

Erikson, Erik and Joan. Feb. 6, 1987

Everett, Dolores. Oct. 17 and 19, 1991

Everett, William. July 23, 2000 (telephone)

Fanton, Jonathan. Dec. 28, 1989

Farley, Philip. Oct. 20, 1983; Feb. 2, 1987 (telephone)

Feld, Bernard. Feb. 28, 1985

Fergusson, Peggy. Aug. 9 and 10, 1993

Feshbach, Herman. Feb. 14, 1990

Fowler, William A. Feb. 2, 1987

Friedman, Paul L. May 31, 1986

Fritchey, Polly (Polly Wisner). June 16, 1989

Fuller, Clarissa Parsons. Sept. 17, 1986

Garwin, Richard. Dec. 9, 1986; Feb. 15, 2000

Gasch, Judge Oliver. Nov. 13, 1991

Gavin, General James M. June 10, 1986

Getting, Ivan. June 24, 1986; Oct. 6, 1989

Gilpatric, Roswell. Nov. 30, 1993

Gingerich, Owen. Feb. 12, 1990

Glauber, Roy. Sept. 12, 1985; Nov. 7, 1985; Jan. 29, 1986; Feb. 18, 1987; Dec. 1, 1988

Goldberger, Marvin. Nov. 15, 1988

Golden, William T. Jan. 3, 1990

Goldstein, Jack. June 20, 1989

Goodwin, Guy. June 15, 1989; July 21, 1989; Dec. 18, 1989

Gorelik, Gennady. April 28, 1993; Nov. 6, 1998; Jan. 20, 1999; Sept. 10, 2001

Graham, Loren. Feb. 1, 1988

Gray, Boyden. May 3, 1991

Gray, Gordon, Jr. April 4, 1989

Gray, Nancy (Mrs. Gordon Gray). June 14, 1989

Green, Harold P. Jan. 25, 1984; Feb. 21, 1984; March 7, 1984; April 27, 1984; May 7, 14, 22, 1984; June 18, 1984; Nov. 13, 1991

Haar, Karl. July 11, 1990

Hancock, Lee. Aug. 22, 1983; Sept. 22, 1983; Dec. 13, 1983; Jan. 16, 1985

Hancock, William. Sept. 25, 1990

Hannifin, Jerry. July 19, 2003 (telephone)

Harrington, Joan (Mrs. David Harrington). Nov. 26–27, 1990

Hawkins, David and Frances. Jan. 30–31, 1985; Feb. 2, 1985; Oct. 4, 1991; May 1, 1994; Jan. 1, 1997; Oct. 12, 1997; Jan. 28, 1999; May 20, 2000

Hein, Hilde Stern. March 7, 1987

Heller, Leon. Oct. 9, 1999

Hempelmann, Louis and Eleanor. Dec. 7, 1987; Dec. 10, 1987

Hewlett, Richard G. May 3, 1990

Hobson, Verna (Mrs. Wilder Hobson). Sept. 20, 1986

Hoffman, Stanley. July 18, 1985

Holbrook, Edythe M. Dec. 17, 1992

Holbrook, John. Nov. 8, 1993

Horsky, Charles. Dec. 19, 1986 (telephone)

Hunt, John. June 26, 1986

Johnson, Lyall. June 14, 1997 (telephone)

Kaufman, William W. Feb. 12, 1996

Kaysen, Carl. March 30, 1999

Keeler, Norris. July 8, 1989

Kempton, Mina. May 7, 1988

Kennan, George F. Dec. 11, 1985

Kerr, Walter. Jan. 5, 1985

Kerst, Don. Oct. 29, 1987

King, Percival L. D. P. Nov. 20, 1983; Dec. 20, 1983; Oct. 12, 1987; Nov. 5, 1987

Kuchment, Mark. May 5, 1985; May 9, 1985; May 27, 1985; Oct. 26, 1985

Lamphere, Robert J. February 1996 (telephone)

Lansdale, John. Nov. 12, 1991

Lawrence, Molly. Feb. 24, 1992

Leva, Marx. Nov. 29, 1990

Lichtenstein, Alice. Jan. 23, 1986

Lichtenstein, Immanuel. Feb. 21, 1987

Lichtenstein, Nancy R. March 3, 1985; Dec. 10, 1985; Feb. 24, 1987; May 7, 1988; Nov. 14, 1988

Lilienthal, James and Betty. Jan. 17–18, 1985; Oct. 28–29, 1987; Nov. 20, 1987

Livingston, Lois. Oct. 31, 1987

Livingston, M. Stanley. Sept. 23, 1983

Lofgren, Edward J. July 19, 1988; Feb. 27, 1992

Luff, Ruth. Jan. 4, 1992 (telephone)

MacKenzie, John. Feb. 13, 1985

MacKinnon, Judge George E. Nov. 13, 1991

Malkov, Viktor. April 29, 1993

Manley, John. Jan. 9, 1985; Jan. 18, 1985; Jan. 23, 1985; March 26, 1986; March 28, 1986; March 29, 1986; April 28, 1986; Oct. 17, 1987; Nov. 1, 1987

Mansfield, J. Kenneth. March 9, 1984; May 27, 1986; May 28, 1986; May 29, 1986; May 31, 1986; June 1, 1986

Mark, Carson. Jan. 6, 1985; Jan. 17, 1985; April 2, 1986; April 3, 1986; Aug. 19, 1986; Aug. 20, 1986; Aug. 21, 1986; Aug. 25, 1986; Aug. 26, 1986; Oct. 17, 1987; Nov. 3, 1987; Dec. 10, 1988; Nov. 17, 1991 (telephone); Dec. 9, 1991 (telephone); June 14, 1993

Marks, Anne Wilson. Aug. 2, 1986; Nov. 11, 1986; June 18, 1994; June 3, 1998; July 21, 1998

McKibbin, Dorothy. Jan. 6, 1985

Meade, Roger. Aug. 22, 1986

Meyer, Cord, Jr. Nov. 7, 1986

Meyner, Robert and Helen. Nov. 4, 1984

Mitchell, John F. B. June 29, 1998 (telephone)

Mitchell, Victor S. and Donna R. Nov. 13, 1990; Nov. 15, 1990

Murray, Daniel Bradley. Nov. 12, 1990

Nabokov, Dominique. June 16, 1986

Nagle, Darragh. July 23, 2001

Nagle, William J. April 30, 1990; May 1, 1990

Nekrich, Alexander M. March 11, 1991

Nelson, Steve. Aug. 28, 1985

Neumann, Honora Fergusson. May 5, 1988; Nov. 14–15, 1988

Nitze, Paul. July 20, 1989

Norton, Garrison. Sept. 28, 1992

O'Keefe, Bernard J. March 27, 1985

Olinger, Chauncey. April 14, 1989; Nov. 11, 2003

Oppenheimer, Frank. Sept. 1, 1983

Oppenheimer, Dr. Judith. Feb. 7, 1987

Oppenheimer, Peter. Jan. 28, 1985; Nov. 16, 1987

Oulahan, Courts. July 13, 1990

Pais, Abraham. April 22, 1986 (telephone); Nov. 18, 1986

Parkinson, Kenneth Wells. Nov. 14, 1991

Peierls, Rudolph. March 6, 1986

Pfau, Richard. July 11, 1989 (telephone); Aug. 4, 1989 (telephone); Nov. 3, 1993 (telephone)

Piel, Gerard. Oct. 4, 1989

Pitzer, Kenneth. March 2, 1992

Pound, John. Nov. 10, 1987

Quesada, Elwood R. Sept. 26, 1992 (telephone)

Rabi, Helen. Aug. 13, 1985; Nov. 13, 1985; April 14, 1989; April 28, 1989; Oct. 5, 1989; April 20, 1991

Rabi, Isidor Isaac. Aug. 13, 1985; Jan. 30, 1986; Jan. 31, 1986; Feb. 21, 1987

Raher, Patrick M. Nov. 11, 1991

Ramsey, Norman. June 7, 1986 (telephone); June 5, 1989

Redman, Leslie. Nov. 20, 1987; Dec. 10, 1987

Robb, Irene Rice. Nov. 11, 1988

Rosen, Louis. April 3, 1986; July 26, 2001

Rosenfeld, Susan F. July 1, 1985

Rota, Gian-Carlo. Sept. 15, 1986; Nov. 1, 1986

Roy, Max. Oct. 11, 1991

Rubel, John. Oct. 9, 1987

Schlesinger, Arthur M., Jr. Dec. 2, 1985

Schreiber, Raemer. Nov. 19, 1987

Seidel, Robert. April 8, 1986; June 8, 1993; March 16, 2001, May 12, 2001

Serber, Robert. Feb. 18, 1985; April 22, 1986

Sherr, Pat. May 5, 1988

Sherwin, Martin. March 1, 1985

Shurcliff, William A. June 29, 1994

Silverman, Samuel J. Oct. 5, 1989; July 2, 1998

Singer, Louise Oppenheimer. June 18, 1986 (telephone)

Slansky, Richard. Jan. 25, 1985; October 1991

Sloss, Leon. March 2, 1998

Smith, Alice K. and Cyril S. March 6, 1985; Nov. 29, 1985; May 20, 1986; Feb. 25, 1987; March 5, 1987; Nov. 3, 1990

Smyth, Henry DeWolf. Dec. 10, 1985

Stern, Philip. Nov. 14, 1986

Stever, Guyford. April 27, 1990 (telephone)

Straus, Donald B. Jan. 18, 1986 (telephone)

Strauss, Alice H. Nov. 28, 1990

Strauss, Lewis H. July 6, 1989

Suid, Larry. April 29, 1985; June 17, 1985; Nov. 23, 1985

Sylves, Richard. Aug. 5–6, 1986; March 30, 1987

Teller, Edward. July 18, 1988; May 8, 1990; June 7, 1993

Thorn, Robert. Nov. 23, 1987

Topkis, Jay. July 1–2, 1998

Tyler, Judge Harold R. Oct. 24, 1989 (telephone)

Unna, Warren. Dec. 20, 1989

Volpe, Joseph, Jr. Nov. 19, 1985; Nov. 21, 1985; July 6–7, 1989; May 12, 1994

Wald, Judge Patricia. Nov. 14, 1991 (telephone)
Walkowicz, Christian Anne. Nov. 9, 1993
Wechsler, Jacob. July 25, 2001; Oct. 19, 2001
Weiner, Charles. Nov. 4, 1985
Weisskopf, Victor. Feb. 25, 1985; Oct. 28, 1986
Wheeler, John Archibald. Nov. 14, 1985
Wheeler, Michael. March 24, 1998
White, Stephen. Aug. 14, 1985; Aug. 24, 1985; Aug. 27, 1985; July 28, 1986; May 1987
Wiesner, Jerome. May 28, 1987 (telephone)
Wilson, Robert R. and Jane. Dec. 3, 1986; June 24, 1987
Woodruff, Roy. June 9, 1993
Wyzanski, Charles. Dec. 27, 1985
Zacharias, Jerrold. Dec. 31, 1985; May 1, 1986
Zuckert, Eugene. Nov. 28, 1990

Interviews by Others

Stanley Goldberg with John Lansdale, Feb. 7, 1990
    Fred "Dusty" Rhodes, Sept. 17, 1991
Jack Holl with Lee Hancock, c. 1972, at Albuquerque Airport motel
Bill Moyers with I. I. Rabi, *A Walk Through the Twentieth Century,* shown on PBS, June 26, 1983
Arthur Lawrence Norberg, for the University of California, Berkeley (Bancroft Library), with Norris E. Bradbury, Feb. 11, 1976
    Darol K. Froman, June 7, 1976
    John H. Manley, July 9 and 11, 1976
    J. Carson Mark, June 8, 1976
    Raemer H. Schreiber, Feb. 13, 1976
Silvan Schweber with George Bell, July 19, 1990
    Norris Bradbury, July 19, 1990
    Charles Critchfield, July 17 and 19, 1990
    Carson Mark, July 16 and 19, 1990
    Nicholas Metropolis, Aug. 20, 1990
    Edward Teller, July 21, 1990
Garry Sturgess with K. D. Nichols, Oct. 30, 1989

INDEX

See also General Advisory
Committee (GAC); Gray board
Atomic Energy for Military Purposes
(*Smyth Report*), 266–67
Atoms for Peace, 183–84, 208,
257–58, 303n8

Bacher, Robert: on AEC, 18; as
"bucking up" Oppenheimer,
209; on panel on long-range
uses of atomic weapons,
285n6; secrecy opposed by, 69;
on Soviet atomic bomb, 20,
21; as speaking out about
dangers of hydrogen bomb, 4;
Strauss's alerting Oppenheimer
opponents of impending
attack, 301n6, visiting
Oppenheimer at Princeton,
251
Ballen, Samuel B., 200
Baruch, Bernard, 60
Bates, Charles W., 189–90, 192,
199–200, 222, 223–24,
263–64
Beckerley, James, 198, 199
Bell, George, 285n3, 287n19
Belmont, Alan, 223
Bentley, Elizabeth, 1
Bethe, Hans: and advanced division
proposed for Los Alamos, 125;
asks Teller not to testify
against Oppenheimer, 212;
Borden's revealing secret
testimony of, 97–98; and
breaches of security before
Gray board, 198; on classified
material lost by Wheeler, 157;
as consultant at Los Alamos
laboratory, 29, 71, 72; on
dangers of hydrogen bomb, 4,
68–71; declines to work on
hydrogen bomb, 30–31,
71–72, 123; at GAC's
Halloween 1949 meeting, 35,
279n1; on hydrogen bomb's

genocidal nature, 67; joins
hydrogen bomb project, 87;
and Mike test, 138, 139, 140,
141, 260, 295n10;
Oppenheimer invited to
American Physical Society
meeting by, 211; at Princeton
AEC meeting of June 1951,
120, 121, 291n22; *Scientific
American* article on hydrogen
bomb, 69–71, 281n9, 281n10;
on skepticism about Super
model, 284n10; on Soviet Joe
Four test, 194; and Strauss's
attempts to have Oppenheimer
fired from Institute for
Advanced Study, 251; and
Taylor, 84; Teller attempts to
recruit to work on hydrogen
bomb, 29–31; Teller blames
for failure of Super, 93; and
Teller meet with Oppenheimer
about hydrogen bomb, 30–31,
32; Teller on delay of
hydrogen bomb development
by, 73, 96; in Teller's "The
Work of Many People," 248;
Teller's wartime failures under,
76, 282n20; on tritium
requirement for hydrogen
bomb, 79–80; Ulam on
arguments between Teller and,
100; on Ulam-Teller concept,
122, 286n9, 287n19; as
understanding meaning of
atomic bomb, 265; U.S. and
Soviet H-bomb progress
compared by, 140; visiting
Oppenheimer at Princeton,
251
Bethe, Rose, 30, 212
Beyer, William, 288n26
Blair, Clay, 240–43, 245–47,
312n10, 313n15
Bohr, Niels, 59, 82
Booster test, 27, 71, 85

about the Oppenheimers, 66, 67; Strauss promises to get Oppenheimer to, 182, 185, 303n1; and Strauss's vendetta against Oppenheimer, 190; Strauss thanks for help in Oppenheimer case, 239; technical surveillance of Oppenheimer requested by, 187–88

Hoyt, Fred, 142

hydrogen bomb (H-bomb): Air Force interest in, 57–58, 94; arms race between U.S. and Soviet Union, 13, 57, 260; Bravo test, 13, 193–94, 260; burning of deuterium in, 80, 81, 85–86, 89, 90, 105; computers for developing, 74–75; debate over whether to develop, 24–33; delivery of, 258–59; detonation of first, 12, 141–42; Eisenhower informed of, 159; and Europe-first school of thought, 88; "Family Committee" for research on, 76; final meeting of committee to advise Truman on, 53–54; first British test of, 256; Fuchs betrayal and, 65–66; GAC reconsiders October 1949 decision, 48–49; GAC's Halloween 1949 meeting on crash program for, 34–47; GAC votes against crash program for, 3, 38–40, 151–52, 201, 262; ignition of, 77–80, 100–103, 284n11; military not informed of potential for developing, 35; Oppenheimer opposes crash program for, 2–4, 10, 13; physicists campaign against development of, 67–72; Princeton AEC meeting of June 1951 and, 120–22; public

concern about, 256; public on development of, 61; radius of destruction of, 57; scientists and politicians divided over, 58; secrecy ordered for debate on, 4, 41–42, 55–56, 67; Soviets working on at time of Truman's announcement, 57; Teller begins recruiting staff for Super program, 72; Teller on Oppenheimer's delay of development of, 72, 73, 95, 96, 116, 146, 155, 212, 213; Teller on recruiting scientists for, 73–74, 86, 96; Teller's Classical Super model of, 37, 58, 81; Teller's estimate of time required to build, 27; tritium requirement for, 78, 79, 80, 89, 117, 282n22, 282n23, 284n11; Truman as not informed about potential for developing, 25, 26; Truman orders production of materials for, 74; Truman orders research on, 2, 55, 60–61, 262. *See also* Super model; Ulam-Teller concept

Hydrogen Bomb, The: The Men, the Menace, the Mechanism (Shepley and Blair), 242–43, 245–47, 313n15

intercontinental missiles, 258, 259
international control of atomic weapons, 10, 59–60
Item test, 106, 120, 286n5

Jackson, C. D., 183
Jackson, Robert H., 117
Jastrow, Robert, 290n14
JCAE. *See* Joint Committee on Atomic Energy of the House and Senate (JCAE)
Jenner, William, 165
Johnson, Edwin, 51, 55

PHOTOGRAPH CREDITS

Insert page 1: Courtesy of LANL Archives; **page 2,** *all:* Courtesy of AP Wide World Photos; **page 3:** Niels Bohr Archive, courtesy of AIP Emilio Segrè Visual Archives; **page 4,** *top:* Photograph by Percival King, courtesy of Nicholas King; *bottom:* Courtesy of Kathleen Mark; **page 5:** AIP Emilio Segrè Visual Archives, W. F. Meggers Gallery of Nobel Laureates; **page 6,** *top:* AIP Emilio Segrè Visual Archives; *bottom:* Courtesy of LANL Archives; **page 7:** Photograph by Frances Simon, courtesy of AIP Emilio Segrè Visual Archives, Frances Simon Collections; **page 8:** Courtesy of Edythe Holbrook; **page 9,** *top:* Courtesy of Herbert Hoover Library; *bottom:* Harris and Ewing, News Service, Massachusetts Institute of Technology, courtesy of AIP Emilio Segrè Visual Archives; **page 10,** *top:* Courtesy of Françoise Ulam; *bottom:* Courtesy of Dolores Everett; **page 11,** *all:* Courtesy of Françoise Ulam; **page 12:** National Archives and Records Administration, courtesy of AIP Emilio Segrè Visual Archives; **page 13,** *top:* Dennis Galloway, courtesy of Emilio Segrè Visual Archives, Physics Today Collection; *bottom:* AIP Emilio Segrè Visual Archives, Physics Today Collection; **page 14:** Photograph by Kenneth Bainbridge, courtesy of AIP Emilio Segrè Visual Archives; **page 15:** Photograph by Fernand Gignon, courtesy of AIP Emilio Segrè Visual Archives, Physics Today Collection; **page 16:** Ulli Steltzer.